THE PHILOSOPHICAL FOUNDATIONS
OF EDUCATION

The Philosophical Foundations of Education

STEVEN M. CAHN

DEPARTMENT OF PHILOSOPHY
NEW YORK UNIVERSITY

HARPER & ROW, PUBLISHERS
NEW YORK • EVANSTON • LONDON

To VICTOR
my brother and my friend

CONTENTS

PREFACE

THIS BOOK is intended to serve both as a text for courses in philosophy of education and as an anthology for those who wish to become acquainted with the finest historical and contemporary work in this field. The book brings together what seem to me to be the most profound and illuminating contributions that philosophers have made to the study of the aims of education.

The selections are long enough to be of value to those who are not acquainted with the other philosophical works of the authors represented. Each selection is preceded by an introduction that seeks to clarify and emphasize the philosophical issues which are at stake without utilizing oversimplified and misleading labels such as realism, scholasticism, and so on. In a number of instances these introductions include criticisms of views that are defended in the selections. This is an indication of the fact that one does not have to agree entirely with a philosopher in order to value highly his opinions.

It is suggested that the material in this book be studied in the order presented. In many cases issues that are raised in one selection are clarified in another, and the introductions often relate to more than one selection.

On a number of occasions I had the privilege of teaching a course in philosophy of education at Vassar College. The students' strong interest in the subject encouraged me greatly in my work on this book.

S. M. C.

INTRODUCTION

"What are the proper aims of education?" This is the question which philosophy of education attempts to answer. A satisfactory answer requires a thorough examination of basic metaphysical, epistemological, moral, and political issues. What is the nature of man? How can a man acquire knowledge? By what moral standards should a man live? How should society be organized? Without answers to these profound questions a philosophy of education is incomplete.

Furthermore, it is not enough for a philosophy of education merely to state the proper aims of education. Unless these aims are sufficiently detailed and the basic methods of carrying them out sufficiently clarified, the aims themselves remain too vague to be of any significant value. It is easy to agree, for example, that students ought to learn to think critically about the important bodies of knowledge possessed by mankind. But what is it to think critically? Is it possible to teach the power of critical thinking? If so, how? What are the most important bodies of knowledge possessed by mankind? Can all knowledge be taught? Should it all be taught in the same way? Should morality, for instance, be taught in the same way as mathematics? A successful philosophy of education must come to grips with issues such as these and not rest content with hazy generalizations.

A philosophy of education is thus a most arduous undertaking. It is, however, an undertaking of vital importance, for upon it all intelligent decisions about educational matters ultimately rest.

Suppose one is asked whether college students ought to be required to take a course in the history of Western civilization. In discussing this issue one is almost immediately plunged into questions such as the following: (1) Is it unwise or unfair to require students to take a particular course? (2) What is the proper relationship between a student and the educational institution he attends? (3) Why is the history of Western civilization worth studying? (4) Even if this subject is important for a historian to study, is it important for a scientist to study? (5) Is history to be studied in order to acquire historical facts or in order to learn the historian's methods of inquiry? (6) Does the investigation of historical events involving human actions necessarily involve an approach that is inapplicable to the scientific study of inanimate objects? Thus, from a seemingly simple question regarding one course, we have moved quickly into complex matters involving moral and political commitments as well as epistemological and metaphysical judgments.

1

To make decisions without consideration of one's ends or goals is the height of intellectual irresponsibility. It is therefore incumbent upon anyone involved in making educational decisions to consider carefully the proper aims of education. It is this complex and demanding inquiry that is referred to as philosophy of education.

PART I

Traditional Philosophies of Education

Plato

(427-347 B.C.)

ALL WORK in philosophy of education must ultimately be measured against the standard of excellence established by Plato, the first systematic philosopher to work in this field.

All of Plato's philosophical writings are in dialogue form, and in almost every dialogue the major figure is Plato's teacher, Socrates. The extent to which the historical Socrates actually espoused the views attributed to the character "Socrates" in Plato's dialogues is a matter of long-standing controversy, which need not detain us. We may reasonably assume that the historical Socrates was concerned with the search for definitions of such terms as "justice," "virtue," "piety," and "courage" and that he defended the thesis that "virtue is knowledge." The Theory of Forms, however, as well as the major ideas presented in *The Republic* appear to be Platonic rather than Socratic in origin.

The *Meno* dialogue is a superb introduction to a number of central issues in philosophy of education. Among these issues are the following: (1) Can virtue be taught? (2) How is it possible for a person who has been taught what is right to act contrary to the principles he has learned? (3) What is the Socratic method of teaching and how effective is this method?

In connection with this third issue, special attention should be paid to Socrates' questioning of the slave boy concerning certain geometric truths. This is the paradigm case of what has come to be known as Socratic questioning. It is interesting to consider how successful Socrates' method of questioning actually is in this case and to what extent the method is applicable to other fields, such as history or science.

Though the *Meno* dialogue concludes with Socrates defending the thesis that virtue cannot be taught and is therefore not knowledge, this is neither Socrates' nor Plato's ultimate view on the matter. This is seen in the

Protagoras dialogue, in which Socrates eventually agrees with Protagoras, a highly respected teacher in Athens, who argues in a profound speech that virtue can be taught.

The Republic is one of Plato's greatest works. It presents a fully developed and brilliantly argued, though not necessarily convincing, philosophy of education. It is interesting to notice how Plato's educational views are a reflection of his epistemological and political views. His denigration of vocational education, for example, follows directly from the separation of knowledge and practical action that is implicit in his Theory of Forms as well as from his creation of an intellectual elite that rules over and is served by the brute labor force.

Bertrand Russell once referred to Plato's *Republic* as a "totalitarian tract." This is a response to Plato's policies of strict censorship as well as his advocacy of the absolute rule of an oligarchy. Defenders of democracy will find *The Republic* a superb whetstone for sharpening the arguments they can bring forth in support of their own opposing political and educational commitments.

MENO

Meno. Can you tell me, Socrates, whether virtue is acquired by teaching or by practice; or if neither by teaching nor by practice, then whether it comes to man by nature, or in what other way?

Socrates. There was a time, Meno, when the Thessalians were famous among the other Hellenes for their riches and their riding; but now, if I am not mistaken, they are famous also for their wisdom, especially at Larisa, which is the native city of your friend Aristippus. And this is Gorgias' doing; for when he came there, he imbued with the love of wisdom the flower of the Aleuadae, among them your admirer Aristippus, and the other chiefs of the Thessalians. And he has taught you the habit of answering questions in the grand and bold style, which is natural to those who know, and may be expected from one who is himself ready and willing to be questioned on any subject by any Hellene, and answers all comers. How different is our lot! my dear Meno. Here at Athens there is a dearth of the commodity, and all wisdom seems to have emigrated from us to you. I am certain that if you were to ask any Athenian whether virtue was natural or acquired, he would laugh in your face, and say: "Stranger, you have far too good an opinion of me, if you think that I can answer your question. For I literally do not know what virtue is, and much less whether it is acquired by teaching or not." And I myself, Meno, living as I do in this region of poverty am as poor as the rest of the world; and I confess with shame that I know literally nothing about virtue; and when I do not know the "quid" of anything how can I know the "quale"? How, if I knew nothing at all of Meno, could I tell if he was handsome, or the opposite; rich and noble, or the reverse of rich and noble? Do you think that I could?

Men. No, indeed. But are you in earnest, Socrates, in saying that you do not know what virtue is? And am I to carry back this report of you to Thessaly?

Soc. Not only that, my dear boy, but you may say further that I have never come across anyone else who did, in my judgement.

Men. Then you have never met Gorgias when he was at Athens?

Soc. Yes, I have.

Men. And did you not think that he knew?

Soc. I have not a good memory, Meno, and therefore I cannot now tell what I thought of him at the time. I dare say that he does know, and that you know what he said: please, therefore, to remind me of what he said; or, if you

From *The Dialogues of Plato*, 4th ed., trans. by Benjamin Jowett, Oxford, The Clarendon Press, 1953, Vol. I, pp. 265–301. Reprinted by permission of the publisher.

would rather, tell me your own view; for I suspect that you and he think much alike.

Men.   Very true.

Soc.   Then as he is not here, never mind him, and do you tell me. I adjure you, Meno, be generous, and tell me what you say that virtue is; for I shall esteem myself truly fortunate if I find that I have been mistaken, and that you and Gorgias do really have this knowledge, when I have been just saying that I have never met anybody who had.

Men.   There will be no difficulty, Socrates, in answering your question. Let us take first the virtue of a man—he should know how to administer the state, and in the administration of it should benefit his friends and harm his enemies; and he must also be careful not to suffer harm himself. A woman's virtue, if you wish to know about that, may also be easily described: her duty is to order her household and keep properly what is indoors, and obey her husband. Every age, every condition of life, young or old, male or female, bond or free, has a different virtue: there are virtues numberless, and consequently there is no difficulty about definitions; for there is a virtue relative to the actions and ages of each of us in all that we do. And I take it the same may be said of vice, Socrates.

Soc.   How fortunate I am, Meno! When I ask you for one virtue, you present me with a swarm of them, which are in your keeping. Suppose that I carried on the figure of the swarm, and asked of you, What is the nature of the bee? and you answered that there are many different kinds of bees, and I replied: But are there many different kinds of bees because they differ *quâ* bees; or, not differing *quâ* bees, are they distinguished from one another by something else, some quality such as beauty, or size, or some other such attribute? How would you answer me?

Men.   I should answer that bees do not differ from one another, *quâ* bees.

Soc.   And if I went on to say: That is what I desire to know, Meno; tell me what is the quality in which they do not differ, but are all alike;—you would presumably be able to answer?

Men.   I should.

Soc.   And so of the virtues, however many and different they may be, they have all a common form which makes them virtues; and on this he who would answer the question, "What is virtue?" would do well to have his eye fixed: Do you understand?

Men.   I am beginning to understand; but I do not as yet take hold of the question as I could wish.

Soc.   When you say, Meno, that there is one virtue of a man, another of a woman, and so on, does this apply only to virtue, or would you say the same of health, and size, and strength? Or is the nature of health always the same, whether in man or woman?

Men.   I should say that health is the same, both in man and woman.

Soc.   And is not this true of size and strength? If a woman is strong, she will be strong by reason of the same form and of the same strength subsisting in her which there is in the man. I mean to say that strength, as strength, whether of man or woman, is the same. Is there any difference?

Men. I think not.

Soc. And will not virtue, as virtue, be the same, whether in a child or in an old man, in a woman or in a man?

Men. I cannot help feeling, Socrates, that this case is different from the others.

Soc. But why? Were you not saying that the virtue of a man was to order a state, and the virtue of a woman was to order a household?

Men. I did say so.

Soc. And can either household or state or anything be well ordered without temperance and without justice?

Men. Certainly not.

Soc. Then they who order a state or a house temperately and justly order them with temperance and justice?

Men. Certainly.

Soc. Then both men and women, if they are to be good men and women, must have the same virtues of temperance and justice?

Men. Clearly.

Soc. And could either a young man or an elder one ever become good, while they were intemperate and unjust?

Men. Certainly not.

Soc. They must be temperate and just?

Men. Yes.

Soc. Then all human beings are good in the same way, and become good by possession of the same virtues?

Men. Such is the inference.

Soc. And they surely would not have been good in the same way, unless their virtue had been the same?

Men. They would not.

Soc. Then now that the sameness of all virtue has been proven, try and remember what Gorgias, and you with him, say that virtue is.

Men. I know not what to say, but that virtue is the power of governing mankind—if you really want to have one definition of them all.

Soc. That is indeed what I want. Now consider this point; can virtue as you define it be the virtue of a child or a slave, Meno? Can the child govern his father, or the slave his master; and would he who governed be any longer a slave?

Men. I think not, Socrates.

Soc. No, indeed; there would be small reason in that. Yet once more, fair friend; according to you, virtue is "the power of governing"; but shall we not add "justly and not unjustly"?

Men. Yes, Socrates; I agree there; for justice is virtue.

Soc.   Would you say "virtue," Meno, or "a virtue"?

Men.   What do you mean?

Soc.   I mean as I might say about anything; that roundness, for example, is "a figure" and not simply "figure," and I should adopt this mode of speaking, because there are other figures.

Men.   Quite right; and that is just what I say about virtue—that there are other virtues as well as justice.

Soc.   What are they? tell me the names of them, as I would tell you the names of the other figures if you asked me.

Men.   Courage and temperance and wisdom and a noble way of life are virtues, it seems to me; and there are many others.

Soc.   Yes, Meno; and again we are in the same case: in searching after one virtue we have found many, though not in the same way as before; but we have been unable to find the common virtue which runs through them all.

Men.   Why, Socrates, even now I am not able to help you in your inquiry and get at one common notion of virtue as in the other cases.

Soc.   No wonder; but I will try to get us nearer if I can. You perhaps understand that this reasoning applies universally: suppose that someone asked you the question which I asked before: Meno, what is figure? if you answered "roundness," he would reply to you, in my way of speaking, by asking whether roundness is "figure" or "a figure"; and you would, of course, answer "a figure."

Men.   Certainly.

Soc.   And for this reason—that there are other figures?

Men.   Yes.

Soc.   And if he proceeded to ask, What other figures are there? you would have told him.

Men.   I should.

Soc.   And if he similarly asked what colour is, and you answered whiteness, and the questioner rejoined, Would you say that whiteness is colour or a colour? you would reply, A colour, because there are other colours as well.

Men.   I should.

Soc.   And if he had said, Tell me what they are?—you would have told him of other colours which are colours just as much as whiteness.

Men.   Yes.

Soc.   And suppose that he were to pursue the matter in my way, he would say: Ever and anon we are landed in particulars, but that is not what I want; tell me then, since you call them by a common name, and say that they are all figures even when opposed to one another, what is that common nature which you designate as figure—which contains round no less than straight, and, you say, belongs to one no more than to the other—that would be your mode of speaking?

Men.   Yes.

Soc.   And in speaking thus, do you mean to say that the round is no more round than straight, or the straight no more straight than round?

Men. Of course not.

Soc. You only assert that the round figure is figure no more than the straight, nor the straight than the round?

Men. Very true.

Soc. To what then do we give the name of figure? Try and answer. Suppose that when a person asked you this question either about figure or colour, you were to reply, My good sir, I do not understand what you want, or know what you mean; he would look rather astonished and say: Do you not understand that I am looking for that which is identical in all the particulars? And then he might put the question in another form: Meno, he might say, what is there identical in the round, the straight, and everything else that you call a figure? Could you not answer that question, Meno? I wish that you would try; the attempt will be good practice for the answer about virtue.

Men. I would rather that you should answer, Socrates.

Soc. Shall I indulge you?

Men. By all means.

Soc. And then you will tell me about virtue?

Men. I will.

Soc. Then I must do my best, for there is a prize to be won.

Men. Certainly.

Soc. Well, I will try and explain to you what figure is. What do you say to this answer?—Figure is the only thing which accompanies colour. Will you be satisfied with it, as I am sure that I should be if you would let me have a similar definition of virtue?

Men. But, Socrates, it is such an artless answer.

Soc. Why artless?

Men. Because, according to you, figure is that which always accompanies colour. Very well; but if a person were to say that he does not know what colour is, any more than what figure is—what sort of answer would you have given him?

Soc. In my opinion, the truth. And if he were a philosopher of the eristic and contentious sort, I should say to him: You have my answer, and if I am wrong, your business is to take up the argument and refute me. But if we were friends, and were talking as you and I are now, I ought of course to reply in a milder strain and more in the dialectician's vein; that is to say, I should not only speak the truth, but I should make use of premises which the person interrogated would be willing to admit. And this is the way in which I shall endeavour to approach you. You will acknowledge, will you not, that there is such a thing as an end, or termination, or extremity?—all which words I use in the same sense, although I am aware that Prodicus might disagree on this point: but still you, I imagine, would speak of a thing as ended or terminated—that is all which I am saying—nothing subtle.

Men. Yes, I should; and I believe that I understand your meaning.

Soc.   And you would speak of a surface and also of a solid, as for example in geometry.

Men.   Yes.

Soc.   Well then, you are now in a condition to understand my definition of figure. I define figure to be always that in which the solid finds its limit; or, more concisely, the limit of solid.

Men.   And now, Socrates, what is colour?

Soc.   You are outrageous, Meno, in thus plaguing a poor old man to give you an answer, when you will not take the trouble of remembering what is Gorgias' definition of virtue.

Men.   When you have told me what I ask, I will tell you, Socrates.

Soc.   A man who was blindfolded has only to hear you talking, and he would know that you are a beautiful creature and still have lovers.

Men.   Why do you think so?

Soc.   Why, because you always speak in imperatives, like proud beauties who reign with absolute power so long as they are in their prime; and also, I suspect, you have found out that I have a weakness for beauty, and therefore to humour you I must answer.

Men.   Please do.

Soc.   Would you like me to answer you after the manner of Gorgias, in which you may find it easier to follow me?

Men.   I should like nothing better.

Soc.   Do not he and you and Empedocles say that there are certain effluences from existing things?

Men.   Certainly.

Soc.   And passages into which and through which the effluences pass?

Men.   Exactly.

Soc.   And some of the effluences fit into the passages, and some of them are too small or too large?

Men.   True.

Soc.   And there is such a thing as sight?

Men.   Yes.

Soc.   And now, as Pindar says, "read my meaning":—colour is an effluence of figures, commensurate with sight, and palpable to sense.

Men.   That, Socrates, appears to me to be an admirable answer.

Soc.   Why, yes, because it happens to be one which you have been in the habit of hearing: and your wit will have discovered, I suspect, that you may explain in the same way the nature of sound and smell, and of many other similar phenomena.

Men.   Quite true.

Soc.   The answer, Meno, was in the solemn language of tragedy, and therefore was more acceptable to you than the other answer about figure.

Men.   Yes.

Soc.   And yet, O son of Alexidemus, I cannot help thinking that the other was the better; and I believe that you would be of the same opinion, if you would only stay and be initiated, and were not compelled, as you said yesterday, to go away before the mysteries.

Men.   But I will stay, Socrates, if you will give me many such answers.

Soc.   Well then, for my own sake as well as for yours, I will do my very best; but I am afraid that I shall not be able to give you very many as good. And now, in your turn, you are to fulfil your promise, and tell me what virtue is in the universal; and do not make a singular into a plural, as the facetious always say of those who break a thing, but leave virtue whole and sound when you tell me its nature. I have given you the pattern.

Men.   Well then, Socrates, virtue, as I take it, is when he, who desires things which are lovely,[1] is able to provide them for himself; so the poet says, and I say too that "virtue is the desire of things that are lovely, with power to attain them."

Soc.   And does he who desires the things that are lovely also desire the good?

Men.   Certainly.

Soc.   Then are there some who desire the evil and others who desire the good? Do not all men, my dear sir, desire good?

Men.   I think not.

Soc.   There are some who desire evil?

Men.   Yes.

Soc.   Do you mean that they think the evils which they desire, to be good; or do they know that they are evil and yet desire them?

Men.   Both, I think.

Soc.   And do you really imagine, Meno, that a man knows evils to be evils and desires them notwithstanding?

Men.   Certainly I do.

Soc.   Desire is of possession?

Men.   Yes, of possession.

Soc.   And does he think that evils do good to him who possesses them, or does he know that their presence does harm?

Men.   There are some who think that the evils do them good, and others who know that they do harm.

Soc.   And, in your opinion, do those who think that they do them good know that they are evils?

Men.   I would not go so far as that.

Soc.   Is it not obvious that those who are ignorant of their nature do not desire them, but desire what they suppose to be goods although they are really evils; and therefore if in their ignorance they suppose the evils to be goods they really desire goods?

Men.   In that case, no doubt.

---

[1] [The Greek word, καλός includes both physical and moral beauty: here the best equivalent seems to be "lovely," in the biblical sense of the word.]

Soc. Again, those who, as you say, desire evils, and think that evils are hurtful to the possessor of them, presumably know that they will be hurt by them?

Men. They must know it.

Soc. And must they not suppose that those who are hurt are miserable in proportion to the hurt which is inflicted upon them?

Men. How can it be otherwise?

Soc. But are not the miserable ill fated?

Men. Yes, indeed.

Soc. And does anyone desire to be miserable and ill fated?

Men. I should say not, Socrates.

Soc. But if there is no one who desires to be miserable, there is no one, Meno, who desires evil; for what is misery but the desire and possession of evil?

Men. That appears to be the truth, Socrates, and I admit that nobody desires evil.

Soc. And yet, were you not saying just now that virtue is the desire and power of attaining good?

Men. Yes, I did say so.

Soc. But of this definition one part, the desire, is common to all, and one man is no better than another in that respect?

Men. Clearly.

Soc. It is obvious then that if one man is indeed better than another, he must be better in the power of attaining good?

Men. Exactly.

Soc. Then, according to your definition, virtue would appear to be the power of attaining good?

Men. I entirely approve, Socrates, of the manner in which you now view this matter.

Soc. Then let us see whether what you now say is true from another point of view; for very likely you may be right:—You affirm virtue to be the power of attaining goods?

Men. Yes.

Soc. And the goods which you mean are such as health and wealth?

Men. And the possession of gold and silver, and having office and honour in the state.

Soc. Those are what you would call goods?

Men. Yes, I should include all those.

Soc. Then, according to Meno, who is the hereditary friend of the great king, virtue is the power of getting silver and gold; and would you add that they must be gained piously, justly, or do you deem this to be of no consequence? And is any mode of acquisition, even if unjust, equally to be deemed virtue?

Men. Not virtue, Socrates.

Soc. But vice?

Men.   Yes.

Soc.   Then justice or temperance or piety, or some other part of virtue, as would appear, must accompany the acquisition, and without them the mere acquisition of goods will not be virtue.

Men.   Why, how can there be virtue without these?

Soc.   On the other hand, the failure to acquire gold and silver in an unjust way for oneself or another, or in other words the want of them, may be equally virtue?

Men.   True.

Soc.   Then the acquisition of such goods is no more virtue than the non-acquisition and want of them, but it seems that whatever is accompanied by justice or honesty is virtue, and whatever is devoid of any such quality is vice.

Men.   It cannot be otherwise, in my judgement.

Soc.   And were we not saying just now that justice, temperance, and the like, were each of them a part of virtue?

Men.   Yes.

Soc.   And so, Meno, this is the way in which you mock me.

Men.   Why do you say that, Socrates?

Soc.   Why, because a short while ago I asked you not to break up virtue and offer it to me in little pieces, and I gave you patterns according to which you were to frame your answer; and you have forgotten already, and tell me that virtue is the power of attaining goods with justice; and justice you acknowledge to be a part of virtue.

Men.   Yes.

Soc.   Then it follows from your own admissions, that virtue consists in doing with one part of virtue whatever a man does do; for justice and the like are said by you to be parts of virtue, each and all of them. Let me explain further. Did not I ask you to tell me the nature of virtue as a whole? And you are very far from telling me this, but declare every action to be virtue which is done with a part of virtue; as though you had told me the nature of virtue as a whole, so that I should recognize it even when you fritter it away into little pieces. And, therefore, my dear Meno, I fear that I must begin again and repeat the same question: What is virtue? for otherwise I can only say that every action done with a part of virtue is virtue; what else is the meaning of saying that every action done with justice is virtue? Ought I not to ask the question over again; for can anyone who does not know the nature of virtue know the nature of a part of virtue?

Men.   No; I do not say that he can.

Soc.   Do you remember how, in the example of figure, we rejected any answer given in terms which were as yet unexplained or unadmitted?

Men.   Yes, Socrates; and we were quite right in doing so.

Soc.   But then, my friend, do not suppose that while the nature of virtue as a whole is still undetermined, you can explain it to anyone by reference to some part of virtue; or indeed explain anything at all in that fashion. We should only have to ask over again the old question, What is this virtue of yours? Am I not right?

Men. I believe that you are.

Soc. Then begin again, and answer me, What, according to you and your friend Gorgias, is the definition of virtue?

Men. O Socrates, I used to be told, before I knew you, that you were always doubting yourself and making others doubt; and now you are casting your spells over me, and I am simply getting bewitched and enchanted and am at my wits' end. And if I may venture to make a jest upon you, you seem to me both in your appearance and in your power over others to be very like the flat torpedo fish, who torpifies those who come near him and touch him, as you have now torpified me, I think. For my soul and my tongue are really torpid, and I do not know how to answer you; and though I have been delivered of an infinite variety of speeches about virtue before now, and to many persons —and very good speeches they were, as I thought—at this moment I cannot even say what virtue is. And I think that you are very wise in not voyaging and going away from home, for if you did in other places as you do in Athens, you would be cast into prison as a magician.

Soc. You are a rogue, Meno, and had all but caught me.

Men. What do you mean, Socrates?

Soc. I can tell why you made a simile about me.

Men. Why?.

Soc. In order that I might make another simile about you. For I know that all beautiful youths like to have similes made about them—as well they may, since beautiful images, I take it, are naturally evoked by beauty—but I shall not return the compliment. As to my being a torpedo, if the torpedo is itself torpid as well as the cause of torpidity in others, then indeed I am a torpedo, but not otherwise; for I perplex others, not because I am clear, but because I am utterly perplexed myself. And now I know not what virtue is, and you seem to be in the same case, although you did once perhaps know before you touched me. However, I have no objection to join with you in the inquiry.

Men. And how will you investigate, Socrates, that of which you know nothing at all? Where can you find a starting-point in the region of the un-known? And even if you happen to come full upon what you want, how will you ever know that this is the thing which you did not know?

Soc. I know, Meno, what you mean; but just see what a tiresome dispute you are introducing. You argue that a man cannot inquire either about that which he knows, or about that which he does not know; for if he knows, he has no need to inquire; and if not, he cannot; for he does not know the very subject about which he is to inquire.

Men. Well, Socrates, and is not the argument sound?

Soc. I think not.

Men. Why not?

Soc. I will tell you why: I have heard from certain men and women skilled in things divine that—

Men. What did they say?

Soc. They spoke of a glorious truth, as I conceive.

Men. What is it? and who are they?

Soc. Some of them are priests and priestesses, who have striven to learn how to give a reasonable account of the things with which they concern themselves: there are poets also, like Pindar, and the many others who are inspired. And they say—mark, now, and see whether their words are true— they say that the soul of man is immortal, and at one time has an end, which is termed dying, and at another time is born again, but is never destroyed. And the moral is, that a man ought to live always in perfect holiness. *"For in the ninth year Persephone sends the souls of those from whom she has received the penalty of ancient crime back again from beneath into the light of the sun above, and these are they who become noble kings and mighty men and great in wisdom and are for ever called saintly heroes."* The soul, then, as being immortal and having been born again many times, and having seen all things that exist, whether in this world or in the world below, has knowledge of them all; and it is no wonder that she should be able to call to remembrance all that she ever knew about virtue, and about everything; for as all nature is akin, and the soul has learned all things, there is no difficulty in a man eliciting out of a single recollection all the rest—the process generally called "learning"—if he is strenuous and does not faint; for all inquiry and all learning is but recollection. And therefore we ought not to listen to this eristic argument about the impossibility of inquiry: for it will make us idle, and it is sweet to the sluggard; but the other doctrine will make us active and inquisitive. In that confiding, I will gladly inquire with you into the nature of virtue.

Men. Yes, Socrates; but what do you mean by saying that we do not learn, and that what we call learning is only a process of recollection? Can you teach me how this is?

Soc. I told you, Meno, just now that you were a rogue, and now you ask whether I can teach you, when I am saying that there is no teaching, but only recollection; and thus you imagine that you will expose me in a contradiction.

Men. Indeed, Socrates, I protest that I had no such intention. I only asked the question from habit; but if you can prove to me that what you say is true, I wish that you would.

Soc. It will be no easy matter, but I am willing to do my best for you. Suppose that you call one of your numerous attendants, whichever you like, that I may demonstrate on him.

Men. Certainly. Come hither, boy.

Soc. He is Greek, and speaks Greek, does he not?

Men. Yes, indeed; he was born in the house.

Soc. Attend now, and observe whether he learns of me or only remembers.

Men. I will.

Soc.   Tell me, boy, do you know that a figure like this is a square?

Boy.   I do.

Soc.   And you know that a square figure has these four lines equal?

Boy.   Certainly.

Soc.   And these lines which I have drawn through the middle of the square are also equal?

Boy.   Yes.

Soc.   A square may be of any size?

Boy.   Certainly.

Soc.   And if one side of the figure be two feet long, and the other side two feet, how much will the whole be? Let me explain: if in one direction the space was two feet long, and in the other direction one foot, the whole space would be two feet taken once?

Boy.   Yes.

Soc.   But since this side is also two feet, there are twice two feet?

Boy.   There are.

Soc.   Then the square is twice two feet?

Boy.   Yes.

Soc.   And how many are twice two feet? count and tell me.

Boy.   Four, Socrates.

Soc.   And might there not be another figure twice as large as this, but of the same kind, and having like this all the lines equal?

Boy.   Yes,

Soc.   And how many feet will that be?

Boy.   Eight feet.

Soc.   And now try and tell me the length of the line which forms the side of that double square: this is two feet—what will that be?

Boy.   Clearly, Socrates, it will be double.

Soc.   Do you observe, Meno, that I am not teaching the boy anything, but only asking him questions; and now he fancies that he knows how long a line is necessary in order to produce a figure of eight square feet; does he not?

Men.   Yes.

Soc.   And does he really know?

Men.   Certainly not.

Soc.   He fancies that because the square is double, the line is double?

Men.   True.

Soc.   Now see him being brought step by step to recollect in regular order. *(To the boy.)* Tell me, boy, do you assert that a double space comes from a double line? Remember that I am not speaking of an oblong, but of a figure equal every way, and twice the size of this—that is to say of eight feet; and I want to know whether you still say that a double square comes from a double line?

Boy.   Yes.

Soc.   But does not this line become doubled if we add another such line here?

Boy. Certainly.

Soc. And four such lines, you say, will make a space containing eight feet?

Boy. Yes.

Soc. Let us describe such a figure: Would you not say that this is the figure of eight feet?

Boy. Yes.

Soc. And are there not these four divisions in the figure, each of which is equal to the figure of four feet?

Boy. True.

Soc. And is not that four times four?

Boy. Certainly.

Soc. And four times is not double?

Boy. No, indeed.

Soc. But how much?

Boy. Four times as much.

Soc. Therefore the double line, boy, has given a space, not twice, but four times as much.

Boy. True.

Soc. Four times four are sixteen—are they not?

Boy. Yes.

Soc. What line would give you a space of eight feet—for that gives a fourfold space, of sixteen feet, does it not?

Boy. Yes.

Soc. And the space of four feet is made from this half line?

Boy. Yes.

Soc. Good; and is not a space of eight feet twice the size of this, and half the size of the other?

Boy. Certainly.

Soc. Such a space, then, will be made out of a line greater than this one, and less than that one?

Boy. Yes; I think so.

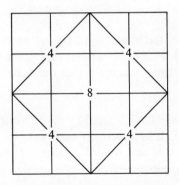

Soc. Very good; I like to hear you say what you think. And now tell me, is not this a line of two feet and that of four?

Boy.   Yes.

Soc.   Then the line which forms the side of the eight foot space ought to be more than this line of two feet, and less than the other of four feet?

Boy.   It ought.

Soc.   Try and see if you can tell me how much it will be.

Boy.   Three feet.

Soc.   Then if we add a half to this line of two, that will be the line of three. Here are two and there is one; and on the other side, here are two also and there is one: and that makes the figure of which you speak?

Boy.   Yes.

Soc.   But if there are three feet this way and three feet that way, the whole space will be three times three feet?

Boy.   That is evident.

Soc.   And how much are three times three feet?

Boy.   Nine.

Soc.   And what was to be the number of feet in the doubled square?

Boy.   Eight.

Soc.   Then the eight foot space is not made out of a line of three feet?

Boy.   No.

Soc.   But from what line?—tell me exactly, and if you would rather not reckon, try and show me the line.

Boy.   Indeed, Socrates, I do not know.

Soc.   Do you see, Meno, what advances he has made in his power of recollection? He did not know at first, and he does not know now, what is the side of a figure of eight feet: but then he thought that he knew, and answered confidently as if he knew, and felt no difficulty; now he feels a difficulty, and neither knows nor fancies that he knows.

Men.   True.

Soc.   Is he not better off in knowing his ignorance?

Men.   I think that he is.

Soc.   If we have made him doubt, and given him the "torpedo's shock," have we done him any harm?

Men.   I think not.

Soc.   We have certainly, as would seem, assisted him in some degree to the discovery of the truth; and now he will wish to remedy his ignorance, but then he would have been ready to tell all the world again and again that the double space should have a double side.

Men.   True.

Soc.   But do you suppose that he would ever have started to inquire into or to learn what he fancied that he knew, though he was really ignorant of it, until he had fallen into perplexity under the idea that he did not know, and had desired to know?

Men.   I think not, Socrates.

Soc.   Then he was the better for the torpedo's touch?

Men. I think so.

Soc. Mark now the further development. I shall only ask him, and not teach him, and he shall share the inquiry with me: and do you watch and see if you find me telling or explaining anything to him, instead of eliciting his opinion. Tell me, boy, is not this a square of four feet which I have drawn?

Boy. Yes.

Soc. And now I add another square equal to the former one?

Boy. Yes.

Soc. And a third, which is equal to either of them?

Boy. Yes.

Soc. Suppose that we fill up the vacant corner?

Boy. Very good.

Soc. Here, then, there are four equal spaces?

Boy. Yes.

Soc. And how many times larger is this space than this other?

Boy. Four times.

Soc. But we wanted one only twice as large, as you will remember.

Boy. True.

Soc. Now, does not this line, reaching from corner to corner, bisect each of these spaces?

Boy. Yes.

Soc. And are there not here four equal lines which contain this space?

Boy. There are.

Soc. Look and see how much this space is.

Boy. I do not understand.

Soc. Has not each interior cut off half of the four spaces?

Boy. Yes.

Soc. And how many such spaces are there in this section?

Boy. Four.

Soc. And how many in this?

Boy. Two.

Soc. And four is how many times two?

Boy. Twice.

Soc. So that this space is of how many feet?

Boy. Of eight feet.

Soc. And from what line do you get this figure?

Boy. From this.

Soc. That is, from the line which extends from corner to corner of the figure of four feet?

Boy. Yes.

Soc. And that is the line which the learned call the diagonal. And if this is the proper name, then you, Meno's slave, are prepared to affirm that the double space is the square of the diagonal?

Boy. Certainly, Socrates.

Soc.   What do you say of him, Meno? Were not all these answers given out of his own head?

Men.   Yes, they were all his own.

Soc.   And yet, as we were just now saying, he did not know?

Men.   True.

Soc.   But still he had in him those notions of his—had he not?

Men.   Yes.

Soc.   Then he who does not know may still have true notions of that which he does not know?

Men.   Apparently.

Soc.   And at present these notions have just been stirred up in him, as in a dream; but if he were frequently asked the same questions, in different forms, he would know as accurately as anyone at last?

Men.   I dare say.

Soc.   Without anyone teaching him he will recover his knowledge for himself, if he is merely asked questions?

Men.   Yes.

Soc.   And this spontaneous recovery of knowledge in him is recollection?

Men.   True.

Soc.   And this knowledge which he now has must he not either have acquired at some time, or else possessed always?

Men.   Yes.

Soc.   But if he always possessed this knowledge he would always have known; or if he has acquired the knowledge he could not have acquired it in this life, unless he has been taught geometry. And he may be made to do the same with all geometry and every other branch of knowledge; has anyone ever taught him all this? You must know about him, if, as you say, he was born and bred in your house.

Men.   And I am certain that no one ever did teach him.

Soc.   And yet he has these notions?

Men.   The fact, Socrates, is undeniable.

Soc.   But if he did not acquire them in this life, then he must have had and learned them at some other time?

Men.   Clearly he must.

Soc.   Which must have been the time when he was not a man?

Men.   Yes.

Soc.   And if there are always to be true notions in him, both while he is and while he is not a man, which only need to be awakened into knowledge by putting questions to him, his soul must remain always possessed of this knowledge; for he must always either be or not be a man.

Men.   Obviously.

Soc.   And if the truth of all things always exists in the soul, then the soul is immortal. Wherefore be of good cheer, and try to discover by recollection what you do not now know, or rather what you do not remember.

Men.   I feel, somehow, that I like what you are saying.

Soc.   And I too like what I am saying. Some things I have said of which I am not altogether confident. But that we shall be better and braver and less helpless if we think that we ought to inquire, than we should have been if we thought that there was no knowing and no duty to seek to know what we do not know;—that is a belief for which I am ready to fight, in word and deed, to the utmost of my power.

Men.   There again, Socrates, your words seem to me excellent.

Soc.   Then, as we are agreed that a man should inquire about that which he does not know, shall you and I make an effort to inquire together into the nature of virtue?

Men.   By all means, Socrates. And yet I would much rather return to my original question, Whether in seeking to acquire virtue we should regard it as a thing to be taught, or as a gift of nature, or as coming to men in some other way?

Soc.   Had I the command of you as well as of myself, Meno, we should not have inquired whether virtue is given by instruction or not, until we had first ascertained "what it is." But since you never think of self-control—such being your notion of freedom—but think only of controlling me and do control me, I must yield to you, for you are irresistible. And therefore it seems we have now to inquire into the qualities of a thing of which we do not as yet know the nature. At any rate, will you loosen the reins a little, and allow the question "Whether virtue is given by instruction, or in any other way," to be argued upon hypothesis? Let me explain. As the geometrician, when he is asked whether a certain triangle is capable of being inscribed in a certain circle, will reply: "I cannot tell you as yet; but I will offer an hypothesis which may assist us in forming a conclusion: If the figure be such that when you have produced a given side of it, the given area of the triangle falls short by an area corresponding to the part produced, then one consequence follows, and if this is impossible then some other; so let me assume an hypothesis, and I am willing to tell you whether this triangle is capable of being inscribed in the circle."—that is a geometrical hypothesis. And we too, as we know not the nature and qualities of virtue, must ask, whether virtue is or is not capable of being taught, upon some hypothesis, as thus: what kind of spiritual good must virtue be in order that it may be taught or not? Let the first hypothesis be that virtue is not within the class "knowledge,"—in that case will it be taught or not? or, as we were just now saying, "recollected"? For there is no use in disputing about the name. But is virtue taught or not? or rather, does not everyone see that knowledge alone is taught?

Men.   I agree.

Soc.   Then if virtue is a kind of knowledge, virtue will be taught?

Men.   Certainly.

Soc.   Then now we have made a quick end of this question: if virtue is of such a nature, it will be taught; and if not, not?

Men.   Certainly.

Soc.   The next question is, whether virtue is knowledge or of another species?

Men.   Yes, that appears to be the question which comes next in order.

Soc.   Very well then; do we not say that virtue is good?—This is an hypothesis which stands firm?

Men.   Certainly.

Soc.   Now, if there be some other good which is separate from knowledge, possibly virtue also is not a kind of knowledge; but if knowledge embraces all good, then we shall be right in supposing that virtue is a kind of knowledge?

Men.   True.

Soc.   And virtue is that which makes us good?

Men.   Yes.

Soc.   And if we are good, then we are profitable; for all good things are profitable?

Men.   Yes.

Soc.   Then virtue is profitable?

Men.   That is the only inference.

Soc.   Then now let us take particular examples of things which profit us. Health and strength, and beauty and wealth—these, and the like of these, we call profitable?

Men.   True.

Soc.   And yet these same things may also sometimes do us harm: would you not think so?

Men.   Yes.

Soc.   And what is the guiding principle which makes them profitable or the reverse? Are they not profitable when they are rightly used, and hurtful when they are not rightly used?

Men.   Certainly.

Soc.   Next, let us consider the goods of the soul: they are temperance, justice, courage, quickness of apprehension, memory, a noble way of life, and the like?

Men.   Surely.

Soc.   And such of these as are not knowledge, but of another sort, are sometimes profitable and sometimes hurtful; as, for example, courage wanting good sense, which is only a sort of confidence? When a man has no sense he is harmed by such confidence, but when he has sense he is profited?

Men.   True.

Soc.   And the same may be said of temperance and quickness of apprehension; whatever things are learned or managed with sense are profitable, but without sense they are hurtful?

Men.   Very true.

Soc.   And in general, all that the soul attempts or endures when under the guidance of wisdom, ends in happiness; but when she is under the guidance of folly, in the opposite?

Men.   That appears to be true.

Soc.   If then virtue is a quality of the soul, and is admitted to be profitable, it must be wisdom or good sense, since none of the things of the soul are either profitable or hurtful in themselves, but they are all made profitable or hurtful by the addition of wisdom or of folly; and therefore if virtue is profitable, virtue must be a sort of wisdom?

Men.   I quite agree.

Soc.   And the other goods, such as wealth and the like, of which we were just now saying that they are sometimes good and sometimes evil, do not they also become profitable or hurtful, accordingly as the soul guides and uses them rightly or wrongly; just as the things of the soul herself become profitable when under the guidance of wisdom and harmful when guided by folly?

Men.   True.

Soc.   And the wise soul guides them rightly, and the foolish soul wrongly?

Men.   Yes.

Soc.   And is not this universally true of human nature? All other things hang upon the soul, and the things of the soul herself hang upon wisdom, if they are to be good; and so wisdom is inferred to be that which profits—and virtue, as we affirm, is profitable?

Men.   Certainly.

Soc.   And thus we arrive at the conclusion that virtue is either wholly or partly wisdom?

Men.   I think that what you are saying, Socrates, is very true.

Soc.   But if this is true, then the good are not by nature good?

Men.   I think not.

Soc.   If they were, there would assuredly be discerners of characters among us who would know our future great men; and on their showing we should have adopted them, and should be keeping them in the citadel out of the way of harm, having set a stamp upon them far rather than upon a piece of gold in order that no one might tamper with them; and that when they grew up they might be useful to the state?

Men.   Yes, Socrates, that would seem the right way.

Soc.   Then if the good are not by nature good, are they made good by instruction?

Men.   There appears to be no other alternative, Socrates. On the supposition that virtue is knowledge, there can be no doubt that virtue is taught.

Soc.   Yes, indeed; but what if the supposition is erroneous?

Men.   I certainly thought just now that we were right.

Soc.   Yes, Meno; but a principle which has any soundness should stand firm not only just now, but always.

Men. Well; and why are you so difficult, so slow to believe that virtue is knowledge?

Soc. I will try and tell you why, Meno. I do not retract the assertion that if virtue is knowledge it may be taught, but I fear that I have some reason in doubting whether it is knowledge. Consider now and say whether virtue, and not only virtue but anything that is taught, must not have teachers and disciples?

Men. Surely.

Soc. And conversely, may not the art of which neither teachers nor disciples exist be presumed to be incapable of being taught?

Men. True; but do you think that there are no teachers of virtue?

Soc. I have certainly often inquired whether there were any, and taken great pains to find them, and have never succeeded; and I have had many companions in the search, by preference the persons whom I thought to have the most experience in that line. And here at the moment when he is wanted Anytus has sat down beside us, and we should be well advised to ask him to join us in our search. In the first place, he is the son of a wealthy and wise father, Anthemion, who acquired his wealth, not by gift or without effort, like Ismenias the Theban (who has recently become as rich as Polycrates), but by his own skill and industry, and who is a well-conditioned modest man, not insolent, nor overbearing, nor annoying; moreover, this son of his has received a good education, as the Athenian people certainly appear to think, for they choose him to fill the highest offices. And these are the sort of men with whose help we ought to inquire whether there are any teachers of virtue, and who they are. Please, Anytus, to help me and your friend Meno in answering our question, Who are the teachers? Consider the matter thus: If we wanted Meno to be a good physician, to whom should we send him? Should we not send him to the physicians?

Any. Certainly.

Soc. Or if we wanted him to be a good cobbler, should we not send him to the cobblers?

Any. Yes.

Soc. And so forth?

Any. Yes.

Soc. Let me trouble you with one more question. When we say that we should be right in sending him to the physicians if we wanted him to be a physician, do we mean that we should be right in sending him to those who profess the art, rather than to those who do not, and to those who demand payment for teaching the art, and publicly offer to teach it to anyone who chooses to come and learn? And if these were our reasons, should we not be right in sending him?

Any. Yes.

Soc. And might not the same be said of flute-playing, and of the other arts?

Would a man who wanted to make another a flute-player refuse to send him to those who promise to teach the art and take money for it, and let him go about plaguing other persons to give him instruction, who are not professed teachers and who never had a single disciple in that branch of knowledge which we expect them to teach him—would not such conduct be the height of folly?

Any. Most certainly, and of ignorance too.

Soc. Very good. And now you are in a position to advise with me about my friend Meno. For some time he has been telling me, Anytus, that he desires to attain that kind of wisdom and virtue by which men order the state or the household, and honour their parents, and know how to receive citizens and strangers and to send them on their way as a good host should. Now, to whom should he go in order that he may learn this virtue? Does not the previous argument imply clearly that we should send him to those who profess to teach virtue and have publicly thrown open their teaching to any Hellene who chooses to come to them and pay the fees they fix?

Any. Whom do you mean, Socrates?

Soc. You surely know, do you not, Anytus, that these are the people whom mankind call sophists?

Any. In heaven's name, Socrates, forbear! I only hope that no friend or kinsman of mine, whether from this city or another, will ever be so mad as to allow himself to be corrupted by them; for they are a manifest pest and corrupting influence to those who have to do with them.

Soc. What, Anytus? Among all the people who profess that they know how to do men good, do you mean to say that these are the only ones who not only do them no good, but positively corrupt those who are entrusted to them, and in return for this disservice have the face to demand money? Indeed, I cannot believe you; for I know of a single man, Protagoras, who made more out of his craft than the illustrious Pheidias, who created such noble works, or any ten other sculptors. How could that be? A mender of old shoes, or patcher up of clothes, who returned shoes or clothes in worse condition than he received them, could not have remained thirty days undetected, and would very soon have starved; whereas during more than forty years, Protagoras was corrupting all Hellas, and sending his disciples from him worse than he received them, and he was never found out. For, if I am not mistaken, he was about seventy years old at his death, forty of which were spent in the practice of his profession; and during all that time he had a good reputation, which to this day he retains: and not only Protagoras, but many others are well spoken of—some who lived before him, and others who are still living. Now, when you say that they deceive and corrupt the youth, are we to suppose that they do it consciously or unconsciously? Can those who are deemed by many to be the wisest of men be out of their minds?

Any. Out of their minds! No, Socrates; the young men who give their money to them are out of their minds, and their relations and guardians who entrust their youth to the care of these men are still more out of their minds, and most of all, the cities who allow them to come in, and do not drive them out, citizen and stranger alike.

Soc. Has any of the sophists wronged you, Anytus? What makes you so angry with them?

Any. No, indeed, neither I nor any of my family has ever had, nor would I suffer them to have, anything to do with them.

Soc. Then you are entirely unacquainted with them?

Any. And I have no wish to be acquainted.

Soc. Then, my dear friend, as you have no acquaintance whatever with the profession, how can you know whether there is any good or bad in it?

Any. Quite well; I am sure that I know what manner of men these are, whether I am acquainted with them or not.

Soc. You must be a diviner, Anytus, for otherwise I really cannot make out, judging from your own words, how you know about them. But I am not inquiring of you who are the teachers who will corrupt Meno (let them be, if you please, the sophists); I only ask you to tell us who there is in this great city who will teach him how to become proficient in the virtue which I was just now describing. He is the friend of your family, and you will oblige him.

Any. Why do you not tell him yourself?

Soc. I have told him whom I supposed to be the teachers of these things; but I learn from you that I am utterly at fault, and I dare say that you are right. And now I wish that you, on your part, would tell me to whom among the Athenians he should go. Whom would you name?

Any. Why single out individuals? Any Athenian gentleman taken at random will do far more good to him than the sophists, if Meno will mind him.

Soc. And did those gentlemen grow of themselves; and without having been taught by anyone, were they nevertheless able to teach others that which they had never learned themselves?

Any. I imagine that they have learned of the previous generation of gentlemen. Have there not been many good men in this city?

Soc. Yes, certainly, Anytus; and many good statesmen also there have been and there are still, in the city of Athens. But the question is whether they were also good teachers of their own virtue;—not whether there are or have been good men in this part of the world, but whether virtue can be taught, is the question which we have been discussing. Now, do we mean to say that the good men of our own and of other times knew how to impart to others that virtue which they had themselves; or is virtue a thing incapable of being communicated by or received from another? That is the question which I and Meno have long been arguing. Look at the matter in your own way: Would you not admit that Themistocles was a good man?

Any. Certainly; no man better.

Soc. And must not he then have been a good teacher, if any man ever was a good teacher of his own virtue?

Any. No doubt,—if he wanted to be so.

Soc. But would he not have wanted? He would, at any rate, have desired to make his own son a good man and a gentleman; he could scarcely have been jealous of him, and have intentionally abstained from imparting to him his own virtue. Did you never hear that he made his son Cleophantus a fine horseman; and had him taught to stand upright on horseback and hurl a javelin, and to do many other marvellous things; and in anything which could be learned from good teachers he was proficient? Have you not heard from our elders of him?

Any. I have.

Soc. So no one could charge his son with natural incompetence?

Any. Very likely not.

Soc. But did anyone, old or young, ever say in your hearing that Cleophantus, son of Themistocles, was a wise or good man in the same respects as his father was?

Any. I have certainly never heard anyone say so.

Soc. And if virtue could have been taught, would his father Themistocles have sought to train him in these minor accomplishments, and allowed him, who was his own son, to be no better than his neighbours in those qualities in which he himself excelled?

Any. Indeed, indeed, I think not.

Soc. Here was a teacher of virtue whom you admit to be among the best men of the past. Let us take another;—Aristides, the son of Lysimachus: would you not acknowledge that he was a good man?

Any. To be sure I should.

Soc. And did not he train his son Lysimachus better than any other Athenian in all that could be done for him by the help of masters? But what has been the result? Is he a bit better than any other mortal? He is an acquaintance of yours, and you see what he is like. There is Pericles, again, magnificent in his wisdom; and he, as you are aware, brought up two sons, Paralus and Xanthippus.

Any. I know.

Soc. And you know, also, that he taught them to be unsurpassed horsemen, and had them trained in music and gymnastics and all sorts of arts—in these respects they were on a level with the best—and had he no wish to make good men of them? Nay, he must have wished it. But virtue, as I suspect, could not be taught. And that you may not suppose the incompetent teachers to have been only the least worthy sort of Athenians and few in number, remember again that Thucydides brought up two sons, Melesias and Stephanus, whom, besides giving them a good education in other things, he trained in wrestling, and they were the best wrestlers in Athens: one of them he committed to the care of Xanthias, and the other of Eudorus, who were celebrated as the finest wrestlers of that day. Do you remember them?

Any. I have heard of them.

Soc. Now, can there be a doubt that Thucydides, whose children were taught things for which he had to spend money, would have taught them to be good men, which would have cost him nothing, if virtue could have been taught? Will you reply that he was a man of no account, and had not many friends among the Athenians and allies? Nay, but he was of a great family, and a man of influence at Athens and in all Hellas, and, if virtue could have been taught, he would have found some Athenian or foreigner to make good men of his sons, if he could not himself spare the time from cares of state. Once more, I suspect, friend Anytus, that virtue is not a thing which can be taught?

Any. Socrates, I think that you are too ready to speak evil of men: and, if you will take my advice, I would recommend you to be careful. Perhaps there is no city in which it is not easier to do men harm than to do them good, and this is certainly the case at Athens, as I believe that you know.

Soc. I think, Meno, that Anytus is in a rage. And he may well be in a rage, for he believes, in the first place, that I am defaming these gentlemen; and in the second place, he is of opinion that he is one of them himself. But today he does not know what is the meaning of defamation, and if he ever does, he will forgive me. Meanwhile I will return to you, Meno; for I suppose that there are gentlemen in your region too?

Men. Certainly there are.

Soc. And will they come forward to teach the young? and do they profess to be teachers? and do they agree that virtue can be taught?

Men. No indeed, Socrates, they are anything but agreed; you may hear them saying at one time that virtue can be taught, and then again the reverse.

Soc. Can we call those teachers who do not even accept the possibility of their own vocation?

Men. I think not, Socrates.

Soc. And what do you think of these sophists, who are the only professors? Do they seem to you to be teachers of virtue?

Men. I often wonder, Socrates, that Gorgias is never heard promising to teach virtue, and when he hears others promising he only laughs at them; but he thinks that men should be taught to speak.

Soc. Then you think that neither are the sophists teachers?

Men. I cannot tell you, Socrates; like the rest of the world, I am in doubt, and sometimes I think that they are teachers and sometimes not.

Soc. And are you aware that not you only and other politicians have doubts whether virtue can be taught or not, but that Theognis the poet says the very same thing?

Men. Where does he say so?

Soc. In these elegiac verses:—

"Eat and drink and sit with the mighty, and make yourself agreeable to them; for from the good you will learn what is good, but if you mix with the bad you will lose the intelligence which you already have."

Do you observe that here he seems to imply that virtue can be taught?

Men.   Clearly.

Soc.   But in some other verses he shifts about and says:—

"If understanding could be created and put into a man, then they [who were able to perform this feat] would be gaining great rewards."

And again:—

"Never would a bad son have sprung from a good sire, for he would have heard the voice of instruction; but not by teaching will you ever make a bad man into a good one."

and this, as you may remark, is a flat contradiction of the other.

Men.   Clearly.

Soc.   And is there anything else of which the professors, so far from being acknowledged as teachers of others, are admitted to be ignorant themselves, and incompetent in the very subject which they are professing to teach? or is there anything else about which even its recognized possessors, in this case the "gentlemen," are sometimes saying that "this thing can be taught," and sometimes the opposite? Can you say that they are teachers in any true sense whose ideas are in such confusion?

Men.   I should say, certainly not.

Soc.   But if neither the sophists nor the gentlemen are teachers, clearly there can be no other teachers?

Men.   No.

Soc.   And if there are no teachers, neither are there disciples?

Men.   Agreed.

Soc.   And we have admitted that a thing cannot be taught of which there are neither teachers nor disciples?

Men.   We have.

Soc.   And there are no teachers of virtue to be found anywhere?

Men.   There are not.

Soc.   And if there are no teachers, neither are there scholars?

Men.   That, I think, is true.

Soc.   Then virtue cannot be taught?

Men.   Not if we have argued correctly. But I cannot believe, Socrates, that there are no good men: And if there are, how did they come into existence?

Soc.   I am afraid, Meno, that you and I are not good for much, and that Gorgias has been as poor an educator of you as Prodicus has been of me. Certainly we shall have to look to ourselves, and try to find someone who will help in some way or other to improve us. This I say, because I observe that, absurdly enough, in the previous discussion none of us remarked that right and good action is possible to man under other guidance than that of knowledge (ἐπιστήμη). Perhaps that is the reason why we have failed to discover how good men are produced.

Men.   How do you mean, Socrates?

Soc.   You will see. Good men are necessarily useful; were we not right in admitting this? It must be so.

Men.   Yes.

Soc.   And in supposing that they will be useful if they are true guides to us of action—there we were also right?

Men.   Yes.

Soc.   But when we said that a man cannot be a good guide unless he have knowledge (φρόνησις) in this we seem to have made a wrong admission.

Men.   What do you mean by "a good guide"?

Soc.   I will explain. If a man knew the way to Larisa, or anywhere else, and went to the place and led others thither, would he not be a right and good guide?

Men.   Certainly.

Soc.   And a person who had a right opinion about the way, but had never been and did not know, would be a good guide also, would he not?

Men.   Certainly.

Soc.   And while he has true opinion about that which the other knows, he will be just as good a guide if he only thinks the truth, as he who knows the truth?

Men.   Exactly.

Soc.   Then true opinion is as good a guide to correct action as knowledge; and that was the point which we omitted in our speculation about the nature of virtue, when we said that knowledge only is the guide of right action; whereas there is also true opinion.

Men.   So it seems.

Soc.   Then right opinion is not less useful than knowledge?

Men.   There is a difference, Socrates; he who has knowledge will always be right, but he who has right opinion will sometimes be right, and sometimes not.

Soc.   What do you mean? Can he be wrong who has right opinion, so long as he has right opinion?

Men.   I admit the cogency of your argument, and therefore, Socrates, I wonder that knowledge should ever be prized far above right opinion—or why they should ever differ.

Soc.   And shall I explain this wonder to you?

Men.   Do tell me.

Soc.   You would not wonder if you had ever observed the images of Daedalus; but perhaps you have not got them in your country?

Men.   What have they to do with the question?

Soc.   Because they require to be fastened in order to keep them, and if they are not fastened they will run away like fugitive slaves.

Men.   Well, what of that?

Soc.   I mean to say that, like runaway slaves, they are not very valuable possessions if they are at liberty, for they will walk off; but when fastened they are of great value, for they are really beautiful works of art. Now this is an illustration of the nature of true opinions: while they abide with us they are beautiful and fruitful of nothing but good, but they run away out of the human soul, and do not care to remain long, and therefore they are not of much value until they are fastened by reasoned understanding of causes; and this fastening of them, friend Meno, is recollection, as you and I have agreed to call it. But when they are bound, in the first place, they attain to be knowledge; and, in the second place, they are abiding. And this is why knowledge is more honourable and excellent than right opinion, because fastened by a chain.

Men.   Indeed, Socrates, something of the kind seems probable.

Soc.   I too speak rather in ignorance; I only conjecture. And yet that knowledge differs from right opinion is no matter of conjecture with me. There are not many things which I profess to know, but this is most certainly one of them.

Men.   Yes, Socrates; and you are quite right in saying so.

Soc.   And am I not also right in saying that true opinion leading the way perfects any action quite as well as knowledge?

Men.   There again, Socrates, I think that you are correct.

Soc.   Then for action right opinion is not a whit inferior to knowledge, nor less useful; nor is the man who has right opinion inferior to him who has knowledge?

Men.   True.

Soc.   And surely the good man has been acknowledged by us to be useful?

Men.   Yes.

Soc.   Seeing then that men become good and useful to states (if they do), not only because they have knowledge, but because they have right opinion, and that neither knowledge nor right opinion is given to man by nature or acquired by him—do you imagine either of them to be given by nature?

Men.   Not I.

Soc.   Then if they are not given by nature, neither are the good by nature good?

Men.   Certainly not.

Soc.   And nature being excluded, then came the question whether virtue is acquired by teaching?

Men.   Yes.

Soc.   If virtue was practical wisdom, then, as we thought, it could be taught?

Men.   Yes.

Soc.   And if it could be taught it was wisdom?

Men.   Certainly.

Soc. And if there were teachers, it could be taught; and if there were no teachers, not?

Men. True.

Soc. But surely we acknowledged that there were no teachers of virtue?

Men. Yes.

Soc. Thus we acknowledged that it could not be taught, and was not wisdom?

Men. Certainly.

Soc. And yet we admitted that it was a good?

Men. Yes.

Soc. And that which guides aright is useful and good?

Men. Certainly.

Soc. And for human beings the only right guides are knowledge and true opinion—things which by some happy chance go aright do not do so by human guidance—and when human guidance leads aright, it must be by one of these two, true opinion or knowledge.

Men. I think so too.

Soc. But if virtue is not taught, neither is virtue knowledge.

Men. Clearly not.

Soc. Then of two good and useful things, one, which is knowledge, has been set aside, and cannot be supposed to be our guide in political life.

Men. I think not.

Soc. And therefore not by any wisdom, and not because they were wise, did Themistocles and those others of whom Anytus spoke govern their states. This was the reason why they were unable to make others like themselves—because their virtue was not grounded on knowledge.

Men. That is probably true, Socrates.

Soc. But if not by knowledge, the only alternative which remains is that statesmen guide their states by right opinion. They stand in the same relation to wisdom as diviners and prophets, who likewise say many things truly when they are inspired, but they know not what they say.

Men. So I suppose.

Soc. And may we not, Meno, truly call those men "divine" who, having no understanding, yet succeed in many a grand deed and word?

Men. Certainly.

Soc. Then we shall also be right in calling divine those whom we were just now speaking of as diviners and prophets, including the whole tribe of poets. Yes, and with these we may class statesmen as no less divine and inspired, being possessed of God and filled with His breath, in which condition they say many grand things, not knowing what they say.

Men. Yes.

Soc. And the women too, Meno, call good men divine—do they not? and the Spartans, when they praise a good man, say "he is a divine man."

Men.   And I think, Socrates, that they are right; although very likely our friend Anytus may take offence at the word.

Soc.   I do not care; as for Anytus, there will be another opportunity of talking with him. To sum up our inquiry—the result seems to be, if we are at all right in our line of argument, that virtue is neither natural nor imparted by teaching, but an instinct given by God to those to whom it is given. Nor is the instinct accompanied by reason, unless there may be supposed to be among statesmen someone who is capable of educating statesmen. And if there be such a one, he may be said to be among the living what Homer says that Tiresias was among the dead, "he alone has understanding, but the rest are flitting shades"; in point of virtue he will be in like manner a reality among shadows.

Men.   That is excellent, Socrates.

Soc.   Then, Meno, the conclusion is that virtue comes by the gift of God to those to whom it does come. But we shall never know the certain truth until, before asking how virtue is given, we set ourselves to inquire into the essential nature of virtue. I fear that I must go away, but do you, now that you are persuaded yourself, persuade our friend Anytus. And do not let him be so exasperated; if you can conciliate him, you will have done good service to the Athenian people.

PROTAGORAS

When we were all seated, Protagoras said: Now that the company are assembled, Socrates, you might repeat what you said to me just now on behalf of this young man.

I replied: I will begin again at the same point, Protagoras, and tell you once more the purport of my visit: this is my friend Hippocrates, who is desirous of your society; he would like to know what will happen to him if he associates with you. I have no more to say.

Protagoras answered: Young man, if you associate with me, on the very first day you will return home a better man than you came, and better on the second day than on the first, and better every day than you were on the day before.

When I heard this, I said: Protagoras, I do not at all wonder at hearing you say this; even at your age, and with all your wisdom, if anyone were to teach you what you did not know before, you would become better no doubt: but please to answer in a different way—I will explain how by an example. Let me suppose that Hippocrates, instead of desiring your society, were suddenly to desire that of the young man Zeuxippus of Heraclea, who has lately arrived on a visit to Athens, and he had come to him as he had come to you, and had heard him say, as he has heard you say, that every day he would grow and become better if he associated with him: and then suppose that he were to ask him, "In what shall I become better, and in what shall I grow?"—Zeuxippus would answer, "In painting." And suppose that he went to Orthagoras the Theban, and heard him say the same thing, and asked him, "In what shall I become better day by day?" he would reply, "In flute-playing." Now I want you to make the same sort of answer to this young man and to me, who am asking questions on his account. When you say that on the first day on which he associates with you he will return home a better man, and on every day will grow in like manner,—in what, Protagoras, will he be better? and about what?

When Protagoras heard me say this, he replied: You ask questions fairly, and I like to answer a question which is fairly put. If Hippocrates comes to me he will not experience the sort of drudgery with which other sophists are in the habit of insulting their pupils; who, when they have just escaped from the arts, are taken against their will and driven back into them by these teachers, and made to learn calculation, and astronomy, and geometry, and music (he gave

From *The Dialogues of Plato*, 4th ed., trans. by Benjamin Jowett, Oxford, The Clarendon Press, 1953, Vol. I, pp. 142–153 (with omissions as indicated in the text). Reprinted by permission of the publisher.

a look at Hippias as he said this); but if he comes to me, he will learn that which he comes to learn. And this is prudence in affairs private as well as public; he will learn to order his own house in the best manner, and he will be fully qualified to speak and act in the affairs of the state.

Do I understand you, I said; and is your meaning that you teach the art of politics, and that you promise to make men good citizens?

That, Socrates, is exactly the profession which I make.

Then, I said, you possess a truly noble art, if there is no mistake about this; for to you, Protagoras, I will speak with entire candour, and admit that I used to think that this art is incapable of being taught, and yet I know not how to disbelieve your assertion. And I ought to tell you why I am of opinion that this art cannot be taught or communicated by man to man. I say that the Athenians are an understanding people, and indeed they are esteemed to be such by the other Hellenes. Now I observe that when we are met together in the assembly, and the matter in hand relate to building, the builders are summoned as advisers; when the question is one of ship-building, then the ship-wrights; and the like of other arts which they think capable of being taught and learned. And if some person offers to give them advice who is not supposed by them to have any skill in the art, even though he be good-looking and rich and noble, they will not listen to him; but laugh and hoot at him, until either he is clamoured down and retires of himself, or he is dragged away or put out by the constables at the command of the prytanes. This is their way of behaving about that which they deem to be the subject of an art. But when the question is an affair of state, then everybody is free to have a say—carpenter, tinker, cobbler, merchant, sea-captain; rich and poor, high and low—anyone who likes gets up, and no one reproaches him, as in the former case, with not having learned, and having no teacher, and yet giving advice; evidently because they are under the impression that this sort of knowledge cannot be taught. And not only is this true of the state, but of individuals; the best and wisest of our citizens are unable to impart their own excellence to others: as for example, Pericles, the father of these young men, who provided them with admirable instruction in all that could be learned from masters, in his own department of politics neither taught them, nor gave them teachers; but they were allowed to wander at their own free will in a sort of hope that they would light upon virtue of their own accord. Or take another example: there was Cleinias the younger brother of our friend Alcibiades, of whom this very same Pericles was the guardian; and he being in fact under the apprehension that Cleinias would be corrupted by Alcibiades snatched him away from his brother, and placed him in the house of Ariphron to be educated; but before six months had elapsed, Pericles sent him back to Alcibiades, not knowing what to do with him. And I could mention numberless other instances of persons who were good themselves, and never yet made any one else good, whether friend or stranger. Now I, Protagoras, when I contemplate these examples, am of opinion that virtue cannot be taught. But then again, when I listen to your words, I waver; and am disposed to think that there must be something in what you say, because I know that you have great experience, and learning, and invention. And I wish that you would, if possible, show me a little more clearly that virtue can be taught. Will you be so good?

That I will, Socrates, and gladly. But what would you like? Shall I, as an elder, speak to you as younger men in an apologue or myth, or shall I argue out the question?

To this several of the company answered that he should choose for himself.

Well, then, he said, I think that the myth will be more interesting.

Once upon a time there were gods only, and no mortal creatures. But when the appointed time came that these also should be created, the gods fashioned them out of earth and fire and various mixtures of both elements in the interior of the earth; and when they were about to bring them into the light of day, they ordered Prometheus and Epimetheus to equip them, and to distribute to them severally their proper qualities. Epimetheus said to Prometheus: "Let me distribute, and do you inspect." This was agreed, and Epimetheus made the distribution. There were some to whom he gave strength without swiftness, while he equipped the weaker with swiftness; some he armed, and others he left unarmed; and devised for the latter some other means of preservation. Upon those whom he clothed in diminutive bodies, he bestowed winged flight or subterranean habitation: those which he aggrandized with magnitude, he protected by their very size: and similarly with the rest of his distribution, always compensating. These devices he used as precautions that no race should be destroyed. And when he had provided against their destruction by one another, he contrived also a means of protecting them against the seasons of heaven; clothing them with close hair and thick skins sufficient to defend them against the winter cold, yet able to resist the summer heat, and serving also as a natural bed of their own when they wanted to rest; also he furnished them with hoofs and hair and hard and callous skins under their feet. Then he gave them varieties of food,—herb of the soil to some, to others fruits of trees, and to others roots, and to some again he gave other animals as food. And some he made to have few young ones, while those who were their prey were very prolific; and in this manner the race was preserved. Thus did Epimetheus, who, not being very wise, forgot that he had distributed among the brute animals all the qualities which he had to give,—and when he came to man, who was still unprovided, he was terribly perplexed. Now while he was in this per-plexity, Prometheus came to inspect the distribution, and he found that the other animals were quite suitably furnished, but that man was naked and shoeless, and had neither bed nor arms of defence. The appointed hour was approaching when man in his turn was to emerge from earth into the light of day; and Prometheus, not knowing how he could devise his salvation, stole the mechanical arts of Hephaestus and Athene, and fire with them (they could neither have been acquired nor used without fire), and gave them to man. Thus man had the wisdom necessary to the support of life, but political wisdom he had not; for that was in the keeping of Zeus, and the power of Prometheus no longer extended to entering into the citadel of heaven, where Zeus dwelt, who moreover had terrible sentinels; but he did enter by stealth into the common workshop of Athene and Hephaestus, in which they used to practise their favourite arts, and carried off Hephaestus' art of working by fire, and also the art of Athene, and gave them to man. And in this way man was supplied with the means of life. But Prometheus is said to have been afterwards prosecuted for theft, owing to the blunder of Epimetheus.

Now man, having a share of the divine attributes, was at first the only one of the animals who had any gods, because he alone was of their kindred; and he would raise altars and images of them. He was not long in inventing articulate speech and names; and he also constructed houses and clothes and shoes and beds, and drew sustenance from the earth. Thus provided, mankind at first lived dispersed, and there were no cities. But the consequence was that they were destroyed by the wild beasts, for they were utterly weak in comparison of them, and their practical attainments were only sufficient to provide them with the means of life, and did not enable them to carry on war against the animals: food they had, but not as yet the art of government, of which the art of war is a part. After a while the desire of self-preservation gathered them into cities; but when they were gathered together, having no art of government, they evilly entreated one another, and were again in process of dispersion and destruction. Zeus feared that the entire race would be exterminated, and so he sent Hermes to them, bearing reverence and justice to be the ordering principles of cities and the bonds of friendship and conciliation. Hermes asked Zeus how he should impart justice and reverence among men:—Should he distribute them as the arts are distributed; that is to say, to a favoured few only, one skilled individual having enough of medicine or of any other art for many unskilled ones? "Shall this be the manner in which I am to distribute justice and reverence among men, or shall I give them to all?" "To all," said Zeus; "I should like them all to have a share; for cities cannot exist, if a few only share in the virtues, as in the arts. And further, make a law by my order, that he who has no part in reverence and justice shall be put to death, for he is a plague of the state."

And this is the reason, Socrates, why the Athenians and mankind in general, when the question relates to carpentering or any other mechanical art, allow but a few to share in their deliberations; and when anyone else interferes, then, as you say, they object, if he be not of the favoured few; which, as I reply, is very natural. But when they meet to deliberate about political virtue, which proceeds only by way of justice and wisdom, they are patient enough of any man who speaks of them, as is also natural, because they think that every man ought to share in this sort of virtue, and that states could not exist if this were otherwise. Such, Socrates, is the reason of this phenomenon.

And that you may not suppose yourself to be deceived in thinking that all men regard every man as having a share of justice or honesty and of every other political virtue, let me give you a further proof. In other cases, as you are aware, if a man says that he is a good flute-player, or skilful in any other art in which he has no skill, people either laugh at him or are angry with him, and his relations think that he is mad and go and admonish him; but when honesty is in question, or some other political virtue, even if they know that he is dishonest, yet, if the man comes forward publicly and tells the truth against himself, then, what in the other case was held by them to be good sense, viz., telling the truth, they now deem to be madness. They say that all men ought to profess honesty whether they are honest or not, and that a man is out of his mind who makes no claim to that virtue. Their notion is, that every man must have it in some degree, or else he ought not to be in the world.

I have been showing that they are right in admitting every man as a counsellor about this sort of virtue, as they are of opinion that every man is a partaker of it. And I will now endeavour to show further that they do not conceive this virtue to be given by nature, or to grow spontaneously, but to be a thing which may be taught; and which comes to those to whom it does come, by taking pains. No one would instruct, no one would rebuke or be angry with those whose calamities they suppose to be due to nature or chance: they do not try to punish or to prevent them from being what they are; they do but pity them. Who is so foolish as to chastise or instruct the ugly, or the diminutive, or the feeble? And for this reason. Because, I take it, everyone knows that good and evil of this kind is the work of nature and of chance; whereas if a man is wanting in those good qualities which are held to be attainable by study and exercise and teaching, and has only the contrary evil qualities, other men are angry with him, and punish and reprove him—of these evil qualities one is impiety, another injustice, and they may be described generally as the very opposite of political virtue. In such cases any man will be angry with another, and reprimand him,—clearly because he thinks that by study and learning the virtue may be acquired. If you think, Socrates, of the effect of punishment upon the wrong-doer, you will see at once that in the opinion of mankind virtue may be acquired; no one punishes the evil-doer under the notion, or for the reason, that he has done wrong,—only the unreasonable fury of a beast acts in that manner. But he who desires to inflict rational punishment does not retaliate for a past wrong, for what has been done cannot be undone; he has regard to the future, and is desirous that the man who is punished, and he who sees him punished, may be deterred from doing wrong again. Now if this is his conception, then he also conceives that virtue may be taught; since it is for the sake of deterrence that he punishes. This is the notion of all who retaliate upon others either privately or publicly. And the Athenians, too, your own citizens, like other men, punish and take vengeance on all whom they regard as evil-doers; and hence we may infer them to be of the number of those who think that virtue may be acquired and taught. Thus far, Socrates, I have shown you clearly enough, if I am not mistaken, that your countrymen are right in admitting the tinker and the cobbler to advise about politics, and also that they deem virtue to be capable of being taught and acquired.

There yet remains one difficulty which has been raised by you about good men. What is the reason why good men teach their sons the knowledge which can be gained from teachers, and make them wise in that, but make them no better than anyone else in the virtues which distinguish themselves? And here, Socrates, I will leave the apologue and resume the argument. Please to consider: Is there or is there not some one quality of which all the citizens must be partakers, if there is to be a city at all? In the answer to this question is contained the only solution of your difficulty; there is no other. For if there be any such quality, and this quality or unity is not the art of the carpenter, or the smith, or the potter, but justice and temperance and holiness and, in a word, manly virtue—if this is the quality of which all men must be partakers, and which is the very condition of their learning or doing anything else, and if he who is wanting in this, whether he be a child only or a grown-up man or woman, must be taught and punished, until by punishment he becomes better, and he who rebels against instruction and punishment must be either exiled or condemned to death as incurable—if what I am saying be true, and yet good men have their sons taught other things and not this, do consider what a strange thing their goodness has become. For we have shown that they think virtue capable of being taught and cultivated both in private and public; and, notwithstanding, they have their sons taught lesser matters, ignorance of which does not involve the punishment of death: but greater things, of which the ignorance may cause death and exile to their own children, if they have no knowledge of virtue or encouragement toward it—aye, and confiscation as well as death, and, in a word, may be the ruin of families—those things, I say, they are supposed not to have them taught,—not to take the utmost care that they should learn. How improbable is this, Socrates!

Education and admonition commence in the first years of childhood, and last to the very end of life. Mother and nurse and father and tutor are vying with one another about the improvement of the child as soon as ever he is able to understand what is being said to him: he cannot say or do anything without their teaching him and setting forth to him that this is just and that is unjust; this is honourable, that is dishonourable; this is holy, that is unholy; do this and abstain from that. And if he obeys, well and good; if not, he is straightened by threats and blows, like a piece of bent or warped wood. At a later stage they send him to teachers, and enjoin them to see to his good behaviour even more than to his reading and music; and the teachers do as they are desired. And when the boy has learned his letters and is beginning to understand what is written, as before he understood only what was spoken, they put on his desk the works of great poets for him to read; in these are contained many admonitions, and many tales and praises and encomia of famous men of old, which he is required to learn by heart, in order that he may imitate or emulate them and desire to become like them. Then, again, the teachers of the lyre take similar care that their young disciple is temperate and gets into no mischief; and when they have taught him the use of the lyre, they introduce him to the poems of other excellent poets, who are the lyric poets; and these they set to music, and make their harmonies and rhythms quite familiar to the children's souls, in order that they may learn to be more gentle, and harmonious, and rhythmical, and so more fitted for speech and action; for the life of man in every part has need of harmony and rhythm. Then they send them to the master of gymnastic, in order that the improvement of their bodies may better minister to the virtuous mind, and that they may not be compelled through bodily weakness to play the coward in war or on any other occasion. This is principally done by those who have the means, and those who have the means are the rich; their children begin to go to school soonest and leave off latest. When they have done with masters, the state again compels them to learn the laws, and live after the pattern which they furnish, and not after their own fancies; and just as the writing-master first traces outlines with a style for the use of the young beginner who is not yet able to write, then gives him the tablet and makes him write along those lines, so the city outlines the laws, which were the invention of good lawgivers living in the olden time, and compels us to exercise and to obey authority in accordance with those; and he who transgresses them is to be corrected, or, in other words, called to account, which is a term used not only in your country, but also in many others, seeing that justice calls men to account. Now when there is all this care about virtue private and public, why, Socrates, do you still wonder and doubt whether virtue can be taught? Cease to wonder, for the opposite would be far more surprising.

But why then do the sons of good fathers often turn out ill? Learn now the cause of this. There is nothing very wonderful in it, if what I said before was true, that the existence of a state implies that no man is unskilled in virtue. If so—and nothing can be truer—then I will further ask you to take as an illustration some other pursuit or branch of knowledge, and reflect upon that. Suppose that there could be no state unless we were all flute-players, as far as each had the capacity, and everybody was freely teaching everybody the art, both in private and public, and reproving the bad player as freely and openly as every man now teaches justice and the laws, not concealing them as he would conceal the other arts, but imparting them—for all of us have a mutual interest in the justice and virtue of one another, and this is the reason why everyone is so ready to propagate and teach justice and the laws;—suppose, I say, that there were the same readiness and liberality among us in teaching one another flute-playing, do you imagine, Socrates, that the sons of good flute-players would be more likely to be good than the sons of bad ones? I think not. Would not their sons grow up to be distinguished or undistinguished according to their own natural capacities as flute-players, and the son of a good player would often turn out to be a bad one, and the son of a bad player to be a good one, but at least they would all play the flute reasonably well in comparison of those who were ignorant and unacquainted with the art of flute-playing? In like manner I would have you consider that he who appears to you to be the worst of those who have been brought up in laws and human society, would appear to be a just man and an artificer of justice if he were to be compared with men who had no education, or courts of justice, or laws, or any constraints forcing them incessantly to the practice of virtue—with savages like those whom the poet Pherecrates exhibited on the stage at last year's Lenaean festival. If you were living among such as the man-haters of his Chorus, you would be only too glad to meet with Eurybates and Phrynondas, and you would sorrowfully long to revisit the rascality of this part of the world. Now you, Socrates, are being fastidious, and why? Because all men are teachers of virtue, each one according to his ability; and you say Where are the teachers? You might as well ask, Who teaches Greek? For of that too there will not be any teachers found. Or you might ask, Who is to teach the sons of our artisans this same art which they have learned of their fathers? He and his fellow workmen have taught them to the best of their ability,—but who will carry them farther in their arts? You would certainly have a difficulty, Socrates, in finding a teacher of them, but there would be no difficulty whatever in finding a teacher of those who are ignorant; this is true of virtue or of anything else. But if there is anyone better able than we are to promote virtue ever so little, we must be content with the result. A teacher of this sort I believe myself to be, excelling all other human beings in the power to raise a man towards nobility and goodness; and I give my pupils their money's-worth, and even more, as they themselves confess. And therefore I have introduced the following mode of payment:—When a man is my pupil, if he likes he pays my fee; if he does not like, he has only to go into a temple and take an oath of the value of the instruction, and he pays no more than that.

Such is my apologue, Socrates, and such is the argument by which I endeavour to show that virtue may be taught, and that this is the opinion of the Athenians. And I have also attempted to show that you are not to wonder at good fathers having bad sons, or at good sons having bad fathers; thus the sons of Polycleitus, who are the companions of our friends here, Paralus and Xanthippus, are nothing in comparison with their father; and this is true of the sons of many other artists. As yet we ought not to bring the same charge against Paralus and Xanthippus themselves, for they are young and there is still hope of them.

Such was the speech of Protagoras, who now held his peace. For a long time I could not take my eyes off him, still spellbound, expecting him to speak further, and eager to hear him. At length, when the truth dawned upon me that he had really finished, not without difficulty I pulled myself together, as it were, and looking at Hippocrates, I said to him: O son of Apollodorus, how deeply grateful I am to you for having urged me to come hither; I would not have missed the speech of Protagoras for a great deal. For I used to imagine that no human care can make men good; but I know better now. . . .

THE REPUBLIC

BOOK II

Glaucon and the rest entreated me . . . to inquire thoroughly into the nature of justice and injustice, and . . . to discover the truth about their relative advantages. I told them, what I really thought, that the inquiry would be of a serious nature, and would require very good eyes. Seeing then, I said, that we are no great wits, I think that we had better adopt a method which I may illustrate thus; suppose that a short-sighted person had been asked to read small letters from a distance; and someone observed that the same inscription was written elsewhere on a larger scale—if they were the same, and he could read the larger letters first and then proceed to the lesser, this would have been thought a rare piece of good fortune.

Very true, said Adeimantus; but how does the illustration apply to our inquiry about justice?

I will tell you, I replied; justice is, as you know, sometimes spoken of as the virtue of an individual, and sometimes as the virtue of a State.

True, he replied.

And is not a State larger than an individual?

It is.

Then in the larger, justice is likely to be more abundant and more easily discernible. I propose therefore that we inquire into the nature of justice and injustice, first as they appear in the State, and secondly in the individual, proceeding from the greater to the lesser and comparing them.

That, he said, is an excellent proposal.

And if we imagine the State in process of creation, we shall see the justice and injustice of the State in process of creation also.

I dare say.

When the State is completed there may be a hope that the object of our search will be more easily discovered.

Yes, far more easily.

But ought we to attempt to construct one? I said; for to do so, as I am inclined to think, will be a very serious task. Reflect therefore.

I have reflected, said Adeimantus, and am anxious that you should proceed.

From *The Dialogues of Plato*, 4th ed., trans. by Benjamin Jowett, Oxford, The Clarendon Press, 1953, Vol. II, pp. 209–407 (with omissions as indicated in the text). Reprinted by permission of the publisher.

A State, I said, arises, as I conceive, out of the needs of mankind; no one is self-sufficing, but all of us have many wants. Can any other origin of a State be imagined?

There can be no other.

Then, as we have many wants, and many persons are needed to supply them, one takes a helper for one purpose and another for another; and when these partners and helpers are gathered together in one habitation the body of inhabitants is termed a State.

True, he said.

And it is in the belief that it is for his own good, that one man gives to another or receives from him in exchange.

Very true.

Then, I said, let us construct a State in theory from the beginning; and yet the true creator, it seems, will be necessity.

Of course, he replied.

Now the first and greatest of necessities is food, which is the condition of life and existence.

Certainly.

The second is a dwelling, and the third clothing and the like.

True.

And now let us see what must be the size of a city able to supply such a demand: We may suppose that one man is a husbandman, another a builder, someone else a weaver—shall we add to them a shoemaker, or perhaps some other purveyor to our bodily wants?

By all means.

The simplest possible State must include four or five men.

Clearly.

And how will they proceed? Will each bring the result of his labours into a common stock?—the individual husbandman, for example, producing for four, and labouring four times as long and as much as he need in the provision of food with which he supplies others as well as himself; or will he have nothing to do with others and not be at the trouble of producing for them, but provide for himself alone a fourth of the food in a fourth of the time, and in the remaining three fourths of his time be employed in making a house or a coat or a pair of shoes, not bothering to form a partnership with others, but supplying himself all his own wants?

Adeimantus thought that he should aim at producing food only and not at producing everything.

Probably, I replied, that would be the better way; and when I hear you say this, I am myself reminded that we are not all alike; there are diversities of natures among us which are adapted to different occupations.

Very true.

And will you have a work better done when every workman tries his hand at many occupations, or when each has only one?

When he has only one.

Further, there can be no doubt that a work is spoilt when not done at the right time?

No doubt.

For business is not disposed to wait until the doer of the business is at leisure; but the doer must follow up his opportunity, and make the business his first object.

He must.

And if so, we must infer that all things are produced more plentifully and easily and of a better quality when one man does one thing which is natural to him and does it at the right time, leaving other crafts alone.

Undoubtedly.

Then more than four citizens will be required to furnish all that has been mentioned; for the husbandman will not make his own plough or mattock, or other implements of agriculture, if they are to be good for anything. Neither will the builder make his tools—and he too needs many; and in like manner the weaver and shoemaker.

True.

Then carpenters, and smiths, and many other artisans, will be sharers in our little State, which is already beginning to grow?

True.

Yet even if we add neatherds, shepherds, and other herdsmen, in order that our husbandmen may have oxen to plough with, and builders as well as husbandmen may have draught cattle, and curriers and weavers fleeces and hides, —still our State will not be very large.

That is true; yet neither will it be a very small State which contains all these.

Then, again, there is the situation of the city—to find a place where nothing need be imported is well nigh impossible.

Impossible.

Then there must be another class of citizens who will bring the required supply from another city?

There must.

But if the trader goes empty-handed, having nothing which they require who would supply his need, he will come back empty-handed.

That is probable.

And therefore what they produce at home must be not only enough for themselves, but such both in quantity and quality as to accommodate those from whom their wants are supplied.

Very true.

Then more husbandmen and more artisans will be required?

They will.

Not to mention those who serve as importers and exporters of goods, who are called, I believe, merchants?

Yes.

Then we shall want merchants?

We shall.

And if merchandise is to be carried over the sea, we shall also require men who have been bred to various nautical occupations.

Yes, a large class.

Then, again, within the city, how will they exchange their productions? To secure such an exchange was, as you will remember, one of our principal objects when we formed them into a society and constituted a State.

Clearly they will buy and sell.

Then they will need a market-place, and a money-token for purposes of exchange.

Certainly.

Suppose now that a husbandman, or an artisan, brings some production to market, and comes at a time when there is no one to exchange with him—is he to sit idle in the market-place, taking a holiday from his work?

Not at all; he will find people there who, seeing the want, undertake the office of salesmen. In well-ordered states they are commonly those who are weakest in bodily strength, and therefore of little use for any other purpose; their duty is to be in the market, and to give money in exchange for goods to those who desire to sell and to take money from those who desire to buy.

This want, then, creates a class of retail-traders in our State. Is not "retailer" the term which is applied to those who sit in the market-place engaged in buying and selling, while those who wander from one city to another are called merchants?

Yes, he said.

And there is another class of servants, who are intellectually hardly on the level of association; still they have plenty of bodily strength for labour, which accordingly they sell, and are called, if I do not mistake, hirelings, hire being the name which is given to the price of their labour.

True.

Then hirelings will help to make up our population?

Yes.

And now, Adeimantus, is our State matured and perfected?

I think so.

Where, then, is justice within it, and where is injustice, and at what stage did they make their entrance?

Probably in the dealings of these citizens with one another. I cannot suggest where else they may be found.

I dare say that you are right in your suggestion, I said; we had better think the matter out, and not shrink from the inquiry.

Let us then consider, first of all, what will be their way of life, now that we have thus established them. Will they not work at the production of corn, and wine, and clothes, and shoes? And when they are housed, in summer they will commonly work stripped and barefoot, but in winter substantially clothed and shod. They will feed on barley-meal and flour of wheat, baking the one and kneading the other, making noble cakes and loaves; these they will serve up on a mat of reeds or on clean leaves, themselves reclining the while upon beds strewn with yew or myrtle. And they and their children will feast, drinking of the wine which they have made, wearing garlands on their heads, and hymning the praises of the gods, in happy converse with one another. And they will take care that their families do not exceed their means; having an eye to poverty or war.

But, said Glaucon, interposing, you have not given them a relish to their meal.

True, I replied, I had forgotten; of course they must have a relish—salt, and olives, and cheese, and they will boil roots and herbs such as country people prepare; for a dessert we shall give them figs, and peas, and beans; and they will roast myrtle-berries and acorns at the fire, sipping their wine in moderation. And with such a diet they may be expected to live in peace and health to a good old age, and bequeath a similar life to their children after them.

Yes, Socrates, he said, and if you were providing for a city of pigs, how else would you feed the beasts?

But what would you have, Glaucon? I replied.

Why, he said, you should give them the ordinary conveniences of life. People who are to be comfortable are accustomed to lie on sofas, and dine off tables, and they should have sauces and sweets in the modern style.

Yes, I said, now I understand: the question which you would have me consider is, not only how a State, but how a luxurious State is created; and possibly there is no harm in this, for by extending our inquiry to such a State we shall be more likely to see how political justice and injustice originate. In my opinion the true and healthy constitution of the State is the one which I have described. But if you wish also to see a State at fever-heat, I have no objection. For I suspect that many will not be satisfied with the simpler way of life. They will be for adding sofas, and tables, and other furniture; also dainties, and perfumes, and incense, and courtezans, and cakes, all these not of one sort only, but in every variety; we must go beyond the necessaries of which I was at first speaking, such as houses, and clothes, and shoes: the arts of the painter and the embroiderer will have to be set in motion, and gold and ivory and all sorts of materials must be procured.

True, he said.

Then we must enlarge our borders; for the original healthy State is no longer sufficient. Now will the city have to fill and swell with a multitude of callings which are not required by any natural want; such as the tribe of hunters, and again imitators, of whom one large class have to do with forms and colours; another will be the votaries of music—poets and their attendant train of rhapsodists, players, dancers, contractors; also makers of divers kinds of articles, including those which serve for the adornment of women. And we shall want more servants. Will not tutors be also in request, and nurses wet and dry, tirewomen and barbers, as well as confectioners and cooks? Then we shall also now need swineherds, who were not needed and therefore had no place in our former State. They must not be forgotten: also a vast number of cattle will be required, if meat is to be eaten.

Certainly.

And living in this way we shall have much greater need of physicians than before?

Much greater.

And the country which was once enough to support the original inhabitants will now have become too small?

Quite true.

Then a slice of our neighbours' land will be wanted by us for pasture and tillage, and they will want a slice of ours, if, like ourselves, they exceed the limit of necessity, and give themselves up to the unlimited accumulation of wealth?

That, Socrates, will be inevitable.

And so we shall go to war, Glaucon. Shall we not?

Most certainly, he replied.

Then, without determining as yet whether war does good or harm, thus much we may affirm, that now we have discovered war to be derived from causes which are also the causes of almost all the evils in States, private as well as public.

Undoubtedly.

And our State must once more enlarge; and this time the enlargement will be nothing short of a whole army, which will have to go out and fight with the invaders for all that we have, as well as for the things and persons whom we were describing above.

Why? he said; are they not capable of defending themselves?

No, I said; not if we were right in the principle which was acknowledged by all of us when we were framing the State: the principle, as you will remember, was that one man cannot practise many arts with success.

Very true, he said.

But is not armed combat in war an art?

Certainly.

And an art requiring as much attention as shoemaking?

Quite true.

And the shoemaker was not allowed by us to be a husbandman, or a weaver, or a builder—in order that we might have our shoes well made; but to him and to every other worker was assigned one work for which he was by nature fitted, and at that he was to continue working all his life long and at no other; he was not to let opportunities slip, and then he would become a good workman. Now can anything be more important than that the work of a soldier should be well done? Or is war an art so easily acquired that a man may be a warrior who is also a husbandman, or shoemaker, or other artisan; although no one in the world would be a good dice- or chess-player who merely took up the game as a recreation, and had not from his earliest years devoted himself to this and nothing else? No equipment will make a man a skilled workman, or athlete, nor be of any use to him who has not learned how to handle it, and has never bestowed sufficient attention upon it. How then will he who takes up shield or other implement of war become a good fighter all in a day, whether with heavy-armed or any other kind of troops?

Yes, he said, the tools which would teach men their own use would be beyond price.

And just as the duties of the guardian surpass all others in importance, I said, so does his business require the most skill and practice, as well as undivided attention.

No doubt, he replied.

Will he not also require natural aptitude for his calling?

Certainly.

Then it will be our duty to select, if we can, natures which are fitted for the task of guarding the city?

It will.

It is no light task, then, that we have undertaken, I said; but we must be brave and do our best.

We must.

Do you agree that the noble youth is very like a well-bred dog in respect of guarding and watching?

What do you mean?

I mean that both of them ought to be quick to see, and swift to overtake the enemy when they see him; and strong too if, when they have caught him, they have to fight with him.

All these qualities, he replied, will certainly be required by them.

Well, and your guardian must be brave if he is to fight well?

Certainly.

And is he likely to be brave who has no spirit, whether horse or dog or any other animal? Have you never observed how invincible and unconquerable is spirit and how the presence of it makes the soul of any creature to be absolutely fearless and indomitable?

I have.

Then now we have a clear notion of the bodily qualities which are required in the guardian.

True.

And also of the mental ones; his soul is to be full of spirit?

True again.

But how can these spirited natures fail to be savage with one another, and with everybody else?

A difficulty by no means easy to overcome, he replied.

Whereas, I said, they ought to be dangerous to their enemies, and gentle to their friends; if not, they will destroy themselves without waiting for their enemies to destroy them.

True, he said.

What is to be done then? I said; how shall we find a gentle nature which has also a high spirit; for the one is the contradiction of the other?

True.

He will not be a good guardian who is wanting in either of these two qualities; and yet the combination of them appears to be impossible; and hence we must infer that to be a good guardian is impossible.

I am afraid that what you say is true, he replied.

Here feeling perplexed I began to think over what had preceded.—My friend, I said, no wonder that we are in a perplexity; for we have lost sight of the image which we had before us.

What do you mean? he said.

It has escaped our notice that there do exist natures gifted with those opposite qualities.

Where?

Many animals, I replied, furnish examples of them, but most of all the dog, to which we compared the guardian: you know the disposition of a well-bred dog, perfectly gentle to its familiars and acquaintances, and the reverse to strangers.

Yes, I know.

Then there is nothing impossible or out of the order of nature in our finding a guardian who has a similar combination of qualities?

Certainly not.

Would not he who is fitted to be a guardian, besides the spirited nature, need to have the qualities of a philosopher?

I do not apprehend your meaning.

The trait of which I am speaking, I replied, may be also seen in the dog, and is remarkable in the animal.

What trait?

Why, a dog, whenever he sees a stranger, is angry; when an acquaintance, he welcomes him, although the one has never done him any harm, nor the other any good. Did this never strike you as curious?

The point never struck me before; but I quite recognize the truth of your remark.

And surely this instinct of the dog is very charming;—your dog is a true philosopher.

Why?

Why, because he distinguishes the face of a friend and of an enemy only by the criterion of knowing and not knowing. And must not an animal be a lover of learning who determines what is or is not friendly to him by the test of knowledge and ignorance?

Most assuredly.

And is not the love of learning the love of wisdom, which is philosophy?

They are the same, he replied.

And may we not say confidently of man also, that he who is likely to be gentle to his friends and acquaintances, must by nature be a lover of wisdom and knowledge?

That we may safely affirm.

Then he who is to be a really good and noble guardian of the State will require to unite in himself philosophy and spirit and swiftness and strength?

Undoubtedly.

Then we have found the desired natures; and now that we have found them, how are they to be reared and educated? Is not this an inquiry which may be expected to throw light on the greater inquiry which is our final end—How do justice and injustice grow up in States? for we do not want either to omit what is to the point or to draw out the argument to an inconvenient length.

Adeimantus thought that the inquiry would be of great service to us.

Then, I said, my dear friend, the task must not be given up, even if somewhat long.

Certainly not.

Come then, and let us pass a leisure hour in story-telling, and our story shall be the education of our heroes.

By all means.

And what shall be their education? It would be hard, I think, to find a better than the traditional system, which has two divisions, gymnastic for the body, and music for the soul.

True.

Presumably we shall begin education with music, before gymnastic can begin.

By all means.

And when you speak of music, do you include literature or not?

I do.

And literature may be either true or false?

Yes.

Both have a part to play in education, but we must begin with the false?

I do not understand your meaning, he said.

You know, I said, that we begin by telling children stories which, though not wholly destitute of truth, are in the main fictitious; and these stories are told them when they are not of an age for gymnastics.

Very true.

That was my meaning when I said that we must teach music before gymnastics.

Quite right, he said.

You know also that the beginning is the most important part of any work, especially in the case of a young and tender thing; for that is the time at which the character is being formed and the desired impression is more readily taken.

Quite true.

And shall we just carelessly allow children to hear any casual tales which may be devised by casual persons, and to receive into their minds ideas for the most part the very opposite of those which we shall wish them to have when they are grown up?

We cannot.

Then the first thing will be to establish a censorship of the writers of fiction, and let the censors receive any tale of fiction which is good, and reject the bad; and we will persuade mothers and nurses to tell their children the authorized ones only. Let them fashion the mind with such tales, even more fondly than they mould the body with their hands; but most of those which are now in use must be discarded.

Of what tales are you speaking? he said.

You may find a model of the lesser in the greater, I said; for they must both be of the same type, and the same spirit ought to be found in both of them.

Very likely, he replied; but I do not as yet know what you would term the greater.

Those, I said, which are narrated by Homer and Hesiod, and the rest of the poets, who have ever been the great story-tellers of mankind.

But which stories do you mean, he said; and what fault do you find with them?

A fault which is fundamental and most serious, I said; the fault of saying what is false, and doing so for no good purpose.

But when is this fault committed?

Whenever an erroneous representation is made of the nature of gods and heroes,—as when a painter paints a picture not having the shadow of a likeness to his subject.

Yes, he said, that sort of thing is certainly very blameable; but what are the stories which you mean?

First of all, I said, there was that greatest of all falsehoods on great subjects, which the misguided poet told about Uranus,—I mean what Hesiod says that Uranus did, and how Cronus retaliated on him. The doings of Cronus, and the sufferings which in turn his son inflicted upon him, even if they were true, ought certainly not to be lightly told to young and thoughtless persons; if possible, they had better be buried in silence. But if there is an absolute necessity for their mention, a chosen few might hear them in a mystery, and they should sacrifice not a common [Eleusinian] pig, but some huge and unprocurable victim, so that the number of the hearers may be very few indeed.

Why, yes, said he, those stories are extremely objectionable.

Yes, Adeimantus, they are stories not to be repeated in our State; the young man should not be told that in committing the worst of crimes he is far from doing anything outrageous; and that even if he chastises in savage fashion his father when he does wrong, he will only be following the example of the first and greatest among the gods.

I entirely agree with you, he said; in my opinion those stories are quite unfit to be repeated.

Neither, if we mean our future guardians to regard the habit of lightly quarrelling among themselves as of all things the basest, should any word be said to them of the wars in heaven, and of the plots and fightings of the gods against one another, for they are not true. No, we shall never mention the battles of the giants, or let them be embroidered on garments; and we shall be silent about the innumerable other quarrels of gods and heroes with their friends and relatives. If we intend to persuade them that quarrelling is unholy, and that never up to this time has there been any hatred between citizens, then the stories which old men and old women tell them as children should be in this strain; and when they grow up, the poets also should be obliged to compose for them in a similar spirit. But the narrative of Hephaestus binding Hera his mother, or how on another occasion his father sent him flying for taking her part when she was being beaten, and all the battles of the gods in Homer— these tales must not be admitted into our State, whether they are supposed to have an allegorical meaning or not. For a young person cannot judge what is allegorical and what is literal; anything that he receives into his mind at that age is likely to become indelible and unalterable; and therefore it is most important that the tales which the young first hear should be models of virtuous thoughts.

There you are right, he replied; but if anyone asks where are such models to be found and of what tales are you speaking—how shall we answer him?

I said to him, You and I, Adeimantus, at this moment are not poets, but founders of a State: now the founders of a State ought to know the general forms in which poets should cast their tales, and the limits which must be observed by them, but to make the tales is not their business.

Very true, he said; but what are these forms of theology which you mean?

Something of this kind, I replied:—God is always to be represented as he truly is, whatever be the sort of poetry, epic, lyric or tragic, in which the representation is given.

Right.

And is he not truly good? and must he not be represented as such?

Certainly.

And no good thing is hurtful?

No, indeed.

And that which is not hurtful hurts not?

Certainly not.

And that which hurts not does no evil?

No.

And can that which does no evil be a cause of evil?

Impossible.

And the good is advantageous?

Yes.

And therefore the cause of well-being?

Yes.

It follows therefore that the good is not the cause of all things, but of those which are as they should be; and it is not to be blamed for evil.

Assuredly.

Then God, if he be good, is not the author of all things, as the many assert, but he is the cause of a few things only, and not of most things that occur to men. For few are the goods of human life, and many are the evils, and the good is to be attributed to God alone; of the evils the causes are to be sought elsewhere, and not in him.

That appears to me to be most true, he said.

Then we must not listen to Homer or to any other poet who is guilty of the folly of saying

.   .   .

"Zeus, who is the dispenser of good and evil to us."

And if anyone asserts that the violation of oaths and treaties, which was really the work of Pandarus, was brought about by Athena and Zeus, or that the strife and competition between the gods was instigated by Themis and Zeus, he shall not have our approval; neither will we allow our young men to hear the words of Aeschylus, that

"God plants guilt among men when he desires utterly to destroy a house."

And if a poet writes of the sufferings of Niobe—the subject of the tragedy in which these iambic verses occur—or of the house of Pelops, or of the Trojan war or on any similar theme, either we must not permit him to say that these are the works of God, or if they are of God, he must devise some explanation of them such as we are seeking: he must say that God did what was just and right, and they were the better for being punished. But that those who are punished are miserable, and that God is the author of their misery—the poet is not to be permitted to say; though he may say that the wicked were miserable because they required to be punished, and were benefited by receiving punishment from God; but that God being good is the author of evil to anyone is to be denied. We shall insist that it is not said or sung or heard in verse or prose by anyone whether old or young in any well-ordered commonwealth. Such a fiction would be impious, disastrous to us, and inconsistent with itself.

I agree with you, he replied, and am ready to give my assent to the law.

Let this then be one of our rules and principles concerning the gods, to which our poets and reciters will be expected to conform,—that God is not the author of all things, but of good only.

That will do, he said.

And what do you think of a second principle? Do you think that God is a magician, and of a nature to appear insidiously now in one shape, and now in another—sometimes really changing and passing into many forms, sometimes deceiving us with the semblance of such transformations; or is he one and the same immutably fixed in his own proper image?

.   .   .

If he change at all he can only change for the worse, for we cannot suppose him to be deficient either in virtue or beauty.

Very true, Adeimantus; but then, would anyone, whether God or man, in your opinion deliberately make himself worse in any respect?

Impossible.

Then it is impossible that God should ever be willing to change; being, as is supposed, the fairest and best that is conceivable, every one of the gods remains absolutely and for ever in his own form.

That necessarily follows, he said, in my judgement.

Then, I said, my dear friend, let none of the poets tell us that

"The gods, taking the disguise of strangers from other lands, walk up and down cities in all sorts of forms";

and let no one slander Proteus and Thetis, neither let anyone, either in tragedy or in any other kind of poetry, introduce Hera disguised in the likeness of a priestess asking an alms

"For the life-giving daughters of Inachus the river of Argos";

—let us have none of that repertoire of falsehoods. Neither must we have mothers under the influence of the poets scaring their children with a bad version of these myths—telling how certain gods, as they say, "go about by night in the likeness of so many strangers and in divers forms"; but let them take heed lest they make cowards of their children, and at the same time speak blasphemy against the gods.

Heaven forbid, he said.

But although the gods are themselves unchangeable, still by witchcraft and deception they may make us think that they appear in various forms?

Perhaps, he replied.

Well, but can you imagine that a god would deign to be false of speech, or false in deed by putting forth a phantom of himself?

I cannot say, he replied.

Do you not know, I said, that true falsehood, if such an expression may be allowed, is hated of all gods and men?

What do you mean? he said.

I mean that no one willingly deceives with that which is the truest and highest part of himself, and about the truest and highest matters; there, above all, he is most afraid of embracing falsehood.

Still, he said, I do not comprehend you.

The reason is, I replied, that you attribute some profound meaning to my words; but I am only saying that deceiving, or being deceived or uninformed, about realities in his very soul, and in that part to have and embrace falsehood, is what every man will least tolerate. Indeed, it is in such circumstances that falsehood is most detested.

By far the most.

Consequently as I was just now remarking, this ignorance in the soul of him who is deceived may be called true falsehood; for the lie in words is only a kind of imitation and shadowy image of a previous affection of the soul, not pure unadulterated falsehood. Am I not right?

Perfectly right.

True falsehood is hated not only by the gods, but also by men?

Yes.

What should be said of the lie in words? When, and in what relationship, may it be useful and not repugnant to us? Presumably in relation to enemies, or again, when those whom we call our friends in a fit of madness or illusion are going to do some harm, then it is useful and is a sort of medicine or preventive; also in the tales of mythology, of which we were just now speaking—because we do not know the truth about ancient times, we make falsehood as much like truth as we can, and so turn it to account.

Very true, he said.

But for which of these reasons might God find falsehood useful? Can we suppose that he is ignorant of antiquity, and therefore has recourse to invention?

That would be ridiculous, he said.

Then the lying poet has no place in our idea of God?

I should say not.

Or perhaps he may tell a lie because he is afraid of enemies?

That is inconceivable.

But he may have friends who are senseless or mad?

But no mad or senseless person can be a friend of God.

Then no motive can be imagined why God should lie?

None whatever.

Then the superhuman and divine is absolutely incapable of falsehood?

Yes.

Then is God perfectly simple and true both in word and deed; he changes not, and does not deceive others, waking or dreaming, either by phantasms or by sign or by word.

Your thoughts, he said, are the reflection of my own.

You agree with me then, I said, that this is the second type or form in which men should write and speak about divine things. The gods are not magicians who transform themselves, neither do they deceive mankind in word or deed.

I grant that.

Then, although we are admirers of Homer, we shall not admire the lying dream which Zeus sends to Agamemnon; neither will we praise the verses of Aeschylus in which Thetis says that Apollo at her nuptials

"Was celebrating in song her fair progeny, whose days were to be long and to know no sickness. And when he had spoken of my lot as in all things blessed of heaven, he raised a note of triumph and cheered my soul. And I thought that the word of Phoebus, being divine and full of prophecy, would not fail. And now he himself who uttered the strain, he who was present at the banquet, and who said this—he it is who has slain my son."

These are the kind of sentiments about the gods which will arouse our anger; and he who utters them shall be refused a chorus; neither shall we allow teachers to make use of them in the instruction of the young, meaning, as we do, that our guardians, as far as men can be, should be god-fearing and godlike.

I entirely agree, he said, in these principles, and would lay them down as laws.

BOOK III

Then as far as the gods are concerned, I said, such tales are to be told, and such others are not to be told to our disciples from their youth upwards, if we mean them to honour the gods and their parents, and to value friendship with one another.

Yes; and I think that our principles are right, he said.

But if they are to be courageous, must they not learn other lessons besides these, and lessons of such a kind as will take away the fear of death? Can any man be courageous who has the fear of death in him?

Certainly not, he said.

And can he be fearless of death, or will he choose death in battle rather than defeat and slavery, who believes the world below to be real and terrible?

Impossible.

Then we must assume a control over the narrators of this class of tales as well as over the others, and beg them not simply to revile, but rather to commend the world below, intimating to them that their descriptions are untrue, and will do harm to our future warriors.

That will be our duty, he said.

Then, I said, we shall have to obliterate many obnoxious passages, beginning with the verses,

"I would rather be a serf on the land of a poor and portionless man than rule over all the dead who have come to nought."

.   .   .

And again:—

"O heavens! verily in the house of Hades there is soul and ghostly form, but no mind at all in them!"

.   .   .

And we must beg Homer and the other poets not to be angry if we strike out these and similar passages, not because they are unpoetical, or unattractive to the popular ear, but because the greater the poetical charm of them, the less are they meet for the ears of boys and men who are meant to be free, and who should fear slavery more than death.

Undoubtedly.

.   .   .

Again, truth should be highly valued; if we were right in saying that falsehood is useless to the gods, and useful only as a medicine to men, then the use of such medicines should be restricted to physicians; private individuals have no business with them.

Clearly not, he said.

Then if anyone at all is to have the privilege of lying, the rulers of the State should be the persons; and they, in their dealings either with enemies or with their own citizens, may be allowed to lie for the public good. But nobody else should meddle with anything of the kind; and although the rulers have this privilege, for a private man to lie to them in return is to be deemed a more heinous fault than for the patient or the pupil of a gymnasium not to speak the truth about his own bodily illnesses to the physician or to the trainer, or for a sailor not to tell the captain what is happening about the ship and the rest of the crew, and how things are going with himself or his fellow sailors.

Most true, he said.

If, then, the ruler catches in a lie anybody beside himself in the State,

"Any of the craftsmen, whether he be priest or physician or carpenter,"

he will punish him for introducing a practice which is equally subversive and destructive of ship or State.

Most certainly, he said, if our talk about the State is ever translated into action.

.   .   .

Enough of the subjects of poetry: let us now speak of the style; and when this has been considered, both matter and manner will have been completely treated.

. . .

You mean, I suspect, to ask whether tragedy and comedy shall be admitted into our State?

Perhaps, I said; but there may be more than this in question: I really do not know as yet, but whither the argument may blow, thither we go.

And go we will, he said.

Then, Adeimantus, let me ask you to consider whether our guardians should or should not be fond of imitation; or rather, has not this question been decided by the rule already laid down that one man can only do one thing well, and not many; and that one who grasps at many will altogether fail of gaining much reputation in any?

Certainly.

And this is equally true of imitation; no one man can imitate many things as well as he would imitate a single one?

He cannot.

Then the same person will hardly be able to play a serious part in life, and at the same time to be an imitator and imitate many other parts as well; for even when two species of imitation are nearly allied, the same persons cannot succeed in both, as, for example, the writers of tragedy and comedy—did you not just now call them imitations?

Yes, I did; and you are right in thinking that the same persons cannot succeed in both.

Any more than they can be rhapsodists and actors at once?

True.

Neither do comic and tragic writers employ the same actors; yet all these things are imitations.

They are so.

And human nature, Adeimantus, appears to have been coined into yet smaller pieces, and to be as incapable of imitating many things well, as of performing well the actions of which the imitations are copies.

Quite true, he replied.

If then we adhere to our original notion and bear in mind that our guardians, released from every other business, are to dedicate themselves wholly to the maintenance of the freedom of the State, making this their craft and engaging in no work which does not bear on this end, then they ought not to practise or even imitate anything else; if they imitate at all, they should imitate from youth upward only those characters which are suitable to their profession— the courageous, temperate, holy, free, and the like; but they should not depict or be skilful at imitating any kind of illiberality or baseness, lest the fruit of imitation should be reality. Did you never observe how imitations, beginning in early youth and continuing far into life, at length grow into habits and become a second nature, affecting body, voice, and mind?

Yes, certainly, he said.

Then, I said, we will not allow those for whom we profess a care and of whom we say that they ought to be good men, to imitate a woman, whether young or old, quarrelling with her husband, or striving and vaunting against the gods in conceit of her happiness, or when she is in affliction, or sorrow, or weeping; and certainly not one who is in sickness, love, or labour.

Very right, he said.

Neither must they represent slaves, male or female, performing the offices of slaves?

They must not.

And surely not bad men, whether cowards or any others, who do the reverse of what we have just been prescribing, who scold or mock or revile one another in drink or out of drink, or who in any other manner sin against themselves and their neighbours in word or deed, as the manner of such is. Neither should they be trained to imitate the action or speech of madmen; they must be able to recognize madness and vice in man or woman, but none of these things is to be practised or imitated.

Very true, he replied.

Neither may they imitate smiths or other artificers, or oarsmen, or boat-swains, or the like?

How can they, he said, when they are not allowed to apply their minds to the callings of any of these?

.   .   .

And this is the reason why in our State, and in our State only, we shall find a shoemaker to be a shoemaker and not a pilot also, and a husbandman to be a husbandman and not a dicast also, and a soldier a soldier and not a trader also, and the same throughout?

True, he said.

And therefore when any one of these pantomimic gentlemen, who are so clever that they can imitate anything, comes to us and makes a proposal to exhibit himself and his poetry, we will fall down and worship him as a sacred, marvellous and delightful being; but we must also inform him that in our State such as he are not permitted to exist; the law will not allow them. And so when we have anointed him with myrrh, and set a garland of wool upon his head, we shall send him away to another city. For we mean to employ for our souls' health the rougher and severer poet or story-teller, who will imitate the style of the virtuous only, and will follow those models which we prescribed at first when we began the education of our soldiers.

We certainly will, he said, if we have the power.

Then now, my friend, I said, that part of music or literary education which relates to the story or myth may be considered to be finished; for the matter and manner have both been discussed.

I think so too, he said.

.   .   .

But shall our superintendence go no further, and are the poets only to be required by us to express the image of the good in their works, on pain, if they do anything else, of expulsion from our State? Or is the same control to be extended to other artists, and are they also to be prohibited from exhibiting the opposite forms of vice and intemperance and meanness and deformity in sculpture and building and the other creative arts; and is he who cannot conform to this rule of ours to be prevented from practising his art in our State, lest the taste of our citizens be corrupted by him? We would not have our guardians grow up amid images of moral deformity, as in some noxious pasture, and there browse and feed upon many a baneful herb and flower day by day, little by little, until they silently gather a festering mass of corruption in their own soul. Let us rather search for artists who are gifted to discern the true nature of the beautiful and graceful; then will our youth dwell in a land of health, amid fair sights and sounds, and receive the good in everything; and beauty, the effluence of fair works, shall flow into the eye and ear, like a health-giving breeze from a purer region, and insensibly draw the soul from earliest years into likeness and sympathy with the beauty of reason.

There can be no nobler training than that, he replied.

And therefore, I said, Glaucon, musical training is a more potent instrument than any other, because rhythm and harmony find their way into the inward places of the soul, on which they mightily fasten, imparting grace, and making the soul of him who is rightly educated graceful, or of him who is ill-educated ungraceful; and also because he who has received this true education of the inner being will most shrewdly perceive omissions or faults in art and nature, and with a true taste, while he praises and rejoices over and receives into his soul the good, and becomes noble and good, he will justly blame and hate the bad, now in the days of his youth, even before he is able to know the reason why; and when reason comes he will recognize and salute the friend with whom his education has made him long familiar.

Yes, he said, I quite agree with you in thinking that it is for such reasons that they should be trained in music.

.   .   .

After music comes gymnastic, in which our youth are next to be trained.

Certainly.

Gymnastic as well as music should begin in early years; the training in it should be careful and should continue through life. Now my belief is,—and this is a matter upon which I should like to have your opinion in confirmation of my own, but my own belief is,—not that the good body by any bodily excellence improves the soul, but, on the contrary, that the good soul by her own excellence improves the body as far as this may be possible. What do you say?

Yes, I agree.

.   .   .

Neither are the two arts of music and gymnastic really designed, as is often supposed, the one for the training of the soul, the other for the training of the body.

What then is the real object of them?

I believe, I said, that the teachers of both have in view chiefly the improvement of the soul.

How can that be? he asked.

Did you never observe, I said, the effect on the mind itself of exclusive devotion to gymnastic, or the opposite effect of an exclusive devotion to music?

In what way shown? he said.

The one producing a temper of hardness and ferocity, the other of softness and effeminacy, I replied.

Yes, he said, I am quite aware that the mere athlete becomes too much of a savage, and that the mere musician is melted and softened beyond what is good for him.

Yet surely, I said, this ferocity only comes from spirit, which if rightly educated would give courage, but if too much intensified is liable to become hard and brutal.

That I quite think.

On the other hand the quality of gentleness must come from the philosophical part of human nature. And this also when too much indulged will turn to softness, but if educated rightly will be gentle and moderate.

True.

.   .   .

And as there are two principles of human nature, one the spirited and the other the philosophical, some god, as I should say, has given mankind two arts answering to them (and only indirectly to the soul and body), in order that these two principles (like the strings of an instrument) may be relaxed or drawn tighter until they are duly harmonized.

That appears to be the intention.

And he who mingles music with gymnastic in the fairest proportions and best attempers them to the soul, may be rightly called the true musician and harmonist in a far higher sense than the tuner of the strings.

You are quite right, Socrates.

And such a presiding genius will be always required in our State if the government is to last.

Yes, he will be absolutely necessary.

Such, then, are our principles of nurture and education: Where would be the use of going into further details about the dances of our citizens, or about their hunting and coursing, their gymnastic and equestrian contests? For these all follow the general principle, and having found that, we shall have no difficulty in discovering them.

I dare say that there will be no difficulty.

Very good, I said; then what is the next question? Must we not ask who are to be rulers and who subjects?

Certainly.

There can be no doubt that the elder must rule the younger.

Clearly.

And that the best of these must rule.

That is also clear.

Now, are the best husbandmen those who are most devoted to husbandry?

Yes.

And as we are to have the best of guardians for our city, must they not be those who have most the character of guardians?

Yes.

And to this end they ought to be wise and efficient, and to have a special care of the State?

True.

And a man will be most likely to care about that which he loves?

To be sure.

And he will be most likely to love that which he regards as having the same interests with himself, and that of which the good or evil fortune is supposed by him at any time most to affect his own?

Very true, he replied.

Then there must be a selection. Let us note among the guardians those who in their whole life show the greatest eagerness to do what they suppose to be for the good of their country, and the greatest repugnance to do what is against her interests.

Those are the right men.

... We must watch them from their youth upwards, and make them perform actions in which they are most likely to forget or to be deceived, and he who remembers and is not deceived is to be selected, and he who fails in the trial is to be rejected. That will be the way?

Yes.

And there should also be toils and pains and conflicts prescribed for them, in which they will be made to give further proof of the same qualities.

Very right, he replied.

And then, I said, we must try them with enchantments—that is the third sort of test—and see what will be their behaviour: like those who take colts amid noise and tumult to see if they are of a timid nature, so must we take our youth amid terrors of some kind, and thence pass them into pleasures, and prove them more thoroughly than gold is proved in the furnace, that we may discover whether they are armed against all enchantments, and of a noble bearing always, good guardians of themselves and of the music which they have learned, and retaining under all circumstances a rhythmical and harmonious nature, such as will be most serviceable to themselves and to the State. And he who at every age, as boy and youth and in mature life, has come out of the trial victorious and pure, shall be appointed a ruler and guardian of the State; he shall be honoured in life and death, and shall receive sepulture and other memorials of honour, the greatest that we have to give. But him who fails, we must reject. I am inclined to think that this is the sort of way in which our rulers and guardians should be chosen and appointed. I speak generally, and not with any pretension to exactness.

And, speaking generally, I agree with you, he said.

And perhaps the word "guardian" in the fullest sense ought to be applied to this higher class only who both preserve us against foreign enemies and maintain peace among our citizens at home, that the one may not have the will, or the others the power, to harm us. The young men whom we before called guardians may be more properly designated auxiliaries and supporters of the principles of the rulers.

I agree with you, he said.

How then may we devise one of those needful falsehoods of which we lately spoke—just one royal lie which may deceive the rulers, if that be possible, and at any rate the rest of the city?

What sort of lie? he said.

Nothing new, I replied; only an old Phoenician tale of what has often occurred before now in other places (as the poets say, and have made the world believe), though not in our time, and I do not know whether such an event could ever happen again, or could now even be made to seem probable.

How your words seem to hesitate on your lips!

You will not wonder, I replied, at my hesitation when you have heard.

Speak, he said, and fear not.

Well then, I will speak, although I really know not how to look you in the face, or in what words to utter the audacious fiction, which I propose to communicate gradually, first to the rulers, then to the soldiers, and lastly to the people. They are to be told that the education and training which they seemed to receive from us in youth was but a dream; in reality during all that time they were being formed and fed in the womb of the earth, where they themselves and their arms and appurtenances were manufactured; when they were completed, the earth, their mother, sent them up; and so, their country being their mother and also their nurse, they are bound to advise for her good, and to defend her against attacks; and the other citizens they are to regard as children of the earth and their own brothers.

You had good reason, he said, to be ashamed of the lie which you were going to tell.

No doubt, I replied, but listen to the continuation of the tale. Citizens, we shall say to them in our tale, you are brothers, yet God has framed you differently. Some of you have the power of command, and in the composition of these he has mingled gold, wherefore also they have the greatest honour; others he has made of silver, to be auxiliaries; others again who are to be husbandmen and craftsmen he has composed of brass and iron; and the species will generally be preserved in the children. But as all are of the same original stock, a golden parent will sometimes have a silver son, a silver parent a golden son, and so forth. And God proclaims as a first principle to the rulers, and above all else, that there is nothing which they should so anxiously guard, or of which they are to be such good guardians, as of the mixture of elements in the soul. First, if one of their own offspring has an admixture of brass or iron, they shall in no wise have pity on it, but give it the rank which is its due and send it down to the husbandmen or artisans. On the other hand, if there are sons of artisans who have an admixture of gold or silver in them, they will be raised to honour, and become guardians or auxiliaries. For an oracle says that when a man of brass or iron guards the State, it will be destroyed. Such is the tale; is there any possibility of making our citizens believe in it?

Not in the first generation, he replied; but their sons may be made to believe in the tale, and their sons' sons, and posterity after them.

I see the difficulty, I replied; yet the fostering of such a belief will make them care more for the city and for one another. Enough, however, of the fiction, which may now fly abroad upon the wings of rumour, while we arm our earth-born heroes, and lead them forth under the command of their rulers. Let them look round and select a spot whence they can best suppress insurrection, if any prove refractory within, and also defend themselves against enemies, who like wolves may come down on the fold from without; there let them encamp, and when they have encamped, let them sacrifice to the proper gods and prepare their lodging.

Just so, he said.

And this must be such as will shield them against the cold of winter and the heat of summer.

I suppose that you mean houses, he replied.

Yes, I said; but they must be the houses of soldiers, and not of shopkeepers.

What is the difference? he said.

That I will endeavour to explain, I replied. To keep watchdogs, who, from want of discipline or hunger, or some evil habit or other, would turn upon the sheep and worry them, and behave not like dogs but wolves, would be a foul and monstrous thing in a shepherd?

Truly monstrous, he said.

And therefore every care must be taken that our auxiliaries, being stronger than our citizens, may not behave in this fashion and become like savage tyrants instead of friends and allies?

Yes, great care should be taken.

And if they have really received a good education, will not that furnish the best safeguard?

But they have received it, he replied.

I cannot be so confident, my dear Glaucon, I said; but I believe the truth is as I said, that a sound education, whatever that may be, will have the greatest tendency to civilize and humanize them in their relations to one another, and to those who are under their protection.

Very true, he replied.

And not only their education, but their habitations, and all that belongs to them, should be such as will neither impair their virtue as guardians, nor tempt them to prey upon the other citizens. Any man of sense must acknowledge that.

He must.

Then now let us consider what will be their way of life, if they are to realize our idea of them. In the first place, none of them should have any property of his own beyond what is absolutely necessary; neither should they have a private house or store closed against anyone who has a mind to enter; their provisions should be only such as are required by trained warriors, who are men of temperance and courage; they should agree to receive from the citizens a fixed rate of pay, enough to meet the expenses of the year and no more; and they will to go mess and live together like soldiers in a camp. Gold and silver we will tell them that they have from God; the diviner metal is within them, and they have therefore no need of the dross which is current among men, and ought not to pollute the divine by any such earthly admixture; for that commoner metal has been the sources of many unholy deeds, but their own is undefiled. And they alone of all the citizens may not touch or handle silver or gold, or be under the same roof with them, or wear them, or drink from them. And this will be their salvation, and they will be the saviours of the State. But should they ever acquire homes or lands or moneys of their own, they will become householders and husbandmen instead of guardians, enemies and tyrants instead of allies of the other citizens; hating and being hated, plotting and being plotted against, they will pass their whole life in much greater terror of internal than of external enemies, and the hour of ruin, both to themselves and to the rest of the State, will be at hand. For all which reasons may we not say that thus shall our State be ordered, and that these shall be the regulations appointed by us for our guardians concerning their lodging and all other matters?

Yes, said Glaucon.

BOOK IV

Here Adeimantus interposed a question: How would you answer, Socrates, said he, if a person were to say that you are not making these men very happy, and that they are themselves to blame; the city in fact belongs to them, but they reap no advantage from it; whereas other men acquire lands, and build large and handsome houses, and have everything handsome about them, offering sacrifices to the gods on their own account, and practising hospitality; moreover, they have the gold and silver which you have just mentioned, and all that is usual among the favourites of fortune; but our poor citizens are no better than mercenaries who are quartered in the city and are always mounting guard?

Yes, I said; and you may add that they are only fed, and not paid in addition to their food like other men; and therefore they cannot, if they would, take a private journey abroad; they have no money to spend on a mistress or any other luxurious fancy, which, as the word goes, is thought to be happiness; and many other accusations of the same nature might be added.

But, said he, let us suppose all this to be included in the charge.

You mean to ask, I said, what will be our answer?

Yes.

If we proceed along the old path, my belief, I said, is that we shall find the answer. And our answer will be that, even as they are, our guardians may very likely be the happiest of men; but that our aim in founding the State was not the disproportionate happiness of any one class, but the greatest happiness of the whole; we thought that in a State which is ordered with a view to the good of the whole we should be most likely to find justice, and in the worst-ordered State injustice: and, having found them, we might then decide upon the answer to our first question. At present, I take it, we are fashioning the happy State, not piecemeal, or with a view of making a few happy citizens, but as a whole, and by-and-by we will proceed to view the opposite kind of State. Suppose that we were painting a statue, and someone came up to us and said, Why do you not put the most beautiful colours on the most beautiful parts of the body— the eyes ought to be purple, but you have made them black—to him we might fairly answer, "Sir, you would not surely have us beautify the eyes to such a degree that they are no longer eyes; consider rather whether, by giving this and the other features their due proportion, we make the whole beautiful." And so I say to you, do not compel us to assign to the guardians a sort of happiness which will make them no guardians at all; for we too can clothe our husbandmen in royal apparel, and set crowns of gold on their heads, and bid them till the ground as much as they like, and no more. Our potters also might be allowed to repose on couches, and feast by the fireside, passing round the winecup, while their wheel is conveniently at hand, so that they may make a few pots when they feel inclined; in this way we might make every class happy —and then, as you imagine, the whole State would be happy. But do not put this idea into our heads; for, if we listen to you, the husbandman will be no longer a husbandman, the potter will cease to be a potter, and no one will have the character of any distinct class in the State. Now this is not of much consequence where the corruption of society, and pretension to be what you are not, is confined to cobblers; but when the guardians of the laws and of the government are only seeming and not real guardians, then see how they turn the State upside down; and on the other hand they alone have the power of giving order and happiness to the State. We mean our guardians to be true saviours and not the destroyers of the State, whereas our opponent is thinking of peasants at a festival, who are enjoying a life of revelry, not of citizens who are doing their duty to the State. But, if so, we mean different things, and he is speaking of something which is not a State. And therefore we must consider whether in appointing our guardians we look to their greatest happiness individually, or whether our aim is not to ensure that happiness appears in the State as a whole. What these guardians or auxiliaries must be compelled or induced to do (and the same may be said of every other trade), is to become as expert as possible in their professional work. And thus the whole State will grow up in a noble order, and the several classes will receive the proportion of happiness which nature assigns to them.

I think that you are quite right.

.   .   .

The regulations which we are prescribing, my good Adeimantus, are not, as might be supposed, a number of great principles, but trifles all, if care be taken, as the saying is, of the one great thing,—a thing, however, which I would rather call, not great, but sufficient for our purpose.

What may that be? he asked.

Education, I said, and nurture: if our citizens are well educated, and grow into sensible men, they will easily see their way through all these, as well as other matters which I omit; such, for example, as marriage, the possession of women and the procreation of children, which will all follow the general principle that friends have all things in common, as the proverb says.

That will be the best way of settling them.

Also, I said, the State, if once started well, moves with accumulating force like a wheel. For where good nurture and education are maintained, they implant good constitutions, and these good constitutions taking root in a good education improve more and more, and this improvement affects the breed in man as in other animals.

Very possibly, he said.

Then to sum up: This is the principle to which our rulers should cling throughout, taking care that neglect does not creep in—that music and gymnastic be preserved in their original form, and no innovation made. They must do their utmost to maintain them intact. And when anyone says that

"Mankind most regard the newest song which the singers have,"

they will be afraid that he may be praising, not new songs, but a new kind of song; and this ought not to be praised, or conceived to be the meaning of the poet; for any musical innovation is to be shunned, as likely to bring danger to the whole State. So Damon tells me, and I can quite believe him;—he says that when modes of music change, the fundamental laws of the State always change with them.

Yes, said Adeimantus; and you may add my suffrage to Damon's and your own.

Then, I said, our guardians must lay the foundations of their fortress in music?

Yes, he said; the lawlessness of which you speak too easily steals in.

Yes, I replied, in the form of amusement, and as though it were harmless.

Why, yes, he said, and harmless it would be; were it not that little by little this spirit of licence, finding a home, imperceptibly penetrates into manners and customs; whence issuing with greater force it invades contracts between man and man, and from contracts goes on to laws and constitutions, in utter recklessness, ending at last, Socrates, by an overthrow of all rights, private as well as public.

Is that true? I said.

That is my belief, he replied.

Then, as I was saying, our boys should be trained from the first in a stricter system, for if childish amusement becomes lawless, it will produce lawless children, who can never grow up into well-conducted and virtuous citizens.

Very true, he said.

And when boys who have made a good beginning in play, have later gained the habit of good order through music, then this habit accompanies them in all their actions and is a principle of growth to them, and is able to correct anything in the State which had been allowed to lapse. It is the reverse of the picture I have just drawn.

Very true, he said.

Thus educated, they will discover for themselves any lesser rules which their predecessors have altogether neglected.

What do you mean?

I mean such things as these:—when the young are to be silent before their elders; how they are to show respect to them by standing and making them sit; what honour is due to parents; what garments or shoes are to be worn; the mode of dressing the hair; deportment and manners in general. You would agree with me?

Yes.

But there is, I think, small wisdom in legislating about such matters,—precise written enactments cannot create these observances, and are not likely to make them lasting.

Impossible.

It would seem, Adeimantus, that the direction in which education starts a man will determine his future life. Does not like always attract like?

To be sure.

Until some one grand result is reached which may be good, and may be the reverse of good?

That is not to be denied.

And for this reason, I said, I, for my part, should not attempt to extend legislation to such details.

Naturally enough, he replied.

.   .   .

So now the foundation of your city, son of Ariston, is finished. What comes next? Provide yourself with a bright light and search, and get your brother and Polemarchus and the rest of our friends to help, and let us see where in it we can discover justice and where injustice, and in what they differ from one another, and which of them the man who would be happy should have for his portion, whether seen or unseen by gods and men.

Nonsense, said Glaucon: did you not promise to search yourself, saying that for you not to help justice in her need would be an impiety?

Your reminder is true, and I will be as good as my word; but you must join.

We will, he replied.

.   .   .

Think, now, and say whether you agree with me or not. Suppose a carpenter sets out to do the business of a cobbler, or a cobbler that of a carpenter; and suppose them to exchange their implements or social position, or the same person to try to undertake the work of both, or whatever be the change; do you think that any great harm would result to the State?

Not much.

But when the cobbler or any other man whom nature designed to be a trader, having his heart lifted up by wealth or strength or the number of his followers or any like advantage, attempts to force his way into the class of warriors, or a warrior into that of legislators and guardians, to which he ought not to aspire, and when these exchange their implements and their social position with those above them; or when one man would be trader, legislator, and warrior all in one, then I think you will agree with me in saying that this interchange and this meddling of one with another is the ruin of the State.

Most true.

Seeing then, I said, that there are three distinct classes, any meddling of one with another, or the change of one into another, is the greatest harm to the State, and may be most justly termed evil-doing?

Precisely.

And the greatest degree of evil-doing to one's own city would be termed by you injustice?

Certainly.

This then is injustice; and on the other hand when the three main classes, traders, auxiliaries, and guardians, each do their own business, that is justice, and will make the city just.

I agree with you.

We will not, I said, be over-positive as yet; but if, on trial, this conception of justice be verified in the individual as well as in the State, there will be no longer any room for doubt; if it be not verified, we must have a fresh inquiry. First let us complete the old investigation, which we began, as you remember, under the impression that, if we could previously examine justice on the larger scale, there would be less difficulty in discerning her in the individual. That larger example appeared to be the State, and accordingly we constructed as good a one as we could, knowing well that in the good State justice would be found. Let the discovery which we made be now applied to the individual— if they agree, we shall be satisfied; or, if there be a difference in the individual, we will come back to the State and have another trial of the theory. The friction of the two when rubbed together may possibly strike the light of justice, from which we can kindle a steady flame in our souls.

That will be in regular course; let us do as you say.

.   .   .

Now are there times when men are thirsty, and yet unwilling to drink?

Yes, he said, it constantly happens.

And in such a case what is one to say? Would you not say that there was something in the soul bidding a man to drink, and something else forbidding him, which is other and stronger than the principle which bids him?

I should say so.

And the prohibition in such cases is derived from reasoning, whereas the motives which lead and attract proceed from passions and diseases?

Clearly.

Then we may fairly assume that they are two, and that they differ from one another; the one with which a man reasons, we may call the rational principle of the soul, the other, with which he loves and hungers and thirsts and feels the flutterings of any other desire, may be termed the irrational or appetitive, the ally of sundry pleasures and satisfactions?

Yes, he said, we may fairly assume them to be different.

So much, then, for the definition of two of the principles existing in the soul. And what now of passion, or spirit? Is it a third, or akin to one of the preceding?

I should be inclined to say—akin to desire.

Well, I said, there is a story which I remember to have heard, and in which I put faith. The story is, that Leontius, the son of Aglaion, coming up one day from the Piraeus, under the north wall on the outside, observed some dead bodies lying on the ground at the place of execution. He felt a desire to see them, and also a dread and abhorrence of them; for a time he struggled and covered his eyes, but at length the desire got the better of him; and forcing them open; he ran up to the dead bodies, saying, Look, ye wretches, take your fill of the fair sight.

I have heard the story myself, he said.

The moral of the tale is that anger at times goes to war with desire, as though they were two distinct things.

Yes; that is the meaning, he said.

And are there not many other cases in which we observe that when a man's desires violently prevail over his reason, he reviles himself, and is angry at the violence within him, and that in this struggle, which is like the struggle of factions in a State, his spirit is on the side of his reason;—but for the passionate or spirited element to take part with the desires when reason decides that she should not be opposed, is a sort of thing which I believe that you never observed occurring in yourself, nor, as I should imagine, in anyone else?

Certainly not.

.   .   .

But a further question arises: Is passion different from reason also, or only a kind of reason; in which latter case, instead of three principles in the soul, there will only be two, the rational and the concupiscent? or rather, as the State was composed of three classes, traders, auxiliaries, counsellors, so may there not be in the individual soul a third element which is passion or spirit, and when not corrupted by bad education is the natural auxiliary of reason?

Yes, he said, there must be a third.

Yes, I replied, if passion, which has already been shown to be different from desire, turn out also to be different from reason.

But that is easily proved:—We may observe even in young children that they are full of spirit almost as soon as they are born, whereas some of them never seem to attain to the use of reason, and most of them late enough.

Excellent, I said, and you may see passion equally in brute animals, which is a further proof of the truth of what you are saying. And we may once more appeal to the words of Homer . . . ,

"He smote his breast, and thus rebuked his heart";

for in this verse Homer has clearly supposed the power which reasons about the better and worse to be different from the unreasoning anger which is rebuked by it.

Very true, he said.

And so, after much tossing, we have reached land, and are fairly agreed that the same principles which exist in the State exist also in the individual, and that they are three in number.

Exactly.

.   .   .

We cannot but remember that the justice of the State consisted in each of the three classes doing the work of its own class?

I do not think we have forgotten, he said.

We must now record in our memory that the individual in whom the several components of his nature do their own work will be just, and will do his own work?

Yes, he said, we must record that important fact.

First, it is proper for the rational principle, which is wise, and has the care of the whole soul, to rule, and for the spirit to be the subject and ally?

Certainly.

And, as we were saying, the blending of music and gymnastic will bring them into accord, nerving and sustaining the reason with noble words and lessons, and moderating and soothing and civilizing the wildness of passion by harmony and rhythm?

Quite true, he said.

And these two, thus nurtured and educated, and having learned truly to know their own functions, will rule over the concupiscent, which in each of us is the largest part of the soul and by nature most insatiable of gain; over this they will keep guard, lest, waxing great and strong with the fullness of bodily pleasures, as they are termed, the concupiscent soul, no longer confined to her own sphere, should attempt to enslave and rule those who are not her natural-born subjects, and overturn the whole life of man?

Very true, he said.

Both together will they not be the best defenders of the whole soul and the whole body against attacks from without; the one counselling, and the other going out to fight as the leader directs, and courageously executing his commands and counsels?

True.

.　.　.

And is justice dimmer in the individual, and is her form different, or is she the same which we found her to be in the State?

There is no difference in my opinion, he said.

... The just man does not permit the several elements within him to interfere with one another, or any of them to do the work of others,—he sets in order his own inner life, and is his own master and his own law, and at peace with himself; and when he has bound together the three principles within him, which may be compared to the higher, lower, and middle notes of the scale, and any that are intermediate between them—when he has bound all these together, and is no longer many, but has become one entirely temperate and perfectly adjusted nature, then he proceeds to act, if he has to act, whether in a matter of property, or in the treatment of the body, or in some affair of politics or private business; always thinking and calling that which preserves and co-operates with this harmonious condition, just and good action, and the knowledge which presides over it, wisdom, and that which at any time impairs this condition, he will call unjust action, and the opinion which presides over it ignorance.

You have said the exact truth, Socrates.

.　.　.

The time has come, then, to answer the final question of the comparative advantage of justice and injustice: Which is the more profitable, to be just and act justly and honourably, whether one's character is or is not known, or to be unjust and act unjustly, if one is unpunished, that is to say unreformed?

In my judgement, Socrates, the question has now become ridiculous. We know that, when the bodily constitution is gone, life is no longer endurable, though pampered with all kinds of meats and drinks, and having all wealth and all power; and shall we be told that when the natural health of our vital principle is undermined and corrupted, life is still worth having to a man, if only he be allowed to do whatever he likes, except to take steps to acquire justice and virtue and escape from injustice and vice; assuming them both to be such as we have described?

Yes, I said, the question is, as you say, ridiculous. . . .

BOOK V

But still I must say, Socrates, that if you are allowed to go on in this way you will entirely forget the other question which at the commencement of this discussion you thrust aside:—Is such an order of things possible, and how, if at all? For I am quite ready to acknowledge that the plan which you propose, if only feasible, would do all sorts of good to the State. . . .

Let me begin by reminding you that we found our way hither in the search after justice and injustice.

True, he replied; but what of that?

I was only going to ask whether, if we have discovered them, we are to require that the just man should in nothing fail of absolute justice; or may we be satisfied with an approximation, and the attainment in him of a higher degree of justice than is to be found in other men?

The approximation will be enough.

.   .   .

Would a painter, in your view, be less expert because, after having delineated with consummate art an ideal of a perfectly beautiful man, he was unable to show that any such man could ever have existed?

No, indeed.

Well, and were we not creating an ideal of a perfect State?

To be sure.

And is our theory a worse theory because we are unable to prove the possibility of a city being ordered in the manner described?

Surely not, he replied.

That is the truth, I said. But if, at your request, I am to try and show how and under what conditions the possibility is highest, I must ask you, having this in view, to repeat your former admissions.

What admissions?

I want to know whether a conception is ever fully realized in action? Must not action, whatever a man may think, always, in the nature of things, have less hold upon the truth than words? What do you say?

I agree.

Then you must not insist on my proving that the actual State will in every respect coincide with the ideal: if we are only able to discover how a city may be governed nearly as we proposed, you will admit that we have discovered the possibility which you demand; and will be contented. I am sure that I should be contented—will not you?

Yes, I will.

Let me next endeavour to show what is that fault in States which is the cause of their present maladministration, and what is the least change which will enable a State to pass into the truer form; and let the change, if possible, be of one thing only, or, if not, of two; at any rate let the changes be as few and slight as possible.

Certainly, he replied.

I think, I said, that there might be a reform of the State if only one change were made, which is not a slight or easy though still a possible one.

What is it? he said.

.   .   .

I said: Until philosophers are kings in their cities, or the kings and princes of this world have the spirit and power of philosophy, and political greatness and wisdom meet in one, and those commoner natures who pursue either to the exclusion of the other are compelled to stand aside, cities will never have rest from their evils,—no, nor the human race, as I believe,—and then only will this our ideal State have a possibility of life and behold the light of day. Such was the thought, my dear Glaucon, which I would fain have uttered if it had not seemed too extravagant; for to be convinced that in no other State can there be happiness private or public is indeed a hard thing.

.   .   .

BOOK VI

Here Adeimantus interposed and said: . . . [A]ny one of us might say, that although in words he is not able to meet you at each step of the argument, he sees as a fact that the votaries of philosophy, when they carry on the study, not only in youth as a part of education, but as the pursuit of their maturer years, most of them become strange monsters, not to say utter rogues, and that those who may be considered the best of them are at least made useless to the world by this occupation which you extol.

Well, and do you think that those who say so are wrong?

I cannot tell, he replied; but I should like to know what is your opinion.

Hear my answer; I am of opinion that they are quite right.

Then how can we be justified in saying that cities will not cease from evil until philosophers rule in them, when we acknowledge that philosophers are useless to the State?

You ask a question, I said, to which a reply can only be given in a parable.

Yes, Socrates; and that is a way of speaking to which you are not at all accustomed, I suppose.

I perceive, I said, that you are vastly amused at having plunged me into such a hopeless discussion; but now hear the parable, and then you will be still more amused at the meagreness of my imagination: for the manner in which the best men are treated in their own States is so grievous that no single thing on earth is comparable to it; and therefore, if I am to plead their cause, I must have recourse to fiction, and put together a figure made up of many things, like the fabulous unions of goats and stags which are found in pictures. Imagine then a fleet or a ship in which the owner is sailing, and he is taller and stronger than any of the crew, but he is a little deaf and has a similar infirmity in sight, and his knowledge of navigation is not much better. The sailors are quarrelling with one another about the steering—everyone is of opinion that he has a right to steer, though he has never learned the art of navigation and cannot tell who taught him or when he learned, and will further assert that it cannot be taught at all, and they are ready to cut in pieces anyone who says the contrary. They throng about the owner, begging and praying him to commit the helm to them; and if at any time they do not prevail, but others are preferred to them, they kill the others or throw them overboard, and having first chained up the excellent shipowner's senses with drink or some narcotic drug, they assume control of the ship and make free with the stores; thus, feasting and drinking, they proceed on their voyage in such manner as might be expected of them. Him who is their partisan and cleverly aids them in their plot for getting the ship out of the owner's hands whether by force or persuasion, they compliment with the name of sailor, pilot, able seaman, and abuse the other sort of man, saying that he is unfit for any service; but that the true pilot must pay attention to the year and seasons and sky and stars and winds, and whatever else belongs to his art, if he intends to be really qualified for the command of a ship,—this has never seriously entered into their thoughts; nor do they think it possible to learn some art, or obtain some experience, whereby a man will remain pilot whether the consent of other people has been granted or no. Yet such is the art of piloting. If all this should occur, how do you suppose that the true pilot will be regarded by the voyagers who sail in such an ill-regulated ship? Will he not be called by them a prater, a star-gazer, a good-for-nothing?

Of course, said Adeimantus.

Then you will hardly need, I said, to hear the interpretation of the figure, which describes the true philosopher in his relation to the State; for you understand already.

Certainly.

Then suppose you now take this parable to the gentleman who is surprised at finding that philosophers have no honour in their cities; explain it to him and try to convince him that their having honour would be far more extraordinary.

I will.

Say to him that, in deeming the best votaries of philosophy to be useless to the rest of the world, he is right; but also tell him to attribute their uselessness to the fault of those who will not use them, and not to themselves. The pilot should not humbly beg the sailors to be commanded by him—that is not the order of nature; neither are "the wise to go to the doors of the rich"—the ingenious author of this saying told a lie—but the truth is that when a man is ill, whether he be rich or poor, to the physician's door he must perforce go, and he who wants to be governed, to him who is able to govern. The ruler who is good for anything ought not to beg his subjects to be ruled by him. However, the present governors of mankind are of a different stamp; they may be justly compared to the sailors in our story, and the true helmsmen to those who are called by them good-for-nothings and star-gazers.

Precisely so, he said.

For these reasons, and among men like these, the noblest occupation of all is not likely to be much esteemed by those who pursue an opposite course of life; but the greatest and most lasting scandal is brought upon philosophy by her own professing followers, the same of whom you suppose the accuser to say that the greater number of them are arrant rogues, and the best are useless; in which opinion I agreed.

Yes.

And the reason why the good are useless has now been explained?

True.

.   .   .

And so with pain and toil we have reached the end of one subject, but more remains to be discussed;—how and by what studies and pursuits will the saviours of the constitution be created, and at what ages are they to apply themselves to their several studies?

Certainly.

.   .   .

And do not suppose that there will be many of them; for the gifts which were deemed by us to be essential rarely grow together; they are mostly found in shreds and patches.

What do you mean? he said.

You are aware, I replied, that quick intelligence, memory, sagacity, cleverness, and similar qualities, do not often grow together, and that persons who possess them and are at the same time high-spirited and magnanimous are not so constituted by nature as to live in an orderly and peaceful and settled manner; they are driven any way by their impulses, and all solid principle goes out of them.

Very true, he said.

On the other hand, those stable and steadfast and, it seems, more trustworthy natures, which in a battle are impregnable to fear and immovable, are equally immovable when there is anything to be learned; they are always in a torpid state, and are apt to yawn and go to sleep over any intellectual toil.

Quite true.

And yet we declare that a right good share of both qualities is necessary in those to whom the higher education is to be imparted, and who are to share in any office or command.

Certainly, he said.

And will they be a class which is rarely found?

Yes, indeed.

Then the aspirant must not only be tested in those labours and dangers and pleasures which we mentioned before, but there is another kind of probation which we did not mention—he must be exercised also in many kinds of knowledge, to see whether the soul will be able to endure the highest of all, or will faint under them, as men do in other studies and exercises.

Yes, he said, you are quite right in testing him. But what do you mean by the highest of all knowledge?

. . . I am certain that you have heard the answer many times, and now you either do not understand me or, as I rather think, you are disposed to make trouble by holding me back; for you have often been told that the Idea of good is the highest knowledge, and that all other things, justice among them, become useful and advantageous only by their use of this. You can hardly be ignorant that this is what I am about to say, and moreover that our knowledge of the Idea of the good is inadequate. Yet you understand that without this knowledge, no other knowledge or possession of any kind will profit us at all. Do you think that the possession of all other things is of any value if it be not good? or a sort of wisdom which includes all else, but has no thought of the honourable or good?

Assuredly not.

You are further aware that most people affirm pleasure to be the good, but the finer sort of wits say it is knowledge?

Yes.

You are aware too that the latter cannot explain what knowledge they mean, but are obliged after all to say knowledge of the good?

True, and very ridiculous it is.

Yes, I said, that they should begin by reproaching us with our ignorance of the good, and then presume our knowledge of it—for the good they define to be knowledge of the good, just as if we understood them when they use the term "good"—this is of course ridiculous.

Most true, he said.

What of those who make pleasure their good? are they not in equal perplexity? for they are compelled to admit that there are bad pleasures as well as good.

Certainly.

And therefore to acknowledge that the same things are both bad and good?
True.

Evidently, then, there are many great differences of opinion about the good.
Undoubtedly.

Is it not likewise evident that many are content to do or to have, or to seem to be, what is just and beautiful without the reality; but no one is satisfied with the appearance of good—the reality is what they seek; in the case of the good, appearance is despised by every one.

Very true, he said.

Of this then, which every soul of man pursues and makes the end of all his actions, having a presentiment that there is such an end, and yet hesitating because neither knowing the nature nor having the same assurance of this as of other things, and therefore losing whatever good there is in other things,—of a principle such and so great as this ought the best men in our State, to whom everything is entrusted, to be in the darkness of ignorance?

Certainly not, he said.

I am sure, I said, that he who does not know how the noble and the just are likewise good will be but a sorry guardian of them; and I suspect that no one who is ignorant of the good will have a true knowledge of them.

That, he said, is a shrewd suspicion of yours.

And if only we have a guardian who has this knowledge our State will be perfectly ordered?

Of course, he replied; but I wish that you would tell me whether you conceive this supreme principle of the good to be knowledge or pleasure, or different from either?

. . . I must first come to an understanding with you, and remind you of what I have mentioned in the course of this discussion, and at many other times.

What?

The old story, that there are many beautiful things and many good. And again there is a true beauty, a true good; and all other things to which the term *many* has been applied, are now brought under a single idea, and, assuming this unity, we speak of it in every case as *that which really is.*

Very true.

The many, as we say, are seen but not known, and the Ideas are known but not seen.

Exactly.

.   .   .

Now take a line which has been cut into two unequal parts, and divide each of them again in the same proportion, and suppose the two main divisions to answer, one to the visible and the other to the intelligible, and then compare the subdivisions in respect of their clearness and want of clearness, and you will find that the first section in the sphere of the visible consists of images. And by images I mean, in the first place, shadows, and in the second place, reflections in water and in solid, smooth and polished bodies and the like: Do you understand?

Yes, I understand.

Imagine, now, the other section, of which this is only the resemblance, to include the animals which we see, and every thing that grows or is made.

Very good.

Would you not admit that both the sections of this division have different degrees of truth, and that the copy is to the original as the sphere of opinion is to the sphere of knowledge?

Most undoubtedly.

Next proceed to consider the manner in which the sphere of the intellectual is to be divided.

In what manner?

Thus:—There are two subdivisions, in the lower of which the soul, using as images those things which themselves were reflected in the former division, is forced to base its enquiry upon hypotheses, proceeding not towards a principle but towards a conclusion; in the higher of the two, the soul proceeds *from* hypotheses, and goes up to a principle which is above hypotheses, making no use of images as in the former case, but proceeding only in and through the Ideas themselves.

I do not quite understand your meaning, he said.

Then I will try again; you will understand me better when I have made some preliminary remarks. You are aware that students of geometry, arithmetic, and the kindred sciences assume the odd and the even and the figures and three kinds of angles and the like in their several branches of science; these are their hypotheses, which they and everybody are supposed to know, and therefore they do not deign to give any account of them either to themselves or others; but they begin with them, and go on until they arrive at last, and in a consistent manner, at the solution which they set out to find?

Yes, he said, I know.

And do you not know also that although they make use of the visible forms and reason about them, they are thinking not of these, but of the ideals which they resemble; not of the figures which they draw, but of the absolute square and the absolute diameter, and so on—the forms which they draw or make, and which themselves have shadows and reflections in water, are in turn converted by them into images; for they are really seeking to behold the things themselves, which can only be seen with the eye of the mind?

That is true.

And this was what I meant by a subdivision of the intelligible, in the search after which the soul is compelled to use hypotheses; not ascending to a first principle, because she is unable to rise above the region of hypothesis, but employing now as images those objects from which the shadows below were derived, even these being deemed clear and distinct by comparison with the shadows.

I understand, he said, that you are speaking of the province of geometry and the sister arts.

And when I speak of the other division of the intelligible, you will understand me to speak of that other sort of knowledge which reason herself attains by the power of dialectic, using the hypotheses not as first principles, but literally as hypotheses—that is to say, as steps and points of departure into a world which is above hypotheses, in order that she may soar beyond them to the first principle of the whole; and clinging to this and then to that which depends on this, by successive steps she descends again without the aid of any sensible object, from Ideas, through Ideas, and in Ideas she ends.

I understand you, he replied; not perfectly, for you seem to me to be describing a task which is really tremendous; but, at any rate, I understand you to say that that part of intelligible Being, which the science of dialectic contemplates, is clearer than that which falls under the arts, as they are termed, which take hypotheses as their principles; and though the objects are of such a kind that they must be viewed by the understanding, and not by the senses, yet, because they start from hypotheses and do not ascend to a principle, those who contemplate them appear to you not to exercise the higher reason upon them, although when a first principle is added to them they are cognizable by the higher reason. And the habit which is concerned with geometry and the cognate sciences I suppose that you would term understanding and not reason, as being intermediate between opinion and reason.

You have quite conceived my meaning, I said; and now, corresponding to these four divisions, let there be four faculties in the soul—reason answering to the highest, understanding to the second, faith (or conviction) to the third, and perception of shadows to the last—and let there be a scale of them, and let us suppose that the several faculties have clearness in the same degree that their objects have truth.

I understand, he replied, and give my assent, and accept your arrangement.

BOOK VII

And now, I said, let me show in a figure how far our nature is enlightened or unenlightened:—Behold! human beings housed in an underground cave, which has a long entrance open towards the light and as wide as the interior of the cave; here they have been from their childhood, and have their legs and necks chained, so that they cannot move and can only see before them, being prevented by the chains from turning round their heads. Above and behind them a fire is blazing at a distance, and between the fire and the prisoners there is a raised way; and you will see, if you look, a low wall built along the way, like the screen which marionette players have in front of them, over which they show the puppets.

I see.

And do you see, I said, men passing along the wall carrying all sorts of vessels, and statues and figures of animals made of wood and stone and various materials, which appear over the wall? While carrying their burdens, some of them, as you would expect, are talking, others silent.

You have shown me a strange image, and they are strange prisoners.

Like ourselves, I replied; for in the first place do you think they have seen anything of themselves, and of one another, except the shadows which the fire throws on the opposite wall of the cave?

How could they do so, he asked, if throughout their lives they were never allowed to move their heads?

And of the objects which are being carried in like manner they would only see the shadows?

Yes, he said.

And if they were able to converse with one another, would they not suppose that the things they saw were the real things?

Very true.

And suppose further that the prison had an echo which came from the other side, would they not be sure to fancy when one of the passers-by spoke that the voice which they heard came from the passing shadow?

No question, he replied.

To them, I said, the truth would be literally nothing but the shadows of the images.

That is certain.

And now look again, and see in what manner they would be released from their bonds, and cured of their error, whether the process would naturally be as follows. At first, when any of them is liberated and compelled suddenly to stand up and turn his neck round and walk and look towards the light, he will suffer sharp pains; the glare will distress him, and he will be unable to see the realities of which in his former state he had seen the shadows; and then conceive someone saying to him that what he saw before was an illusion, but that now, when he is approaching nearer to being and his eye is turned towards more real existence, he has a clearer vision,—what will be his reply? And you may further imagine that his instructor is pointing to the objects as they pass and requiring him to name them,—will he not be perplexed? Will he not fancy that the shadows which he formerly saw are truer than the objects which are now shown to him?

Far truer.

And if he is compelled to look straight at the light, will he not have a pain in his eyes which will make him turn away to take refuge in the objects of vision which he can see, and which he will conceive to be in reality clearer than the things which are now being shown to him?

True, he said.

And suppose once more, that he is reluctantly dragged up that steep and rugged ascent, and held fast until he is forced into the presence of the sun himself, is he not likely to be pained and irritated? When he approaches the light his eyes will be dazzled, and he will not be able to see anything at all of what are now called realities.

Not all in a moment, he said.

He will require to grow accustomed to the sight of the upper world. And first he will see the shadows best, next the reflections of men and other objects in the water, and then the objects themselves; and, when he turned to the heavenly bodies and the heaven itself, he would find it easier to gaze upon the light of the moon and the stars at night than to see the sun or the light of the sun by day?

Certainly.

Last of all he will be able to see the sun, not turning aside to the illusory reflections of him in the water, but gazing directly at him in his own proper place, and contemplating him as he is.

Certainly.

He will then proceed to argue that this is he who gives the seasons and the years, and is the guardian of all that is in the visible world, and in a certain way the cause of all things which he and his fellows have been accustomed to behold?

Clearly, he said, he would arrive at this conclusion after what he had seen.

And when he remembered his old habitation, and the wisdom of the cave and his fellow-prisoners, do you not suppose that he would felicitate himself on the change, and pity them?

Certainly, he would.

And if they were in the habit of conferring honours among themselves on those who were quickest to observe the passing shadows and to remark which of them went before and which followed after and which were together, and who were best able from these observations to divine the future, do you think that he would be eager for such honours and glories, or envy those who attained honour and sovereignty among those men? Would he not say with Homer,

"Better to be a serf, labouring for a landless master,"

and to endure anything, rather than think as they do and live after their manner?

Yes, he said, I think that he would consent to suffer anything rather than live in this miserable manner.

Imagine once more, I said, such a one coming down suddenly out of the sunlight, and being replaced in his old seat; would he not be certain to have his eyes full of darkness?

To be sure, he said.

And if there were a contest, and he had to compete in measuring the shadows with the prisoners who had never moved out of the cave, while his sight was still weak, and before his eyes had become steady (and the time which would be needed to acquire this new habit of sight might be very considerable), would he not make himself ridiculous? Men would say of him that he had returned from the place above with his eyes ruined; and that it was better not even to think of ascending; and if anyone tried to loose another and lead him up to the light, let them only catch the offender, and they would put him to death.

No question, he said.

This entire allegory, I said, you may now append, dear Glaucon, to the previous argument; the prison-house is the world of sight, the light of the fire is the power of the sun, and you will not misapprehend me if you interpret the journey upwards to be the ascent of the soul into the intellectual world according to my surmise, which, at your desire, I have expressed—whether rightly or wrongly God knows. But, whether true or false, my opinion is that in the world of knowledge the Idea of good appears last of all, and is seen only with an effort; although, when seen, it is inferred to be the universal author of all things beautiful and right, parent of light and of the lord of light in the visible world, and the immediate and supreme source of reason and truth in the intellectual; and that this is the power upon which he who would act rationally either in public or private life must have his eye fixed.

I agree, he said, as far as I am able to understand you.

Moreover, I said, you must agree once more, and not wonder that those who attain to this vision are unwilling to take any part in human affairs; for their souls are ever hastening into the upper world where they desire to dwell; which desire of theirs is very natural, if our allegory may be trusted.

Yes, very natural.

And is there anything surprising in one who passes from divine contemplations to the evil state of man, appearing grotesque and ridiculous; if, while his eyes are blinking and before he has become accustomed to the surrounding darkness, he is compelled to fight in courts of law, or in other places, about the images or the shadows of images of justice, and must strive against some rival about opinions of these things which are entertained by men who have never yet seen the true justice?

Anything but surprising, he replied.

Anyone who has common sense will remember that the bewilderments of the eyes are of two kinds and arise from two causes, either from coming out of the light or from going into the light, and, judging that the soul may be affected in the same way, will not give way to foolish laughter when he sees anyone whose vision is perplexed and weak; he will first ask whether that soul of man has come out of the brighter life and is unable to see because unaccustomed to the dark, or having turned from darkness to the day is dazzled by excess of light. And he will count the one happy in his condition and state of being, and he will pity the other; or, if he have a mind to laugh at the soul which comes from below into the light, this laughter will not be quite so laughable as that which greets the soul which returns from above out of the light into the cave.

That, he said, is a very just distinction.

But then, if I am right, certain professors of education must be wrong when they say that they can put a knowledge into the soul which was not there before, like sight into blind eyes.

They undoubtedly say this, he replied.

Whereas our argument shows that the power and capacity of learning exists in the soul already; and that just as if it were not possible to turn the eye from darkness to light without the whole body, so too the instrument of knowledge can only by the movement of the whole soul be turned from the world of becoming to that of being, and learn by degrees to endure the sight of being, and of the brightest and best of being, or in other words, of the good.

Very true.

And must there not be some art which will show how the conversion can be effected in the easiest and quickest manner; an art which will not implant the faculty of sight, for that exists already, but will set it straight when it has been turned in the wrong direction, and is looking away from the truth?

Yes, he said, such an art may be presumed.

And whereas the other so-called virtues of the soul seem to be akin to bodily qualities, for even when they are not originally innate they can be implanted later by habit and exercise, the virtue of wisdom more than anything else contains a divine element which never loses its power, and by this conversion is rendered useful and profitable; or, by conversion of another sort, hurtful and useless. Did you never observe the narrow intelligence flashing from the keen eye of a clever rogue—how eager he is, how clearly his paltry soul sees the way to his end; he is the reverse of blind, but his keen eye-sight is forced into the service of evil, and he is mischievous in proportion to his cleverness?

Very true, he said.

But what if such natures had been gradually stripped, beginning in childhood, of the leaden weights which sink them in the sea of Becoming, and which, fastened upon the soul through gluttonous indulgence in eating and other such pleasures, forcibly turn its vision downwards—if, I say, they had been released from these impediments and turned in the opposite direction, the very same faculty in them would have seen the truth as keenly as they see what their eyes are turned to now.

Very likely.

Yes, I said; and there is another thing which is likely, or rather a necessary inference from what has preceded, that neither the uneducated and uninformed of the truth, nor yet those who are suffered to prolong their education without end, will be able ministers of State; not the former, because they have no single aim of duty which is the rule of all their actions, private as well as public; nor the latter, because they will not act at all except upon compulsion, fancying that they are already dwelling apart in the islands of the blest.

Very true, he replied.

Then, I said, the business of us who are the founders of the State will be to compel the best minds to attain that knowledge which we have already shown to be the greatest of all, namely, the vision of the good; they must make the ascent which we have described; but when they have ascended and seen enough we must not allow them to do as they do now.

What do you mean?

They are permitted to remain in the upper world, refusing to descend again among the prisoners in the cave, and partake of their labours and honours, whether they are worth having or not.

But is not this unjust? he said; ought we to give them a worse life, when they might have a better?

You have again forgotten, my friend, I said, the intention of our law, which does not aim at making any one class in the State happy above the rest; it seeks rather to spread happiness over the whole State, and to hold the citizens together by persuasion and necessity, making each share with others any benefit which he can confer upon the State; and the law aims at producing such citizens, not that they may be left to please themselves, but that they may serve in binding the State together.

True, he said, I had forgotten.

Observe, Glaucon, that we shall do no wrong to our philosophers but rather make a just demand, when we oblige them to have a care and providence of others; we shall explain to them that in other States, men of their class are not obliged to share in the toils of politics: and this is reasonable, for they grow up spontaneously, against the will of the governments in their several States; and things which grow up of themselves, and are indebted to no one for their nurture, cannot fairly be expected to pay dues for a culture which they have never received. But we have brought you into the world to be rulers of the hive, kings of yourselves and of the other citizens, and have educated you far better and more perfectly than they have been educated, and you are better able to share in the double duty. Wherefore each of you, when his turn comes, must go down to rejoin his companions, and acquire with them the habit of seeing things in the dark. As you acquire that habit, you will see ten thousand times better than the inhabitants of the cave, and you will know what the several images are and what they represent, because you have seen the beautiful and just and good in their truth. And thus our State, which is also yours, will be a reality and not a dream only, and will be administered in a spirit unlike that of other States, in which men fight with one another about shadows only and are distracted in the struggle for power, which in their eyes is a great good. Whereas the truth is that the State in which those who are to govern have least ambition to do so is always the best and most quietly governed, and the State in which they are most eager, the worst.

Quite true, he replied.

And will our pupils, when they hear this, refuse to take their turn at the toils of State, when they are allowed to spend the greater part of their time with one another in the heavenly light?

Impossible, he answered; for they are just men, and the commands which we impose upon them are just. But there can be no doubt that every one of them will take office as a stern necessity, contrary to the spirit of our present rulers of State.

Yes, my friend, I said; and there lies the point. You must contrive for your future rulers another and a better life than that of a ruler, and then you may have a well-ordered State; for only in the State which offers this, will they rule who are truly rich, not in gold, but in virtue and wisdom, which are the true blessings of life. Whereas if men who are destitute and starved of such personal goods go to the administration of public affairs, thinking to enrich themselves at the public expense, order there can never be; for they will be fighting about office, and the civil and domestic broils which thus arise will be the ruin of the rulers themselves and of the whole State.

Most true, he replied.

And the only life which looks down upon the life of political ambition is that of true philosophy. Do you know of any other?

Indeed, I do not, he said.

And those who govern should not "make love to their employment"? For, if they do there will be rival lovers, and they will fight.

No question.

Whom, then, will you compel to become guardians of the State? Surely those who excel in judgement of the means by which a State is administered, and who at the same time have other honours and another and a better life than that of politics?

None but these, he replied.

And now shall we consider in what way such guardians will be produced, and how they are to be brought from darkness to light,—as some are said to have ascended from the world below to the gods?

By all means, he replied.

The process, I said, is not the turning over of an oyster-shell, but the turning round of a soul passing from a day which is little better than night to the true day; an ascent towards reality, which we shall affirm to be true philosophy?

Quite so.

And should we not inquire what sort of knowledge has the power of effecting such a change?

Certainly.

. . . What branch of knowledge is there, my dear Glaucon, which is of the desired nature; since all the useful arts were reckoned mean by us?

Undoubtedly; and yet what study remains, distinct both from music and gymnastic and from the arts?

Well, I said, if nothing remains outside them, let us select something which is a common factor in all.

What may that be?

Something, for instance, which all arts and sciences and intelligences use in common, and which everyone has to learn among the first elements of education.

What is that?

The little matter of distinguishing one, two, and three—in a word, number and calculation:—do not all arts and sciences necessarily partake of them?

Yes.

Then the art of war partakes of them?

To be sure.

.   .   .

Can we deny that a warrior should have a knowledge of arithmetic?

Certainly he should, if he is to have the smallest understanding of military formations, or indeed, I should rather say, if he is to be a man at all.

I should like to know whether you have the same notion which I have of this study?

What is your notion?

It appears to me to be a study of the kind which we are seeking, and which leads naturally to reflection, but never to have been rightly used; for it has a strong tendency to draw the soul towards being.

How so? he said.

I will try to explain my meaning, I said; and I wish you would share the inquiry with me and say "yes" or "no" when I attempt to distinguish in my own mind what branches of knowledge have this attracting power, in order that we may have clearer proof that arithmetic is, as I suspect, one of them.

Explain, he said.

Do you follow me when I say that objects of sense are of two kinds? some of them do not invite the intelligence to further inquiry because the sense is an adequate judge of them; while in the case of other objects sense is so untrustworthy that inquiry by the mind is imperatively demanded.

You are clearly referring, he said, to the appearance of objects at a distance, and to painting in light and shade.

No, I said, you have not quite caught my meaning.

Then what things do you mean?

When speaking of uninviting objects, I mean those which do not pass straight from one sensation to the opposite; inviting objects are those which do; in this latter case the sense coming upon the object, whether at a distance or near, does not give one particular impression more strongly than its opposite. An illustration will make my meaning clearer:—here are three fingers— a little finger, a second finger, and a middle finger.

Very good.

You may suppose that they are seen quite close: And here comes the point. What is it?

Each of them equally appears a finger, and in this respect it makes no difference whether it is seen in the middle or at the extremity, whether white or black, or thick or thin, or anything of that kind. In these cases a man is not compelled to ask of thought the question what is a finger? for the sight never intimates to the mind that a finger is the opposite of a finger.

True.

And therefore, I said, there is nothing here which is likely to invite or excite intelligence.

There is not, he said.

But is this equally true of the greatness and smallness of the fingers? Can sight adequately perceive them? and is no difference made by the circumstance that one of the fingers is in the middle and another at the extremity? And in like manner does the touch adequately perceive the qualities of thickness or thinness, of softness or hardness? And so of the other senses; do they give perfect intimations of such matters? Is not their mode of operation on this wise —the sense which is concerned with the quality of hardness is necessarily concerned also with the quality of softness, and only intimates to the soul that the same thing is felt to be both hard and soft?

It is, he said.

And must not the soul be perplexed at this intimation which this sense gives of a hard which is also soft? What, again, is the meaning of light and heavy, if the sense pronounces that which is light to be also heavy, and that which is heavy, light?

Yes, he said, these intimations which the soul receives are very curious and require to be explained.

Yes, I said, and in these perplexities the soul naturally summons to her aid calculation and intelligence, that she may see whether the several objects announced to her are one or two.

True.

And if they turn out to be two, is not each of them one and different?

Certainly.

And if each is one, and both are two, she will conceive the two as in a state of division, for if they were undivided they could only be conceived of as one?

True.

The eye, also, certainly did see both small and great, but only in a confused manner; they were not distinguished.

Yes.

Whereas on the contrary the thinking mind, intending to light up the chaos, was compelled to reconsider the small and great viewing them as separate and not in that confusion.

Very true.

Is it not in some such way that there arises in our minds the inquiry "What is great?" and "What is small?"

Exactly so.

And accordingly we made the distinction of the visible and the intelligible.

A very proper one.

This was what I meant just now when I spoke of impressions which invited the intellect, or the reverse—those which strike our sense simultaneously with opposite impressions, invite thought; those which are not simultaneous with them, do not awaken it.

I understand now, he said, and agree with you.

And to which class do unity and number belong?

I do not know, he replied.

Think a little and you will see that what has preceded will supply the answer; for if simple unity could be adequately perceived by the sight or by any other sense, then, as we were saying in the case of the finger, there would be nothing to attract towards being; but when something contrary to unity is always seen at the same time, so that there seems to be no more reason for calling it one than the opposite, some discriminating power becomes necessary, and in such a case the soul in perplexity, is obliged to rouse her power of thought and to ask: "What *is* absolute unity?" This is the way in which the study of the one has a power of drawing and converting the mind to the contemplation of true being.

And surely, he said, this occurs notably in the visual perception of unity; for we see the same thing at once as one and as infinite in multitude?

Yes, I said; and this being true of one must be equally true of all number?

Certainly.

And all arithmetic and calculation have to do with number?

Yes.

And they appear to lead the mind towards truth?

Yes, in a very remarkable manner.

Then this is a discipline of the kind for which we are seeking; for the man of war must learn the art of number or he will not know how to array his troops, and the philosopher also, because he has to rise out of the sea of change and lay hold of true being, or be for ever unable to calculate and reason.

That is true.

But our guardian is, in fact, both warrior and philosopher?

Certainly.

Then this is a kind of knowledge which legislation may fitly prescribe; and we must endeavour to persuade those who are to be the principal men of our State to go and learn arithmetic, and take up the study in no amateurish spirit but pursue it until they can view the nature of numbers with the unaided mind; nor again, like merchants or retail-traders, with a view to buying or selling, but for the sake of their military use, and of the soul herself, because this will be the easiest way for her to pass from becoming to truth and being.

That is excellent, he said.

Yes, I said, and now having spoken of it, I must add how charming the science is! and in how many ways it conduces to our desired end, if pursued in the spirit of a philosopher, and not of a shopkeeper!

How do you mean?

I mean that arithmetic has, in a marked degree, that elevating effect of which we were speaking, compelling the soul to reason about abstract number, and rebelling against the introduction of numbers which have visible or tangible bodies into the argument. You know how steadily the masters of the art repel and ridicule anyone who attempts to divide the perfect unit when he is calculating, and if you divide, they multiply, taking care that the unit shall continue one and not appear to break up into fractions.

That is very true.

Now, suppose a person were to say to them: O my friends, what are these wonderful numbers about which you are reasoning, in which, as you say, there is a unity such as you demand, and each unit is equal, invariable, indivisible, —what would they answer?

They would answer, as I should conceive, that they were speaking of those numbers which can only be grasped by thought, and not handled in any other way.

Then you see that this study may be truly called necessary for our purpose, since it evidently compels the soul to use the pure intelligence in the attainment of pure truth?

Yes; that is a marked characteristic of it.

And have you further observed, that those who have a natural talent for calculation are generally quick at every other kind of study; and even the dull, if they have been trained and exercised in this, although they may derive no other advantage from it, always become much quicker than they would otherwise have been?

Very true, he said.

And indeed, you will not easily find a study of which the learning and exercise require more pains, and not many which require as much.

You will not.

And, for all these reasons, arithmetic is a kind of knowledge in which the best natures should be trained, and which must not be given up.

I agree.

Let this then be adopted as one of our subjects of education. And next, shall we inquire whether the kindred science also concerns us?

You mean geometry?

Exactly so.

Clearly, he said, we are concerned with that part of geometry which relates to war; for in pitching a camp, or taking up a position, or closing or extending the lines of an army, or any other military manoeuvre, whether in actual battle or on a march, it will make all the difference whether a general is or is not a geometrician.

Yes, I said, but for that purpose a very little of either geometry or calculation will be enough; the question relates rather to the greater and more advanced part of geometry—whether that tends in any degree to make more easy the vision of the Idea of good; and thither, as I was saying, all things tend which compel the soul to turn her gaze towards that place where is the full perfection of being, which she ought, by all means, to behold.

True, he said.

Then if geometry compels us to view being, it concerns us; if becoming only, it does not concern us?

Yes, that is what we assert.

Yet anybody who has the least acquaintance with geometry will not deny that such a conception of the science is in flat contradiction to the ordinary language of geometricians.

How so?

They speak, as you doubtless know, in terms redolent of the workshop. As if they were engaged in action, and had no other aim in view in all their reasoning, they talk of squaring, applying, extending and the like, whereas, I presume, the real object of the whole science is knowledge.

Certainly, he said.

Then must not a further admission be made?

What admission?

That the knowledge at which geometry aims is knowledge of eternal being, and not of aught which at a particular time comes into being and perishes.

That, he replied, may be readily allowed, and is true.

Then, my noble friend, geometry will draw the soul towards truth, and create the spirit of philosophy, and raise up that which is now unhappily allowed to fall down.

Nothing will be more likely to have such an effect.

Then nothing should be more sternly laid down than that the inhabitants of your fair city should by no means remain unversed in geometry. Moreover the science has indirect effects, which are not small.

Of what kind? he said.

There are the military advantages of which you spoke, I said; and further, we know that for the better apprehension of any branch of knowledge, it makes all the difference whether a man has a grasp of geometry or not.

Yes indeed, he said, all the difference in the world.

Then shall we propose this as a second branch of knowledge which our youth will study?

Let us do so, he replied. . . .

And suppose we make astronomy the third—what do you say?

I am strongly inclined to it, he said; the observation of the seasons and of months and years is as essential to the general as it is to the farmer or sailor.

I am amused, I said, at your fear of the world, lest you should appear as an ordainer of useless studies; and I quite admit that it is by no means easy to believe that in every man there is an eye of the soul which, when by other pursuits lost and dimmed, is purified and reillumined by these studies; and is more precious far than ten thousand bodily eyes, for by it alone is truth seen. Now there are two classes of persons: some who will agree with you and will take your words as a revelation; another class who have never perceived this truth will probably find them unmeaning, for they see no noticeable profit which is to be obtained from them. And therefore you had better decide at once with which of the two you are proposing to argue. You will very likely say with neither, and that your chief aim in carrying on the argument is your own improvement, while at the same time you would not grudge to others any benefit which they may receive.

I should prefer, he said, to speak and inquire and answer mainly on my own behalf.

Then take a step backward, for we have gone wrong in the order of the sciences.

What was the mistake? he said.

After plane geometry, I said, we proceeded at once to solids in revolution, instead of taking solids in themselves; whereas after the second dimension the third, which is concerned with cubes and dimensions of depth, ought to have followed.

That is true, Socrates; but so little seems to have been discovered as yet about these subjects.

Why, yes, I said, and for two reasons;—in the first place, no government patronizes them; this leads to a want of energy in the pursuit of them, and they are difficult; in the second place, students cannot learn them unless they have a director. But then a director can hardly be found, and even if he could, as matters now stand, the students, who are very conceited, would not attend to him. That, however, would be otherwise if the whole State were to assist the director of these studies by giving honour to them; then disciples would show obedience, and there would be continuous and earnest search, and discoveries would be made; since even now, disregarded as they are by the world, and maimed of their fair proportions, because those engaged in the research have no conception of its use, still these studies force their way by their natural charm, and it would not be surprising if they should some day emerge into light.

Yes, he said, there is a remarkable charm in them. But I do not clearly understand the change in the order. By geometry, I suppose that you meant the theory of plane surfaces?

Yes, I said.

And you placed astronomy next, and then you made a step backward?

Yes, and my haste to cover the whole field has made me less speedy; the ludicrous state of research in solid geometry, which, in natural order, should have followed, made me pass over this branch and go on to astronomy, or motion of solids.

True, he said.

Then assuming that the science now omitted would come into existence if encouraged by the State, let us take astronomy as our fourth study.

The right order, he replied. And now, Socrates, as you rebuked the vulgar manner in which I praised astronomy before, my praise shall be given in your own spirit. For everyone, as I think, must see that astronomy compels the soul to look upwards and leads us from this world to another.

Everyone but myself, I said; for I am not sure that it is so.

And what then would you say?

I should rather say that those who elevate astronomy into philosophy treat it in such a way as to make us look downwards and not upwards.

What do you mean? he asked.

You, I replied, have in your mind a truly sublime conception of our knowledge of the things above. And I dare say that if a person were to throw his head back and study the fretted ceiling, you would still think that his mind was the percipient, and not his eyes. And you are very likely right, and I may be a simpleton: but, in my opinion, that knowledge only which is concerned with true being and the unseen can make the soul look upwards, and whether a man gapes at the heavens or blinks on the ground, when seeking to learn some particular of sense, I would deny that he can learn, for nothing of that sort is matter of science; and I say that his soul is looking downwards, not upwards, even though, in the quest for knowledge he floats face upwards on the sea, or on the land.

I acknowledge, he said, the justice of your rebuke. Still, I should like to ascertain how astronomy can be learned in any manner more conducive than the present system to that knowledge of which we are speaking?

I will tell you, I said: The starry heaven which we behold is wrought upon a visible ground, and therefore although the fairest and most perfect of visible things, must necessarily be deemed inferior far to the true motions with which the real swiftness and the real slowness move in their relation to each other, carrying with them that which is contained in them, in the true number and in true figures of every kind. Now, these are to be apprehended by reason and intelligence, but not by sight. Do you doubt that?

No, he replied.

The spangled heavens should be used as a pattern and with a view to that higher knowledge; they may be compared to diagrams which one might find excellently wrought by the hand of Daedalus, or some other great artist. For any geometrician who saw them would doubtless appreciate the exquisiteness of their workmanship, but he would never dream of thinking that in them he could find the true equal or the true double, or the truth of any other proportion.

No, he replied, such an idea would be ridiculous.

And will not a true astronomer have the same feeling when he looks at the movements of the stars? Will he not think that heaven and the things in heaven are framed by the Craftsman who made them in the most perfect manner in which such things can be framed? But if he finds someone supposing that the proportions of night and day, or of both to the month, or of the month to the year, or of the stellar movements generally to these and to one another, being, as they are, embodied and visible, are eternal and unchanging, and never deviate in any direction, and that it is worth while to investigate their exact truth at any cost—will he not think him a queer fellow?

I quite agree, now that I hear it from you.

Then, I said, in astronomy, as in geometry, we should employ problems, and let the heavens alone if we would approach the subject in the right way and so make the natural gift of reason to be of any real use.

That, he said, is a work infinitely beyond our present astronomers.

Yes, I said; and I think we must prescribe the rest of our studies in the same spirit, if our legislation is to be of any value. But can you tell me of any other suitable study?

No, he said, not without thinking.

Motion, I said, has many forms, and not one only; a wise man will, perhaps, be able to name them all; but two of them are obvious enough even to wits no better than ours.

What are they?

There is a second, I said, which is the counterpart of the one already named.

And what may that be?

It appears, I said, that as the eyes are designed to look up at the stars, so are the ears to hear harmonious motions; and these are sister sciences—as the Pythagoreans say, and we, Glaucon, agree with them?

Yes, he replied.

But this, I said, is a laborious study, and therefore we shall inquire what they have to say on these points, or on any others. For our own part, we shall in all this preserve our own principle.

What is that?

There is a perfection which all knowledge ought to reach, and which our pupils ought also to attain, and not to fall short of, as I was saying that they did in astronomy. For in the science of harmony, as you probably know, the same thing happens. The teachers of harmony compare only the sounds and consonances which are heard, and their labour, like that of the astronomers, is in vain.

Yes, by heaven! he said; and 'tis as good as a play to hear them talking about their close intervals, whatever they may be; they put their ears close alongside of the strings like persons catching a sound from their neighbour's wall—one set of them declaring that they distinguish an intermediate note and have found the least interval which should be the unit of measurement; the others insisting that the two sounds have passed into the same—either party setting their ears before their understanding.

You mean, I said, those gentlemen who tease and torture the strings and rack them on the pegs of the instrument: I might carry on the metaphor and speak after their manner of the blows which the plectrum gives, and of accusations against the strings, and of their reticence or forwardness;[1] but this would be tedious, and therefore I will only say that these are not the men, and that I am referring to the Pythagoreans, of whom I was just now proposing to inquire about harmony. For they too are in error, like the astronomers; they investigate the numbers of the harmonies which are heard, but they never attain to problems—to inquiring which numbers are harmonious and which are not, and for what reason.

That, he said, is a thing of more than mortal knowledge.

A thing, I replied, which I would rather call useful; that is, if sought after with a view to the beautiful and good; but if pursued in any other spirit, useless.

Very true, he said.

Now, when all these studies reach the point of inter-communion and connexion with one another, and come to be considered in their mutual affinities, then, I think, but not till then, will the pursuit of them have a value for our objects; otherwise there is no profit in them.

I suspect so; but you are speaking, Socrates, of a vast work.

What do you mean? I said; the prelude or what? Do you not know that all these are but preludes to the actual strain which must be learnt? For you surely would not regard those skilled in these sciences as dialecticians?

Assuredly not, he said; apart from a very few whom I have met.

But do you imagine that men who are unable to give and take a reason will have the knowledge which we require of them?

Neither can this be supposed.

And so, Glaucon, I said, we have at last arrived at the hymn of dialectic. This is that strain which is of the intellect only, but which the faculty of sight will nevertheless be found to imitate; for sight, as you may remember, was

[1][These are metaphors from the behaviour of persons on the rack.]

imagined by us after a while to behold the real animals and stars, and last of all the sun himself. And so with dialectic; when a person starts on the discovery of the real by the light of reason only, and without any assistance of sense, and perseveres until by pure intelligence he arrives at the perception of the absolute good, he at last finds himself at the end of the intellectual world, as in the case of sight at the end of the visible.

. . . Say, then, what is the nature and what are the divisions of the power of dialectic, and what are the paths which lead to our destination, where we can rest from the journey.

Dear Glaucon, I said, you will no longer be able to follow me here, though I would do my best, and would endeavour to show you not an image only but the absolute truth, according to my notion. Whether that notion is or is not correct, it would not be right for me to affirm. But that it is something like this that you must see, of that I am confident.

Doubtless, he replied.

But I must also remind you, that the power of dialectic alone can reveal this, and only to one who is a disciple of the previous sciences.

Of that assertion you may be as confident as of the last.

And assuredly no one will argue that there is any other method of comprehending by any regular process all true existence or of ascertaining what each thing is in its own nature; for the arts in general are concerned with the desires or opinions of men, or with processes of growth and construction; or they have been cultivated in order to care for things grown and constructed; and as to the mathematical sciences which, as we were saying, have some apprehension of true being—geometry and the like—they only dream about being, but never can they behold the waking reality so long as they leave unmoved the hypotheses which they use, and are unable to give an account of them. For when a man knows not his own first principle, and when the conclusion and intermediate steps are also constructed out of he knows not what, how can he imagine that such a fabric of convention can ever become science?

Impossible, he said.

Then dialectic, and dialectic alone, goes directly to the first principle and is the only science which does away with hypotheses in order to make her ground secure; the eye of the soul, which is really buried in an outlandish slough, is by her gentle aid lifted upwards; and in this work she uses as handmaids and helpers the sciences which we have been discussing. We have often used the customary name sciences, but they ought to have some other name, implying greater clearness than opinion and less clearness than science: and this, in our previous sketch, was called understanding. But why should we dispute about names when we have realities of such importance to consider?

Why indeed, he said, when any name will do which expresses the thought of the mind with clearness?

At any rate, we are satisfied, as before, to have four divisions; two for intellect and two for opinion, and to call the first division science, the second understanding, the third belief, and the fourth perception of shadows, opinion being concerned with becoming, and intellect with being; and so to make a proportion:—

As being is to becoming, so is pure intellect to opinion.

And as intellect is to opinion, so is science to belief, and understanding to the perception of shadows.

But let us defer the further correlation and subdivision of the *objects* of opinion and of intellect, for it will be a long inquiry, many times longer than this has been.

Apart from that, then, he said, as far as I understand, I agree.

And do you also agree, I said, in describing the dialectician as one who attains a conception of the essence of each thing? And he who does not possess and is therefore unable to impart this conception, in whatever degree he fails, may in that degree also be said to fail in intelligence? Will you admit so much?

Yes, he said; how can I deny it?

And you would say the same of the conception of the good? Unless the person is able to abstract from all else and define rationally the Idea of good, and unless he can run the gauntlet of all objections, and is keen to disprove them by appeals not to opinion but to absolute truth, never faltering at any step of the argument—unless he can do all this, you would say that he knows neither the Idea of good nor any other good; he apprehends only a shadow, if anything at all, which is given by opinion and not by science;—dreaming and slumbering in this life, before he is well awake here, he arrives at the world below, and has his final quietus.

In all that I should most certainly agree with you.

And surely you would not have the children of your imaginary State, whom you are nurturing and educating—if your imagination ever becomes a reality —you would not allow the future rulers to be mere irrational quantities, and yet to be set in authority over the highest matters?

Certainly not.

Then you will make a law that they shall have such an education as will enable them to attain the greatest skill in asking and answering questions?

Yes, he said, you and I together will make it.

Dialectic, then, as you will agree, is the coping-stone of the sciences, and is set over them; no other study can rightly be built on and above this, and our treatment of the studies required has now reached its end?

I agree, he said.

But to whom we are to assign these studies, and in what way they are to be assigned, are questions which remain to be considered.

Yes, clearly.

You remember, I said, the character which was preferred in our former choice of rulers?

Certainly, he said.

I would have you think that, in other respects, the same natures must still be chosen, and the preference again given to the surest and the bravest, and, if possible, to the fairest; but now we must look for something more than a noble and virile temper; they should also have the natural gifts which accord with this higher education.

And what are these?

Such gifts as keenness and ready powers of acquisition; for the mind more often faints from the severity of study than from the severity of gymnastics: the toil is more entirely the mind's own, and is not shared with the body.

Very true, he replied.

Further, he of whom we are in search should have a good memory, and be an unwearied solid man who is a lover of labour in any line; or he will never be able, besides enduring some bodily exercise, to go through all the intellectual discipline and study which we require of him.

He will not, he said, unless he is gifted by nature in every way.

. . . This, however, is the point which we must not forget, that although in our former selection we chose old men, we must not do so in this. Solon was under a delusion when he said that a man when he grows old may learn many things—for he can no more learn much than he can run much; youth is the time for great and frequent toil.

Of course.

And, therefore, calculation and geometry and all the other elements of instruction, which are to be a preparation for dialectic, should be presented to the mind in childhood; not, however, under any notion of forcing our system of education.

Why not?

Because a freeman ought not to acquire knowledge of any kind like a slave. Bodily exercise, when compulsory, does no harm to the body; but knowledge which is acquired under compulsion obtains no hold on the mind.

Very true.

Then, my good friend, I said, do not use compulsion, but let early education be a sort of amusement; you will then also be better able to find out the natural bent.

There is reason in your remark, he said.

Do you remember that the children were even to be taken to see the battle on horseback; and that if there were no danger they were to be brought close up and, like young hounds, have a taste of blood given them?

Yes, I remember.

The same practice may be followed, I said, in all these things—labours, lessons, dangers—and he who is most at home in all of them ought to be enrolled in a select number.

At what age?

At the age when the necessary gymnastics are over: the period whether of two or three years which passes in this sort of training is useless for any other purpose, for sleep and tiring exercise are unpropitious to learning. Moreover the trial of their quality in gymnastic exercises is one of the most important tests to which our youth are subjected.

Certainly, he replied.

After that time those who are selected from the class of twenty years old will be promoted to higher honour than the rest, and the sciences which they learned without any order in their early education will now be brought together, and they will be able to see the natural relationship of them to one another and to true being.

Yes, he said, that is the only kind of knowledge which, in a few fortunate persons, takes lasting root.

Yes, I said; and the capacity for such knowledge is the great criterion of dialectical talent: the comprehensive mind is always the dialectical.

I agree with you, he said.

These, I said, are the points which you must consider; and those who have most of this comprehension, and who are most steadfast in their learning, and in their military and other appointed duties, when they pass the age of thirty will have to be chosen by you out of the select class, and elevated to higher honour; and you will have to prove them by the help of dialectic, in order to learn which of them is able to give up the use of sight and the other senses, and in company with truth to attain absolute being: And here, my friend, great caution is required.

Why great caution?

. . . They should not taste the dear delight too early; for youngsters, as you may have observed, when they first get the taste in their mouths, argue for amusement, and are always contradicting and refuting others in imitation of those who refute them; like puppy-dogs, they rejoice in pulling and tearing at all who come near them.

Yes, he said, there is nothing which they like better.

And when they have made many conquests and received defeats at the hands of many, they violently and speedily get into a way of not believing anything which they believed before, and hence not only they, but philosophy and all that relates to it is apt to have a bad name with the rest of the world.

Too true, he said.

But when a man begins to get older, he will no longer be guilty of such insanity; he will imitate the dialectician who is seeking for truth, and not the eristic who is contradicting for the sake of amusement; and he will not only attain greater moderation of character, but will increase instead of diminishing the honour of the pursuit.

Very true, he said.

And have not all our previous provisions been designed to avert this danger, when we said that those who are to be trained in reasoning must be orderly and steadfast, not, as now, any chance aspirant or intruder?

Very true.

Suppose, I said, the training in logic to be continued diligently and earnestly and exclusively for twice the number of years which were passed in equivalent bodily exercise—will that be enough?

Would you say six or four years? he asked.

Say five years, I replied; at the end of the time they must be sent down again into the cave and compelled to hold any military or other office which young men are qualified to hold, so that they may not be behind others in experience of life, and here again they must be tested, to show whether, when they are drawn all manner of ways by temptation, they will stand firm or flinch.

And how long is this stage of their lives to last?

Fifteen years, I answered; and when they have reached fifty years of age, then let those who still survive and have distinguished themselves in every action of their lives and in every branch of knowledge be brought at last to their consummation: the time has now arrived at which they must raise the eye of the soul to the universal light which lightens all things, and behold the absolute good; for that is the pattern according to which they are to order the State and the lives of individuals, and the remainder of their own lives also; making philosophy their chief pursuit, but, when their turn comes, toiling also at politics and ruling for the public good, not as though they were performing some heroic action, but simply as a necessity; and when they have brought up in each generation others like themselves and left them in their place to be governors of the State, then they will depart to the Islands of the Blest and dwell there; and the city will give them public memorials and sacrifices and honour them, if the Pythian oracle consent, as demigods, but if not, as in any case blessed and divine.

You are a sculptor, Socrates, and have wrought statues of our governors faultless in beauty.

Yes, I said, Glaucon, and of our governesses too; for you must not suppose that what I have been saying applies to men only and not to women as far as their natures can go.

There you are right, he said, since we have made them to share in all things like the men.

Well, I said, and you would agree (would you not?) that what has been said about the State and the government is not a mere dream, and although difficult not impossible, but only possible in the way which has been supposed; that is to say, when true philosophers are born in the reigning family in a State, one or more of them, despising the honours of this present world which they deem mean and worthless, esteeming above all things right and the honour that springs from right, and regarding justice as the greatest and most necessary of all things, whose ministers they are, and whose principles will be exalted by them when they set in order their own city?

How will they proceed?

They will begin by sending out into the country all the inhabitants of the city who are more than ten years old, and will take possession of their children, who will be unaffected by the habits of their parents; these they will train in their own habits and laws, which will be such as we have described: and in this way the State and constitution of which we were speaking will soonest and most easily attain happiness, and the nation which has such a constitution will gain most.

Yes, that will be the best way. And I think, Socrates, that you have very well described how, if ever, such a constitution might come into being.

Enough then of the perfect State, and of the man who bears its image—there is no difficulty, I suppose, in seeing how we shall describe him also.

There is no difficulty, he replied; and I agree with you in thinking that nothing more need be said.

Aristotle

(384-324 B.C.)

ARISTOTLE did not formulate a total philosophy of education as did his teacher, Plato. He did, however, make a number of vitally important contributions to this field of inquiry.

The *Nicomachean Ethics* is one of the most subtle philosophical works ever written. It contains Aristotle's discussion of whether virtue can be taught, his reflections on the Socratic doctrine that virtue is knowledge, and his arguments in behalf of the life of the intellect as the supreme life for man. The crucial distinction which he draws between intellectual virtue and moral virtue provides him with an answer to the question raised at the opening of the *Meno* dialogue as to "whether virtue is acquired by teaching or by practice." According to Aristotle, intellectual virtue is acquired by teaching, whereas moral virtue is acquired by practice.

Aristotle's conception of the ideal state is presented in *The Politics*. Unfortunately, the book concludes abruptly without presenting much of the detailed discussion concerning educational matters that we are led to expect. This is a result of the fact that some of Aristotle's treatises, including *The Politics*, are actually texts of his lectures, as they are preserved for us in his students' notes. This accounts for many of the stylistic and organizational difficulties which appear in his writings.

His views concerning the ideal state are similar in a number of ways to those of Plato, though Aristotle argues in favor of a society in which Plato's two higher classes are combined into one. A member of Aristotle's aristocracy serves first as soldier, then as ruler, and finally as priest.

Of particular interest is Aristotle's view that one important indication of a good education is the proper use of one's leisure time. This insight is of special importance in light of the current increase in the amount of leisure time available to all members of society.

In his discussion of musical education Aristotle claims that "it is difficult, if not impossible, for those who do not perform to be good judges of the performance of others." If this statement is true, then one ought to consider the extent to which it can be generalized to other activities, such as writing or teaching.

NICHOMACHEAN ETHICS

BOOK I

Every art and every investigation, and likewise every practical pursuit or undertaking, seems to aim at some good: hence it has been well said that the Good is that at which all things aim. . . . But as there are numerous pursuits and arts and sciences it follows that their ends are correspondingly numerous: for instance, the end of the science of medicine is health, that of the art of shipbuilding a vessel, that of strategy victory, that of domestic economy wealth. Now in cases where several such pursuits are subordinate to some single faculty—as bridle-making and the other trades concerned with horses' harness are subordinate to horsemanship, and this and every other military pursuit to the science of strategy . . .—in all these cases, I say, the ends of the master arts are things more to be desired than the ends of the arts subordinate to them; since the latter ends are only pursued for the sake of the former. . . .

If therefore among the ends at which our actions aim there be one which we will for its own sake, while we will the others only for the sake of this, and if we do not choose everything for the sake of something else (which would obviously result in a process *ad infinitum,* so that all desire would be futile and vain), it is clear that this one ultimate End must be the Good, and indeed the Supreme Good. Will not then a knowledge of this Supreme Good be also of great practical importance for the conduct of life? Will it not better enable us to attain our proper object, like archers having a target to aim at? If this be so, we ought to make an attempt to comprehend at all events in outline what exactly this Supreme Good is . . . .

Now there do appear to be several ends at which our actions aim; but as we choose some of them—for instance wealth, or flutes, and instruments generally —as a means to something else, it is clear that not all of them are final ends; whereas the Supreme Good seems to be something final or perfect. Consequently if there be some one thing which alone is a final end, this thing—or if there be several final ends, the one among them which is the most final— will be the Good which we are seeking. In speaking of degrees of finality, we mean that a thing pursued as an end in itself is more final than one pursued as a means to something else, and that a thing never chosen as a means to

From *The Nicomachean Ethics* by Aristotle, trans. by H. Rackham, Cambridge, Mass., Harvard University Press, 1926, pp. 3–619 (with omissions as indicated in the text). Reprinted by permission of the publisher and The Loeb Classical Library.

anything else is more final than things chosen both as ends in themselves and as means to that thing; and accordingly a thing chosen always as an end and never as a means we call absolutely final. Now happiness above all else appears to be absolutely final in this sense, since we always choose it for its own sake and never as a means to something else; whereas honour, pleasure, intelligence, and excellence in its various forms, we choose indeed for their own sakes (since we should be glad to have each of them although no extraneous advantage resulted from it), but we also choose them for the sake of happiness, in the belief that they will be a means to our securing it. But no one chooses happiness for the sake of honour, pleasure, etc., nor as a means to anything whatever other than itself.

.   .   .

Happiness, therefore, being found to be something final and self-sufficient, is the End at which all actions aim.

To say however that the Supreme Good is happiness will probably appear a truism; we still require a more explicit account of what constitutes happiness. Perhaps then we may arrive at this by ascertaining what is man's function. For the goodness or efficiency of a flute-player or sculptor or craftsman of any sort, and in general of anybody who has some function or business to perform, is thought to reside in that function; and similarly it may be held that the good of man resides in the function of man, if he has a function.

Are we then to suppose that, while the carpenter and the shoemaker have definite functions or businesses belonging to them, man as such has none, and is not designed by nature to fulfil any function? Must we not rather assume that, just as the eye, the hand, the foot and each of the various members of the body manifestly has a certain function of its own, so a human being also has a certain function over and above all the functions of his particular members? What then precisely can this function be? The mere act of living appears to be shared even by plants, whereas we are looking for the function peculiar to man; we must therefore set aside the vital activity of nutrition and growth. Next in the scale will come some form of sentient life; but this too appears to be shared by horses, oxen, and animals generally. There remains therefore what may be called the practical life of the rational part of man. (This part has two divisions, one rational as obedient to principle, the other as possessing principle and exercising intelligence.) Rational life again has two meanings; let us assume that we are here concerned with the active exercise of the rational faculty, since this seems to be the more proper sense of the term. If then the function of man is the active exercise of the soul's faculties in conformity with rational principle, or at all events not in dissociation from rational principle, and if we acknowledge the function of an individual and of a good individual of the same class (for instance, a harper and a good harper, and so generally with all classes) to be generically the same, the qualification of the latter's superiority in excellence being added to the function in his case (I mean that if the function of a harper is to play the harp, that of a good harper is to play the harp well): if this is so, and if we declare that the function of man is a certain form of life, and define that form of life as the exercise of the soul's faculties and activities in association with rational principle, and say that the function of a good man is to perform these activities well and rightly, and if a function is well performed when it is performed in accordance with its own proper excellence—if then all this be so, the Good of man proves to be the active exercise of his soul's faculties in conformity with excellence or virtue, or if there be several human excellences or virtues, in conformity with the best and most perfect among them.

Moreover, to be happy takes a complete lifetime. For one swallow does not make summer, nor does one fine day; and similarly one day or a brief period of happiness does not make a man supremely blessed and happy.

.   .   .

But inasmuch as happiness is a certain activity of soul in conformity with perfect virtue, it is necessary to examine the nature of virtue. For this will probably assist us in our investigation of the nature of happiness. Also, the true statesman seems to be one who has made a special study of virtue, since his aim is to make the citizens good and law-abiding men—witness the lawgivers of Crete and Sparta, and the other great legislators of history; but if the study of virtue falls within the province of Political Science, it is clear that in investigating virtue we shall be keeping to the plan which we laid down at the outset.

Now the virtue that we have to consider is clearly human virtue, since the good or happiness which we set out to seek is human good and human happiness. But human virtue means in our view excellence of soul, not excellence of body, indeed our definition of happiness is an activity of the soul. Now if this is so, clearly it behoves the statesman to have some acquaintance with psychology, just as the physician who is to heal the eye or the other parts of the body must know their anatomy. Indeed a foundation of science is even more requisite for the statesman, inasmuch as politics is a higher and more honourable art than medicine; but physicians of the better class devote much attention to the study of the human body. The student of politics therefore as well as the psychologist must study the nature of the soul, though he will do so as an aid to politics, and only so far as is requisite for the objects of enquiry that he has in view: to pursue the subject in further detail would doubtless be more laborious than is necessary for his purpose.

Now on the subject of psychology some of the teaching current in extraneous discourses is satisfactory, and may be adopted here: namely that the soul consists of two parts, one irrational and the other capable of reason. . . . Of the irrational part of the soul again one division appears to be common to all living things, and of a vegetative nature: I refer to the part that causes nutrition and growth . . . .

But there also appears to be another element in the soul, which, though irrational, yet in a manner participates in rational principle. In self-restrained and unrestrained people we approve their principle, or the rational part of their souls, because it urges them in the right way and exhorts them for their good; but their nature seems also to contain another element beside that of rational principle, which combats and resists that principle. Exactly the same thing may take place in the soul as occurs with the body in a case of paralysis: when the patient wills to move his limbs to the right they swerve to the left; and similarly in unrestrained persons their impulses run counter to their principle. But whereas in the body we see the erratic member, in the case of the soul we do not see it; nevertheless it cannot be doubted that in the soul also there is an element beside that of principle, which opposes and runs counter to principle (though in what sense the two are distinct does not concern us here). But this second element also seems, as we said, to participate in rational principle; at least in the self-restrained man it obeys the behest of principle—and no doubt in the temperate and brave man it is still more amenable, for all parts of his nature are in harmony with principle.

Thus we see that the irrational part, as well as the soul as a whole, is double. One division of it, the vegetative, does not share in rational principle at all; the other, the seat of the appetites and of desire in general, does in a sense participate in principle, as being amenable and obedient to it (in the sense in fact in which we speak of "paying heed" to one's father and friends, not in the sense of the term "rational" in mathematics). And that principle can in a manner appeal to the irrational part, is indicated by our practice of admonishing delinquents, and by our employment of rebuke and exhortation generally.

If on the other hand it be more correct to speak of the appetitive part of the soul also as rational, in that case it is the rational part which, as well as the whole soul, is divided into two, the one division having rational principle in the proper sense and in itself, the other in the sense in which a child listens to its father.

Now virtue also is differentiated in correspondence with this division of the soul. Some forms of virtue are called intellectual virtues, others moral virtues: Wisdom, Understanding, and Prudence are intellectual, Liberality and Temperance are moral virtues. When describing a man's moral character we do not say that he is wise or intelligent, but gentle or temperate; but a wise man also is praised for his disposition, and praiseworthy dispositions we term virtues.

BOOK II

Virtue being, as we have seen, of two kinds, intellectual and moral, intellectual virtue is for the most part both produced and increased by instruction, and therefore requires experience and time; whereas moral or ethical virtue is the product of habit *(ethos)*, and has indeed derived its name, with a slight variation of form, from that word. And therefore it is clear that none of the moral virtues is engendered in us by nature, for no natural property can be altered by habit. For instance, it is the nature of a stone to move downwards, and it cannot be trained to move upwards, even though you should try to train it to do so by throwing it up into the air ten thousand times; nor can fire be trained to move downwards, nor can anything else that naturally behaves in one way be trained into a habit of behaving in another way. The virtues therefore are engendered in us neither by nature nor yet in violation of nature; nature gives us the capacity to receive them, and this capacity is brought to maturity by habit.

Moreover, the faculties given us by nature are bestowed on us first in a potential form; we develop their actual exercise afterwards. This is clearly so with our senses: we did not acquire the faculty of sight or hearing by repeatedly seeing or repeatedly listening, but the other way about—because we had the senses we began to use them, we did not get them by using them. The virtues on the other hand we acquire by first having actually practised them, just as we do the arts. We learn an art or craft by doing the things that we shall have to do when we have learnt it: for instance, men become builders by building houses, harpers by playing on the harp. Similarly we become just by doing just acts, temperate by doing temperate acts, brave by doing brave acts. This truth is attested by the experience of states: lawgivers make the citizens good by training them in habits of right action—this is the aim of all legislation, and if it fails to do this it is a failure; this is what distinguishes a good form of constitution from a bad one. Again, the actions from or through which any virtue is produced are the same as those through which it also is destroyed—just as is the case with skill in the arts, for both the good harpers and the bad ones are produced by harping, and similarly with builders and all the other craftsmen: as you will become a good builder from building well, so you will become a bad one from building badly. Were this not so, there would be no need for teachers of the arts, but everybody would be born a good or bad craftsman as the case might be. The same then is true of the virtues. It is by taking part in transactions with our fellow-men that some of us become just and others unjust; by acting in dangerous situations and forming a habit of fear or of confidence we become courageous or cowardly. And the same holds good of our dispositions with regard to the appetites, and anger; some men become temperate and gentle, others profligate and irascible, by actually comporting themselves in one way or the other in relation to those passions. In a word, our moral dispositions are formed as a result of the corresponding activities. Hence it is incumbent on us to control the character of our activities, since on the quality of these depends the quality of our dispositions. It is therefore not of small moment whether we are trained from childhood in one set of habits or another; on the contrary it is of very great, or rather of supreme, importance.

As then our present study, unlike the other branches of philosophy, has a practical aim (for we are not investigating the nature of virtue for the sake of knowing what it is, but in order that we may become good, without which result our investigation would be of no use), we have consequently to carry our enquiry into the region of conduct, and to ask how we are to act rightly; since our actions, as we have said, determine the quality of our dispositions.

.   .   .

But let it be granted to begin with that the whole theory of conduct is bound to be an outline only and not an exact system, in accordance with the rule we laid down at the beginning, that philosophical theories must only be required to correspond to their subject matter; and matters of conduct and expediency have nothing fixed or invariable about them, any more than have matters of health. And if this is true of the general theory of ethics, still less is exact precision possible in dealing with particular cases of conduct; for these come under no science or professional tradition, but the agents themselves have to consider what is suited to the circumstances on each occasion, just as is the case with the art of medicine or of navigation. But although the theory we are now investigating is thus necessarily inexact, we must do our best to help it out.

First of all then we have to observe, that moral qualities are so constituted as to be destroyed by excess and by deficiency—as we see is the case with bodily strength and health (for one is forced to explain what is invisible by means of visible illustrations). Strength is destroyed both by excessive and by deficient exercise; and similarly health is destroyed both by too much and by too little food and drink, while it is produced, increased, and preserved by a suitable quantity. The same therefore is true of Temperance, Courage, and the other virtues. The man who runs away from everything in fear and never endures anything becomes a coward; the man who fears nothing whatsoever but encounters everything becomes foolhardy. Similarly he that indulges in every pleasure and refrains from none turns out a profligate, and he that shuns all pleasure, as boorish persons do, becomes what may be called insensible. Thus Temperance and Courage are destroyed by excess and deficiency, and preserved by the observance of the mean.

But not only are the virtues both generated and fostered on the one hand, and destroyed on the other, from and by the same actions, but they will also find their full exercise in the same actions. This is clearly the case with the other more visible qualities, such as bodily strength: for strength is produced by taking much food and undergoing much exertion, while also it is the strong man who will be able to eat most food and endure most exertion. The same holds good with the virtues. We become temperate by abstaining from pleasures, and at the same time we are best able to abstain from pleasures when we have become temperate. And so with Courage: we become brave by training ourselves to despise and endure terrors, and we shall be best able to endure terrors when we have become brave.

.   .   .

A difficulty may however be raised as to what we mean by saying that in order to become just men must do just actions, and in order to become temperate they must do temperate actions. For if they do just and temperate actions, they are just and temperate already, just as, if they spell or play music correctly, they are scholars or musicians.

But perhaps this is not the case even with the arts. It is possible to spell a word correctly by chance, or because some one else prompts you; hence you will be a scholar only if you spell correctly in the scholar's way, that is, in virtue of the scholarly knowledge which you yourself possess.

Moreover the case of the arts is not really analogous to that of the virtues. Works of art have their merit in themselves, so that it is enough if they are produced having a certain quality of their own; but acts done in conformity with the virtues are not done justly or temperately if they themselves are of a certain sort, but only if the agent also is in a certain state of mind when he does them: first he must act with knowledge; secondly he must deliberately choose the act, and choose it for its own sake; and thirdly the act must spring from a fixed and permanent disposition of character. For the possession of an art, none of these conditions is included, except the mere qualification of knowledge; but for the possession of the virtues, knowledge is of little or no avail, whereas the other conditions, so far from being of little moment, are all-important, inasmuch as virtue results from the repeated performance of just and temperate actions. Thus although actions are entitled just and temperate when they are such acts as just and temperate men would do, the agent is just and temperate not when he does these acts merely, but when he does them in the way in which just and temperate men do them. It is correct therefore to say that a man becomes just by doing just actions and temperate by doing temperate actions; and no one can have the remotest chance of becoming good without doing them. But the mass of mankind, instead of doing virtuous acts, have recourse to discussing virtue, and think that they are pursuing philosophy and that this will make them good men. In so doing they act like invalids who listen carefully to what the doctor says, but entirely neglect to carry out his prescriptions. That sort of philosophy will no more lead to a healthy state of soul than will that mode of treatment produce health of body.

.   .   .

Virtue then is a settled disposition of the mind as regards the choice of actions and feelings, consisting essentially in the observance of the mean relative to us, this being determined by principle, that is, as the prudent man would determine it.

And it is a mean state between two vices, one of excess and one of defect.

Furthermore, it is a mean state in that whereas the vices either fall short of or exceed what is right in feelings and in actions, virtue ascertains and adopts the mean. Hence while in respect of its essence and the definition that states its original being virtue is the observance of the mean, in point of excellence and rightness it is an extreme.

Not every action or feeling however admits of the observance of a due mean. Indeed the very names of some essentially denote evil, for instance malice, shamelessness, envy, and, of actions, adultery, theft, murder. All these and similar actions and feelings are blamed as being bad in themselves; it is not the excess or deficiency of them that we blame. It is impossible therefore ever to go right in regard to them—one must always be wrong; nor does right or wrong in their case depend on the circumstances, for instance, whether one commits adultery with the right woman, at the right time, and in the right manner; the mere commission of any of them is wrong. One might as well suppose there could be a due mean and excess and deficiency in acts of injustice or cowardice or profligacy, which would imply that one could have a medium amount of excess and of deficiency, an excessive amount of excess and a deficient amount of deficiency.

But just as there can be no excess or deficiency in temperance and justice, because the mean is in a sense an extreme, so there can be no observance of the mean nor excess nor deficiency in the corresponding vicious acts mentioned above, but however they are committed, they are wrong; since, to put it in general terms, there is no such thing as observing a mean in excess or deficiency, nor as exceeding or falling short in the observance of a mean.

.   .   .

Enough has now been said to show that moral virtue is a mean, and in what sense this is so, namely that it is a mean between two vices, one of excess and the other of defect; and that it is such a mean because it aims at hitting the middle point in feelings and in actions. This is why it is a hard task to be good, for it is hard to find the middle point in anything: for instance, not everybody can find the centre of a circle, but only someone who knows geometry. So also anybody can become angry—that is easy, and so it is to give and spend money; but to be angry with or give money to the right person, and to the right amount, and at the right time, and for the right purpose, and in the right way—this is not within everybody's power and is not easy; so that to do these things properly is rare, praiseworthy, and noble.

Hence the first rule in aiming at the mean is to avoid that extreme which is the more opposed to the mean, as Calypso advises—

"Steer the ship clear of yonder spray and surge."

For of the two extremes one is a more serious error than the other. Hence, inasmuch as to hit the mean extremely well is difficult, the second best way to sail, as the saying goes, is to take the least of the evils; and the best way to do this is the way we enjoin.

The second rule is to notice what are the errors to which we are ourselves most prone (as different men are inclined by nature to different faults)—and we shall discover what these are by observing the pleasure or pain that we experience—; then we must drag ourselves away in the opposite direction, for by steering wide of our besetting error we shall make a middle course. This is the method adopted by carpenters to straighten warped timber.

Thirdly, we must in everything be most of all on our guard against what is pleasant and against pleasure; for when pleasure is on her trial we are not impartial judges. The right course is therefore to feel towards pleasure as the elders of the people felt towards Helen, and to apply their words to her on every occasion; for if we roundly bid her be gone, we shall be less likely to err.

These then, to sum up the matter, are the precautions that will best enable us to hit the mean. But no doubt it is a difficult thing to do, and especially in particular cases: for instance, it is not easy to define in what manner and with what people and on what sort of grounds and how long one ought to be angry; and in fact we sometimes praise men who err on the side of defect in this matter and call them gentle, sometimes those who are quick to anger and style them manly. However, though we do not blame one who diverges only a little from the right course, whether on the side of the too much or of the too little, we do blame one who diverges more widely, and to a noticeable extent. Yet to what degree and how seriously a man must err to be blamed is not easy to define on principle. For in fact no object of perception is easy to define; and such questions of degree depend on particular circumstances, and the decision lies with perception.

Thus much then is clear, that it is the middle disposition in each department of conduct that is to be praised, but that one should lean sometimes to the side of excess and sometimes to that of deficiency, since this is the easiest way of hitting the mean and the right course.

BOOK VII

... How can a man fail in self-restraint when believing correctly that what he does is wrong? Some people say that he cannot do so when he *knows* the act to be wrong; since, as Socrates held, it would be strange if, when a man possessed Knowledge, some other thing should overpower it, and drag it about like a slave. In fact Socrates used to combat the view altogether, maintaining that there is no such thing as Unrestraint, since no one, he held, acts contrary to what is best, believing what he does to be bad, but only through ignorance. Now this theory is manifestly at variance with plain facts; and we ought to investigate the state of mind in question more closely. ...

(1) ... [The] word *know* is used in two senses. A man who has knowledge but is not exercising it is said to know, and so is a man who is actually

exercising his knowledge. It will make a difference whether a man does wrong having the knowledge that it is wrong but not consciously thinking of his knowledge, or with the knowledge consciously present to his mind. The latter would be felt to be surprising; but it is not surprising that a man should do what he knows to be wrong if he is not conscious of the knowledge at the time.

(2) Again, reasoning on matters of conduct employs premises of two forms. Now it is quite possible for a man to act against knowledge when he knows both premises but is only exercising his knowledge of the universal premise and not of the particular; for action has to do with particular things. Moreover, there is a distinction as regards the universal term: one universal is predicated of the man himself, the other of the thing; for example, he may know and be conscious of the knowledge that dry food is good for every man and that he himself is a man, or even that food of a certain kind is dry, but either not possess or not be actualizing the knowledge whether the particular food before him is food of that kind. Now clearly the distinction between these two ways of knowing will make all the difference in the world. It will not seem at all strange that the unrestrained man should "know" in one way, but it would be astonishing if he knew in another way.

(3) Again, it is possible for men to "have knowledge" in yet another way besides those just discussed; for even in the state of having knowledge without exercising it we can observe a distinction: a man may in a sense both have it and not have it; for instance, when he is asleep, or mad, or drunk. But persons under the influence of passion are in the same condition; for it is evident that anger, sexual desire, and certain other passions, actually alter the state of the body, and in some cases even cause madness. It is clear therefore that we must pronounce the unrestrained to "have knowledge" only in the same way as men who are asleep or mad or drunk. Their using the language of knowledge is no proof that they possess it. Persons in the states mentioned repeat propositions of geometry and verses of Empedocles; students who have just begun a subject reel off its formulae, though they do not yet know their meaning, for knowledge has to become part of the tissue of the mind, and this takes time. Hence we must conceive that men who fail in self-restraint talk in the same way as actors speaking a part.

(4) Again, one may also study the cause of Unrestraint scientifically, thus: In a practical syllogism, the major premise is an opinion, while the minor premise deals with particular things, which are the province of perception. Now when the two premises are combined, just as in theoretic reasoning the mind is compelled to *affirm* the resulting conclusion, so in the case of practical premises you are forced at once to *do* it. For example, given the premises "All sweet things ought to be tasted" and "Yonder thing is sweet"—a particular instance of the general class—, you are bound, if able and not prevented, immediately to taste the thing. When therefore there is present in the mind on the one hand a universal judgement forbidding you to taste and on the other hand a universal judgement saying "All sweet things are pleasant," and a minor

premise "Yonder thing is sweet," and this minor premise is actually operant, and when desire is present at the same time, then, though the former universal judgement says "Avoid that thing," the desire leads you to it (since desire can put the various parts of the body in motion). Thus it comes about that when men fail in self-restraint, they act in a sense under the influence of a principle or opinion, but an opinion not in itself but only accidentally opposed to the right principle (for it is the desire, and not the opinion, that is really opposed). Hence the lower animals cannot be called unrestrained, if only for the reason that they have no power of forming universal concepts, but only mental images and memories of particular things.

If we ask how the unrestrained man's ignorance is dissipated and he returns to a state of knowledge, the explanation is the same as in the case of drunkenness and sleep, and is not peculiar to failure of self-restraint. We must go for it to physiology.

But inasmuch as the last premise, which originates action, is an opinion as to some object of sense, and it is this opinion which the unrestrained man when under the influence of passion either does not possess, or only possesses in a way which as we saw does not amount to knowing it but only makes him repeat it as the drunken man repeats the maxims of Empedocles, and since the ultimate term is not a universal, and is not deemed to be an object of Scientific Knowledge in the same way as a universal term is, we do seem to be led to the conclusion which Socrates sought to establish. For the knowledge which is present when failure of self-restraint occurs is not what is held to be Knowledge in the true sense, nor is it true Knowledge which is dragged about by passion, but knowledge derived from sense-perception.

So much for the question whether failure of self-restraint can go with knowledge or not, and with knowledge in what sense.

.   .   .

BOOK X

Having now discussed the various kinds of Virtue, of Friendship and of Pleasure, it remains for us to treat in outline of Happiness, inasmuch as we count this to be the End of human life. But it will shorten the discussion if we recapitulate what has been said already.

Now we stated that happiness is not a certain disposition of character; since if it were it might be possessed by a man who passed the whole of his life asleep, living the life of a vegetable, or by one who was plunged in the deepest misfortune. If then we reject this as unsatisfactory, and feel bound to class happiness rather as some form of activity, as has been said in the earlier part of this treatise, and if activities are of two kinds, some merely necessary means and desirable only for the sake of something else, others desirable in themselves, it is clear that happiness is to be classed among activities desirable in themselves, and not among those desirable as a means to something else; since happiness lacks nothing, and is self-sufficient.

But those activities are desirable in themselves which do not aim at any result beyond the mere exercise of the activity. Now this is felt to be the nature of actions in conformity with virtue; for to do noble and virtuous deeds is a thing desirable for its own sake.

But agreeable amusements also are desirable for their own sake; we do not pursue them as a means to something else, for as a matter of fact they are more often harmful than beneficial, causing men to neglect their health and their estates. Yet persons whom the world counts happy usually have recourse to such pastimes; and this is why adepts in such pastimes stand in high favour with princes, because they make themselves agreeable in supplying what their patrons desire: and what they want is amusement. So it is supposed that amusements are a component part of happiness, because princes and potentates devote their leisure to them.

But (i) perhaps princes and potentates are not good evidence. Virtue and intelligence, which are the sources of man's higher activities, do not depend on the possession of power; and if these persons, having no taste for pure and liberal pleasure, have recourse to the pleasures of the body, we must not on that account suppose that bodily pleasures are the more desirable. Children imagine that the things they themselves value are actually the best; it is not surprising therefore that, as children and grown men have different standards of value, so also should the worthless and the virtuous. Therefore, as has repeatedly been said, those things are actually valuable and pleasant which appear so to the good man; but each man thinks that activity most desirable which suits his particular disposition, and therefore the good man thinks virtuous activity most desirable. It follows therefore that happiness is not to be found in amusements.

(ii) Indeed it would be strange that amusement should be our End—that we should toil and moil all our life long in order that we may amuse ourselves. For virtually every object we adopt is pursued as a means to something else, excepting happiness, which is an end in itself; to make amusement the object of our serious pursuits and our work seems foolish and childish to excess: Anacharsis's motto, Play in order that you may work, is felt to be the right rule. For amusement is a form of rest; but we need rest because we are not able to go on working without a break, and therefore it is not an end, since we take it as a means to further activity.

(iii) And the life that conforms with virtue is thought to be a happy life; but virtuous life involves serious purpose, and does not consist in amusement.

(iv) Also we pronounce serious things to be superior to things that are funny and amusing; and the nobler a faculty or a person is, the more serious, we think, are their activities; therefore, the activity of the nobler faculty or person is itself superior, and therefore more productive of happiness.

(v) Also anybody can enjoy the pleasures of the body, a slave no less than the noblest of mankind; but no one allows a slave any measure of happiness, any more than a life of his own. Therefore happiness does not consist in pastimes and amusements, but in activities in accordance with virtue, as has been said already.

But if happiness consists in activity in accordance with virtue, it is reasonable that it should be activity in accordance with the highest virtue; and this will be the virtue of the best part of us. Whether then this be the intellect, or whatever else it be that is thought to rule and lead us by nature, and to have cognizance of what is noble and divine, either as being itself also actually divine, or as being relatively the divinest part of us, it is the activity of this part of us in accordance with the virtue proper to it that will constitute perfect happiness; and it has been stated already that this activity is the activity of contemplation.

And that happiness consists in contemplation may be accepted as agreeing both with the results already reached and with the truth. For contemplation is at once the highest form of activity, since the intellect is the highest thing in us, and the objects with which the intellect deals are the highest things that can be known; and also it is the most continuous, for we can reflect more continuously than we can carry on any form of action. And again we suppose that happiness must contain an element of pleasure; now activity in accordance with wisdom is admittedly the most pleasant of the activities in accordance with virtue: at all events it is held that philosophy or the pursuit of wisdom contains pleasures of marvellous purity and permanence, and it is reasonable to suppose that the enjoyment of knowledge is a still pleasanter occupation than the pursuit of it. Also the activity of contemplation will be found to possess in the highest degree the quality that is termed self-sufficiency; for while it is true that the wise man equally with the just man and the rest requires the necessaries of life, yet, these being adequately supplied, whereas the just man needs other persons towards whom or with whose aid he may act justly, and so likewise do the temperate man and the brave man and the others, the wise man on the contrary can also contemplate by himself, and the more so the wiser he is; no doubt he will study better with the aid of fellow-workers, but still he is the most self-sufficient of men. Also the activity of contemplation may be held to be the only activity that is loved for its own sake: it produces no result beyond the actual act of contemplation, whereas from practical pursuits we look to secure some advantage, greater or smaller, beyond the action itself. Also happiness is thought to involve leisure; for we do business in order that we may have leisure, and carry on war in order that we may have peace. Now the practical virtues are exercised in politics or in warfare; but the pursuits of politics and war seem to be unleisured—those of war indeed entirely so, for no one desires to be at war for the sake of being at war, nor deliberately takes steps to cause a war: a man would be thought an utterly bloodthirsty character if he declared war on a friendly state for the sake of causing battles and massacres. But the activity of the politician also is un-leisured, and aims at securing something beyond the mere participation in politics—positions of authority and honour, or, if the happiness of the politi-cian himself and of his fellow-citizens, this happiness conceived as something distinct from political activity (and in fact we are investigating it as so distinct). If then among practical pursuits displaying the virtues, politics and war stand out pre-eminent in nobility and grandeur, and yet they are unleisured, and directed to some further end, not chosen for their own sakes: whereas the activity of the intellect is felt to excel in serious worth, consisting as it does in contemplation, and to aim at no end beyond itself, and also to contain a pleasure peculiar to itself, and therefore augmenting its activity: and if accord-ingly the attributes of this activity are found to be self-sufficiency, leisuredness, such freedom from fatigue as is possible for man, and all the other attributes of blessedness: it follows that it is the activity of the intellect that constitutes complete human happiness—provided it be granted a complete span of life, for nothing that belongs to happiness can be incomplete.

Such a life as this however will be higher than the human level: not in virtue of his humanity will a man achieve it, but in virtue of something within him that is divine; and by as much as this something is superior to his composite nature, by so much is its activity superior to the exercise of the other forms of virtue. If then the intellect is something divine in comparison with man, so is the life of the intellect divine in comparison with human life. Nor ought we to obey those who enjoin that a man should have man's thoughts and a mortal the thoughts of mortality, but we ought so far as possible to achieve immortal-ity, and do all that man may to live in accordance with the highest thing in him; for though this be small in bulk, in power and value it far surpasses all the rest.

It may even be held that this is the true self of each, inasmuch as it is the ruling and better part; and therefore it would be a strange thing if a man should choose to live not his own life but the life of some other than himself.

Moreover what was said before will apply here also: that which is best and most pleasant for each creature is that which is proper to the nature of each; accordingly the life of the intellect is the best and the pleasantest life for man, inasmuch as the intellect especially is man; therefore this life will be the happiest.

.   .   .

THE POLITICS

BOOK VII

. . . [T]he first point to be considered is what should be the conditions of the ideal or perfect state; for the perfect state cannot exist without a due supply of the means of life. And therefore we must presuppose many purely imaginary conditions, but nothing impossible. There will be, a certain number of citizens, a country in which to place them, and the like. As the weaver or shipbuilder or any other artisan must have the material proper for his work (and in proportion as this is better prepared, so will the result of his art be nobler), so the statesman or legislator must also have the materials suited to him.

First among the materials required by the statesman is population: he will consider what should be the number . . . of the citizens . . . . Experience shows that a very populous city can rarely, if ever, be well governed; since all cities which have a reputation for good government have a limit of population. We may argue on grounds of reason, and the same result will follow. For law is order, and good law is good order; but a very great multitude cannot be orderly: to introduce order into the unlimited is the work of a divine power —of such a power as holds together the universe. Beauty is realized in number and magnitude, and the state which combines magnitude with good order must necessarily be the most beautiful. To the size of states there is a limit, as there is to other things, plants, animals, implements; for none of these retain their natural power when they are too large or too small, but they either wholly lose their nature, or are spoiled. For example, a ship which is only a span long will not be a ship at all, nor a ship a quarter of a mile long; yet there may be a ship of a certain size, either too large or too small, which will still be a ship, but bad for sailing. In like manner a state when composed of too few is not as a state ought to be, self-sufficing; when of too many, though self-sufficing in all mere necessaries, it is a nation and not a state, being almost incapable of constitutional government. . . .

A state then only begins to exist when it has attained a population sufficient for a good life in the political community: it may indeed somewhat exceed this number. But, as I was saying, there must be a limit. What should be the limit

From *The Politics of Aristotle*, trans. by Benjamin Jowett, Oxford, The Clarendon Press, 1885, Vol. I, pp. 213–255 (with omissions as indicated in the text). Reprinted by permission of the publisher.

will be easily ascertained by experience. For both governors and governed have duties to perform; the special functions of a governor are to command and to judge. But if the citizens of a state are to judge and to distribute offices according to merit, then they must know each other's characters; where they do not possess this knowledge, both the election to offices and the decision of lawsuits will go wrong. When the population is very large they are manifestly settled at haphazard, which clearly ought not to be. . . . Clearly then the best limit of the population of a state is the largest number which suffices for the purposes of life, and can be taken in at a single view.

. . . We must see also how many things are indispensable to the existence of a state. . . . Let us then enumerate the functions of a state, and we shall easily elicit what we want:

First, there must be food; secondly, arts, for life requires many instruments; thirdly, there must be arms, for the members of a community have need of them in order to maintain authority both against disobedient subjects and against external assailants; fourthly, there must be a certain amount of revenue, both for internal needs, and for the purposes of war; fifthly or rather first, there must be a care of religion, which is commonly called worship; sixthly, and most necessary of all, there must be a power of deciding what is for the public interest, and what is just in men's dealings with one another.

These are the things which every state may be said to need. For a state is not a mere aggregate of persons, but a union of them sufficing for the purposes of life; and if any of these things be wanting, it is simply impossible that the community can be self-sufficing. A state then should be framed with a view to the fulfilment of these functions. There must be husbandmen to procure food, and artisans, and a warlike and a wealthy class, and priests, and judges to decide what is just and expedient.

Having determined these points, we have in the next place to consider whether all ought to share in every sort of occupation. Shall every man be at once husbandman, artisan, councillor, judge, or shall we suppose the several occupations just mentioned assigned to different persons? or, thirdly, shall some employments be assigned to individuals and others common to all? The question, however, does not occur in every state . . . for in democracies all share in all, in oligarchies the opposite practice prevails. Now, since we are here speaking of the best form of government, and that under which the state will be most happy (and happiness, as has been already said, cannot exist without virtue), it clearly follows that in the state which is best governed the citizens who are absolutely and not merely relatively just men must not lead the life of mechanics or tradesmen, for such a life is ignoble and inimical to virtue. Neither must they be husbandmen, since leisure is necessary both for the development of virtue and the performance of political duties.

Again, there is in a state a class of warriors, and another of councillors, who advise about the expedient and determine matters of law, and these seem in an especial manner parts of a state. Now, should these two classes be distinguished, or are both functions to be assigned to the same persons? Here again there is no difficulty in seeing that both functions will in one way belong to the same, in another, to different persons. To different persons in so far as their employments are suited to different ages of life, for the one requires wisdom, and the other strength. But on the other hand, since it is an impossible thing that those who are able to use or to resist force should be willing to remain always in subjection, from this point of view the persons are the same; for those who carry arms can always determine the fate of the constitution. It remains therefore that both functions of government should be entrusted to the same persons, not, however, at the same time, but in the order prescribed by nature, who has given to young men strength and to older men wisdom. Such a distribution of duties will be expedient and also just, and is founded upon a principle of proportion. Besides, the ruling class should be the owners of property for they are citizens, and the citizens of a state should be in good circumstances; whereas mechanics or any other class whose art excludes the art of virtue have no share in the state. This follows from our first principle, for happiness cannot exist without virtue, and a city is not to be termed happy in regard to a portion of the citizens, but in regard to them all. And clearly property should be in their hands, since the husbandmen will of necessity be slaves or barbarians. . . .

Of the classes enumerated there remain only the priests, and the manner in which their office is to be regulated is obvious. No husbandman or mechanic should be appointed to it; for the Gods should receive honour from the citizens only. Now since the body of the citizens is divided into two classes, the warriors and the councillors; and it is beseeming that the worship of the Gods should be duly performed, and also a rest provided in their service for those who from age have given up active life—to the old men of these two classes should be assigned the duties of the priesthood.

We have shown what are the necessary conditions, and what the parts of a state: husbandmen, craftsmen, and labourers of all kinds are necessary to the existence of states, but the parts of the state are the warriors and councillors. . . .

We conclude that from one point of view governors and governed are identical, and from another different. And therefore their education must be the same and also different. For he who would learn to command well must, as men say, first of all learn to obey. . . . There is one rule which is for the sake of the rulers and another rule which is for the sake of the ruled; the former is a despotic, the latter a free government. Some commands differ not in the thing commanded, but in the intention with which they are imposed. Wherefore, many apparently menial offices are an honour to the free youth by whom they are performed; for actions do not differ as honourable or dishonourable in themselves so much as in the end and intention of them. But since we say that the virtue of the citizen and ruler is the same as that of the good man, and that the same person must first be a subject and then a ruler, the legislator has to see that they become good men, and by what means this may be accomplished, and what is the end of the perfect life.

Now the soul of man is divided into two parts, one of which has reason in itself, and the other, not having reason in itself, is able to obey reason. And we call a man good because he has the virtues of these two parts. In which of them the end is more likely to be found is no matter of doubt to those who adopt our division; for in the world both of nature and of art the inferior always exists for the sake of the better or superior, and the better or superior is that which has reason. The reason too, in our ordinary way of speaking, is divided into two parts, for there is a practical and a speculative reason, and there must be a corresponding division of actions; the actions of the naturally better principle are to be preferred by those who have it in their power to attain to both or to all, for that is always to every one the most eligible which is the highest attainable by him. The whole of life is further divided into two parts, business and leisure, war and peace, and all actions into those which are necessary and useful, and those which are honourable. And the preference given to one or the other class of actions must necessarily be like the preference given to one or other part of the soul and its actions over the other; there must be war for the sake of peace, business for the sake of leisure, things useful and necessary for the sake of things honourable. All these points the statesman should keep in view when he frames his laws; he should consider the parts of the soul and their functions, and above all the better and the end; he should also remember the diversities of human lives and actions. For men must engage in business and go to war, but leisure and peace are better; they must do what is necessary and useful, but what is honourable is better. In such principles children and persons of every age which requires education should be trained. . . .

After . . . children have been born, the manner of rearing them may be supposed to have a great effect on their bodily strength. . . . To accustom children to the cold from their earliest years is . . . an excellent practice, which greatly conduces to health, and hardens them for military service. . . . For human nature should be early habituated to endure all which by habit it can be made to endure; but the process must be gradual. . . . Such care should attend them in the first stage of life.

The next period lasts to the age of five; during this no demand should be made upon the child for study or labour, lest its growth be impeded; and there should be sufficient motion to prevent the limbs from being inactive. This can be secured, among other ways, by amusement, but the amusement should not be vulgar or tiring or riotous. The Directors of Education, as they are termed, should be careful what tales or stories the children hear, for the sports of children are designed to prepare the way for the business of later life, and should be for the most part imitations of the occupations which they will hereafter pursue in earnest. . . . Besides other duties, the Directors of Education should have an eye to their bringing up, and should take care that they are left as little as possible with slaves. For until they are seven years old they must live at home; and therefore, even at this early age, all that is mean and low should be banished from their sight and hearing. Indeed, there is nothing which the legislator should be more careful to drive away than indecency of speech; for the light utterance of shameful words is akin to shameful actions. The young especially should never be allowed to repeat or hear anything of the sort. A freeman who is found saying or doing what is forbidden, if he be too young as yet to have the privilege of a place at the public tables, should be disgraced and beaten, and an elder person degraded as his slavish conduct deserves. And since we do not allow improper language, clearly we should also banish pictures or tales which are indecent. Let the rulers take care that there be no image or picture representing unseemly actions, except in the temples of those Gods at whose festivals the law permits even ribaldry, and whom the law also permits to be worshipped by persons of mature age on behalf of themselves, their children, and their wives. But the legislator should not allow youth to be hearers of satirical Iambic verses or spectators of comedy until they are of an age to sit at the public tables and to drink strong wine; by that time education will have armed them against the evil influences of such representations.

. . . Theodorus, the tragic actor, was quite right in saying that he would not allow any other actor, not even if he were quite second-rate, to enter before himself, because the spectators grew fond of the voices which they first heard. And the same principle of association applies universally to things as well as persons, for we always like best whatever comes first. And therefore youth should be kept strangers to all that is bad, and especially to things which suggest vice or hate. When the five years have passed away, during the two following years they must look on at the pursuits which they are hereafter to learn. There are two periods of life into which education has to be divided, from seven to the age of puberty, and onwards to the age of one and twenty. [The poets] who divide ages by sevens are not always right: we should rather adhere to the divisions actually made by nature; for the deficiencies of nature are what art and education seek to fill up.

Let us then first enquire if any regulations are to be laid down about children, and secondly, whether the care of them should be the concern of the state or of private individuals, which latter is in our own day the common custom, and in the third place, what these regulations should be.

BOOK VIII

No one will doubt that the legislator should direct his attention above all to the education of youth, or that the neglect of education does harm to states.

The citizen should be moulded to suit the form of government under which he lives. For each government has a peculiar character which originally formed and which continues to preserve it. The character of democracy creates democracy, and the character of oligarchy creates oligarchy; and always the better the character, the better the government.

Now for the exercise of any faculty or art a previous training and habituation are required; clearly therefore for the practice of virtue. And since the whole city has one end, it is manifest that education should be one and the same for all, and that it should be public, and not private,—not as at present, when every one looks after his own children separately, and gives them separate instruction of the sort which he thinks best; the training in things which are of common interest should be the same for all. Neither must we suppose that any one of the citizens belongs to himself, for they all belong to the state, and are each of them a part of the state, and the care of each part is inseparable from the care of the whole. In this particular the Lacedaemonians are to be praised, for they take the greatest pains about their children, and make education the business of the state.

That education should be regulated by law and should be an affair of state is not to be denied, but what should be the character of this public education, and how young persons should be educated, are questions which remain to be considered. For mankind are by no means agreed about the things to be taught, whether we look to virtue or the best life. Neither is it clear whether education is more concerned with intellectual or with moral virtue. The existing practice is perplexing; no one knows on what principle we should proceed—should the useful in life, or should virtue, or should the higher knowledge, be the aim of our training; all three opinions have been entertained. Again, about the means there is no agreement; for different persons, starting with different ideas about the nature of virtue, naturally disagree about the practice of it. There can be no doubt that children should be taught those useful things which are really necessary, but not all things; for occupations are divided into liberal and illiberal; and to young children should be imparted only such kinds of knowledge as will be useful to them without vulgarizing them. And any occupation, art, or science, which makes the body or soul or mind of the freeman less fit for the practice or exercise of virtue, is vulgar; wherefore we call those arts vulgar which tend to deform the body, and likewise all paid employments, for they absorb and degrade the mind. There are also some liberal arts quite proper for a freeman to acquire, but only in a certain degree, and if he attend to them too closely, in order to attain perfection in them, the same evil effects will follow. The object also which a man sets before him makes a great difference; if he does or learns anything for his own sake or for the sake of his friends, or with a view to excellence, the action will not appear illiberal; but if done for the sake of others, the very same action will be thought menial and servile. The received subjects of instruction, as I have already remarked, are partly of a liberal and partly of an illiberal character.

The customary branches of education are in number four; they are—(1) reading and writing, (2) gymnastic exercises, (3) music, to which is sometimes added (4) drawing. Of these, reading and writing and drawing are regarded as useful for the purposes of life in a variety of ways, and gymnastic exercises are thought to infuse courage. Concerning music a doubt may be raised—in our own day most men cultivate it for the sake of pleasure, but originally it was included in education, because nature herself, as has been often said, requires that we should be able, not only to work well, but to use leisure well; for, as I must repeat once and again, the first principle of all action is leisure. Both are required, but leisure is better than occupation; and therefore the question must be asked in good earnest, what ought we to do when at leisure? Clearly we ought not to be amusing ourselves, for then amusement would be the end of life. But if this is inconceivable, and yet amid serious occupations amusement is needed more than at other times (for he who is hard at work has need of relaxation, and amusement gives relaxation, whereas occupation is always accompanied with exertion and effort), at suitable times we should introduce amusements, and they should be our medicines, for the emotion which they create in the soul is a relaxation, and from the pleasure we obtain rest. Leisure of itself gives pleasure and happiness and enjoyment of life, which are experienced, not by the busy man, but by those who have leisure. For he who is occupied has in view some end which he has not attained; but happiness is an end which all men deem to be accompanied with pleasure and not with pain. This pleasure, however, is regarded differently by different persons, and varies according to the habit of individuals; the pleasure of the best man is the best, and springs from the noblest sources. It is clear then that there are branches of learning and education which we must study with a view to the enjoyment of leisure, and these are to be valued for their own sake; whereas those kinds of knowledge which are useful in business are to be deemed necessary, and exist for the sake of other things. And therefore our fathers admitted music into education, not on the ground either of its necessity or utility, for it is not necessary, nor indeed useful in the same manner as reading and writing, which are useful in money-making, in the management of a household, in the acquisition of knowledge and in political life, nor like drawing, useful for a more correct judgment of the works of artists, nor again like gymnastic, which gives health and strength; for neither of these is to be gained from music. There remains, then, the use of music for intellectual enjoyment in leisure; which appears to have been the reason of its introduction, this being one of the ways in which it is thought that a freeman should pass his leisure; as Homer says—

"How good is it to invite men to the pleasant feast,"

and afterwards he speaks of others whom he describes as inviting

"The bard who would delight them all."

And in another place Odysseus says there is no better way of passing life than when

"Men's hearts are merry and the banqueters in the hall, sitting in order, hear the voice of the minstrel."

It is evident, then, that there is a sort of education in which parents should train their sons, not as being useful or necessary, but because it is liberal or noble. Whether this is of one kind only, or of more than one, and if so, what they are, and how they are to be imparted, must hereafter be determined. Thus much we are now in a position to say that the ancients witness to us; for their opinion may be gathered from the fact that music is one of the received and traditional branches of education. Further, it is clear that children should be instructed in some useful things,—for example, in reading and writing,—not only for their usefulness, but also because many other sorts of knowledge are acquired through them. With a like view they may be taught drawing, not to prevent their making mistakes in their own purchases, or in order that they may not be imposed upon in the buying or selling of articles, but rather because it makes them judges of the beauty of the human form. To be always seeking after the useful does not become free and exalted souls. Now it is clear that in education habit must go before reason, and the body before the mind; and therefore boys should be handed over to the trainer, who creates in them the proper habit of body, and to the wrestling-master, who teaches them their exercises.

Of those states which in our own day seem to take the greatest care of children, some aim at producing in them an athletic habit, but they only injure their forms and stunt their growth. Although the Lacedaemonians have not fallen into this mistake, yet they brutalize their children by laborious exercises which they think will make them courageous. But in truth, as we have often repeated, education should not be exclusively directed to this or to any other single end. And even if we suppose the Lacedaemonians to be right in their end, they do not attain it. For among barbarians and among animals courage is found associated, not with the greatest ferocity, but with a gentle and lion-like temper. . . . It is notorious that the Lacedaemonians, while they were themselves assiduous in their laborious drill, were superior to others, but now they are beaten both in war and gymnastic exercises. For their ancient superiority did not depend on their mode of training their youth, but only on the circumstance that they trained them at a time when others did not. Hence we may infer that what is noble, not what is brutal, should have the first place; no wolf or other wild animal will face a really noble danger; such dangers are for the brave man. And parents who devote their children to gymnastics while they neglect their necessary education, in reality vulgarize them; for they make them useful to the state in one quality only, and even in this the argument proves them to be inferior to others. We should judge the Lacedaemonians not from what they have been, but from what they are; for now they have rivals who compete with their education; formerly they had none.

It is an admitted principle, that gymnastic exercises should be employed in education, and that for children they should be of a lighter kind, avoiding severe regimen or painful toil, lest the growth of the body be impaired. The evil of excessive training in early years is strikingly proved by the example of the Olympic victors; for not more than two or three of them have gained a prize both as boys and as men; their early training and severe gymnastic exercises exhausted their constitutions. When boyhood is over, three years should be spent in other studies; the period of life which follows may then be devoted to hard exercise and strict regimen. Men ought not to labour at the same time with their minds and with their bodies; for the two kinds of labour are opposed to one another, the labour of the body impedes the mind, and the labour of the mind the body.

Concerning music there are some questions which we have already raised; these we may now resume and carry further; and our remarks will serve as a prelude to this or any other discussion of the subject. It is not easy to determine the nature of music, or why any one should have a knowledge of it. Shall we say, for the sake of amusement and relaxation, like sleep or drinking, which are not good in themselves, but are pleasant, and at the same time "make care to cease," as Euripides says? And therefore men rank them with music, and make use of all three,—sleep, drinking, music,—to which some add dancing. Or shall we argue that music conduces to virtue, on the ground that it can form our minds and habituate us to true pleasures as our bodies are made by gymnastic to be of a certain character? Or shall we say that it contributes to the enjoyment of leisure and mental cultivation, which is a third alternative? Now obviously youth are not to be instructed with a view to their amusement, for learning is no pleasure, but is accompanied with pain. Neither is intellectual enjoyment suitable to boys of that age, for it is the end, and that which is imperfect cannot attain the perfect or end. But perhaps it may be said that boys learn music for the sake of the amusement which they will have when they are grown up. If so, why should they learn themselves, and not, like the Persian and Median kings, enjoy the pleasure and instruction which is derived from hearing others? (for surely skilled persons who have made music the business and profession of their lives will be better performers than those who practise only to learn). If they must learn music, on the same principle they should learn cookery, which is absurd. And even granting that music may form the character, the objection still holds: why should we learn ourselves? Why cannot we attain true pleasure and form a correct judgment from hearing others, like the Lacedaemonians?—for they, without learning music, nevertheless can correctly judge, as they say, of good and bad melodies. Or again, if music should be used to promote cheerfulness and refined intellectual enjoyment, the objection still remains—why should we learn ourselves instead of enjoying the performances of others? We may illustrate what we are saying by our conception of the Gods; for in the poets Zeus does not himself sing or play on the lyre. Nay, we call professional performers vulgar; no freeman would play or sing unless he were intoxicated or in jest. But these matters may be left for the present.

The first question is whether music is or is not to be a part of education. Of the three things mentioned in our discussion, which is it?—Education or amusement or intellectual enjoyment, for it may be reckoned under all three, and seems to share in the nature of all of them. Amusement is for the sake of relaxation, and relaxation is of necessity sweet, for it is the remedy of pain caused by toil, and intellectual enjoyment is universally acknowledged to contain an element not only of the noble but of the pleasant, for happiness is made up of both. All men agree that music is one of the pleasantest things, whether with or without song; as Musaeus says,

"Song is to mortals of all things the sweetest."

Hence and with good reason it is introduced into social gatherings and entertainments, because it makes the hearts of men glad: so that on this ground alone we may assume that the young ought to be trained in it. For innocent pleasures are not only in harmony with the perfect end of life, but they also provide relaxation. And whereas men rarely attain the end, but often rest by the way and amuse themselves, not only with a view to some good, but also for the pleasure's sake, it may be well for them at times to find a refreshment in music. It sometimes happens that men make amusement the end, for the end probably contains some element of pleasure, though not any ordinary or lower pleasure; but they mistake the lower for the higher, and in seeking for the one find the other, since every pleasure has a likeness to the end of action. For the end is not eligible, nor do the pleasures which we have described exist, for the sake of any future good but of the past, that is to say, they are the alleviation of past toils and pains. And we may infer this to be the reason why men seek happiness from common pleasures. But music is pursued, not only as an alleviation of past toil, but also as providing recreation. And who can say whether, having this use, it may not also have a nobler one? In addition to this common pleasure, felt and shared in by all (for the pleasure given by music is natural, and therefore adapted to all ages and characters), may it not have also some influence over the character and the soul? It must have such an influence if characters are affected by it. And that they are so affected is proved by the power which the songs of Olympus and of many others exercise; for beyond question they inspire enthusiasm, and enthusiasm is an emotion of the ethical part of the soul. Besides, when men hear imitations, even unaccompanied by melody or rhythm, their feelings move in sympathy. Since then music is a pleasure, and virtue consists in rejoicing and loving and hating aright, there is clearly nothing which we are so much concerned to acquire and to cultivate as the power of forming right judgments, and of taking delight in good dispositions and noble actions. Rhythm and melody supply imitations of anger and gentleness, and also of courage and temperance and of virtues and vices in general, which hardly fall short of the actual affections, as we know from our own experience, for in listening to such strains our souls undergo a change. The habit of feeling pleasure or pain at mere representations is not far removed from the same feeling about realities; for example, if any one delights in the sight of a statue for its beauty only, it necessarily follows that the sight of the original will be pleasant to him. No other sense, such as taste or touch, has any resemblance to moral qualities; in sight only there is a little, for figures are to some extent of a moral character, and [so far] all participate in the feeling about them. Again, figures and colours are not imitations, but signs of moral habits, indications which the body gives of states of feeling. The connexion of them with morals is slight, but in so far as there is any, young men should be taught to look, not at the works of Pauson but at those of Polygnotus, or any other painter or statuary who expresses moral ideas. On the other hand, even in mere melodies there is an imitation of character, for the musical modes differ essentially from one another, and those who hear them are differently affected by each. Some of them make men sad and grave, like the so-called Mixolydian, others enfeeble the mind, like the relaxed harmonies, others, again, produce a moderate and settled temper, which appears to be the peculiar effect of the Dorian; the Phrygian inspires enthusiasm. The whole subject has been well treated by philosophical writers on this branch of education, and they confirm their arguments by facts. The same principles apply to rhythms: some have a character of rest, others of motion, and of these latter again, some have a more vulgar, others a nobler movement. Enough has been said to show that music has a power of forming the character, and should therefore be introduced into the education of the young. The study is suited to the stage of youth, for young persons will not, if they can help, endure anything which is not sweetened by pleasure, and music has a natural sweetness. There seems to be in us a sort of affinity to harmonies and rhythms, which makes some philosophers say that the soul is a harmony, others, that she possesses harmony.

And now we have to determine the question which has been already raised, whether children should be themselves taught to sing and play or not. Clearly there is a considerable difference made in the character by the actual practice of the art. It is difficult, if not impossible, for those who do not perform to be good judges of the performance of others. Besides, children should have something to do, and the rattle of Archytas, which people give to their children in order to amuse them and prevent them from breaking anything in the house, was a capital invention, for a young thing cannot be quiet. The rattle is a toy suited to the infant mind, and [musical] education is a rattle or toy for children of a larger growth. We conclude then that they should be taught music in such a way as to become not only critics but performers.

The question what is or is not suitable for different ages may be easily answered; nor is there any difficulty in meeting the objection of those who say that the study of music is vulgar. We reply (1) in the first place, that they who are to be judges must also be performers, and that they should begin to practise early, although when they are older they may be spared the execution; they must have learned to appreciate what is good and to delight in it, thanks to the knowledge which they acquired in their youth. As to (2) the vulgarizing effect which music is supposed to exercise . . . it is quite possible that certain methods of teaching and learning music do really have a degrading effect. It is evident then that the learning of music ought not to impede the business of riper years, or to degrade the body or render it unfit for civil or military duties, whether for the early practice or for the later study of them.

The right measure will be attained if students of music stop short of the arts which are practised in professional contests, and do not seek to acquire those fantastic marvels of execution which are now the fashion in such contests, and from these have passed into education. Let the young pursue their studies until they are able to feel delight in noble melodies and rhythms, and not merely in that common part of music in which every slave or child and even some animals find pleasure.

.   .   .

John Locke

(1632-1704)

NOT EVERY philosopher who considers matters concerning educational policy can be said to have formulated a philosophy of education. As was pointed out earlier, philosophy of education involves discussion of the aims of education within the context of metaphysical, epistemological, moral, and political considerations. If an author treats these considerations sketchily or not at all, it is misleading to refer to his work as a philosophy of education. We might more appropriately refer to it as "suggestions concerning educational policy" or, as Locke titled it, *Some Thoughts Concerning Education.*

In some cases, however, those who discuss educational policy without placing this discussion in philosophical perspective rely implicitly upon considerations of a philosophical sort that lie submerged in their works. It is a challenge for the reader to spot such considerations and bring them to the surface. In Part III Israel Scheffler, a leading figure in contemporary philosophy of education, shows how this can be done with the works of Locke and others.

Locke's educational writings are remarkably perceptive and enlightening. Among his major themes are (1) the need to instill self-discipline in the young, (2) the importance of reasoning with children, and (3) the significance of the development of a student's character, not merely his intellect. These points seemed heretical to many educators of Locke's time, but these men are forgotten, while Locke's ideas still exert a powerful influence on modern education.

It is true that Locke was concerned with education within a social order that enabled a pupil to have his own tutor, while education today is of a very different sort. Many of Locke's insights, however, are as useful to a teacher facing an entire classroom of students as they are to a tutor with just one student.

SOME THOUGHTS
CONCERNING EDUCATION

. . . 1. A sound mind in a sound body, is a short but full description of a happy state in this world: he that has these two, has little more to wish for; and he that wants either of them, will be but little the better for any thing else. Men's happiness or misery is [for the] most part of their own making. He whose mind directs not wisely, will never take the right way; and he whose body is crazy and feeble, will never be able to advance in it. I confess, there are some men's constitutions of body and mind so vigorous, and well framed by nature, that they need not much assistance from others; but, by the strength of their natural genius, they are, from their cradles, carried towards what is excellent; and, by the privilege of their happy constitutions, are able to do wonders. But examples of this kind are but few; and I think I may say, that, of all the men we meet with, nine parts of ten are what they are, good or evil, useful or not, by their education. It is that which makes the great difference in mankind. The little, or almost insensible, impressions on our tender infancies, have very important and lasting consequences: and there it is, as in the fountains of some rivers, where a gentle application of the hand turns the flexible waters into channels, that make them take quite contrary courses; and by this little direction, given them at first, in the source, they receive different tendencies, and arrive at last at very remote and distant places.

.   .   .

32. . . . [W]e have reason to conclude, that great care is to be had of the forming children's minds, and giving them that seasoning early, which shall influence their lives always after. For when they do well or ill, the praise or blame will be laid there: and when any thing is done awkwardly, the common saying will pass upon them, that it is suitable to their breeding.

33. As the strength of the body lies chiefly in being able to endure hardships, so also does that of the mind. And the great principle and foundation of all virtue and worth is placed in this, that a man is able to deny himself his own desires, cross his own inclinations, and purely follow what reason directs as best, though the appetite lean the other way.

34. The great mistake I have observed in people's breeding their children has been, that this has not been taken care enough of in its due season; that the mind has not been made obedient to discipline, and pliant to reason, when at

From *Works of John Locke*, London, Thomas Tegg, *et al.*, 1823, Vol. IX, pp. 67–176 (with omissions as indicated in the text).

first it was most tender, most easy to be bowed. Parents being wisely ordained by nature to love their children, are very apt, if reason watch not that natural affection very warily; are apt, I say, to let it run into fondness. They love their little ones, and it is their duty: but they often with them cherish their faults too. They must not be crossed, forsooth; they must be permitted to have their wills in all things; and they being in their infancies not capable of great vices, their parents think they may safely enough indulge their little irregularities, and make themselves sport with that pretty perverseness, which they think well enough becomes that innocent age. But to a fond parent, that would not have his child corrected for a perverse trick, but excused it, saying it was a small matter; Solon very well replied, "Ay, but custom is a great one."

. . .

38. It seems plain to me, that the principle of all virtue and excellency lies in a power of denying ourselves the satisfaction of our own desires, where reason does not authorize them. This power is to be got and improved by custom, made easy and familiar by an early practice. If therefore I might be heard, I would advise, that, contrary to the ordinary way, children should be used to submit their desires, and go without their longings, even from their very cradles. The very first thing they should learn to know, should be, that they were not to have any thing, because it pleased them, but because it was thought fit for them. If things suitable to their wants were supplied to them, so that they were never suffered to have what they once cried for, they would learn to be content without it . . .

39. I say not this as if children were not to be indulged in any thing, or that I expected they should, in hanging-sleeves, have the reason and conduct of counsellors. I consider them as children, who must be tenderly used, who must play, and have play things. That which I mean is, that whenever they craved what was not fit for them to have, or do, they should not be permitted it, because they were little and desired it: nay, whatever they were importunate for, they should be sure, for that very reason, to be denied. I have seen children at a table, who, whatever was there, never asked for any thing, but contentedly took what was given them: and at another place I have seen others cry for every thing they saw, must be served out of every dish, and that first too. What made this vast difference but this, that one was accustomed to have what they called or cried for, the other to go without it? The younger they are, the less, I think, are their unruly and disorderly appetites to be complied with; and the less reason they have of their own, the more are they to be under the absolute power and restraint of those, in whose hands they are. From which I confess, it will follow, that none but discreet people should be about them. If the world commonly does otherwise, I cannot help that. I am saying what I think should be; which, if it were already in fashion, I should not need to trouble the world with a discourse on this subject. But yet I doubt not but, when it is considered, there will be others of opinion with me, that the sooner this way is begun with children, the easier it will be for them, and their governors too: and that this ought to be observed as an inviolable maxim, that whatever once is denied them, they are certainly not to obtain by crying or importunity; unless one has a mind to teach them to be impatient and troublesome, by rewarding them for it, when they are so.

40. Those therefore that intend ever to govern their children, should begin it whilst they are very little; and look that they perfectly comply with the will of their parents. Would you have your son obedient to you, when past a child? Be sure then to establish the authority of a father, as soon as he is capable of submission, and can understand in whose power he is. If you would have him stand in awe of you, imprint it in his infancy; and, as he approaches more to a man, admit him nearer to your familiarity: so shall you have him your obedient subject (as is fit) whilst he is a child, and your affectionate friend when he is a man. For methinks they mightily misplace the treatment due to their children, who are indulgent and familiar when they are little, but severe to them, and keep them at a distance, when they are grown up. For liberty and indulgence can do no good to children: their want of judgment makes them stand in need of restraint and discipline. And, on the contrary, imperiousness and severity is but an ill way of treating men, who have reason of their own to guide them, unless you have a mind to make your children, when grown up, weary of you; and secretly to say within themselves, "When will you die, father?"

41. I imagine every one will judge it reasonable, that their children, when little, should look upon their parents as their lords, their absolute governors; and, as such, stand in awe of them: and that, when they come to riper years, they should look on them as their best, as their only sure friends: and, as such, love and reverence them. The way I have mentioned, if I mistake not, is the only one to obtain this. We must look upon our children, when grown up, to be like ourselves; with the same passions, the same desires. We would be thought rational creatures, and have our freedom; we love not to be uneasy under constant rebukes and brow-beatings; nor can we bear severe humours, and great distance, in those we converse with. Whoever has such treatment when he is a man, will look out other company, other friends, other conversation, with whom he can be at ease. If therefore a strict hand be kept over children from the beginning, they will in that age be tractable, and quietly submit to it, as never having known any other: and if, as they grow up to the use of reason, the rigour of government be, as they deserve it, gently relaxed, the father's brow more smoothed to them, and the distance by degrees abated: his former restraints will increase their love, when they find it was only a kindness for them, and a care to make them capable to deserve the favour of their parents, and the esteem of every body else.

42. Thus much for the settling your authority over children in general. Fear and awe ought to give you the first power over their minds, and love and friendship in riper years to hold it: for the time must come, when they will be

past the rod and correction; and then, if the love of you make them not obedient and dutiful; if the love of virtue and reputation keep them not in laudable courses; I ask, what hold will you have upon them, to turn them to it? Indeed, fear of having a scanty portion, if they displease you, may make them slaves to your estate; but they will be nevertheless ill and wicked in private, and that restraint will not last always. Every man must some time or other be trusted to himself, and his own conduct; and he that is a good, a virtuous, and able man, must be made so within. And therefore, what he is to receive from education, what is to sway and influence his life, must be something put into him betimes: habits woven into the very principles of his nature; and not a counterfeit carriage, and dissembled outside, put on by fear, only to avoid the present anger of a father, who perhaps may disinherit him.

43. This being laid down in general, as the course ought to be taken, it is fit we come now to consider the parts of the discipline to be used, a little more particularly. I have spoken so much of carrying a strict hand over children, that perhaps I shall be suspected of not considering enough what is due to their tender age and constitutions. But that opinion will vanish, when you have heard me a little farther. For I am very apt to think, that great severity of punishment does but very little good; nay, great harm in education: and I believe it will be found, that, *caeteris paribus*, those children who have been most chastised, seldom make the best men. All that I have hitherto contended for, is, that whatsoever rigour is necessary, it is more to be used, the younger children are; and, having by a due application wrought its effect, it is to be relaxed, and changed into a milder sort of government.

44. A compliance, and suppleness of their wills, being by a steady hand introduced by parents, before children have memories to retain the beginnings of it, will seem natural to them, and work afterwards in them, as if it were so; preventing all occasions of struggling, or repining. The only care is, that it be begun early, and inflexibly kept to, till awe and respect be grown familiar, and there appears not the least reluctancy in the submission and ready obedience of their minds. When this reverence is once thus established, (which it must be early, or else it will cost pains and blows to recover it, and the more, the longer it is deferred) it is by it, mixed still with as much indulgence as they made not an ill use of, and not by beating, chiding, or other servile punishments, they are for the future to be governed, as they grow up to more understanding.

45. That this is so, will be easily allowed, when it is but considered what is to be aimed at, in an ingenuous education; and upon what it turns.

1. He that has not a mastery over his inclinations, he that knows not how to resist the importunity of present pleasure or pain, for the sake of what reason tells him is fit to be done, wants the true principle of virtue and industry; and is in danger of never being good for any thing. This temper, therefore, so contrary to unguided nature, is to be got betimes; and this habit, as the true foundation of future ability and happiness, is to be wrought into the mind, as

early as may be, even from the first dawnings of any knowledge or apprehension in children; and so to be confirmed in them, by all the care and ways imaginable, by those who have the oversight of their education.

46. 2. On the other side, if the mind be curbed, and humbled too much in children; if their spirits be abased and broken much, by too strict an hand over them; they lose all their vigour and industry, and are in a worse state than the former. For extravagant young fellows, that have liveliness and spirit, come sometimes to be set right, and so make able and great men: but dejected minds, timorous and tame, and low spirits, are hardly ever to be raised, and very seldom attain to any thing. To avoid the danger that is on either hand is the great art: and he that has found a way how to keep up a child's spirit, easy, active, and free; and yet, at the same time, to restrain him from many things he has a mind to, and to draw him to things that are uneasy to him; he, I say, that knows how to reconcile these seeming contradictions, has, in my opinion, got the true secret of education.

47. The usual lazy and short way by chastisement, and the rod, which is the only instrument of government that tutors generally know, or ever think of, is the most unfit of any to be used in education; because it tends to both those mischiefs; which as we have shown, are the Scylla and Charybdis, which, on the one hand or the other, ruin all that miscarry.

48. 1. This kind of punishment contributes not at all to the mastery of our natural propensity to indulge corporal and present pleasure and to avoid pain at any rate; but rather encourages it; and thereby strengthens that in us, which is the root, from whence spring all vicious actions and the irregularities of life. From what other motive, but of sensual pleasure, and pain, does a child act, who drudges at his book against his inclination, or abstains from eating unwholesome fruit, that he takes pleasure in, only out of fear of whipping? He in this only prefers the greater corporal pleasure, or avoids the greater corporal pain. And what is it to govern his actions, and direct his conduct, by such motives as these? what is it, I say, but to cherish that principle in him, which it is our business to root out and destroy? And therefore I cannot think any correction useful to a child, where the shame of suffering for having done amiss does not work more upon him than the pain.

49. 2. This sort of correction naturally breeds an aversion to that which it is the tutor's business to create a liking to. How obvious is it to observe, that children come to hate things which were at first acceptable to them, when they find themselves whipped, and chid, and teazed about them? And it is not to be wondered at in them; when grown men would not be able to be reconciled to any thing by such ways. Who is there that would not be disgusted with any innocent recreation, in itself indifferent to him, if he should with blows, or ill language, be hauled to it, when he had no mind? or be constantly so treated, for some circumstances in his application to it? This is natural to be so. Offensive circumstances ordinarily infect innocent things, which they are joined with: and the very sight of a cup, wherein any one uses to take nauseous physic, turns his stomach; so that nothing will relish well out of it, though the cup be ever so clean, and well-shaped, and of the richest materials.

50. 3. Such a sort of slavish discipline makes a slavish temper. The child submits, and dissembles obedience, whilst the fear of the rod hangs over him; but when that is removed, and, by being out of sight, he can promise himself impunity, he gives the greater scope to his natural inclination; which by this way is not at all altered, but on the contrary heightened and increased in him; and after such restraint, breaks out usually with the more violence. Or,

51. 4. If severity carried to the highest pitch does prevail, and works a cure upon the present unruly distemper, it is often bringing in the room of it worse and more dangerous disease, by breaking the mind; and then, in the place of a disorderly young fellow, you have a low-spirited moped creature: who, however with his unnatural sobriety he may please silly people, who commend tame inactive children, because they make no noise, nor give them any trouble; yet, at last, will probably prove as uncomfortable a thing to his friends, as he will be, all his life, an useless thing to himself and others.

52. Beating then, and all other sorts of slavish and corporal punishments, are not the discipline fit to be used in the education of those who would have wise, good, and ingenuous men; and therefore very rarely to be applied, and that only on great occasions, and cases of extremity. On the other side, to flatter children by rewards of things that are pleasant to them, is as carefully to be avoided. He that will give to his son apples, or sugar-plums, or what else of this kind he is most delighted with, to make him learn his book, does but authorise his love of pleasure, and cocker up that dangerous propensity, which he ought by all means to subdue and stifle in him. You can never hope to teach him to master it, whilst you compound for the check you give his inclination in one place, by the satisfaction you propose to it in another. To make a good, a wise, and a virtuous man, it is fit he should learn to cross his appetite, and deny his inclination to riches, finery, or pleasing his palate, &c. whenever his reason advises the contrary, and his duty requires it. But when you draw him to do any thing that is fit, by the offer of money; or reward the pains of learning his book, by the pleasure of a luscious morsel; when you promise him a lace-cravat, or a fine new suit, upon performance of some of his little tasks; what do you, by proposing these as rewards, but allow them to be the good things he should aim at, and thereby encourage his longing for them, and accustom him to place his happiness in them? Thus people, to prevail with children to be industrious about their grammar, dancing, or some other such matter, of no great moment to the happiness or usefulness of their lives, by misapplied rewards and punishments, sacrifice their virtue, invert the order of their education, and teach them luxury, pride, or covetousness, &c. For in this way, flattering those wrong inclinations, which they should restrain and suppress, they lay the foundations of those future vices, which cannot be avoided, but by curbing our desires and accustoming them early to submit to reason.

.   .   .

54. But if you take away the rod on one hand, and these little encouragements, which they are taken with, on the other; how then (will you say) shall children be governed? Remove hope and fear, and there is an end of all discipline. I grant, that good and evil, reward and punishment, are the only motives to a rational creature; these are the spur and reins, whereby all mankind are set on work and guided, and therefore they are to be made use of to children too. For I advise their parents and governors always to carry this in their minds, that children are to be treated as rational creatures.

55. Rewards, I grant, and punishments must be proposed to children, if we intend to work upon them. The mistake, I imagine, is, that those that are generally made use of, are ill chosen. The pains and pleasures of the body are, I think, of ill consequence, when made the rewards and punishments whereby men would prevail on their children: for, as I said before, they serve but to increase and strengthen those inclinations, which it is our business to subdue and master. . . .

56. The rewards and punishments then whereby we should keep children in order are quite of another kind; and of that force, that when we can get them once to work, the business, I think, is done, and the difficulty is over. Esteem and disgrace are, of all others, the most powerful incentives to the mind, when once it is brought to relish them. If you can once get into children a love of credit, and an apprehension of shame and disgrace, you have put into them the true principle, which will constantly work, and incline them to the right. But it will be asked, How shall this be done?

I confess, it does not, at first appearance, want some difficulty; but yet I think it worth our while to seek the ways (and practise them when found) to attain this, which I look on as the great secret of education.

57. First, children (earlier perhaps than we think) are very sensible of praise and commendation. They find a pleasure in being esteemed and valued, especially by their parents, and those whom they depend on. If therefore the father caress and commend them, when they do well; show a cold and neglectful countenance to them upon doing ill; and this accompanied by a like carriage of the mother, and all others that are about them; it will in a little time make them sensible of the difference: and this, if constantly observed, I doubt not but will of itself work more than threats or blows, which lose their force, when once grown common, and are of no use when shame does not attend them; and therefore are to be forborn, and never to be used, but in the case hereafter mentioned, when it is brought to extremity.

58. But, secondly, to make the sense of esteem or disgrace sink the deeper, and be of the more weight, other agreeable or disagreeable things should constantly accompany these different states; not as particular rewards and punishments of this or that particular action, but as necessarily belonging to, and constantly attending one, who by his carriage has brought himself into a state of disgrace or commendation. By which way of treating them, children may as much as possible be brought to conceive, that those that are commended and in esteem for doing well, will necessarily be beloved and cherished by every body, and have all other good things as a consequence of it; and, on the other side, when any one by miscarriage falls into dis-esteem, and cares not to preserve his credit, he will unavoidably fall under neglect and contempt: and, in that state, the want of whatever might satisfy or delight him, will follow. In this way the objects of their desires are made assisting to virtue; when a settled experience from the beginning teaches children, that the things they delight in, belong to, and are to be enjoyed by those only, who are in a state of reputation. If by these means you can come once to shame them out of their faults, (for besides that, I would willingly have no punishment) and make them in love with the pleasure of being well thought on, you may turn them as you please, and they will be in love with all the ways of virtue.

·   ·   ·

63. But if a right course be taken with children, there will not be so much need of the application of the common reward and punishments, as we imagined, and as the general practice has established. For all their innocent folly, playing, and childish actions, are to be left perfectly free and unrestrained, as far as they can consist with the respect due to those that are present; and that with the greatest allowance. If these faults of their age, rather than of the children themselves, were, as they should be, left only to time, and imitation, and riper years to cure, children would escape a great deal of misapplied and useless correction; which either fails to overpower the natural disposition of their childhood, and so, by an ineffectual familiarity, makes correction in other necessary cases of less use; or else if it be of force to restrain the natural gaiety of that age, it serves only to spoil the temper both of body and mind. If the noise and bustle of their play prove at any time inconvenient, or unsuitable to the place or company they are in, (which can only be where their parents are) a look or a word from the father or mother, if they have established the authority they should, will be enough either to remove, or quiet them for that time. But this gamesome humour, which is wisely adapted by nature to their age and temper, should rather be encouraged, to keep up their spirits, and improve their strength and health, than curbed or restrained: and the chief art is to make all that they have to do, sport and play too.

64. And here give me leave to take notice of one thing I think a fault in the ordinary method of education; and that is, the charging of children's memories, upon all occasions, with rules and precepts, which they often do not understand, and are constantly as soon forgot as given. If it be some action you would have done, or done otherwise; whenever they forget, or do it awkwardly, make them do it over and over again, till they are perfect: whereby you will get these two advantages: first, to see whether it be an action they can do, or is fit to be expected of them. For sometimes children are bid to do things,

which, upon trial, they are found not able to do; and had need be taught and exercised in, before they are required to do them. But it is much easier for a tutor to command, than to teach. Secondly, another thing got by it will be this, that by repeating the same action, till it be grown habitual in them, the performance will not depend on memory, or reflection, the concomitant of prudence and age, and not of childhood; but will be natural in them. Thus, bowing to a gentleman when he salutes him, and looking in his face when he speaks to him, is by constant use as natural to a well-bred man, as breathing; it requires no thought, no reflection. Having this way cured in your child any fault, it is cured for ever: and thus, one by one, you may weed them out all, and plant what habits you please.

65. I have seen parents so heap rules on their children, that it was impossible for the poor little ones to remember a tenth part of them, much less to observe them. However, they were either by words or blows corrected for the breach of those multiplied and often very impertinent precepts. Whence it naturally followed, that the children minded not what was said to them; when it was evident to them, that no attention they were capable of, was sufficient to preserve them from transgression, and the rebukes which followed it.

Let therefore your rules to your son be as few as is possible, and rather fewer than more than seem absolutely necessary. For if you burden him with many rules, one of these two things must necessarily follow, that either he must be very often punished, which will be of ill consequence, by making punishment too frequent and familiar; or else you must let the transgressions of some of your rules go unpunished, whereby they will of course grow contemptible, and your authority become cheap to him. Make but few laws but see they be well observed, when once made. Few years require but few laws; and as his age increases, when one rule is by practice well established, you may add another.

66. But pray remember, children are not to be taught by rules, which will be always slipping out of their memories. What you think necessary for them to do, settle in them by an indispensable practice, as often as the occasion returns; and, if it be possible, make occasions. This will beget habits in them, which, being once established, operate of themselves easily and naturally, without the assistance of the memory. But here let me give two cautions: 1. The one is, that you keep them to the practice of what you would have grow into a habit in them, by kind words and gentle admonitions, rather as minding them of what they forget, than by harsh rebukes and chiding, as if they were wilfully guilty. 2dly, Another thing you are to take care of, is, not to endeavour to settle too many habits at once, lest by a variety you confound them, and so perfect none. When constant custom has made any one thing easy and natural to them, and they practise it without reflection, you may then go on to another.

This method of teaching children by a repeated practice, and the same action done over and over again, under the eye and direction of the tutor, till they have got the habit of doing it well, and not by relying on rules trusted to their memories; has so many advantages, which way soever we consider it, that I cannot but wonder (if ill customs could be wondered at in any thing) how it could possibly be so much neglected. I shall name one more that comes now in my way. By this method we shall see, whether what is required of him be adapted to his capacity, and any way suited to the child's natural genius and constitution: for that too must be considered in a right education. We must not hope wholly to change their original tempers, nor make the gay pensive and grave, nor the melancholy sportive, without spoiling them. God has stamped certain characters upon men's minds, which, like their shapes, may perhaps be a little mended; but can hardly be totally altered and transformed into the contrary.

He therefore, that is about children, should well study their natures and aptitudes, and see, by often trials, what turn they easily take, and what becomes them; observe what their native stock is, how it may be improved, and what it is fit for: he should consider what they want, whether they be capable of having it wrought into them by industry, and incorporated there by practice; and whether it be worth while to endeavour it. For, in many cases, all that we can do, or should aim at, is, to make the best of what nature has given; to prevent the vices and faults to which such a constitution is most inclined, and give it all the advantages it is capable of. Every one's natural genius should be carried as far as it could; but to attempt the putting another upon him; will be but labour in vain; and what is so plaistered on will at best sit but untowardly, and have always hanging to it the ungracefulness of constraint and affectation.

.   .   .

71. . . . I must here take the liberty to mind parents of this one thing, viz. that he that will have his son have a respect for him and his orders, must himself have a great reverence for his son. *"Maxima debetur pueris reverentia."* You must do nothing before him, which you would not have him imitate. If any thing escape you, which you would have pass for a fault in him, he will be sure to shelter himself under your example, and shelter himself so, as that it will not be easy to come at him to correct it in him the right way. If you punish him for what he sees you practise yourself, he will not think that severity to proceed from kindness in you, or carefulness to amend a fault in him; but will be apt to interpret it the peevishness and arbitrary imperiousness of a father, who, without any ground for it, would deny his son the liberty and pleasures he takes himself. Or if you assume to yourself the liberty you have taken, as a privilege belonging to riper years, to which a child must not aspire, you do but add new force to your example, and recommend the action the more powerfully to him. For you must always remember, that children affect to be men earlier than is thought: and they love breeches, not for their cut, or ease, but because the having them is a mark or a step towards manhood. What

I say of the father's carriage before his children, must extend itself to all those who have any authority over them, or for whom he would have them have any respect.

.   .   .

73. 1. None of the things they are to learn should ever be made a burden to them, or imposed on them as a task. Whatever is so proposed presently becomes irksome: the mind takes an aversion to it, though before it were a thing of delight or indifferency. Let a child be but ordered to whip his top at a certain time every day, whether he has or has not a mind to it; let this be but required of him as a duty, wherein he must spend so many hours morning and afternoon, and see whether he will not soon be weary of any play at this rate. Is it not so with grown men? What they do cheerfully of themselves, do they not presently grow sick of, and can no more endure, as soon as they find it is expected of them as a duty? Children have as much a mind to show that they are free that their own good actions come from themselves, that they are absolute and independent, as any of the proudest of you grown men, think of them as you please.

74. 2. As a consequence of this, they should seldom be put about doing even those things you have got an inclination in them to, but when they have a mind and disposition to it. He that loves reading, writing, music, &c. finds yet in himself certain seasons wherein those things have no relish to him: and, if at that time he forces himself to it, he only pothers and wearies himself to no purpose. So it is with children. This change of temper should be carefully observed in them, and the favourable seasons of aptitude and inclination be heedfully laid hold of: and if they are not often enough forward to themselves, a good disposition should be talked into them, before they be set upon any thing.

.   .   .

81. It will perhaps be wondered, that I mention reasoning with children: and yet I cannot but think that the true way of dealing with them. They understand it as early as they do language; and, if I misobserve not, they love to be treated as rational creatures sooner than is imagined. It is a pride should be cherished in them, and, as much as can be, made the greatest instrument to turn them by.

But when I talk of reasoning, I do not intend any other but such as is suited to the child's capacity and apprehension. Nobody can think a boy of three or seven years old should be argued with as a grown man. Long discourses, and philosophical reasonings, at best amaze and confound, but do not instruct, children. When I say, therefore, that they must be treated as rational creatures, I mean, that you should make them sensible, by the mildness of your carriage, and the composure, even in your correction of them, that what you do is reasonable in you, and useful and necessary for them; and that it is not out of caprice, passion, or fancy, that you command or forbid them any thing. This they are capable of understanding; and there is no virtue they should be excited to, nor fault they should be kept from, which I do not think they may be convinced of: but it must be by such reasons as their age and understanding are capable of, and those proposed always in very few and plain words. The foundations on which several duties are built, and the fountains of right and wrong, from which they spring, are not, perhaps, easily to be let into the minds of grown men, not used to abstract their thoughts from common received opinions. Much less are children capable of reasonings from remote principles. They cannot conceive the force of long deductions: the reasons that move them must be obvious, and level to their thoughts, and such as may (if I may so say) be felt and touched. But yet, if their age, temper, and inclinations, be considered, they will never want such motives as may be sufficient to convince them. If there be no other more particular, yet these will always be intelligible, and of force, to deter them from any fault fit to be taken notice of in them, viz. that it will be a discredit and disgrace to them, and displease you.

· · ·

95. . . . [A] father will do well, as his son grows up, and is capable of it, to talk familiarly with him; nay, ask his advice, and consult with him, about those things wherein he has any knowledge or understanding. By this the father will gain two things, both of great moment. The one is, that it will put serious considerations into his son's thoughts, better than any rules or advices he can give him. The sooner you treat him as a man, the sooner he will begin to be one: and if you admit him into serious discourses sometimes with you, you will insensibly raise his mind above the usual amusements of youth, and those trifling occupations which it is commonly wasted in. For it is easy to observe, that many young men continue longer in the thought and conversation of schoolboys, than otherwise they would, because their parents keep them at that distance, and in that low rank, by all their carriage to them.

· · ·

118. Curiosity in children . . . is but an appetite after knowledge, and therefore ought to be encouraged in them, not only as a good sign, but as the great instrument nature has provided, to remove that ignorance they were born with, and which without this busy inquisitiveness will make them dull and useless creatures. The ways to encourage it, and keep it active and busy, are, I suppose, these following:

1. Not to check or discountenance any inquiries he shall make, nor suffer them to be laughed at; but to answer all his questions, and explain the matters he desires to know, so as to make them as much intelligible to him, as suits the capacity of his age and knowledge. But confound not his understanding with explications or notions that are above it, or with the variety or number of things that are not to his present purpose. Mark what it is his mind aims

at in the question, and not what words he expresses it in: and, when you have informed and satisfied him in that, you shall see how his thoughts will enlarge themselves, and how by fit answers he may be led on farther than perhaps you could imagine. For knowledge is grateful to the understanding, as light to the eyes: children are pleased and delighted with it exceedingly, especially if they see that their inquiries are regarded, and that their desire of knowing is encouraged and commended. And I doubt not but one great reason, why many children abandon themselves wholly to silly sports, and trifle away all their time insipidly, is, because they have found their curiosity baulked, and their inquiries neglected. But had they been treated with more kindness and respect, and their questions answered, as they should, to their satisfaction, I doubt not but they would have taken more pleasure in learning, and improving their knowledge, wherein there would be still newness and variety, which is what they are delighted with, than in returning over and over to the same play and play things.

119. 2. To this serious answering their questions, and informing their understandings in what they desire, as if it were a matter that needed it, should be added some peculiar ways of commendation. Let others, whom they esteem, be told before their faces of the knowledge they have in such and such things; and since we are all, even from our cradles, vain and proud creatures, let their vanity be flattered with things that will do them good; and let their pride set them on work on something which may turn to their advantage. Upon this ground you shall find, that there cannot be a greater spur to the attaining what you would have the elder learn and know himself, than to set him upon teaching it his younger brothers and sisters.

120. 3. As children's inquires are not to be slighted, so also great care is to be taken, that they never receive deceitful and illuding answers. They easily perceive when they are slighted or deceived, and quickly learn the trick of neglect, dissimulation, and falsehood, which they observe others to make use of. We are not to intrench upon truth in any conversation, but least of all with children; since, if we play false with them, we not only deceive their expectation, and hinder their knowledge, but corrupt their innocence, and teach them the worst of vices. They are travellers newly arrived in a strange country, of which they know nothing: we should therefore make conscience not to mislead them. And though their questions seem sometimes not very material, yet they should be seriously answered; for however they may appear to us (to whom they are long since known) inquiries not worth the making, they are of moment to those who are wholly ignorant. Children are strangers to all we are acquainted with; and all the things they meet with, are at first unknown to them, as they once were to us: and happy are they who meet with civil people, that will comply with their ignorance, and help them to get out of it.

·   ·   ·

133. This is what I have thought concerning the general method of educating a young gentleman; which, though I am apt to suppose may have some influence on the whole course of his education, yet I am far from imagining it contains all those particulars which his growing years, or peculiar temper, may require. But this being premised in general, we shall, in the next place, descend to a more particular consideration of the several parts of his education.

134. That which every gentleman (that takes any care of his education) desires for his son, besides the estate he leaves him, is contained (I suppose) in these four things, virtue, wisdom, breeding, and learning. . . .

135. I place virtue as the first and most necessary of those endowments that belong to a man or a gentleman, as absolutely requisite to make him valued and beloved by others, acceptable or tolerable to himself. Without that, I think, he will be happy neither in this, nor the other world.

.   .   .

140. Wisdom I take, in the popular acceptation, for a man's managing his business ably, and with foresight, in this world. . . . To accustom a child to have true notions of things, and not to be satisfied till he has them; to raise his mind to great and worthy thoughts; and to keep him at a distance from falsehood, and cunning, which has always a broad mixture of falsehood in it; is the fittest preparation of a child for wisdom. The rest, which is to be learned from time, experience, and observation, and an acquaintance with men, their tempers and designs, is not to be expected in the ignorance and inadvertency of childhood, or the inconsiderate heat and unwariness of youth: all that can be done towards it, during this unripe age, is, as I have said, to accustom them to truth and sincerity; to a submission to reason; and, as much as may be, to reflection on their own actions.

141. The next good quality belonging to a gentleman, is good-breeding. There are two sorts of ill-breeding; the one, a sheepish bashfulness; and the other, a misbecoming negligence and disrespect in our carriage; both which are avoided, by duly observing this one rule, Not to think meanly of ourselves, and not to think meanly of others.

.   .   .

147. You will wonder, perhaps, that I put learning last, especially if I tell you I think it the least part. This may seem strange in the mouth of a bookish man: and this making usually the chief, if not only bustle and stir about children, this being almost that alone which is thought on, when people talk of education, makes it the greater paradox. When I consider what ado is made about a little Latin and Greek, how many years are spent in it, and what a noise and business it makes to no purpose, I can hardly forbear thinking, that the parents of children still live in fear of the schoolmaster's rod, which they look on as the only instrument of education; as if a language or two were its whole business. How else is it possible, that a child should be chained to the oar seven, eight, or ten of the best years of his life, to get a language or two, which I think might be had at a great deal cheaper rate of pains and time, and be learned almost in playing?

Forgive me, therefore, if I say, I cannot with patience think, that a young gentleman should be put into the herd, and be driven with a whip and scourge, as if he were to run the gantlet through the several classes, *"ad capiendum ingenii cultum."* "What then, say you, would you not have him write and read? Shall he be more ignorant than the clerk of our parish, who takes Hopkins and Sternhold for the best poets in the world, whom yet he makes worse than they are, by his ill reading?" Not so, not so fast, I beseech you. Reading, and writing, and learning, I allow to be necessary, but yet not the chief business. I imagine you would think him a very foolish fellow, that should not value a virtuous, or a wise man, infinitely before a great scholar. Not but that I think learning a great help to both, in well disposed minds; but yet it must be confessed also, that in others not so disposed, it helps them only to be the more foolish, or worse men. . . .

148. When he can talk, it is time he should begin to learn to read. But as to this, give me leave here to inculcate again what is very apt to be forgotten, viz. that a great care is to be taken, that it be never made as a business to him, nor he look on it as a task. We naturally, as I said, even from our cradles, love liberty, and have therefore an aversion to many things, for no other reason, but because they are enjoined us. I have always had a fancy, that learning might be made a play and recreation to children; and that they might be brought to desire to be taught, if it were proposed to them as a thing of honour, credit, delight, and recreation, or as a reward for doing something else, and if they were never chid or corrected for the neglect of it. That which confirms me in this opinion is, that amongst the Portuguese, it is so much a fash.on and emulation amongst their children to learn to read and write, that they cannot hinder them from it: they will learn it one from another, and are as intent on it as if it were forbid them. I remember, that being at a friend's house, whose younger son, a child in coats, was not easily brought to his book (being taught to read at home by his mother); I advised to try another way than requiring it of him as his duty. We therefore, in a discourse on purpose amongst ourselves, in his hearing, but without taking any notice of him, declared, that it was the privilege and advantage of heirs and elder brothers, to be scholars; that this made them fine gentlemen, and beloved by every body: and that for younger brothers, it was a favour to admit them to breeding; to be taught to read and write was more than came to their share; they might be ignorant bumpkins and clowns, if they pleased. This so wrought upon the child, that afterwards he desired to be taught; would come himself to his mother to learn; and would not let his maid be quiet, till she heard him his lesson. I doubt not but some way like this might be taken with other children; and, when their tempers are found, some thoughts be instilled into them, that might set them upon desiring of learning themselves, and make them seek it, as another sort of play or recreation. But then, as I said before, it must never be imposed as a task, nor made a trouble to them.

. . .

167. . . . There is yet a farther reason, why masters and teachers should raise no difficulties to their scholars; but, on the contrary, should smooth their way, and readily help them forwards, where they find them stop. Children's minds are narrow and weak, and usually susceptible but of one thought at once. Whatever is in a child's head, fills it for the time, especially if set on with any passion. It should therefore be the skill and art of the teacher, to clear their heads of all other thoughts, whilst they are learning of any thing, the better to make room for what he would instil into them, that it may be received with attention and application, without which it leaves no impression. The natural temper of children disposes their minds to wander. Novelty alone takes them; whatever that presents, they are presently eager to have a taste of, and are as soon satiated with it. They quickly grow weary of the same thing, and so have almost their whole delight in change and variety. It is a contradiction to the natural state of childhood, for them to fix their fleeting thoughts. Whether this be owing to the temper of their brains, or the quickness or instability of their animal spirits, over which the mind has not yet got a full command; this is visible, that it is a pain to children to keep their thoughts steady to any thing. A lasting continued attention is one of the hardest tasks can be imposed on them: and therefore, he that requires their application, should endeavour to make what he proposes as grateful and agreeable as possible; at least, he ought to take care not to join any displeasing or frightful idea with it. If they come not to their books with some kind of liking and relish, it is no wonder their thoughts should be perpetually shifting from what disgusts them, and seek better entertainment in more pleasing objects, after which they will unavoidably be gadding.

It is, I know, the usual method of tutors, to endeavour to procure attention in their scholars, and to fix their minds to the business in hand, by rebukes and corrections, if they find them ever so little wandering. But such treatment is sure to produce the quite contrary effect. Passionate words or blows from the tutor fill the child's mind with terror and affrightment, which immediately takes it wholly up, and leaves no room for other impressions. I believe there is nobody, that reads this, but may recollect, what disorder hasty or imperious words from his parents or teachers have caused in his thoughts; how for the time it has turned his brains, so that he scarce knew what was said by, or to him: he presently lost the sight of what he was upon; his mind was filled with disorder and confusion, and in that state was no longer capable of attention to any thing else.

It is true, parents and governors ought to settle and establish their authority, by an awe over the minds of those under their tuition; and to rule them by that:

but when they have got an ascendant over them, they should use it with great moderation, and not make themselves such scarecrows, that their scholars should always tremble in their sight. Such an austerity may make their government easy to themselves but of very little use to their pupils. It is impossible children should learn any thing, whilst their thoughts are possessed and disturbed with any passion, especially fear, which makes the strongest impression on their yet tender and weak spirits. Keep the mind in an easy calm temper, when you would have it receive your instructions, or any increase of knowledge. It is as impossible to draw fair and regular characters on a trembling mind, as on a shaking paper.

The great skill of a teacher is to get and keep the attention of his scholar: whilst he has that, he is sure to advance as fast as the learner's abilities will carry him; and without that, all his bustle and pother will be to little or no purpose. To attain this, he should make the child comprehend (as much as may be) the usefulness of what he teaches him; and let him see, by what he has learned, that he can do something which he could not do before; something which gives him some power and real advantage above others, who are ignorant of it. To this he should add sweetness in all his instructions; and by a certain tenderness in his whole carriage, make the child sensible that he loves him, and designs nothing but his good; the only way to beget love in the child, which will make him hearken to his lessons, and relish what he teaches him.

Nothing but obstinacy should meet with any imperiousness or rough usage. All other faults should be corrected with a gentle hand; and kind encouraging words will work better and more effectually upon a willing mind, and even prevent a good deal of that perverseness, which rough and imperious usage often produces in well-disposed and generous minds. It is true, obstinacy and wilful neglects must be mastered, even though it costs blows to do it: but I am apt to think perverseness in the pupils is often the effect of forwardness in the tutor; and that most children would seldom have deserved blows, if needless and misapplied roughness had not taught them ill-nature, and given them an aversion to their teacher, and all that comes from him.

Inadvertency, forgetfulness, unsteadiness, and wandering of thought, are the natural faults of childhood: and therefore, when they are not observed to be wilful, are to be mentioned softly, and gained upon by time. If every slip of this kind produces anger and rating, the occasions of rebuke and corrections will return so often, that the tutor will be a constant terror and uneasiness to his pupils; which one thing is enough to hinder their profiting by his lessons, and to defeat all his methods of instruction.

Let the awe he has got upon their minds be so tempered with the constant marks of tenderness and good will, that affection may spur them to their duty, and make them find a pleasure in complying with his dictates. This will bring them with satisfaction to their tutor; make them hearken to him, as to one who is their friend, that cherishes them, and takes pains for their good; this will keep their thoughts easy and free, whilst they are with him, the only temper wherein the mind is capable of receiving new informations, and of admitting into itself those impressions, which if not taken and retained, all that they and their teacher do together is lost labour; there is much uneasiness, and little learning.

. . .

177. . . . [U]nder whose care soever a child is put to be taught, during the tender and flexible years of his life, this is certain, it should be one who thinks Latin and language the least part of education; one, who knowing how much virtue, and a well-tempered soul, is to be preferred to any sort of learning or language, makes it his chief business to form the mind of his scholars, and give that a right disposition: which, if once got, though all the rest should be neglected, would, in due time, produce all the rest; and which if it be not got, and settled, so as to keep out ill and vicious habits, languages and sciences, and all the other accomplishments of education, will be to no purpose, but to make the worse or more dangerous man.

. . .

216. Though I am now come to a conclusion of what obvious remarks have suggested to me concerning education, I would not have it thought, that I look on it as a just treatise on this subject. There are a thousand other things that may need consideration; especially if one should take in the various tempers, different inclinations, and particular defaults, that are to be found in children; and prescribe proper remedies. The variety is so great, that it would require a volume; nor would that reach it. Each man's mind has some peculiarity, as well as his face, that distinguishes him from all others; and there are possibly scarce two children, who can be conducted by exactly the same method. Besides that, I think a prince, a nobleman, and an ordinary gentleman's son, should have different ways of breeding. But having had here only some general views, in reference to the main end and aims in education, and those designed for a gentleman's son, whom, being then very little, I considered only as white paper, or wax, to be moulded and fashioned as one pleases; I have touched little more than those heads, which I judged necessary for the breeding, of a young gentleman of his condition in general; and have now published these my occasional thoughts, with this hope, that, though this be far from being a complete treatise on this subject, or such as that every one may find what will just fit his child in it; yet it may give some small light to those, whose concern for their dear little ones makes them so irregularly bold, that they dare venture to consult their own reason, in the education of their children, rather than wholly to rely upon old custom.

Jean Jacques Rousseau

(1712-1778)

ROUSSEAU'S *Emile* contains a remarkable number of powerful ideas. Its insight into the special nature of a child's mind, its insistence that a child be treated as a person in his own right, and its stress on the importance of motivating a student to want to learn combine to make this work a landmark in the history of educational thought.

It must be noted, however, that a number of Rousseau's views are open to serious criticism. Chief among these are his claims that nature provides the goals of education and that, therefore, a child ought not to be allowed to acquire any habits. These claims are simply untenable, and a careful reading of *Emile* shows that Rousseau himself did not consistently defend them.

He argues, for example, that once you refuse to give a child something, your refusal should be irrevocable. This will soon result in the child's not pestering you for things which he has been refused. But he has thus developed a habit, viz., the habit of not pestering you for things which he has been refused.

The fact of the matter is that no human being can live effectively without developing habits. If walking never became a habit, we should all spend hours just attempting to walk. The question is not whether we should develop habits. The question is which habits we ought to develop.

That some action is "natural" is no reason to perform it. We often have "natural" desires to harm other individuals. These are desires that we must control if we are to live in society. Some impulses are good and some are not. The only way to decide whether a particular impulse is good is to consider its consequences. That it is an impulse is no reason why it ought to be followed.

Furthermore, it is difficult even to establish what is meant by the claim that a particular course of action is "natural." According to the most obvious sense of that term, any human action is natural, since it is according to the laws of nature. Only miracles are unnatural, and no child has to be taught to refrain from performing miracles.

Rousseau was not the first thinker to fall into the trap of attempting to utilize the hopelessly vague notion of what is "natural" as a justification for a social policy. Plato argued that each man ought to occupy himself with the one task which is "natural" to him, though it is certainly not clear how the choice of this task was to be determined. And it was Aristotle, in one of his less sublime moments, who defended slavery on the grounds that it was "nature's intention" for this institution to exist, though how he discovered this "intention" remains a mystery. The fact of the matter is that any action or policy can be defended on the grounds that it is "natural" and in no case is such a defense valid.

Despite these shortcomings, however, Rousseau's *Emile* merits serious study, for the work exerted a profound, and not undeserved, influence on subsequent developments in education.

EMILE

BOOK I

Everything is good as it comes from the hands of the Maker of the world but degenerates once it gets into the hands of man. Man makes one land yield the products of another, disregards differences of climates, elements and seasons, mutilates his dogs and horses, perverts and disfigures everything. Not content to leave anything as nature has made it, he must needs shape man himself to his notions, as he does the trees in his garden.

But under present conditions, human beings would be even worse than they are without this fashioning. A man left entirely to himself from birth would be the most misshapen of creatures. Prejudices, authority, necessity, example, the social institutions in which we are immersed, would crush out nature in him without putting anything in its place. He would fare like a shrub that has grown up by chance in the middle of a road, and got trampled under foot by the passers-by.

Plants are fashioned by cultivation, men by education. We are born feeble and need strength; possessing nothing, we need assistance; beginning without intelligence, we need judgment. All that we lack at birth and need when grown up is given us by education. This education comes to us from nature, from men, or from things. The internal development of our faculties and organs is the education of nature. The use we learn to make of this development is the education of men. What comes to us from our experience of the things that affect us is the education of things. Each of us therefore is fashioned by three kinds of teachers. When their lessons are at variance the pupil is badly educated, and is never at peace with himself. When they coincide and lead to a common goal he goes straight to his mark and lives single-minded. Now, of these three educations the one due to nature is independent of us, and the one from things only depends on us to a limited extent. The education that comes from men is the only one within our control, and even that is doubtful. Who can hope to have the entire direction of the words and deeds of all the people around a child?

It is only by good luck that the goal can be reached. What is this goal? It is nature's own goal. Since the three educations must work together for a

From *The "Emile" of Jean Jacques Rousseau: Selections,* William Boyd (ed.), New York, Teachers College Press, 1956, pp. 11–128 (with omissions as indicated in the text). Copyright 1962, Teachers College, Columbia University. Reprinted by permission of the publisher.

perfect result, the one that cannot be modified determines the course of the other two. But perhaps "nature" is too vague a word. We must try to fix its meaning. Nature, it has been said, is only habit. Is that really so? Are there not habits which are formed under pressure, leaving the original nature unchanged? One example is the habit of plants which have been forced away from the upright direction. When set free, the plant retains the bent forced upon it; but the sap has not changed its first direction and any new growth the plant makes returns to the vertical. It is the same with human inclinations. So long as there is no change in conditions the inclinations due to habits, however unnatural, remain unchanged, but immediately the restraint is removed the habit vanishes and nature reasserts itself.

We are born capable of sensation and from birth are affected in diverse ways by the objects around us. As soon as we become conscious of our sensations we are inclined to seek or to avoid the objects which produce them: at first, because they are agreeable or disagreeable to us, later because we discover that they suit or do not suit us, and ultimately because of the judgments we pass on them by reference to the idea of happiness or perfection we get from reason. These inclinations extend and strengthen with the growth of sensibility and intelligence, but under the pressure of habit they are changed to some extent with our opinions. The inclinations before this change are what I call our nature. In my view everything ought to be in conformity with these original inclinations.

There would be no difficulty if our three educations were merely different. But what is to be done when they are at cross purposes? Consistency is plainly impossible when we seek to educate a man for others, instead of for himself. If we have to combat either nature or society, we must choose between making a man or making a citizen. We cannot make both. There is an inevitable conflict of aims, from which come two opposing forms of education: the one communal and public, the other individual and domestic.

To get a good idea of communal education, read Plato's *Republic.* It is not a political treatise, as those who merely judge books by their titles think. It is the finest treatise on education ever written. Communal education in this sense, however, does not and can not now exist. There are no longer any real fatherlands and therefore no real citizens. The words "fatherland" and "citizen" should be expunged from modern languages.

I do not regard the instruction given in those ridiculous establishments called colleges as "public," any more than the ordinary kind of education. This education makes for two opposite goals and reaches neither. The men it turns out are double-minded, seemingly concerned for others, but really only concerned for themselves. From this contradiction comes the conflict we never cease to experience in ourselves. We are drawn in different directions by nature and by man, and take a midway path that leads us nowhere. In this state of confusion we go through life and end up with our contradictions unsolved, never having been any good to ourselves or to other people.

There remains then domestic education, the education of nature. But how will a man who has been educated entirely for himself get on with other people? If there were any way of combining in a single person the twofold aim, and removing the contradictions of life, a great obstacle to happiness would be removed. But before passing judgment on this kind of man it would be necessary to follow his development and see him fully formed. It would be necessary, in word, to make the acquaintance of the natural man. This is the subject of our quest in this book.

What can be done to produce this very exceptional person? In point of fact all we have to do is to prevent anything being done. When it is only a matter of sailing against the wind it is enough to tack, but when the sea runs high and you want to stay where you are, you must throw out the anchor.

In the social order where all stations in life are fixed, every one needs to be brought up for his own station. The individual who leaves the place for which he has been trained is useless in any other. In Egypt, where the son was obliged to follow in his father's footsteps, education had at least an assured aim: in our country where social ranks are fixed, but the men in them are constantly changing, nobody knows whether he is doing his son a good or a bad turn when he educates him for his own rank.

In the natural order where all men are equal, manhood is the common vocation. One who is well educated for that will not do badly in the duties that pertain to it. The fact that my pupil is intended for the army, the church or the bar, does not greatly concern me. Before the vocation determined by his parents comes the call of nature to the life of human kind. Life is the business I would have him learn. When he leaves my hands, I admit he will not be a magistrate, or a soldier, or a priest. First and foremost, he will be a man. All that a man must be he will be when the need arises, as well as anyone else. Whatever the changes of fortune he will always be able to find a place for himself.

.   .   .

A man of high rank once suggested that I should be his son's tutor. But having had experience already I knew myself unfit and I refused. Instead of the difficult task of educating a child, I now undertake the easier task of writing about it. To provide details and examples in illustration of my views and to avoid wandering off into airy speculations, I propose to set forth the education of Emile, an imaginary pupil, from birth to manhood. I take for granted that I am the right man for the duties in respect of age, health, knowledge and talents.

A tutor is not bound to his charge by the ties of nature as the father is, and so is entitled to choose his pupil, especially when as in this case he is providing a model for the education of other children. I assume that Emile is no genius, but a boy of ordinary ability: that he is the inhabitant of some temperate climate, since it is only in temperate climates that human beings develop completely; that he is rich, since it is only the rich who have need of the natural education that would fit them to live under all conditions; that he is to all intents and purposes an orphan, whose tutor having undertaken the parents' duties will also have their right to control all the circumstances of his upbringing; and, finally, that he is a vigorous, healthy, well-built child.

. . .

We are born with a capacity for learning, but know nothing and distinguish nothing. The mind is cramped by imperfect half-formed organs and has not even the consciousness of its own existence. The movements, and cries of the new born child are purely mechanical, quite devoid of understanding and will.

Children's first sensations are wholly in the realm of feeling. They are only aware of pleasure and pain. With walking and grasp undeveloped, it takes a long time for them to construct the representative sensations which acquaint them with external objects; but even before these objects reach up to and depart from their eyes, if one may put it so, the recurrence of the sensations begins to subject them to the bondage of habit. You see their eyes always turning to the light and unconsciously taking the direction from which the light comes, so that you have to be careful to keep them facing the light in order to prevent them acquiring a squint or becoming cross-eyed. Similarly, they have to be accustomed quite early to darkness, or soon they will wail and cry if they find themselves in the dark. Food and sleep, if too precisely organised, come to be necessary at definite intervals, and soon the desire for them is due not to need but to habit. Or rather, habit adds a new need to that of nature. That is something to be avoided.

The only habit the child should be allowed to acquire is to contract none. He should not be carried on one arm more than the other or allowed to make use of one hand more than the other, or to want to eat, sleep or do things at definite hours; and he should be able to remain alone by night or day. Prepare in good time for the reign of freedom and the exercise of his powers, by allowing his body its natural habits and accustoming him always to be his own master and follow the dictates of his will as soon as he has a will of his own.

. . .

BOOK II

. . . The more children can do for themselves the less help they need from other people. Added strength brings with it the sense needed for its direction. With the coming of self-consciousness at this second stage individual life really begins. Memory extends the sense of identity over all the moments of the child's existence. He becomes one and the same person, capable of happiness or sorrow. From this point on it is essential to regard him as a moral being.

.   .   .

Your first duty is to be humane. Love childhood. Look with friendly eyes on its games, its pleasures, its amiable dispositions. Which of you does not sometimes look back regretfully on the age when laughter was ever on the lips and the heart free of care? Why steal from the little innocents the enjoyment of a time that passes all too quickly?

Already I hear the clamour of the false wisdom that regards the present as of no account and is for ever chasing a future which flees as we advance. This is the time to correct the evil inclinations of mankind, you reply. Suffering should be increased in childhood when it is least felt, to reduce it at the age of reason. But how do you know that all the fine lessons with which you oppress the feeble mind of the child will not do more harm than good? Can you prove that these bad tendencies you profess to be correcting are not due to your own misguided efforts rather than to nature?

If we are to keep in touch with reality we must never forget what befits our condition. Humanity has its place in the scheme of things. Childhood has its place in the scheme of human life. We must view the man as a man, and the child as a child. The best way to ensure human well-being is to give each person his place in life and keep him there, regulating the passions in accordance with the individual constitution. The rest depends on external factors without our control.

We can never know absolute good or evil. Everything in this life is mixed. We never experience a pure sentiment, or remain in the same state for two successive moments. Weal and woe are common to us all, but in differing measure. The happiest man is the one who suffers least: the most miserable the one who has least pleasure. Always the sufferings outweigh the enjoyments. The felicity of man here below is therefore a negative state, to be measured by the fewness of his ills. Every feeling of pain is inseparable from the desire to escape from it: every idea of pleasure inseparable from the desire for its enjoyment. Privation is implicit in desire, and all privations are painful. Consequently unhappiness consists in the excess of desire over power. A conscious being whose powers equalled his desires would be absolutely happy.

In what then does the human wisdom that leads to true happiness consist? Not simply in the diminution of desires, for if they fell below our power to achieve, part of our faculties would be unemployed and our entire being would not be satisfied. Neither does it consist in the extension of our faculties, for a disproportionate increase in our desires would only make us more miserable. True happiness comes with equality of power and will. The only man who gets his own way is the one who does not need another's help to get it: from which it follows that the supreme good is not authority, but freedom. The true freeman wants only what he can get, and does only what pleases him. This is my fundamental maxim. Apply it to childhood and all the rules of education follow.

There are two kinds of dependence: dependence on things, which is natural, and dependence on men, which is social. Dependence on things being non-moral is not prejudicial to freedom and engenders no vices: dependence on men being capricious engenders them all. The only cure for this evil in society would be to put the law in place of the individual, and to arm the general will with a real power that made it superior to every individual will.

Keep the child in sole dependence on things and you will follow the natural order in the course of his education. Put only physical obstacles in the way of indiscreet wishes and let his punishments spring from his own actions. Without forbidding wrong-doing, be content to prevent it. Experience or impotence apart from anything else should take the place of law for him. Satisfy his desires, not because of his demands but because of his needs. He should have no consciousness of obedience when he acts, nor of mastery when someone acts for him. Let him experience liberty equally in his actions and in yours.

Be specially careful not to give the child empty formulae of politeness, to serve as magic words for subjecting his surroundings to his will and getting him what he wants at once. For my part I am less afraid of rudeness than of arrogance in Emile, and would rather have him say "Do this" as a request, than "Please" as a command. I am not concerned with the words he uses, but with what they imply.

Excessive severity and excessive indulgence are equally to be avoided. If you let children suffer you endanger health and life. If you are over-careful in shielding them from trouble of every kind you are laying up much unhappiness for the future: you are withdrawing them from the common lot of man, to which they must one day become subject in spite of you.

You will tell me that I am making the same mistake as those bad fathers whom I blamed for sacrificing their children's happiness for the sake of a distant time that may never come. That is not so, for the liberty I allow my pupil amply compensates for the slight hardships I let him experience. I see little scamps playing in the snow, blue and stiff with cold and scarcely able to move a finger. There is nothing to hinder them warming themselves, but they don't. If they were forced to come indoors they would feel the rigours of constraint a hundred times more than the cold. What then is there to complain about? Am I making the child unhappy by exposing him to hardships which he is quite willing to endure? I am doing him good at the present moment by leaving him free. I am doing him good in the future by arming him against inevitable evils. If he had to choose between being my pupil or yours, do you think he would hesitate for an instant?

The surest way to make your child unhappy is to accustom him to get everything he wants. With desire constantly increasing through easy satisfaction, lack of power will sooner or later force you to a refusal in spite of yourself, and the unwonted refusal will cause him deeper annoyance than the mere lack of what he desires. First he will want the stick in your hand, then the bird that flies past, then the star that shines above him. Everything he sees he will want: and unless you were God you could never hope to satisfy him. How could such a child possibly be happy? Happy! He is a despot, at once the meanest of slaves and the most wretched of creatures. Let us get back to the primitive way. Nature made children to be loved and helped, not to be obeyed and feared. Is there in the world a being more feeble and unhappy, more at the mercy of his environment, more in need of pity and protection than a child? Surely then there is nothing more offensive or more unseemly than the sight of a dictatorial headstrong child, issuing orders to those around him and assuming the tone of a master to people without whom he would perish.

On the other hand, it should be obvious that with the many restrictions imposed on children by their own weakness it is barbarous for us to add subjection to our caprices to the natural subjection, and take from them such limited liberty as they possess. Social servitude will come with the age of reason. Why anticipate it by a domestic servitude? Let one moment of life be free from this yoke which nature has not imposed, and leave the child to the enjoyment of his natural liberty.

I come back to practice. I have already said that what your child gets he should get because he needs it, not because he asks for it, and that he should never act from obedience but only from necessity. For this reason, the words "obey" and "command" must be banished from his vocabulary, still more the words "duty" and "obligation"; but "force," "necessity," "weakness" and "constraint" should be emphasised. It is impossible to form any idea of moral facts or social relations before the age of reason. Consequently the use of terms which express such ideas should as far as possible be avoided, for fear the child comes to attach to these words false ideas which cannot or will not be eradicated at a later time.

"Reason with children" was Locke's chief maxim. It is the one most popular today, but it does not seem to me justified by success. For my part I do not see any children more stupid than those who have been much reasoned with. Of all the human faculties, reason which may be said to be compounded of all the rest develops most slowly and with greatest difficulty. Yet it is reason that people want to use in the development of the first faculties. A reasonable man is the masterwork of a good education: and we actually pretend to be educating children by means of reason! That is beginning at the end. If children appreciated reason they would not need to be educated.

Instead of appealing to reason, say to the child: "You must not do that!" "Why not?" "Because it is wrong." "Why is it wrong?" "Because it is forbidden." "Why is it forbidden?" "Because it is wrong." That is the inevitable circle. To distinguish right from wrong and appreciate the reason for the duties of man is beyond a child's powers.

Nature wants children to be children before they are men. If we deliberately depart from this order we shall get premature fruits which are neither ripe nor well flavoured and which soon decay. We shall have youthful sages and grown up children. Childhood has ways of seeing, thinking and feeling peculiar to itself: nothing can be more foolish than to seek to substitute our ways for them. I should as soon expect a child of ten to be five feet in height as to be possessed of judgment.

Treat your pupil according to his age. Begin by putting him in his place and keep him in it so firmly that he will not think of leaving it. Then he will practice the most important lesson of wisdom before he knows what wisdom is. Give him absolutely no orders of any kind. Do not even let him imagine that you claim any authority over him. Let him only know that he is weak and you are strong, and that therefore he is at your mercy. Quite early let him feel the heavy yoke which nature imposes on man, the yoke of the necessity in things as opposed to human caprice. If there is anything he should not do, do not forbid him, but prevent him without explanation or reasoning. Whatever you give, give at the first word without prayers or entreaty, and above all without conditions. Give with pleasure, refuse with regret, but let your refusals be irrevocable. Your "No" once uttered must be a wall of brass which the child will stop trying to batter down once he has exhausted his strength on it five or six times.

It is strange that all the time people have been bringing up children nobody has thought of any instruments for their direction but emulation, jealousy, envy, vanity, greed or base fear; most dangerous passions all of them, sure to corrupt the soul. Foolish teachers think they are working wonders when they are simply making the children wicked in the attempt to teach them about goodness. Then they announce gravely: such is man. Yes, such is the man you have made. All the instruments have been tried but one, and that as it happens is the only one that can succeed: well regulated liberty.

Avoid verbal lessons with your pupil. The only kind of lesson he should get is that of experience. Never inflict any punishment, for he does not know what it is to be at fault. Being devoid of all morality in his actions he can do nothing morally wrong, nothing that deserves either punishment or reprimand.

Let us lay it down as an incontestable principle that the first impulses of nature are always right. There is no original perversity in the human heart. Of every vice we can say how it entered and whence it came. The only passion natural to man is self-love, or self-esteem in a broad sense. This self-esteem has no necessary reference to other people. In so far as it relates to ourselves it is good and useful. It only becomes good or bad in the social application we make of it. Until reason, which is the guide of self-esteem, makes its appearance, the child should not do anything because he is seen or heard by other people, but only do what nature demands of him. Then he will do nothing but what is right.

I do not mean to say that he will never do any mischief: that he will never hurt himself, for example, or break a valuable bit of furniture. He might do a great deal that was bad without being bad, because the wrong action depends on harmful intention and that he will never have.

.   .   .

I have now brought my pupil through the land of the sensations right up to the bounds of childish reason. The first step beyond this should take him towards manhood. But before entering on this new stage let us cast our eyes backward for a moment on the one we have traversed. Each age and state of life has its own proper perfection, its own distinctive maturity. People sometimes speak about a complete man. Let us think rather of a complete child. This vision will be new for us and perhaps not less agreeable.

When I picture to myself a boy of ten or twelve, healthy, strong and well built for his age, only pleasant thoughts arise in me, whether for his present or for his future. I see him bright, eager, vigorous, care-free, completely absorbed in the present, rejoicing in abounding vitality. I see him in the years ahead using senses, mind and power as they develop from day to day. I view him as a child and he pleases me. I think of him as a man and he pleases me still more. His warm blood seems to heat my own. I feel as if I were living in his life and am rejuvenated by his vivacity.

The clock strikes and all is changed. In an instant his eye grows dull and his merriment disappears. No more mirth, no more games! A severe, hard-faced man takes him by the hand, says gravely, "Come away, sir," and leads him off. In the room they enter I get a glimpse of books. Books! What a cheerless equipment for his age. As he is dragged away in silence, he casts a regretful look around him. His eyes are swollen with tears he dare not shed, his heart heavy with sighs he dare not utter.

Come, my happy pupil, and console us for the departure of the wretched boy. Here comes Emile, and at his approach I have a thrill of joy in which I see he shares. It is his friend and comrade, the companion of his games to whom he comes. His person, his bearing, his countenance reveal assurance and contentment. Health glows in his face. His firm step gives him an air of vigour. His complexion is refined without being effeminate; sun and wind have put on it the honourable imprint of his sex. His eyes are still unlighted by the fires of sentiment and have all their native serenity. His manner is open and free without the least insolence or vanity.

His ideas are limited but precise. If he knows nothing by heart, he knows a great deal by experience. If he is not as good a reader in books as other children, he reads better in the book of nature. His mind is not in his tongue but in his head. He has less memory but more judgment. He only knows one language, but he understands what he says; and if he does not talk as well as other children he can do things better than they can.

Habit, routine and custom mean nothing to him. What he did yesterday has no effect on what he does today. He never follows a fixed rule and never accepts authority or example. He only does or says what seems good to himself. For this reason you must not expect stock speeches or studied manners from him but just the faithful expression of his ideas and the conduct that comes from his inclinations.

You will find in him a few moral notions relating to his own situation, but not being an active member of society he has none relating to manhood. Talk to him about liberty, property and even convention, and he may understand you thus far. But speak to him about duty and obedience, and he will not know what you mean. Command him to do something, and he will pay no heed. But say to him: "If you will do me this favour, I will do the same for you another time"; and immediately he will hasten to oblige. For his part, if he needs any help he will ask the first person he meets as a matter of course. If you grant his request he will not thank you, but will feel that he has contracted a debt. If you refuse, he will neither complain nor insist. He will only say: "It could not be done." He does not rebel against necessity once he recognises it.

Work and play are all the same to him. His games are his occupations: he is not aware of any difference. He goes into everything he does with a pleasing interest and freedom. It is indeed a charming spectacle to see a nice boy of this age with open smiling countenance, doing the most serious things in his play or profoundly occupied with the most frivolous amusements.

Emile has lived a child's life and has arrived at the maturity of childhood, without any sacrifice of happiness in the achievement of his own perfection. He has acquired all the reason possible for his age, and in doing so has been as free and as happy as his nature allowed him to be. If by chance the fatal scythe were to cut down the flower of our hopes we would not have to bewail at the same time his life and his death, nor add to our griefs the memory of those we caused him. We would say that at any rate he had enjoyed his childhood and that nothing we had done had deprived him of what nature gave.

BOOK III

The whole course of life up to adolescence is a time of weakness, but there is one point during this first age of man at which strength exceeds the demands made on it by needs, and the growing creature though still absolutely weak becomes relatively strong. With needs incompletely developed, his powers more than suffice. As a man he would be very feeble: as a child he is very strong. This is the third stage of early life which for lack of a better word I continue to call childhood. It is not yet the age of puberty, but adolescence draws near.

At twelve or thirteen the child's powers develop much more rapidly than his needs. The sex passions, the most violent and terrible of all, have not yet awakened. He is indifferent to the rigours of weather and seasons, and braves them light-heartedly. His growing body heat takes the place of clothing. Appetite is his sauce, and everything nourishing tastes good. When he is tired he stretches himself out on the ground and goes to sleep. He is not troubled by imaginary wants. What people think does not trouble him. Not only is he self-sufficient but his strength goes beyond his requirements. . . .

Nevertheless, it will probably be necessary to give him a little guidance. But let it be very little, and avoid the appearance of it. If he goes wrong, do not correct his errors. Say nothing till he sees them and corrects them himself; or at most, arrange some practical situation which will make him realise things personally. If he never made mistakes he would never learn properly. In any case, the important thing is not that he should know the topography of the country, but that he should be able to get his information for himself. It does not matter greatly whether he has maps in his head, provided he knows what they represent and has a clear idea of the art of their construction.

. . . It is not a question of teaching him the sciences, but of giving him a taste for them, and methods of acquiring them when this taste is better developed. This is most certainly a fundamental principle in all good education.

. . .

With the child's advance in intelligence other considerations compel greater care in the choice of his occupations. As soon as he comes to know himself well enough to understand what constitutes happiness for him and can judge what is fitting and what is not, he is in a position to appreciate the difference between work and play, and to regard play as relaxation from work. Thereafter matters of real utility may enter into his studies and lead him to apply himself more diligently than he did to mere amusements. The law of necessity, always operative, soon teaches man to do what he does not like, in order to avoid evils he would like still less. Such is the practice of foresight; and from foresight, well or ill directed, comes all the wisdom or all the unhappiness of mankind.

When children foresee their needs their intelligence has made real progress. They begin to know the value of time. For this reason, it is important to accustom them to employ their time on objects of an obvious utility that are within their understanding. All that pertains to the moral order and to social usage should not be put before them yet, because it does not mean anything for them. Why do you want to set a child to the studies of an age he may never reach, to the detriment of studies suited for the present? But you will ask: "Will there be time for him to learn what he ought to know when the occasion for its use arises?" That I do not know. What I do know is that it is impossible for him to learn it sooner. Our real teachers are experience and feeling, and no one ever appreciates what is proper to manhood till he enters into its situations. A child knows that he is destined to become a man. Such of the ideas of adult life as are within his comprehension are occasions of instruction for him, but he ought to be kept in absolute ignorance of all the rest. This whole book is one long demonstration of this educational principle.

.   .   .

Your main endeavour should be to keep away from your pupil all the notions of social relations which are beyond his comprehension; but when the inter-relation of knowledge forces you to show him the mutual dependence of men, avoid the moral aspects and direct his attention to industry and the mechanical arts which make them useful to each other. As you take him from one work-shop to another, never let him see any kind of work without putting his hand to it, and never let him leave till he knows perfectly the reason for all that he has observed. With that in view, set him an example by working yourself in the different occupations. To make him a master become an apprentice. You can be sure that he will learn more from an hour's work than he would remember after a day's explanations.

.   .   .

Reader, do not give too much thought to the bodily activity and the skill of hand of our pupil. Consider rather the direction we are giving to his childish curiosities. Consider his senses, his inventive mind, his foresight. Consider the good head he will have. He will want to know all about everything he sees and does, and will take nothing for granted. He will refuse to learn anything until he acquires the knowledge that is implied in it. When he sees a spring made he will want to know how the steel was got from the mine. If he sees the pieces of a box put together, he will want to know how the tree was cut. When he is using a tool himself he will not fail to say of the tool he uses: "If I did not have this tool, how would I make one like it, or manage without it?"

At the begining of this period of life we have taken advantage of the fact that our strength greatly exceeds our needs, to get away beyond ourselves. We have soared into the heavens and have surveyed the earth. We have studied the laws of nature. In a word, we have traversed the whole of our island. Now we come back gradually to our own dwelling. What is there for us to do when we have completed the study of our surroundings? We must convert them as much as we can to our own purposes. Up to this point, we have provided ourseves with all kinds of instruments without knowing which of them we will need. It may be that those which are of no use to us may be of service to other people and that we in turn may need theirs. In this way we will all find ourselves gaining by these exchanges. For this we must know the mutual needs of men; what each of us has to give and to get. Suppose there are ten men, each with ten kinds of needs, each applying himself to ten different kinds of work to provide for the necessities of life. The ten, because of differences of gift and talent, are likely to be less apt at some tasks than others, and all will be badly served when each does everything. But make a society of these ten, and let each man apply himself for his own benefit and that of the other nine to the kind of work that suits him best. Each one will profit by the talents of the others as if he personally had them all, and at the same time grow more perfect in his own line of work by constant practice. So it will come that the whole ten are perfectly provided for and will still have something left for others. This is the obvious basis of all our social institutions.

In this way the ideas of social relations take shape in the child's mind little by little, even before he becomes an active member of society himself. Emile sees that in order to have things for his own use he must have some he can exchange with other people. It is easy to lead him to feel the need for such exchanges and put himself in a position to profit by them.

As soon as he knows what life is, my first concern will be to teach him to preserve it. Up to this point I have ignored differences of station, rank or fortune, and I shall say little more about them in what follows, because man is the same in all stations. The rich man's stomach is no bigger than the poor man's, and his digestion no better. The master's arms are no longer and no stronger than the slave's. A "great" man is no greater than a man of the people. Natural needs being everywhere alike, the means of satisfying them should likewise be equal. Fit man's education to what man really is. Do you not see that if you try to fit him exclusively for one way of life you make him useless for every other? You put your trust in the existing social order and do not take into account the fact that that order is subject to inevitable revolutions, and that you can neither foresee nor prevent the revolution that may affect your children.

. . .

Here is our child, ready to cease being a child and to enter on an individual life. More than ever he feels the necessity which binds him to things. After training his body and his senses, we have trained his mind and his judgment. In short, we have combined the use of his limbs with that of his faculties. We have made him an efficient thinking being and nothing further remains for us in the production of a complete man but to make him a loving, sensitive being: in fact, to perfect reason through sentiment. But before entering on this new order of things let us look back over the one we are leaving, and see where we have reached.

To begin with, our pupil had only sensations, now he has ideas: he had only feelings, now he judges; for from the comparison of several sensations, whether successive or simultaneous, and the judgment passed on them, there comes a sort of mixed or complex sensation which I call an idea. It is the particular way of forming ideas that gives its character to the human mind. A solid mind forms its ideas on real relations: a superficial one is content with appearances.

Greater or less aptitude in the comparison of ideas and the discovery of relations is what makes the difference in the mental capacity of different people.

In sensation, judgment is purely passive—we feel what we feel: in perception or idea, it is active—it connects, compares, determines relations. It is never the sensation that is wrong but the judgment passed on it. The child says about the ice cream that it burns. That is a right sensation but a wrong judgment. So with the experiences of those who see a mirror for the first time, or enter a cellar at different times of the year, or dip a warm or cold hand into lukewarm water, or see the clouds passing over the moon as if they were stationary, or think the stick immersed in water is broken. All our mistakes in these cases come from judgment. Unfortunately social man is dependent on a great many things about which he has to judge. He must therefore be taught to reason correctly.

I will be told that in training the child to judge, I am departing from nature. I do not think so. Nature chooses her instruments, and makes use of them not according to opinion but according to necessity. There is a great difference between natural man living in nature and natural man living in the social state. Emile is not a savage to be banished to the deserts: he is a savage made to live in a town. He must know how to get a living in towns, and how to get on with their inhabitants, and to live with them, if not to live like them.

The best way of learning to judge correctly is to simplify our sense experiences as much as possible. To do this we must learn to check the reports of each sense by itself, over and above the check from the other senses. Then each sensation will become an idea, and this idea will always conform to the truth. This is the kind of acquirement I have tried to secure in this third stage of childhood.

Emile, who has been compelled to learn for himself and use his reason, has a limited knowledge, but the knowledge he has is his own, none of it half-known. Among the small number of things he really knows the most important is that there is much he does not know which he may one day come to know, much more that other people know that he will never know, and an infinity of things that nobody will ever know. He has a universal mind, not because of what he knows but from his faculty for acquiring knowledge: a mind open, intelligent, responsive, and (as Montaigne says) if not instructed, capable of being instructed. I am content if he knows the "wherefore" of all he does, and the "why" of all he believes.

The only knowledge Emile has at this stage is in the sphere of natural and physical facts. He does not even know the name of history, nor what metaphysics and ethics are. He knows the essential relations between man and things, but none of the moral relations between man and man. He has little ability to form general ideas or abstractions. He sees the qualities common to certain bodies without reasoning about the qualities in themselves. He knows abstract space by means of geometrical figures, and abstract quantity by means of algebraic symbols. These figures and signs are the basis of the abstractions, on which his senses rest. He does not seek to know things in themselves, but through the relations which interest him. He only judges external facts by their relation to himself, but this judgment of his is sound. Nothing fantastic or conventional enters into it. He sets most store on what is useful for him, and as he never departs from this method of evaluation, he is not swayed by accepted opinion.

Emile is hard working, temperate, patient, stable and courageous. His imagination, still unstimulated, does not exaggerate dangers. Few evils affect him and he can endure suffering calmly because he has learned not to fight against fate. As for death, he does not yet know what it is, but being accustomed to submit unresistingly to the laws of nature, he will die if he must without a struggle. To live a free man and hold human affairs lightly is the best way to prepare for death. In a word, Emile has every personal virtue. To add the social virtues he only needs to know the relations which call them into being. That knowledge his mind is now quite ready to receive.

He still thinks of himself without regard to others and is quite satisfied that others should give no thought to him. He asks nothing from other people and does not believe that he owes anything to them. Thus far he stands alone in human society. He is self-dependent and is better entitled to be so than any other person, since he is all that a child could be at his age. He has no mistaken ideas and no vices, other than those that nobody can avoid. He has a healthy body, agile limbs, a true mind free from prejudice, a free heart devoid of passion. Self-esteem, the first and most natural of all the passions, has still to awaken in him. Without disturbing anybody's peace he has lived happy, contented and free within the bounds of nature. Do you think that a child who has reached his fifteenth year like this has wasted his childhood?

BOOK IV

We are born twice over; the first time for existence, the second for life; once as human beings and later as men or as women. Up to puberty, children of the two sexes have nothing obvious to distinguish them. They are similar in features, in figure, in complexion, in voice. Girls are children, boys are children. The same name suffices for beings so much alike.

But man is not meant to remain a child for ever. At the time prescribed by nature he passes out of his childhood. As the fretting of the sea precedes the distant storm, this disturbing change is announced by the murmur of nascent passions. A change of mood, frequent tantrums, a constant unease of mind make the child hard to manage. He no longer listens to his master's voice. He is a lion in a fever. He mistrusts his guide and is averse to control.

With the moral signs of changing mood go patent physical changes. His countenance develops and takes on the imprint of a definite character. The soft slight down on his cheeks grows darker and firmer. His voice breaks, or rather, gets lost. He is neither child nor man, and he speaks like neither. His eyes, organs of the soul, which have hitherto said nothing, find language and expression as they light up with a new fire. He is becoming conscious that they can tell too much and he is learning to lower them and blush. He is disturbed for no reason whatever.

This is the second birth of which I spoke. Now is the time that man really enters into life and finds nothing alien to him. So far his guardian's responsibility has been child's play: it is only now that his task comes to have real importance. This stage at which ordinary educations end is just that when ours should begin.

The passions are the chief instruments for our preservation. The child's first sentiment is self-love, the only passion that is born with man. The second, which is derived from it, is the love he has for the people he sees ready to help him, and from this develops a kindly feeling for mankind. But with fresh needs and growing dependence on others comes the consciousness of social relations and with it the sense of duties and preferences. It is at this point that the child may become domineering, jealous, deceitful, vindictive. Self-love being concerned only with ourselves is content when our real needs are satisfied, but self-esteem which involves comparisons with other people never is and never can be content because it makes the impossible demand that others should prefer us to themselves. That is how it comes that the gentle kindly passions issue from self-love, while hate and anger spring from self-esteem. Great care and skill are required to prevent the human heart being depraved by the new needs of social life.

The proper study of man is that of his relationships. So long as he is aware of himself only as a physical being he should study himself in his relations with things. That is the task of childhood. When he comes to consciousness of himself as a moral being he should study himself in his relations with his fellows. This is the occupation of his whole life, beginning at the point we have now reached.

.   .   .

Here it is important to take the opposite course from the one we have been following so far, and let the young man learn from other people's experience rather than his own. I would have you choose a young man's associates so that he may think well of those who live with him, and at the same time I would have you teach him to know the world so well that he may think ill of all that goes on in it. You want him to know and feel that man is naturally good, and to judge his neighbour by himself: equally, you want him to see how society corrupts men and to find in their prejudices the source of all their vices. This method, I have to admit, has its drawbacks and it is not easy to put into practice. If a young man is set to observe men too early and too close up, he will take a hateful pleasure in interpreting everything as badness and fail to see anything good in what is really good. Soon the general perversity will serve him as an excuse rather than as a warning, and he will say that if this is what man is, he himself has no wish to be different.

To get over this obstacle and bring him to an understanding of the human heart without risk of spoiling himself I would show him men in other times and places, in such a way that he can look on the scene as an outsider. This is the time for history. By means of it he will read the hearts of men without the lessons of philosophy, and look on them as a mere spectator without prejudice and without passion: judging them, but neither their accomplice nor their accuser.

Unfortunately this study has dangers and drawbacks of various kinds. It is difficult to put one's self at a point of view from which to judge one's fellows fairly. One of the great vices of history is the portrayal of men by what is bad in them rather than by what is good. It is from revolutions and catastrophes that it derives its interest. So long as a nation grows and prospers in the calm of peaceful government, history has nothing to say about it. It only begins to tell about nations when they are no longer self-sufficient and have got mixed up in their neighbours' affairs. It only records their story when they enter on their decline. Our historians all begin where they ought to finish. Only bad men achieve fame: the good are either forgotten or held up to ridicule. Like philosophy, history always slanders mankind.

Moreover, the facts described in history never give an exact picture of what actually happened. They change form in the historian's head. They get moulded by his interests and take on the hue of his prejudices. Who can put the reader at the precise point where an event can be seen just as it took place? Ignorance or partisanship distorts everything. Without even altering a single feature a quite different face can be put on events by a broader or a narrower view of the relevant circumstances. How often a tree more or less, a rock to the right or the left, a cloud of dust blown up by the wind, have decided the outcome of a battle without anybody being aware of it! But that does not prevent the historian telling you the causes of defeat or victory with as much assurance as if he had been everywhere himself. In any case, what do the facts matter when the reason for them is unknown? And what lessons can I draw from an event when I am ignorant of the real cause of it? The historian gives me an explanation, but it is his own invention. And is not criticism itself, of which there is so much talk, only an art of guessing, the art of choosing among various lies the one most like the truth?

I will be told that historical precision is of less consequence than the truth about men and manners. So long as the human heart is well depicted, it will be said, it does not greatly matter whether events are accurately narrated or not. That is right, if the pictures are drawn close enough to nature. If, however, most of them are coloured by the historian's imagination, we are back again to the difficulty we set out to avoid, and are allowing writers an authority which has been denied the teacher. If my pupil is only to see pictures of fancy, I prefer to have them traced by my own hand. They will at least be those best suited for him.

The worst historians for a young man are those who pass judgment. Give him the facts and let him judge for himself. That is how he will learn to know men. If he is always guided by some author's judgment, he only sees through another's eyes: when he lacks these eyes he cannot see.

.   .   .

To all these considerations must be added the fact that history is more concerned with actions than with men. It takes men at certain chosen moments when they are in full dress. It only depicts the public man when he is prepared to be seen, and does not follow him into the intimacies of friendship and private life. It is the coat rather than the person that is portrayed.

I would much rather have the study of human nature begin with the reading of the life story of individual men. In these stories the historian gets on the track of the man, and there is no escape from his scrutiny. . . .

It is true that the genius of nations, or of men in association, is very different from the character of man as an individual; and the knowledge of human nature got without examination of the form it assumes in the multitude, would be very imperfect. But it is no less true that it is necessary to begin with the study of man in order to form a judgment about men, and that one who had a complete knowledge of the dispositions of the constituent individuals might be able to foresee their joint effects in the body politic.

.   .   .

One step more and we reach the goal. Self-esteem is a useful instrument but it has its dangers. Often it wounds the hand that employs it and rarely does good without also doing evil. Emile, comparing himself with other human beings and finding himself very fortunately situated, will be tempted to give credit to his own reason for the work of his guardian, and to attribute to his own merit the effects of his good fortune. He will say: "I am wise, and men are foolish." This is the error most to be feared, because it is the one hardest to eradicate. If choice had to be made I do not know whether I would not prefer the illusion of prejudice to the illusion of pride.

There is no remedy for vanity but experience. It is doubtful indeed if it can be cured at all; but at any rate its growth may be checked when it appears. Do not waste your time on fine arguments and try to convince an adolescent that he is a man like other men and subject to the same weaknesses. Make him feel it for himself, or he will never learn it. Once again, I have to make an exception to my own rules, by deliberately exposing my pupil to the mischances which may prove to him that he is no wiser than the rest of us. I will let flatterers get the better of him. If fools were to entice him into some extravagance or other I would let him run the risk. I will allow him to be duped by card sharpers, and leave him to be swindled by them. The only snares from which I would guard him with special care would be those of prostitutes. Actually Emile would not be readily tempted in these ways. It should be kept in mind that my constant plan is to take things at their worst. I try in the first place to prevent the vice, and then I assume its existence in order to show how it can be remedied.

The time for faults is the time for fables. Censure of an offender under cover of a fiction gives instruction without offence. The young man learns in this way that the moral of the tale is not a lie, from the truth that finds application in his own case. The child who has never been deceived by flattery sees no point in the fable of *The Fox and the Crow,* but the silly person who has been gulled by a flatterer understands perfectly what a fool the crow was. From a fact he draws a moral, and the experience which would speedily have been forgotten is engraved in his mind by the fable. There is no moral knowledge which cannot be acquired either through the experience of other people or of ourselves. Where the experience is too dangerous for the young man to get it at first hand, the lesson can be drawn from history. When the test has no serious consequences it is good for him to be exposed to it and to have the particular cases known to him summed up as maxims. I do not mean, however, that these maxims should be expounded or even stated. The moral at the end of most fables is badly conceived. Before I put the inimitable fables of La Fontaine into the hands of a young man I would cut out all the conclusions in which he takes the trouble to explain what he had just said so clearly and agreeably. If your pupil does not understand the fable without the explanation, you can be sure that he will not understand it in any case. Only men can learn from fables and now is the time for Emile to begin.

When I see young people confined to the speculative studies at the most active time of life and then cast suddenly into the world of affairs without the least experience, I find it as contrary to reason as to nature and am not at all surprised that so few people manage their lives well. By some strange perversity we are taught all sorts of useless things, but nothing is done about the art of conduct. We are supposed to be getting trained for society but are taught as if each one of us were going to live a life of contemplation in a solitary cell. You think you are preparing children for life when you teach them certain bodily contortions and meaningless strings of words. I also have been a teacher of the art of conduct. I have taught my Emile to live his own life, and more than that to earn his own bread. But that is not enough. To live in the world one must get on with people and know how to get a hold on them. It is necessary also to be able to estimate the action and reaction of individual interests in civil society and so forecast events as to be rarely at fault in one's enterprises.

It is by doing good that we become good. I know of no surer way. Keep your pupil occupied with all the good deeds within his power. Let him help poor people with money and with service, and get justice for the oppressed. Active benevolence will lead him to reconcile the quarrels of his comrades and to be concerned about the sufferings of the afflicted. By putting his kindly feelings into action in this way and drawing his own conclusions from the outcome of his efforts, he will get a great deal of useful knowledge. In addition to college lore he will acquire the still more important ability of applying his knowledge to the purposes of life.

.   .   .

Let us now look at Emile as he enters into society, not to become a leader but to become acquainted with it and to find his mate. Whatever the rank into which he may be born, whatever the society he enters, his first appearance will be simple and unpretentious. He neither has nor desires the qualities that make an immediate impression. He sets too little store by the opinions of men to be concerned about their prejudices, and is not concerned to have people esteem him till they know him. His way of presenting himself is neither modest nor conceited, but just natural and sincere. He knows neither constraint nor concealment. He is the same in company as when he is alone. He speaks little, because he has no desire to attract notice. For the same reason he only speaks about things that are of practical value, being too well informed ever to be a babbler. Far from despising the ways of other people, he conforms quite readily to them: not for the sake of appearing versed in the conventions or affecting fashionable airs, but simpy to avoid notice. He is never more at his ease than when nobody is paying him any attention.

When he studies the ways of men in society as he formerly studied their passions in history, he will often have occasion to reflect on the things that gratify or offend the human heart. This will lead him to philosophise on the principles of taste, and this is the study that is most fitting for this period of life.

There is no need to go far for a definition of taste. Taste is simply the faculty of judging what pleases or displeases the greatest number of people. This does not mean that there are more people of taste than others. For though the majority judge sanely about any particular thing, there are few who possess this sanity about everything. Taste is like beauty. Though the most general tastes put together make good taste, there are not many people of taste, just as beauty is constituted by an assemblage of the most common traits and yet there are few beautiful persons.

We are not concerned here with the things we like because they are useful, or dislike because they are harmful. Taste has nothing to do with the necessities of life: it applies to things which are indifferent to us or at most have the interest that goes with our amusements. This is what makes decisions of taste so difficult and seemingly so arbitrary. I should add that taste has local rules which make it dependent in very many ways on region, custom, government and institutions, as well as other rules relating to age, sex and character. That is why there can be no disputing about tastes.

Taste is natural to all men, but all do not possess it in equal measure. The degree of taste we may have depends on native sensibility: the form it takes under cultivation depends on the social groups in which we have lived. In the first place, it is necessary to live in numerous social groups and make many comparisons. In the second place, these must be groups for amusement and leisure, for in those that have to do with practical affairs it is interest and not pleasure that has to be considered. In the third place, there must not be too great inequality in the group and the tyranny of opinion must not be excessive: otherwise fashion stifles taste and people no longer desire what pleases but what gives distinction.

This matter of taste is one to which Emile cannot be indifferent in his present enquiries. The knowledge of what may be agreeable or disagreeable to men is essential to one who has need of them, and no less to one who wants to be useful to them. It is important to please people if you want to serve them.

. . .

To keep his taste pure and healthy I will . . . arrange to have useful conversations with him, and by directing the talk to topics that please him I will make these conversations both amusing and instructive. Now is the time to read agreeable books, and to teach him to analyse speech and appreciate all the beauties of eloquence and diction. Contrary to the general belief, there is little to be gained from the study of languages for themselves; but the study of languages leads to the study of the general principles of grammar. It is necessary to know Latin to get a proper knowledge of French. To learn the rules of the art of speech we must study and compare the two languages.

There is moreover a certain simplicity of taste that goes to the heart, which is to be found only in the writings of the ancients. In oratory, in poetry, in every kind of literature, the pupil will find them, as in history, abundant in matter and sober in judgment. In contrast with this our authors talk much and say little. To be always accepting their judgment as right is not the way to acquire a judgment of our own.

. . .

Generally speaking Emile will have more liking for the writings of the ancients than our own, for the good reason that coming first they are nearer nature and their genius is more distinctive. Whatever may be said to the contrary the human reason shows no advance. What is gained in one direction is lost in another. All minds start from the same point, and the time spent in learning what others think is so much time lost for learning to think for ourselves. As time goes on there is more acquired knowledge and less vigour of mind.

It is not for the study of morals but of taste that I take Emile to the theatre, for it is there above all that taste reveals itself to thinking people. "Give no thought to moral precepts," I will say to him: "it is not here that you will learn them." The theatre is not intended to give truth but to humour and amuse. Nowhere can the art of pleasing men and touching the human heart be so well learned. The study of drama leads to the study of poetry: their object is the same. If Emile has even a glimmering of taste for poetry he will cultivate Greek, Latin and Italian—the languages of the poets—with great pleasure. The study of them will give him unlimited entertainment, and will profit him all the more on that account. They will bring him delight at an age and in circumstances when the heart finds charm in every kind of beauty. Imagine on the one hand my Emile, and, on the other, some young college scamp, reading the Fourth Book of the *Aeneid*, or Tibullus, or Plato's *Banquet*. What a difference there is: the heart of the one stirred to its depth by something that does not impress the other at all. Stop the reading, young man: you are too greatly moved. I want you to find pleasure in the language of love, but not to be carried away by it. Be a man of feeling, but also a wise man. Actually, it is of no consequence whether Emile succeeds in the dead languages, in literature, in poetry or not. It would not matter greatly if he were ignorant of them all. His education is not really concerned with such diversions.

My main object in teaching him to feel and love beauty in every form is to fix his affections and his tastes on it and prevent his natural appetites from deteriorating so that he comes to look for the means of happiness in his wealth instead of finding it within himself. As I have said elsewhere, taste is simply the art of appreciating the little things, but since the pleasure of life depends on a multitude of little things such concern is not unimportant. It is by means of them that we come to enrich our lives with the good things at our disposal. . . .

Immanuel Kant

(1724-1804)

DESPITE Kant's immense influence on the history of philosophy, his writings in education have been curiously neglected. This is unfortunate, since his work in this area contains many points of vital importance.

Kant believes that "the greatest and most difficult problem to which man can devote himself is the problem of education." He claims that it is through education that human nature can be constantly improved. He points out that students may either be "trained" or "enlightened." Animals are trained; children must be taught to think. Kant also emphasizes the importance of experimentation in education, the advantages of public education, and the fact that "the best way to understand is to do."

Since Kant's views on ethics are so widely studied, it is of special interest to consider his views on moral education. His rule that no child should be shown special preference, that all should be treated with equal respect, is related to his basic moral principle that each human being is an end in himself, something whose existence has in itself an absolute worth. Kant's emphasis on the importance of "maxims" in teaching a child morality is directly related to Kant's general ethical position, according to which the moral worth of an action depends on the principle upon which it is based rather than on the actual consequences of performing the action. These two examples serve as a reminder of the close relationship between a thinker's moral views and his educational views.

Among the unusual aspects of Kant's educational thought is his belief that "novel reading is the worst thing for children, since they can make no further use of it." One may disagree with Kant on this matter, but his view calls attention to the fact that a philosophy of education must supply a justification for each subject which it proposes as a part of the curriculum. Why should one study literature, history, science, mathematics, foreign languages, art, or music? If there is no reason, then these subjects should be replaced with others of greater value.

Careful consideration of the reasons why a particular subject ought to be studied is a rich source of insight into the proper approach which teachers of that subject ought to employ in presenting it to students. If it is understood, for instance, why history ought to be studied, teachers of history will be in a far better position to decide which aspects of history they ought to emphasize in class. In this case, as in so many others, intelligent decisions concerning educational policy necessarily rest on one's views concerning issues in philosophy of education.

THOUGHTS
ON EDUCATION

CHAPTER I
INTRODUCTION

1. Man is the only being who needs education. For by education we must understand nurture (the tending and feeding of the child), discipline *(Zucht)*, and teaching, together with culture.[1] According to this, man is in succession infant (requiring nursing), child (requiring discipline), and scholar (requiring teaching).

2. Animals use their powers, as soon as they are possessed of them, according to a regular plan—that is, in a way not harmful to themselves.

It is indeed wonderful, for instance, that young swallows, when newly hatched and still blind, are careful not to defile their nests.

Animals therefore need no nurture, but at the most, food, warmth, and guidance, or a kind of protection. It is true, most animals need feeding, but they do not require nurture. For by nurture we mean the tender care and attention which parents must bestow upon their children, so as to prevent them from using their powers in a way which would be harmful to themselves. For instance, should an animal cry when it comes into the world, as children do, it would surely become a prey to wolves and other wild animals, which would gather round, attracted by its cry.

3. Discipline changes animal nature into human nature. Animals are by their instinct all that they ever can be; some other reason has provided everything for them at the outset. But man needs a reason of his own. Having no instinct, he has to work out a plan of conduct for himself. Since, however, he is not able to do this all at once, but comes into the world undeveloped, others have to do it for him.

4. All the natural endowments of mankind must be developed little by little out of man himself, through his own effort.

One generation educates the next. The first beginnings of this process of educating may be looked for either in a rude and unformed, or in a fully developed condition of man. If we assume the latter to have come first, man must at all events afterwards have degenerated and lapsed into barbarism.

It is discipline, which prevents man from being turned aside by his animal

[1]Culture *(Bildung)* is used here in the sense of moral training. (Tr.)

From *Kant on Education*, trans. by Annette Churton, London, Routledge & Kegan Paul, Ltd., 1899, pp. 1–94 (with omissions as indicated in the text).

impulses from humanity, his appointed end. Discipline, for instance, must restrain him from venturing wildly and rashly into danger. Discipline, thus, is merely negative, its action being to counteract man's natural unruliness. The positive part of education is instruction.

Unruliness consists in independence of law. By discipline men are placed in subjection to the laws of mankind, and brought to feel their constraint. This, however, must be accomplished early. Children, for instance, are first sent to school, not so much with the object of their learning something, but rather that they may become used to sitting still and doing exactly as they are told. And this to the end that in later life they should not wish to put actually and instantly into practice anything that strikes them.

5. The love of freedom is naturally so strong in man, that when once he has grown accustomed to freedom, he will sacrifice everything for its sake. For this very reason discipline must be brought into play very early; for when this has not been done, it is difficult to alter character later in life. Undisciplined men are apt to follow every caprice.

We see this also among savage nations, who, though they may discharge functions for some time like Europeans, yet can never become accustomed to European manners. With them, however, it is not the noble love of freedom which Rousseau and others imagine, but a kind of barbarism—the animal, so to speak, not having yet developed its human nature. Men should therefore accustom themselves early to yield to the commands of reason, for if a man be allowed to follow his own will in his youth, without opposition, a certain lawlessness will cling to him throughout his life. And it is no advantage to such a man that in his youth he has been spared through an over-abundance of motherly tenderness, for later on all the more will he have to face opposition from all sides, and constantly receive rebuffs, as soon as he enters into the business of the world.

.   .   .

7. Man can only become man by education. He is merely what education makes of him. It is noticeable that man is only educated by man—that is, by men who have themselves been educated. Hence with some people it is want of discipline and instruction on their own part, which makes them in turn unfit educators of their pupils. Were some being of higher nature than man to undertake our education, we should then be able to see what man might become. It is, however, difficult for us accurately to estimate man's natural capabilities, since some things are imparted to man by education, while other things are only developed by education. Were it possible, by the help of those in high rank, and through the united forces of many people, to make an experiment on this question, we might even by this means be able to gain some information as to the degree of eminence which it is possible for man to attain. But it is as important to the speculative mind, as it is sad to one who loves his fellow-men, to see how those in high rank generally care only for their own concerns, and take no part in the important experiments of education, which bring our nature one step nearer to perfection.

There is no one who, having been neglected in his youth, can come to years of discretion without knowing whether the defect lies in discipline or culture (for so we may call instruction). The uncultivated man is crude, the undisciplined is unruly. Neglect of discipline is a greater evil than neglect of culture, for this last can be remedied later in life, but unruliness cannot be done away with, and a mistake in discipline can never be repaired. It may be that education will be constantly improved, and that each succeeding generation will advance one step towards the perfecting of mankind; for with education is involved the great secret of the perfection of human nature. It is only now that something may be done in this direction, since for the first time people have begun to judge rightly, and understand clearly, what actually belongs to a good education. It is delightful to realise that through education human nature will be continually improved, and brought to such a condition as is worthy of the nature of man. This opens out to us the prospect of a happier human race in the future.

8. The prospect of a *theory of education* is a glorious ideal, and it matters little if we are not able to realise it at once. Only we must not look upon the idea as chimerical, nor decry it as a beautiful dream, notwithstanding the difficulties that stand in the way of its realisation.

An idea is nothing else than the conception of a perfection which has not yet been experienced. For instance, the idea of a perfect republic governed by principles of justice—is such an idea impossible, because it has not yet been experienced?

Our idea must in the first place be correct, and then, notwithstanding all the hindrances that still stand in the way of its realisation, it is not at all impossible. Suppose, for instance, lying to become universal, would truth-speaking on that account become nothing but a whim? And the idea of an education which will develop all man's natural gifts is certainly a true one.

9. Under the present educational system man does not fully attain to the object of his being; for in what various ways men live! Uniformity can only result when all men act according to the same principles, which principles would have to become with them a second nature. What we can do is to work out a scheme of education better suited to further its objects, and hand down to posterity directions as to how this scheme may be carried into practice, so that they might be able to realise it gradually. . . .

10. There are many germs lying undeveloped in man. It is for us to make these germs grow, by *developing his natural gifts* in their due proportion, and to see that he fulfils his destiny. Animals accomplish this for themselves unconsciously. Man must strive to attain it, but this he cannot do if he has not even a conception as to the object of his existence. For the individual it is absolutely impossible to attain this object. Let us suppose the first parents to have been fully developed, and see how they educate their children. These first parents set their children an example, which the children imitate and in this way develop some of their own natural gifts. All their gifts cannot, however, be developed in this way, for it all depends on occasional circumstances what examples children see. In times past men had no conception of the perfection to which human nature might attain—even now we have not a very clear idea of the matter. This much, however, is certain: that no individual man, no matter what degree of culture may be reached by his pupils, can insure their attaining their destiny. To succeed in this, not the work of a few individuals only is necessary, but that of the whole human race.

11. Education is an *art* which can only become perfect through the practice of many generations. Each generation, provided with the knowledge of the foregoing one, is able more and more to bring about an education which shall develop man's natural gifts in their due proportion and in relation to their end, and thus advance the whole human race towards its destiny. Providence has willed, that man shall bring forth for himself the good that lies hidden in his nature, and has spoken, as it were, thus to man: "Go forth into the world! I have equipped thee with every tendency towards the good. Thy part let it be to develop those tendencies. Thy happiness and unhappiness depend upon thyself alone."

12. Man must develop his tendency towards *the good.* Providence has not placed goodness ready formed in him, but merely as a tendency and without the distinction of moral law. Man's duty is to improve himself; to cultivate his mind; and, when he finds himself going astray, to bring the moral law to bear upon himself. Upon reflection we shall find this very difficult. Hence the greatest and most difficult problem to which man can devote himself is the problem of education. For insight depends on education, and education in its turn depends on insight. It follows therefore that education can only advance by slow degrees, and a true conception of the method of education can only arise when one generation transmits to the next its stores of experience and knowledge, each generation adding something of its own before transmitting them to the following. . . .

14. Since the development of man's natural gifts does not take place of itself, all education is an art. Nature has placed no instinct in him for that purpose. The *origin* as well as the *carrying out* of this art is either *mechanical* and without plan, ruled by given circumstances, or it involves the exercise of *judgment.* The art of education is only then mechanical, when on chance occasions we learn by experience whether anything is useful or harmful to man. All education which is merely mechanical must carry with it many mistakes and deficiencies, because it has no sure principle to work upon. If education is to develop human nature so that it may attain the object of its being, it must involve the exercise of judgment. Educated parents are examples which children use for their guidance. If, however, the children are to progress beyond their parents, education must become a study, otherwise we can hope for nothing from it, and one man whose education has been spoilt will only repeat his own mistakes in trying to educate others. The mechanism of education must be changed into a science, and one generation may have to pull down what another had built up.

15. One *principle of education* which those men especially who form educational schemes should keep before their eyes is this—children ought to be educated, not for the present, but for a possibly improved condition of man in the future; that is, in a manner which is adapted to the *idea of humanity* and the whole destiny of man. This principle is of great importance. Parents usually educate their children merely in such a manner that, however bad the world may be, they may adapt themselves to its present conditions. But they ought to give them an education so much better than this, that a better condition of things may thereby be brought about in the future.

.   .   .

18. Through education, then, man must be made—

First, subject to *discipline;* by which we must understand that influence which is always restraining our animal nature from getting the better of our manhood, either in the individual as such, or in man as a member of society. Discipline, then, is merely restraining unruliness.

Secondly, education must also supply men with *culture.* This includes information and instruction. It is culture which brings out ability. Ability is the possession of a faculty which is capable of being adapted to various ends. Ability, therefore, does not determine any ends, but leaves that to circumstances as they arise afterwards.

Some accomplishments are essentially good for everybody—reading and writing, for instance; others, merely in the pursuit of certain objects, such as music, which we pursue in order to make ourselves liked. Indeed, the various purposes to which ability may be put are almost endless.

Thirdly, education must also supply a person with *discretion (Klugheit),* so that he may be able to conduct himself in society, that he may be liked, and that he may gain influence. For this a kind of culture is necessary which we call *refinement (Civilisierung).* The latter requires manners, courtesy, and a kind of discretion which will enable him to use all men for his own ends. ...

Fourthly, *moral training* must form a part of education. It is not enough that a man shall be fitted for any end, but his disposition must be so trained that he shall choose none but good ends—good ends being those which are necessarily approved by everyone, and which may at the same time be the aim of everyone.

19. Man may be either broken in, trained, and mechanically taught, or he may be really enlightened. Horses and dogs are broken in; and man, too, may be broken in.

It is, however, not enough that children should be merely broken in; for it is of greater importance that they shall learn to *think.* By learning to think, man comes to act according to fixed principles and not at random. Thus we see that a real education implies a great deal. But as a rule, in our private education *the fourth and most important point is still too much neglected,* children being for the most part educated in such a way that moral training is left to the Church. And yet how important it is that children should learn from their youth up to detest vice!—not merely on the ground that God has forbidden it, but because vice is detestable in itself. If children do not learn this early, they are very likely to think that, if only God had not forbidden it, there would be no harm in practising wickedness, and that it would otherwise be allowed, and that therefore He would probably make an exception now and then. But God is the most holy being, and wills only what is good, and desires that we may love virtue for its own sake, and not merely because He requires it.

· · ·

27. In the first period of childhood the child must learn submission and positive obedience. In the next stage he should be allowed to think for himself, and to enjoy a certain amount of freedom, although still obliged to follow certain rules. In the first period there is a mechanical, in the second a moral constraint.

28. The child's submission is either *positive* or *negative. Positive* in that he is obliged to do what he is told, because he cannot judge for himself, and the faculty of imitation is still strong in him; or *negative*, in that he is obliged to do what others wish him to do, if he wishes others to do him a good turn. In the former case, the consequence of not obeying is punishment; in the latter, the fact that people do not comply with his wishes. He is in this case, though capable of thinking for himself, dependent on others with regard to his own pleasure.

29. One of the greatest problems of education is how to unite submission to the necessary *restraint* with the child's capability of exercising his *freewill* —for restraint is necessary. How am I to develop the sense of freedom in spite of the restraint? I am to accustom my pupil to endure a restraint of his freedom, and at the same time I am to guide him to use his freedom aright. Without this all education is merely mechanical, and the child, when his education is over, will never be able to make a proper use of his freedom. He should be made to feel early the inevitable opposition of society, that he may learn how difficult it is to support himself, to endure privation, and to acquire those things which are necessary to make him independent.

30. Here we must observe the following:—First, we must allow the child from his earliest childhood perfect liberty in every respect (except on those occasions when he might hurt himself—as, for instance, when he clutches at a knife), provided that in acting so he does not interfere with the liberty of others. For instance, as soon as he screams or is too boisterously happy, he annoys others.

Secondly, he must be shown that he can only attain his own ends by allowing others to attain theirs. For instance, should he be disobedient, or refuse to learn his lessons, he ought to be refused any treat he may have been looking forward to.

Thirdly, we must prove to him that restraint is only laid upon him that he may learn in time to use his liberty aright, and that his mind is being cultivated so that one day he may be free; that is, independent of the help of others. This is the last thing a child will come to understand. It is much later in life that children realise such facts as that they will afterwards have to support themselves; for they imagine that they can always go on as they are in their parents' house, and that food and drink will always be provided for them without any trouble on their part. . . .

. . . [W]e see the advantage of public education in that under such a system, we learn to measure our powers with those of others, and to know the limits imposed upon us by the rights of others. Thus we can have no preference shown us, because we meet with opposition everywhere, and we can only make our mark and obtain an advantage over others by real merit. Public education is the best school for future citizens.

.   .   .

31. Education is either *physical* or "practical." One part of physical education is that which man has in common with animals, namely, feeding and tending. *"Practical"* or *moral* training is that which teaches a man how to live as a free being. (We call anything *"practical"* which has reference to freedom.) This is the education of a personal character, of a free being, who is able to maintain himself, and to take his proper place in society, keeping at the same time a proper sense of his own individuality.

32. This *"practical"* education consists, then, of three parts:—

(a) The *ordinary curriculum of the school,* where the child's general ability is developed—the work of the schoolmaster.

(b) Instruction in the practical matters of life—to act with wisdom and discretion—the work of the private tutor or governess.

(c) The training of moral character.

Men need the training of school-teaching or instruction to develop the ability necessary to success in the various vocations of life. School-teaching bestows upon each member an individual value of his own.

Next, by learning the lesson of discretion in the practical matters of life, he is educated as a citizen, and becomes of value to his fellow-citizens, learning both how to accommodate himself to their society and also how to profit by it.

Lastly, moral training imparts to man a value with regard to the whole human race.

33. Of these three divisions of education school-teaching comes *first* in order of time; for a child's abilities must first be developed and trained, otherwise he is incapable of gaining knowledge in the practical matters of life. Discretion is the faculty of using our abilities aright.

Moral training, in as far as it is based upon fundamental principles which a man must himself comprehend, comes last in order of time. In so far, however, as it is based on common sense merely, it must be taken into account from the beginning, at the same time with physical training; for if moral training be omitted, many faults will take root in the child, against which all influences of education at a later stage will be powerless. As to ability and the general knowledge of life, everything must depend entirely upon the age of the pupil. Let a child be clever after the manner of children; let him be shrewd and good-natured in a childish way, but not cunning *(listig)* like a man. The latter is as unsuitable for a child as a childish mind is for a grown-up person.

CHAPTER II
PHYSICAL EDUCATION

47. With regard to the training of character—which we may indeed call also, in a certain sense, physical culture—we must chiefly bear in mind that *discipline* should not be slavish. For a child ought always to be conscious of his freedom, but always in such a way as not to interfere with the liberty of others —in which case he must be met with opposition. Many parents refuse their children everything they ask, in order that they may exercise their patience, but in doing so they require from their children more patience than they have themselves. This is cruel. One ought rather to give a child as much as will agree with him, and then tell him "that is enough"; but this decision must be absolutely final. No attention should ever be given to a child when he cries for anything, and children's wishes should never be complied with if they try to extort something by crying; but if they ask properly, it should be given them, provided it is for their good. By this the child will also become accustomed to being open-minded; and since he does not annoy anyone by his crying, everybody will be friendly towards him.

Providence seems indeed to have given children happy, winning ways, in order that they may gain people's hearts. Nothing does children more harm than to exercise a vexatious and slavish discipline over them with a view to breaking their self-will.

. . .

50. No better than this vexatious system of bringing up children is that of perpetually *playing with* and *caressing* the child; this makes him self-willed and deceitful, and by betraying to him their weakness, parents lose the necessary respect in the eyes of the child. If, on the other hand, he is so trained that he gets nothing by crying for it, he will be frank without being bold, and modest without being timid. *Boldness*, or, what is almost the same thing, *insolence*, is insufferable. There are many men whose constant insolence has given them such an expression that their very look leads one to expect rudeness from them, while you have only to look at others to see at once that they are incapable of being rude to anyone. Now we can always be frank in our demeanour, provided our frankness be united with a certain kindness.

.   .   .

54. The *will* of children . . . must not be broken, but merely bent in such a way that it may yield to natural obstacles. At the beginning, it is true, the child must obey blindly. It is unnatural that a child should command by his crying, and that the strong should obey the weak. Children should never, even in their earliest childhood, be humoured because they cry, nor allowed to extort anything by crying. Parents often make a mistake in this, and then, wishing to undo the result of their over-indulgence, they deny their children in later life whatever they ask for. It is, however, very wrong to refuse them without cause what they may naturally expect from the kindness of their parents, merely for the sake of opposing them, and that they, being the weaker, should be made to feel the superior power of their parents.

55. To grant children their wishes is to *spoil* them; to thwart them purposely is an utterly *wrong way of bringing them up.* The former generally happens as long as they are the playthings of their parents, and especially during the time when they are beginning to talk. By spoiling a child, however, very great harm is done, affecting its whole life. Those who thwart the wishes of children prevent them (and must necessarily prevent them) at the same time from showing their anger; but their inward rage will be all the stronger, for children have not yet learned to control themselves.

The following rules should accordingly be observed with children from their earliest days:—When they cry, and we have reason to believe they are hurt, we should go to their help. On the other hand, when they cry simply from temper, they should be left alone. And this way of dealing with them should be continued as they grow older. In this case the opposition the child meets with is quite natural, and, properly speaking, merely negative, consisting simply in his not being indulged. Many children, on the other hand, get all they want from their parents by persistent asking. If children are allowed to get whatever they want by crying, they become ill-tempered; while if they are allowed to get whatever they want by asking, their characters are weakened. Should there, then, be no important reason to the contrary, a child's request should be granted; should there be a reason to the contrary, it should not be granted, no matter how often the request is repeated. A refusal should always be final. This will shortly have the effect of making its repetition unnecessary.

56. Supposing—what is of extremely rare occurrence—that a child should be naturally inclined to be *stubborn*, it is best to deal with him in this way:— If he refuses to do anything to please us, we must refuse to do anything to please him.

Breaking a child's will makes him a slave, while natural opposition makes him docile.

.   .   .

CHAPTER IV
CULTIVATION OF THE MIND

63. We come now to the *cultivation of the mind,* which also we may call, in a certain sense, physical. . . .

This physical cultivation of the mind, however, must be distinguished from moral training, in that it aims only at nature, while moral training aims at freedom. A man may be highly cultivated physically, he may have a well-cultivated mind; but if he lacks moral culture, he will be a wicked man.

.   .   .

65. Various plans of education have been drawn up by different people, in order to discover the best methods—a most praiseworthy undertaking. One among others suggests that children should be allowed to *learn everything as it were in play.* . . . This is an utterly preposterous notion. A child must play, must have his hours of recreation; but he must also learn to work. It is a good thing, doubtless, to exercise skill, as it is to cultivate the mind, but these two kinds of culture should have their separate hours. Moreover, it is a great misfortune for man that he is by nature so inclined to inaction. The longer a man gives way to this inclination, the more difficult will he find it to make up his mind to work.

66. In *work* the occupation is not pleasant in itself, but it is undertaken for the sake of the end in view. In *games,* on the other hand, the occupation is pleasant in itself without having any other end in view. When we go for a walk, we do so for the sake of the walk, and therefore the further we go the pleasanter it is; while when we go to a certain place, our object is the company which we shall find there, or something else, and therefore we shall naturally choose the shortest way. The same thing happens in card games. It is really extraordinary how reasonable men can sit by the hour and shuffle cards. It is not, it seems, so easy for men to leave off being children. For how is this a better game than the children's game of ball? It is true that grown men do not care to ride hobby-horses, but they ride other hobbies.

67. It is of the greatest importance that children should learn to work. Man is the only animal who is obliged to work. He must go through a long apprenticeship before he can enjoy anything for his own sustenance. The question whether Heaven would not have shown us greater kindness by supplying all our wants without the necessity of work on our part must certainly be answered in the negative, for man needs occupation, even occupation that involves a certain amount of restraint. Just as false a notion is it that if Adam and Eve had only remained in Paradise they would have done nothing there but sit together singing pastoral songs and admiring the beauty of Nature. Were this so, they would have been tormented with *ennui,* just as much as other people in the same position.

Men ought to be occupied in such a way that, filled with the idea of the end which they have before their eyes, they are not conscious of themselves, and the best rest for them is the rest which follows work. In the same way a child must become accustomed to work, and where can the inclination to work be cultivated so well as at school? School is a place of compulsory culture. It is very bad for a child to learn to look upon everything as play. He must, it is true, have his time for recreation, but he must also have his time for work. Even though the child does not at once understand the use of this restraint, later in life he will recognise its value. It would be merely training the child to bad habits of inquisitiveness were one always to answer his questions: "What is the use of this?" or, "What is the use of that?" Education must be compulsory, but it need not therefore be slavish.

68. With regard to the *"free"* cultivation of the *mental faculties,* we must remember that this cultivation is going on constantly. It really deals with the superior faculties. The inferior faculties must be cultivated along with them, but only with a view to the superior; for instance, the intelligence with a view to the understanding—the principal rule that we should follow being that no mental faculty is to be cultivated by itself, but always in relation to others; for instance, the imagination to the advantage of the understanding.

The inferior faculties have no value in themselves; for instance, a man who has a good memory, but no judgment. Such a man is merely a walking dictionary. These beasts of burden of Parnassus are of some use, however, for if they cannot do anything useful themselves they at least furnish material out of which others may produce something good. Intelligence divorced from judgment produces nothing but foolishness. Understanding is the knowledge of the general. Judgment is the application of the general to the particular. Reason is the power of understanding the connection between the general and the particular. This free culture runs its course from childhood onwards till the time that the young man is released from all education. When a young man, for instance, quotes a general rule, we may make him quote examples drawn from history or fable in which this rule is disguised, passages from the poets where it is expressed, and thus encourage him to exercise both his intelligence and his memory, &c.

69. The maxim *Tantum scimus, quantum memoria tenemus*[2] is quite true —hence it is very necessary to cultivate the memory. Things are so constituted that the understanding first follows the mental impression, and the memory must preserve this impression. So it is, for instance, in languages. We learn them either by the formal method of committing them to memory or by conversation—this last being the best method for modern languages. The learning of words is really necessary, but the best plan is for the youth to learn words as he comes across them in the author he is reading. The youth should have a certain set task. In the same way geography is best learnt mechanically. What is learnt in a mechanical way is best retained by the memory, and in a great many cases this way is indeed very useful. The proper mechanism for the study of history has yet to be found. An attempt has been made in this direction consisting of a system of tables, but the result has not been very satisfactory. History, however, is an excellent means of exercising the understanding in judging rightly. Learning by heart is very necessary, but doing it merely for the sake of exercising the memory is of no use educationally—for instance, the learning of a speech by heart. At all events, it only serves to encourage forwardness. Besides this, declamation is only proper for grown-up men. The same may be said of all those things which we learn merely for some future examination or with a view to *futuram oblivionem*.[3] The memory should only be occupied with such things as are important to be retained, and which will be of service to us in real life. Novel-reading is the worst thing for children, since they can make no further use of it, and it merely affords them entertainment for the moment. Novel-reading weakens the memory. For it would be ridiculous to remember novels in order to relate them to others. Therefore all novels should be taken away from children. Whilst reading them they weave, as it were, an inner romance of their own, rearranging the circumstances for themselves; their fancy is thus imprisoned, but there is no exercise of thought.

Distractions must never be allowed, least of all in school, for the result will be a certain propensity in that direction which might soon grow into a habit. Even the finest talents may be wasted when once a man is subject to distraction. Although children are inattentive at their games, they soon recall their attention. We may notice, however, that they are most distracted when they are thinking of some mischief, for then they are contriving either how to hide it, or else how to repair the evil done. They then only half hear anything, give wrong answers, and know nothing about what they are reading, &c.

70. The memory must be cultivated early, but we must be careful to cultivate the understanding at the same time.

The memory is cultivated (i) by learning the names which are met with in tales, (ii) by reading and writing. But as to reading, children should practise it with the head, without depending on the spelling. (iii) By languages, which children should first learn by hearing, before they read anything.

[2] We know just so much as we remember.
[3] Future forgetfulness.

Then a well-constructed so-called *orbis pictus* will prove very useful. We might begin with botany, mineralogy, and natural history in general. In order to make sketches of these objects, drawing and modelling will have to be learned, and for this some knowledge of mathematics is necessary. The first lessons in science will most advantageously be directed to the study of geography, mathematical as well as physical. Tales of travel, illustrated by pictures and maps, will lead on to political geography. From the present condition of the earth's surface we go back to its earlier condition, and this leads us to ancient geography, ancient history, and so on.

But in teaching children we must seek insensibly to unite knowledge with the carrying out of that knowledge into practice. Of all the sciences, mathematics seems to be the one that best fulfils this. Further, knowledge and speech (ease in speaking, fluency, eloquence) must be united. The child, however, must learn also to distinguish clearly between knowledge and mere opinion and belief. Thus we prepare the way for a right understanding, and a *right*—not a *refined* or *delicate*—taste. This taste must at first be that of the senses, especially the eyes, but ultimately of ideas.

71. It is necessary to have rules for everything which is intended to cultivate the understanding. It is very useful mentally to separate the rules, that the understanding may proceed not merely mechanically, but with the consciousness of following a rule.

It is also very useful to bring these rules into a set form, and thus commit them to memory. If we keep the rule in our memory, though we forget its application, we shall soon find our way again.

Here the question arises whether the rules shall first be studied *in abstracto*, and whether they ought to be studied after they have been applied, or whether the rule and its application should be studied side by side. This last is the only advisable course; otherwise the application of the rule is very uncertain till the rule itself is learned.

But from time to time the rules must also be arranged in classes, for it is difficult to keep them in memory when they are not associated together. Consequently in learning languages the study of grammar must always, to a certain extent, come first.

72. We must now give a systematic idea of the whole aim of education, and the means of obtaining it.

I. *The general cultivation of the mental faculties, as distinguished from the cultivation of particular mental faculties.*—This aims at skill and perfection, and has not for its object the imparting of any particular knowledge, but the general strengthening of the mental faculties.

This culture is either (a) *physical*—here everything depends upon exercise and discipline, without the child needing to learn any "maxims"; it is passive for the pupil, who has only to follow the guidance of others—or (b) it is moral. This depends not upon discipline, but upon "maxims."[4] All will be spoilt if

---

[4] "Maxim" is an important term in Kant's *Moral Philosophy*, and by it must be understood general principles of right and wrong. (Tr.)

moral training rests upon examples, threats, punishments, and so on. It would then be merely discipline. We must see that the child does right on account of his own "maxims," and not merely from habit; and not only that he does right, but that he does it because it is right. For the whole moral value of actions consists in "maxims" concerning the good.

Physical education, then, is distinguished from moral in the former being passive, while the latter is active, for the child. He should always understand the principle of an action, and its relation to the idea of duty.

73. II. The cultivation of particular mental faculties.—This includes the cultivation of the faculty of cognition, of the senses, the imagination, memory, power of attention, and intelligence—in a word, the inferior powers of the understanding.

Of the cultivation of the senses—eyesight, for instance—we have already spoken. As to the cultivation of the imagination, the following is to be noticed: —Children generally have a very lively imagination, which does not need to be expanded or made more intense by the reading of fairy tales. It needs rather to be curbed and brought under rule, but at the same time should not be left quite unoccupied. There is something in maps which attracts everybody, even the smallest children. When they are tired of everything else, they will still learn something by means of maps. And this is a good amusement for children, for here their imagination is not allowed to rove, since it must, as it were, confine itself to certain figures. We might really begin with geography in teaching children. Figures of animals, plants, and so on, might be added at the same time; these will make the study of geography more lively. History, however, would probably have to come later on.

With regard to the power of attention, we may remark that this faculty needs general strengthening. The power of rigidly fixing our thoughts upon one object is not so much a talent as a weakness of our mind, which in this case is inflexible, and does not allow itself to be applied at pleasure. But distraction is the enemy of all education. Memory depends upon our attention.

74. As regards the cultivation of the *superior mental faculties,* this includes the cultivation of the understanding, judgment, and reason. The understanding may at first be cultivated, in a certain way, passively also, either by quoting examples which prove the rules, or, on the contrary, by discovering rules for particular cases. The judgment shows us what use to make of the understanding. Understanding is necessary in order that we may understand what we learn or say, and that we may not repeat anything without understanding it. How many people hear and read things which they do not understand, though they believe them! Of that kind are both images and real things.

It is through reason that we get an insight into principles. But we must remember that we are speaking here of a reason which still needs guidance. Hence the child should not be encouraged to be always reasoning, nor should we indulge in reasoning in the presence of children, about things which surpass their conception.

We are not dealing here with speculative reason, but only with reflection upon actual occurrences, according to their causes and effects. It is in its arrangement and working a practical reason.

75. The best way of cultivating the mental faculties is to *do ourselves* all that we wish to accomplish; for instance, by carrying out into practice the grammatical rule which we have learnt. We understand a map best when we are able to draw it out for ourselves. The best way to understand is to do. That which we learn most thoroughly, and remember the best, is what we have in a way taught ourselves. There are but few men, however, who are capable of doing this. They are called self-taught (αὐτοδίδακτοι).

76. In the culture of *reason* we must proceed according to the Socratic method. Socrates, who called himself the midwife of his hearers' knowledge, gives examples in his dialogues, which Plato has in a manner preserved for us, of the way in which, even in the case of grown-up people, ideas may be drawn forth from their own individual reason. In many respects children need not exercise their reason. They must not be allowed to argue about everything. It is not necessary for them to know the principles of everything connected with their education; but when the question of duty arises, they should be made to understand those principles. But on the whole we should try to draw out their own ideas, founded on reason, rather than to introduce such ideas into their minds. The Socratic method should form, then, the rule for the catechetical method. True it is somewhat slow, and it is difficult to manage so that in drawing ideas out of one child the others shall also learn something. The mechanical method of catechising is also useful in some sciences; for instance, in the explanation of revealed religion. In universal religion, on the other hand, we must employ the Socratic method. As to what has to be learnt historically, the mechanical method of catechising is much to be commended.

CHAPTER V
MORAL CULTURE

77. *Moral culture* must be based upon "maxims," not upon discipline; the one prevents evil habits, the other trains the mind to think. We must see, then, that the child should accustom himself to act in accordance with "maxims," and not from certain ever-changing springs of action. Through discipline we form certain habits, moreover, the force of which becomes lessened in the course of years. The child should learn to act according to "maxims," the reasonableness of which he is able to see for himself. One can easily see that there is some difficulty in carrying out this principle with young children, and that moral culture demands a great deal of insight on the part of parents and teachers.

Supposing a child tells a lie, for instance, he ought not to be punished, but treated with contempt, and told that he will not be believed in the future, and the like. If you punish a child for being naughty, and reward him for being good, he will do right merely for the sake of the reward; and when he goes out into the world and finds that goodness is not always rewarded, nor wickedness always punished, he will grow into a man who only thinks about how he may get on in the world, and does right or wrong according as he finds either of advantage to himself.

78. *"Maxims"* ought to originate in the human being as such. In moral training we should seek early to infuse into children ideas as to what is right and wrong. If we wish to establish morality, we must abolish punishment. Morality is something so sacred and sublime that we must not degrade it by placing it in the same rank as discipline. The first endeavour in moral education is the formation of character. Character consists in readiness to act in accordance with "maxims." At first they are school "maxims," and later "maxims" of mankind. At first the child obeys rules. "Maxims" are also rules, but subjective rules. They proceed from the understanding of man. No infringement of school discipline must be allowed to go unpunished, although the punishment must always fit the offence.

79. If we wish to *form the characters* of children, it is of the greatest importance to point out to them a certain plan, and certain rules, in everything; and these must be strictly adhered to. For instance, they must have set times for sleep, for work, and for pleasure; and these times must be neither shortened nor lengthened. With indifferent matters children might be allowed to choose for themselves, but having once made a rule they must always follow it. We must, however, form in children the character of a child, and not the character of a citizen.

Unmethodical men are not to be relied on; it is difficult to understand them, and to know how far we are to trust them. It is true we often blame people who always act by rule—for instance, the man who does everything by the clock, having a fixed hour for every one of his actions—but we blame them often unreasonably, for this exactness, though it looks like pedantry, goes far towards helping the formation of character.

80. Above all things, obedience is an essential feature in the character of a child, especially of a school boy or girl. This obedience is twofold, including absolute obedience to his master's commands, and obedience to what he feels to be a good and reasonable will. Obedience may be the result of compulsion; it is then *absolute:* or it may arise out of confidence; it is then obedience of the second kind. This *voluntary* obedience is very important, but the former is also very necessary, for it prepares the child for the fulfilment of laws that he will have to obey later, as a citizen, even though he may not like them.

81. Children, then, must be subject to a certain law of *necessity.* This law, however, must be a general one—a rule which has to be kept constantly in view, especially in schools. The master must not show any predilection or preference for one child above others; for thus the law would cease to be general. As soon as a child sees that the other children are not all placed under the same rules as himself, he will at once become refractory.

82. One often hears it said that we should put everything before children in such a way that they shall do it from *inclination*. In some cases, it is true, this is all very well, but there is much besides which we must place before them as *duty*. And this will be of great use to them throughout their life. For in the paying of rates and taxes, in the work of the office, and in many other cases, we must be led, not by inclination, but by duty. Even though a child should not be able to see the reason of a duty, it is nevertheless better that certain things should be prescribed to him in this way; for, after all, a child will always be able to see that he has certain duties as a child, while it will be more difficult for him to see that he has certain duties as a human being. Were he able to understand this also—which, however, will only be possible in the course of years—his obedience would be still more perfect.

83. Every transgression of a command in a child is a want of obedience, and this brings *punishment* with it. Also, should a command be disobeyed through inattention, punishment is still necessary. This punishment is either *physical* or *moral.* It is *moral* when we do something derogatory to the child's longing to be honoured and loved (a longing which is an aid to moral training); for instance, when we humiliate the child by treating him coldly and distantly. This longing of children should, however, be cultivated as much as possible. Hence this kind of punishment is the best, since it is an aid to moral training —for instance, if a child tells a lie, a look of contempt is punishment enough, and punishment of a most appropriate kind.

Physical punishment consists either in refusing a child's requests or in the infliction of pain. The first is akin to moral punishment, and is of a negative kind. The second form must be used with caution, lest an *indoles servilis*[5] should be the result. It is of no use to give children rewards; this makes them selfish, and gives rise to an *indoles mercenaria.*[6]

84. Further, obedience is either that of the child or that of the *youth.* Disobedience is always followed by punishment. This is either a really *natural* punishment, which a man brings upon himself by his own behaviour—for instance, when a child gets ill from over-eating—and this kind of punishment is the best, since a man is subject to it throughout his life, and not merely during his childhood; or, on the other hand, the punishment is artificial. By taking into consideration the child's desire to be loved and respected, such punishments may be chosen as will have a lasting effect upon its character. Physical punishments must merely supplement the insufficiency of moral punishment. If moral punishment have no effect at all, and we have at last to resort to physical punishment, we shall find after all that no good character is formed in this way. At the beginning, however, physical restraint may serve to take the place of reflection.

[5] A slavish disposition.
[6] The disposition of a hireling.

85. Punishments inflicted with signs of *anger* are useless. Children then look upon the punishment simply as the result of anger, and upon themselves merely as the victims of that anger; and as a general rule punishment must be inflicted on children with great caution, that they may understand that its one aim is their improvement.... If physical punishment is often repeated, it makes a child stubborn; and if parents punish their children for obstinacy, they often become all the more obstinate. Besides, it is not always the worst men who are obstinate, and they will often yield easily to kind remonstrance.

86. The obedience of the growing *youth* must be distinguished from the obedience of the *child.* The former consists in submission to rules of duty. To do something for the sake of duty means obeying reason. It is in vain to speak to children of duty. They look upon it in the end as something which if not fulfilled will be followed by the rod. A child may be guided by mere instinct. As he grows up, however, the idea of duty must come in. Also the idea of shame should not be made use of with children, but only with those who have left childhood for youth. For it cannot exist with them till the idea of honour has first taken root.

87. The second principal feature in the formation of a child's character is *truthfulness.* This is the foundation and very essence of character. A man who tells lies has no character, and if he has any good in him it is merely the result of a certain kind of temperament. Some children have an inclination towards lying, and this frequently for no other reason than that they have a lively imagination. It is the father's business to see that they are broken of this habit, for mothers generally look upon it as a matter of little or no importance, even finding in it a flattering proof of the cleverness and ability of their children. This is the time to make use of the sense of shame, for the child in this case will understand it well. The blush of shame betrays us when we lie, but it is not always a proof of it, for we often blush at the shamelessness of others who accuse us of guilt. On no condition must we punish children to force the truth from them, unless their telling a lie immediately results in some mischief; *then* they may be punished for that mischief. The withdrawal of respect is the only fit punishment for lying.

Punishments may be divided into *negative* and *positive* punishments. The first may be applied to laziness or viciousness; for instance, lying, disobedience. Positive punishment may be applied to acts of spitefulness. But above all things we must take care never to bear children a grudge.

88. A third feature in the child's character is *sociableness.* He must form friendships with other children, and not be always by himself. Some teachers, it is true, are opposed to these friendships in schools, but this is a great mistake. Children ought to prepare themselves for the sweetest enjoyment of life.

If a teacher allows himself to prefer one child to another, it must be on account of its character, and not for the sake of any talents the child may possess; otherwise jealousy will arise, which is opposed to friendship.

Children ought to be open-hearted and cheerful in their looks as the sun. A joyful heart alone is able to find its happiness in the good. A religion which makes people gloomy is a false religion; for we should serve God with a joyful heart, and not of constraint.

Children should sometimes be released from the narrow constraint of school, otherwise their natural joyousness will soon be quenched. When the child is set free he soon recovers his natural elasticity. Those games in which children, enjoying perfect freedom, are ever trying to outdo one another, will serve this purpose best, and they will soon make their minds bright and cheerful again.

89. Many people imagine that the years of their youth are the pleasantest and best of their lives; but it is not really so. They are the most troublesome; for we are then under strict discipline, can seldom choose our own friends, and still more seldom can we have our freedom. As Horace says: *Multa tulit, fecitque puer, sudavit et alsit.*[7]

90. Children should only be taught those things which are suited to their age. Many parents are pleased with the precocity of their offspring; but as a rule, nothing will come of such children. A child should be clever, but only as a child. He should not ape the manners of his elders. For a child to provide himself with moral sentences proper to manhood is to go quite beyond his province and to become merely an imitator. He ought to have merely the understanding of a child, and not seek to display it too early. A precocious child will never become a man of insight and clear understanding. It is just as much out of place for a child to follow all the fashions of the time, to curl his hair, wear ruffles, and even carry a snuff-box. He will thus acquire affected manners not becoming to a child. Polite society is a burden to him, and he entirely lacks a man's heart. For that very reason we must set ourselves early to fight against all signs of vanity in a child; or, rather, we must give him no occasion to become vain. This easily happens by people prattling before children, telling them how beautiful they are, and how well this or that dress becomes them, and promising them some finery or other as a reward. Finery is not suitable for children. They must accept their neat and simple clothes as necessaries merely.

At the same time the parents must not set great store by their own clothes, nor admire themselves; for here, as everywhere, example is all-powerful, and either strengthens or destroys good precepts. . . .

[7]The lad [who hopes to win the race] has borne and done much; he has endured extremes of heat and cold.

PART II

Modern Philosophies of Education

John Dewey

(1859-1952)

JOHN DEWEY is the only thinker who has constructed a philosophy of education comparable in scope and depth to that of Plato. While Plato's educational philosophy rests upon his belief in aristocracy and the power of pure reason, Dewey's educational philosophy rests upon his belief in democracy and the power of scientific method.

A democratic society, according to Dewey, is one "which makes provision for participation in its good of all its members on equal terms and which secures flexible readjustment of its institutions through interaction of the different forms of associated life." It is Dewey's view that the class society outlined in *The Republic* results in the subordination of individuality. What Plato failed to note is that "each individual constitutes his own class."

Dewey considers scientific method to consist in "observation, reflection, and testing . . . deliberately adopted to secure a settled, assured subject matter." It is the essence of his position that utilization of this method is effective not only in science but in all aspects of life. "Science is experience becoming rational," and rationality or reasonableness has proven to be the most reliable method of reaching the truth, no matter what the field of inquiry. What Plato overlooked is that "there is no such thing as genuine knowledge and fruitful understanding except as the offspring of *doing*" and that "knowledge furnishes the means of understanding . . . what is to be done." In short, one acquires knowledge by intelligent action, and the possession of knowledge enables one to act more intelligently.

Dewey's insights into the educational process are so numerous and so subtle that it is impossible to summarize them adequately. It is important, however, to warn the reader that Dewey's ideas have been constantly misinterpreted, and views are attributed to him which are exactly the opposite of those which he explicitly espouses.

It is often said, for example, that Dewey defended the idea that children should not be disciplined and should be left free to do whatever they choose. Nothing could be further from the truth. Dewey's actual view, which he stated on numerous occasions, is that "it is . . . fatal . . . to permit capricious or discontinuous action in the name of spontaneous self-expression."

Dewey is also often accused of defending the view that subject matter should be taught only for its future practical value and not for its present intrinsic value. Again, nothing could be further from the truth. As Dewey wrote, "it is true of arithmetic as it is of poetry that . . . it ought to be a good to be appreciated on its own account—just as an enjoyable experience. . . . Every subject at some phase of its development should possess, what is for the individual concerned with it, an aesthetic quality."

The first selection that follows is taken from Dewey's masterpiece, *Democracy and Education.* It is strongly recommended that, if time permits, this work should be read in its entirety. The second selection is a booklet that Dewey wrote in response to certain developments in education, which under the guise of carrying out his educational principles actually distorted and misapplied them. This booklet contains a remarkably clear and concise presentation of Dewey's philosophy of education, and a careful reading should help to forestall future misinterpretations of his thought.

DEMOCRACY
AND EDUCATION

CHAPTER XII
THINKING IN EDUCATION

1. THE ESSENTIALS OF METHOD

No one doubts, theoretically, the importance of fostering in school good habits of thinking. But apart from the fact that the acknowledgment is not so great in practice as in theory, there is not adequate theoretical recognition that all which the school can or need do for pupils, so far as their *minds* are concerned (that is, leaving out certain specialized muscular abilities), is to develop their ability to think. The parceling out of instruction among various ends such as acquisition of skill (in reading, spelling, writing, drawing, reciting); acquiring information (in history and geography), *and* training of thinking is a measure of the ineffective way in which we accomplish all three. Thinking which is not connected with increase of efficiency in action, and with learning more about ourselves and the world in which we live, has something the matter with it just as thought. . . . And skill obtained apart from thinking is not connected with any sense of the purposes for which it is to be used. It consequently leaves a man at the mercy of his routine habits and of the authoritative control of others, who know what they are about and who are not especially scrupulous as to their means of achievement. And information severed from thoughtful action is dead, a mind-crushing load. Since it simulates knowledge and thereby develops the poison of conceit, it is a most powerful obstacle to further growth in the grace of intelligence. The sole direct path to enduring improvement in the methods of instruction and learning consists in centering upon the conditions which exact, promote, and test thinking. Thinking *is* the method of intelligent learning, of learning that employs and rewards mind. We speak, legitimately enough, about the method of thinking, but the important thing to bear in mind about method is that thinking is method, the method of intelligent experience in the course which it takes.

1. The initial stage of that developing experience which is called thinking is *experience*. This remark may sound like a silly truism. It ought to be one; but unfortunately it is not. On the contrary, thinking is often regarded both in philosophic theory and in educational practice as something cut off from experience, and capable of being cultivated in isolation. In fact, the inherent limitations of experience are often urged as the sufficient ground for attention to thinking. Experience is then thought to be confined to the senses and appetites; to a mere material world, while thinking proceeds from a higher faculty (of reason), and is occupied with spiritual or at least literary things. So, oftentimes, a sharp distinction is made between pure mathematics as a peculiarly fit subject matter of thought (since it has nothing to do with physical existences) and applied mathematics, which has utilitarian but not mental value.

Speaking generally, the fundamental fallacy in methods of instruction lies in supposing that experience on the part of pupils may be assumed. What is here insisted upon is the necessity of an actual empirical situation as the initiating phase of thought. Experience is here taken as previously defined: trying to do something and having the thing perceptibly do something to one in return. The fallacy consists in supposing that we can begin with ready-made subject matter of arithmetic, or geography, or whatever, irrespective of some direct personal experience of a situation. Even the kindergarten and Montessori techniques are so anxious to get at intellectual distinctions, without "waste of time," that they tend to ignore—or reduce—the immediate crude handling of the familiar material of experience, and to introduce pupils at once to material which expresses the intellectual distinctions which adults have made. But the first stage of contact with any new material, at whatever age of maturity, must inevitably be of the trial and error sort. An individual must actually try, in play or work, to do something with material in carrying out his own impulsive activity, and then note the interaction of his energy and that of the material employed. This is what happens when a child at first begins to build with blocks, and it is equally what happens when a scientific man in his laboratory begins to experiment with unfamiliar objects.

Hence the first approach to any subject in school, if thought is to be aroused and not words acquired, should be as unscholastic as possible. To realize what an experience, or empirical situation, means, we have to call to mind the sort of situation that presents itself outside of school; the sort of occupations that interest and engage activity in ordinary life. And careful inspection of methods which are permanently successful in formal education, whether in arithmetic or learning to read, or studying geography, or learning physics or a foreign language, will reveal that they depend for their efficiency upon the fact that they go back to the type of the situation which causes reflection out of school in ordinary life. They give the pupils something to do, not something to learn; and the doing is of such a nature as to demand thinking, or the intentional noting of connections; learning naturally results.

That the situation should be of such a nature as to arouse thinking means of course that it should suggest something to do which is not either routine or capricious—something, in other words, presenting what is new (and hence uncertain or problematic) and yet sufficiently connected with existing habits to call out an effective response. An effective response means one which accomplishes a perceptible result, in distinction from a purely haphazard activity, where the consequences cannot be mentally connected with what is done. The most significant question which can be asked, accordingly, about any situation or experience proposed to induce learning is what quality of problem it involves.

At first thought, it might seem as if usual school methods measured well up to the standard here set. The giving of problems, the putting of questions, the assigning of tasks, the magnifying of difficulties, is a large part of school work. But it is indispensable to discriminate between genuine and simulated or mock problems. The following questions may aid in making such discrimination. (a) Is there anything *but* a problem? Does the question naturally suggest itself within some situation of personal experience? Or is it an aloof thing, a problem only for the purposes of conveying instruction in some school topic? Is it the sort of trying that would arouse observation and engage experimentation outside of school? (b) Is it the pupil's own problem, or is it the teacher's or textbook's problem, made a problem for the pupil only because he cannot get the required mark or be promoted or win the teacher's approval, unless he deals with it? Obviously, these two questions overlap. They are two ways of getting at the same point: Is the experience a personal thing of such a nature as inherently to stimulate and direct observation of the connections involved, and to lead to inference and its testing? Or is it imposed from without, and is the pupil's problem simply to meet the external requirement?

Such questions may give us pause in deciding upon the extent to which current practices are adapted to develop reflective habits. The physical equipment and arrangements of the average schoolroom are hostile to the existence of real situations of experience. What is there similar to the conditions of everyday life which will generate difficulties? Almost everything testifies to the great premium put upon listening, reading, and the reproduction of what is told and read. It is hardly possible to overstate the contrast between such conditions and the situations of active contact with things and persons in the home, on the playground, in fulfilling of ordinary responsibilities of life. Much of it is not even comparable with the questions which may arise in the mind of a boy or girl in conversing with others or in reading books outside of the school. No one has ever explained why children are so full of questions outside of the school (so that they pester grown-up persons if they get any encouragement), and the conspicuous absence of display of curiosity about the subject matter of school lessons. Reflection on this striking contrast will throw light upon the question of how far customary school conditions supply a context of experience in which problems naturally suggest themselves. No amount of improvement in the personal technique of the instructor will wholly remedy this state of things. There must be more actual material, more *stuff,* more appliances, and more opportunities for doing things, before the gap can be overcome. And where children are engaged in doing things and in discussing what arises in the course of their doing, it is found, even with comparatively indifferent modes of instruction, that children's inquiries are spontaneous and numerous, and the proposals of solution advanced, varied, and ingenious.

As a consequence of the absence of the materials and occupations which generate real problems, the pupil's problems are not his; or, rather, they are his *only* as a pupil, not as a human being. Hence the lamentable waste in carrying over such expertness as is achieved in dealing with them to the affairs of life beyond the schoolroom. A pupil has a problem, but it is the problem of meeting the peculiar requirements set by the teacher. His problem becomes that of finding out what the teacher wants, what will satisfy the teacher in recitation and examination and outward deportment. Relationship to subject matter is no longer direct. The occasions and material of thought are not found in the arithmetic or the history or geography itself, but in skillfully adapting that material to the teacher's requirements. The pupil studies, but unconsciously to himself the objects of his study are the conventions and standards of the school system and school authority, not the nominal "studies." The thinking thus evoked is artificially one-sided at the best. At its worst, the problem of the pupil is not how to meet the requirements of school life, but how to *seem* to meet them—or, how to come near enough to meeting them to slide along without an undue amount of friction. The type of judgment formed by these devices is not a desirable addition to character. If these statements give too highly colored a picture of usual school methods, the exaggeration may at least serve to illustrate the point: the need of active pursuits, involving the use of material to accomplish purposes, if there are to be situations which normally generate problems occasioning thoughtful inquiry.

2. There must be *data* at command to supply the considerations required in dealing with the specific difficulty which has presented itself. Teachers following a "developing" method sometimes tell children to think things out for themselves as if they could spin them out of their own heads. The material of thinking is not thoughts, but actions, facts, events, and the relations of things. In other words, to think effectively one must have had, or now have, experiences which will furnish him resources for coping with the difficulty at hand. A difficulty is an indispensable stimulus to thinking, but not all difficulties call out thinking. Sometimes they overwhelm and submerge and discourage. The perplexing situation must be sufficiently like situations which have already been dealt with so that pupils will have some control of the means of handling it. A large part of the art of instruction lies in making the difficulty of new problems large enough to challenge thought, and small enough so that, in addition to the confusion naturally attending the novel elements, there shall be luminous familiar spots from which helpful suggestions may spring.

In one sense, it is a matter of indifference by what psychological means the subject matter for reflection is provided. Memory, observation, reading, communication, are all avenues for supplying data. The relative proportion to be obtained from each is a matter of the specific features of the particular problem in hand. It is foolish to insist upon observation of objects presented to the senses if the student is so familiar with the objects that he could just as well recall the facts independently. It is possible to induce undue and crippling dependence upon sense-presentations. No one can carry around with him a museum of all the things whose properties will assist the conduct of thought. A well-trained mind is one that has a maximum of resources behind it, so to speak, and that is accustomed to go over its past experiences to see what they yield. On the other hand, a quality or relation of even a familiar object may previously have been passed over, and be just the fact that is helpful in dealing with the question. In this case direct observation is called for. The same principle applies to the use to be made of observation on one hand and of reading and "telling" on the other. Direct observation is naturally more vivid and vital. But it has its limitations; and in any case it is a necessary part of education that one should acquire the ability to supplement the narrowness of his immediately personal experiences by utilizing the experiences of others. Excessive reliance upon others for data (whether got from reading or listening) is to be depreciated. Most objectionable of all is the probability that others, the book or the teacher, will supply solutions ready-made, instead of giving material that the student has to adapt and apply to the question in hand for himself.

There is no inconsistency in saying that in schools there is usually both too much and too little information supplied by others. The accumulation and acquisition of information for purposes of reproduction in recitation and examination is made too much of. "Knowledge," in the sense of information, means the working capital, the indispensable resources, of further inquiry; of finding out, or learning, more things. Frequently it is treated as an end itself, and then the goal becomes to heap it up and display it when called for. This static, cold-storage ideal of knowledge is inimical to educative development. It not only lets occasions for thinking go unused, but it swamps thinking. No one could construct a house on ground cluttered with miscellaneous junk. Pupils who have stored their "minds" with all kinds of material which they have never put to intellectual uses are sure to be hampered when they try to think. They have no practice in selecting what is appropriate, and no criterion to go by; everything is on the same dead static level. On the other hand, it is quite open to question whether, if information actually functioned in experience through use in application to the student's own purposes, there would not be need of more varied resources in books, pictures, and talks than are usually at command.

3. The correlate in thinking of facts, data, knowledge already acquired, is suggestions, inferences, conjectured meanings, suppositions, tentative expla-

nations:—*ideas*, in short. Careful observation and recollection determine what is given, what is already there, and hence assured. They cannot furnish what is lacking. They define, clarify, and locate the question; they cannot supply its answer. Projection, invention, ingenuity, devising come in for that purpose. The data *arouse* suggestions, and only by reference to the specific data can we pass upon the appropriateness of the suggestions. But the suggestions run beyond what is, as yet, actually *given* in experience. They forecast possible results, things *to* do, not facts (things already done). Inference is always an invasion of the unknown, a leap from the known.

In this sense, a thought (what a thing suggests but is not as it is presented) is creative,—an incursion into the novel. It involves some inventiveness. What is suggested must, indeed, be familiar in *some* context; the novelty, the inventive devising, clings to the new light in which it is seen, the different use to which it is put. When Newton thought of his theory of gravitation, the creative aspect of his thought was not found in its materials. They were familiar; many of them commonplaces—sun, moon, planets, weight, distance, mass, square of numbers. These were not original ideas; they were established facts. His originality lay in the *use* to which these familiar acquaintances were put by introduction into an unfamiliar context. The same is true of every striking scientific discovery, every great invention, every admirable artistic production. Only silly folk identify creative originality with the extraordinary and fanciful; others recognize that its measure lies in putting everyday things to uses which had not occurred to others. The operation is novel, not the materials out of which it is constructed.

The educational conclusion which follows is that *all* thinking is original in a projection of considerations which have not been previously apprehended. The child of three who discovers what can be done with blocks, or of six who finds out what he can make by putting five cents and five cents together, is really a discoverer, even though everybody else in the world knows it. There is a genuine increment of experience; not another item mechanically added on, but enrichment by a new quality. The charm which the spontaneity of little children has for sympathetic observers is due to perception of this intellectual originality. The joy which children themselves experience is the joy of intellectual constructiveness—of creativeness, if the word may be used without misunderstanding.

The educational moral I am chiefly concerned to draw is not, however, that teachers would find their own work less of a grind and strain if school conditions favored learning in the sense of discovery and not in that of storing away what others pour into them; nor that it would be possible to give even children and youth the delights of personal intellectual productiveness—true and important as are these things. It is that no thought, no idea, can possibly be conveyed as an idea from one person to another. When it is told, it is, to the one to whom it is told, another given fact, not an idea. The communication may stimulate the other person to realize the question for himself and to think out a like idea, or it may smother his intellectual interest and suppress his dawning effort at thought. But what he *directly* gets cannot be an idea. Only by wrestling with the conditions of the problem at first hand, seeking and finding his own way out, does he think. When the parent or teacher has provided the conditions which stimulate thinking and has taken a sympathetic attitude toward the activities of the learner by entering into a common or conjoint experience, all has been done which a second party can do to instigate learning. The rest lies with the one directly concerned. If he cannot devise his own solution (not of course in isolation, but in correspondence with the teacher and other pupils) and find his own way out he will not learn, not even if he can recite some correct answer with one hundred per cent accuracy. We can and do supply ready-made "ideas" by the thousand; we do not usually take much pains to see that the one learning engages in significant situations where his own activities generate, support, and clinch ideas—that is, perceived meanings or connections. This does not mean that the teacher is to stand off and look on; the alternative to furnishing ready-made subject matter and listening to the accuracy with which it is reproduced is not quiescence, but participation, sharing, in an activity. In such shared activity, the teacher is a learner, and the learner is, without knowing it, a teacher—and upon the whole, the less consciousness there is, on either side, of either giving or receiving instruction, the better.

4. Ideas, as we have seen, whether they be humble guesses or dignified theories, are anticipations of possible solutions. They are anticipations of some continuity or connection of an activity and a consequence which has not as yet shown itself. They are therefore tested by the operation of acting upon them. They are to guide and organize further observations, recollections, and experiments. They are intermediate in learning, not final. All educational reformers, as we have had occasion to remark, are given to attacking the passivity of traditional education. They have opposed pouring in from without, and absorbing like a sponge; they have attacked drilling in material as into hard and resisting rock. But it is not easy to secure conditions which will make the getting of an idea identical with having an experience which widens and makes more precise our contact with the environment. Activity, even self-activity, is too easily thought of as something merely mental, cooped up within the head, or finding expression only through the vocal organs.

While the need of application of ideas gained in study is acknowledged by all the more successful methods of instruction, the exercises in application are sometimes treated as devices for *fixing* what has already been learned and for getting greater practical skill in its manipulation. These results are genuine and not to be despised. But practice in applying what has been gained in study ought primarily to have an intellectual quality. As we have already seen, thoughts just as thoughts are incomplete. At best they are tentative; they are suggestions, indications. They are standpoints and methods for dealing with situations of experience. Till they are applied in these situations they lack full point and reality. Only application tests them, and only testing confers full meaning and a sense of their reality. Short of use made of them, they tend to segregate into a peculiar world of their own. It may be seriously questioned whether the philosophies . . . which isolate mind and set it over against the world did not have their origin in the fact that the reflective or theoretical class of men elaborated a large stock of ideas which social conditions did not allow them to act upon and test. Consequently men were thrown back into their own thoughts as ends in themselves.

However this may be, there can be no doubt that a peculiar artificiality attaches to much of what is learned in schools. It can hardly be said that many students consciously think of the subject matter as unreal; but it assuredly does not possess for them the kind of reality which the subject matter of their vital experiences possesses. They learn not to expect that sort of reality of it; they become habituated to treating it as having reality for the purposes of recitations, lessons, and examinations. That it should remain inert for the experiences of daily life is more or less a matter of course. The bad effects are twofold. Ordinary experience does not receive the enrichment which it should; it is not fertilized by school learning. And the attitudes which spring from getting used to and accepting half-understood and ill-digested material weaken vigor and efficiency of thought.

If we have dwelt especially on the negative side, it is for the sake of suggesting positive measures adapted to the effectual development of thought. Where schools are equipped with laboratories, shops, and gardens, where dramatizations, plays, and games are freely used, opportunities exist for reproducing situations of life, and for acquiring and applying information and ideas in the carrying forward of progressive experiences. Ideas are not segregated, they do not form an isolated island. They animate and enrich the ordinary course of life. Information is vitalized by its function; by the place it occupies in direction of action.

The phrase "opportunities exist" is used purposely. They may not be taken advantage of; it is possible to employ manual and constructive activities in a physical way, as means of getting just bodily skill; or they may be used almost exclusively for "utilitarian," *i.e.*, pecuniary, ends. But the disposition on the part of upholders of "cultural" education to assume that such activities are merely physical or professional in quality, is itself a product of the philosophies which isolate mind from direction of the course of experience and hence from action upon and with things. When the "mental" is regarded as a self-contained separate realm, a counterpart fate befalls bodily activity and movements. They are regarded as at the best mere external annexes to mind. They may be necessary for the satisfaction of bodily needs and the attainment of external decency and comfort, but they do not occupy a necessary place in mind nor enact an indispensable rôle in the completion of thought. Hence they have no place in a liberal education—*i.e.*, one which is concerned with the interests of intelligence. If they come in at all, it is as a concession to the material needs of the masses. That they should be allowed to invade the education of the élite is unspeakable. This conclusion follows irresistibly from the isolated conception of mind, but by the same logic it disappears when we perceive what mind really is—namely, the purposive and directive factor in the development of experience.

While it is desirable that all educational institutions should be equipped so as to give students an opportunity for acquiring and testing ideas and information in active pursuits typifying important social situations, it will, doubtless, be a long time before all of them are thus furnished. But this state of affairs does not afford instructors an excuse for folding their hands and persisting in methods which segregate school knowledge. Every recitation in every subject gives an opportunity for establishing cross connections between the subject matter of the lesson and the wider and more direct experiences of everyday life. Classroom instruction falls into three kinds. The least desirable treats each lesson as an independent whole. It does not put upon the student the responsibility of finding points of contact between it and other lessons in the same subject, or other subjects of study. Wiser teachers see to it that the student is systematically led to utilize his earlier lessons to help understand the present one, and also to use the present to throw additional light upon what has already been acquired. Results are better, but school subject matter is still isolated. Save by accident, out-of-school experience is left in its crude and comparatively irreflective state. It is not subject to the refining and expanding influences of the more accurate and comprehensive material of direct instruction. The latter is not motivated and impregnated with a sense of reality by being intermingled with the realities of everyday life. The best type of teaching bears in mind the desirability of affecting this interconnection. It puts the student in the habitual attitude of finding points of contact and mutual bearings.

SUMMARY

Processes of instruction are unified in the degree in which they center in the production of good habits of thinking. While we may speak, without error, of the method of thought, the important thing is that thinking is the method of an educative experience. The essentials of method are therefore identical with the essentials of reflection. They are first that the pupil have a genuine situation of experience—that there be a continuous activity in which he is interested for its own sake; secondly, that a genuine problem develop within this situation as a stimulus to thought; third, that he possess the information and make the observations needed to deal with it; fourth, that suggested solutions occur to him which he shall be responsible for developing in an orderly way; fifth, that he have opportunity and occasion to test his ideas by application, to make their meaning clear and to discover for himself their validity.

CHAPTER XXVI
EDUCATIONAL VALUES

2. THE VALUATION OF STUDIES

. . . To value means primarily to prize, to esteem; but secondarily it means to apprize, to estimate. It means, that is, the act of cherishing something, holding it dear, and also the act of passing judgment upon the nature and amount of its value as compared with something else. To value in the latter sense is to valuate or evaluate. The distinction coincides with that sometimes made between intrinsic and instrumental values. Intrinsic values are not objects of judgment, they cannot (as intrinsic) be compared, or regarded as greater and less, better or worse. They are invaluable; and if a thing is invaluable, it is neither more nor less so than any other invaluable. But occasions present themselves when it is necessary to choose, when we must let one thing go in order to take another. This establishes an order of preference, a greater and less, better and worse. Things judged or passed upon have to be estimated in relation to some third thing, some further end. With respect to that, they are means, or instrumental values.

We may imagine a man who at one time thoroughly enjoys converse with his friends, at another the hearing of a symphony; at another the eating of his meals; at another the reading of a book; at another the earning of money, and so on. As an appreciative realization, each of these is an intrinsic value. It occupies a particular place in life; it serves its own end, which cannot be supplied by a substitute. There is no question of comparative value, and hence none of valuation. Each is the specific good which it is, and that is all that can be said. In its own place, none is a means to anything beyond itself. But there may arise a situation in which they compete or conflict, in which a choice has to be made. Now comparison comes in. Since a choice has to be made, we want to know the respective claims of each competitor. What is to be said for it? What does it offer in comparison with, as balanced over against, some other possibility? Raising these questions means that a particular good is no longer an end in itself, an intrinsic good. For if it were, its claims would be incomparable, imperative. The question is now as to its status as a means of realizing something else, which is then the invaluable of *that* situation. If a man has just eaten, or if he is well fed generally and the opportunity to hear music is a rarity, he will probably prefer the music to eating. In the given situation that will render the greater contribution. If he is starving, or if he is satiated with music for the time being, he will naturally judge food to have the greater worth. In the abstract or at large, apart from the needs of a particular situation in which choice has to be made, there is no such thing as degrees or order of value.

Certain conclusions follow with respect to educational values. We cannot establish a hierarchy of values among studies. It is futile to attempt to arrange them in an order, beginning with one having least worth and going on to that of maximum value. In so far as any study has a unique or irreplaceable function in experience, in so far as it marks a characteristic enrichment of life, its worth is intrinsic or incomparable. Since education is not a means to living, but is identical with the operation of living a life which is fruitful and inherently significant, the only ultimate value which can be set up is just the process of living itself. And this is not an end to which studies and activities are subordinate means; it is the whole of which they are ingredients. And what has been said about appreciation means that every study in one of its aspects ought to have just such ultimate significance. It is as true of arithmetic as it is of poetry that in some place and at some time it ought to be a good to be appreciated on its own account—just as an enjoyable experience, in short. If it is not, then when the time and place come for it to be used as a means or instrumentality, it will be in just that much handicapped. Never having been realized or appreciated for itself, one will miss something of its capacity as a resource for other ends.

It equally follows that when we compare studies as to their values, that is, treat them as means to something beyond themselves, that which controls their proper valuation is found in the specific situation in which they are to be used. The way to enable a student to apprehend the instrumental value of arithmetic is not to lecture him upon the benefit it will be to him in some remote and uncertain future, but to let him discover that success in something he is interested in doing depends upon ability to use number.

It also follows that the attempt to distribute distinct sorts of value among different studies is a misguided one, in spite of the amount of time recently devoted to the undertaking. Science for example may have *any* kind of value, depending upon the situation into which it enters as a means. To some the value of science may be military; it may be an instrument in strengthening means of offense or defense; it may be technological, a tool for engineering; or it may be commercial—an aid in the successful conduct of business; under other conditions, its worth may be philanthropic—the service it renders in relieving human suffering; or again it may be quite conventional—of value in establishing one's social status as an "educated" person. As matter of fact, science serves all these purposes, and it would be an arbitrary task to try to fix upon one of them as its "real" end. All that we can be sure of educationally is that science should be taught so as to be an end in itself in the lives of students—something worth while on account of its own unique intrinsic contribution to the experience of life. Primarily it must have "appreciation value." If we take something which seems to be at the opposite pole, like poetry, the same sort of statement applies. It may be that, at the present time, its chief value is the contribution it makes to the enjoyment of leisure. But that may represent a degenerate condition rather than anything necessary. Poetry has historically been allied with religion and morals; it has served the purpose of penetrating the mysterious depths of things. It has had an enormous patriotic value. Homer to the Greeks was a Bible, a textbook of morals, a history, and a national inspiration. In any case, it may be said that an education which does not succeed in making poetry a resource in the business of life as well as in its leisure, has something the matter with it—or else the poetry is artificial poetry.

The same considerations apply to the value of a study or a topic of a study with reference to its motivating force. Those responsible for planning and teaching the course of study should have grounds for thinking that the studies and topics included furnish both direct increments to the enriching of lives of the pupils and also materials which they can put to use in other concerns of direct interest. Since the curriculum is always getting loaded down with purely inherited traditional matter and with subjects which represent mainly the energy of some influential person or group of persons in behalf of something dear to them, it requires constant inspection, criticism, and revision to make sure it is accomplishing its purpose. Then there is always the probability that it represents the values of adults rather than those of children and youth, or those of pupils a generation ago rather than those of the present day. Hence a further need for a critical outlook and survey. But these considerations do not mean that for a subject to have motivating value to a pupil (whether intrinsic or instrumental) is the same thing as for him to be aware of the value, or to be able to tell what the study is good for.

In the first place, as long as any topic makes an immediate appeal, it is not necessary to ask what it is good for. This is a question which can be asked only about instrumental values. Some goods are not good *for* anything; they are just goods. Any other notion leads to an absurdity. For we cannot stop asking the question about an instrumental good, one whose value lies in its being good *for* something, unless there is at some point something intrinsically good, good for itself. To a hungry, healthy child, food is a good of the situation; we do not have to bring him to consciousness of the ends subserved by food in order to supply a motive to eat. The food in connection with his appetite *is* a motive. The same thing holds of mentally eager pupils with respect to many topics. Neither they nor the teacher could possibly foretell with any exactness the purposes learning is to accomplish in the future; nor as long as the eagerness continues is it advisable to try to specify particular goods which are to come of it. The proof of a good is found in the fact that the pupil responds; his response *is* use. His response to the material shows that the subject functions in his life. It is unsound to urge that, say, Latin has a value *per se* in the abstract, just as a study, as a sufficient justification for teaching it. But it is equally absurd to argue that unless teacher or pupil can point out some definite assignable future use to which it is to be put, it lacks justifying value. When pupils are genuinely concerned in learning Latin, that is of itself proof that it possesses value. The most which one is entitled to ask in such cases is whether in view of the shortness of time, there are not other things of intrinsic value which in addition have greater instrumental value.

This brings us to the matter of instrumental values—topics studied because of some end beyond themselves. If a child is ill and his appetite does not lead him to eat when food is presented, or if his appetite is perverted so that he prefers candy to meat and vegetables, conscious reference to results is indicated. He needs to be made conscious of consequences as a justification of the positive or negative value of certain objects. Or the state of things may be normal enough, and yet an individual not be moved by some matter because he does not grasp how his attainment of some intrinsic good depends upon active concern with what is presented. In such cases, it is obviously the part of wisdom to establish consciousness of connection. In general what is desirable is that a topic be presented in such a way that it either have an immediate value, and require no justification, or else be perceived to be a means of achieving something of intrinsic value. An instrumental value then has the intrinsic value of being a means to an end.

It may be questioned whether some of the present pedagogical interest in the matter of values of studies is not either excessive or else too narrow. Sometimes it appears to be a labored effort to furnish an apologetic for topics which no longer operate to any purpose, direct or indirect, in the lives of pupils. At other times, the reaction against useless lumber seems to have gone to the extent of supposing that no subject or topic should be taught unless some quite definite future utility can be pointed out by those making the course of study or by the pupil himself, unmindful of the fact that life is its own excuse for being; and that definite utilities which can be pointed out are themselves justified only because they increase the experienced content of life itself.

.   .   .

CHAPTER XXVII
THEORIES OF MORALS

3. INTELLIGENCE AND CHARACTER

A noteworthy paradox often accompanies discussions of morals. On the one hand, there is an identification of the moral with the rational. Reason is set up as a faculty from which proceed ultimate moral intuitions, and sometimes, as in the Kantian theory, it is said to supply the only proper moral motive. On the other hand, the value of concrete, everyday intelligence is constantly underestimated, and even deliberately depreciated. Morals is often thought to

be an affair with which ordinary knowledge has nothing to do. Moral knowledge is thought to be a thing apart, and conscience is thought of as something
radically different from consciousness. This separation, if valid, is of especial
significance for education. Moral education in school is practically hopeless
when we set up the development of character as a supreme end, and at the
same time treat the acquiring of knowledge and the development of understanding, which of necessity occupy the chief part of school time, as having
nothing to do with character. On such a basis, moral education is inevitably
reduced to some kind of catechetical instruction, or lessons about morals.
Lessons "about morals" signify as matter of course lessons in what other
people think about virtues and duties. It amounts to something only in the
degree in which pupils happen to be already animated by a sympathetic and
dignified regard for the sentiments of others. Without such a regard, it has no
more influence on character than information about the mountains of Asia;
with a servile regard, it increases dependence upon others, and throws upon
those in authority the responsibility for conduct. As a matter of fact, direct
instruction in morals has been effective only in social groups where it was a
part of the authoritative control of the many by the few. Not the teaching as
such but the reënforcement of it by the whole régime of which it was an
incident made it effective. To attempt to get similar results from lessons about
morals in a democratic society is to rely upon sentimental magic.

At the other end of the scale stands the Socratic-Platonic teaching which
identifies knowledge and virtue—which holds that no man does evil knowingly
but only because of ignorance of the good. This doctrine is commonly attacked
on the ground that nothing is more common than for a man to know the good
and yet do the bad: not knowledge, but habituation or practice, and motive are
what is required. Aristotle, in fact, at once attacked the Platonic teaching on
the ground that moral virtue is like an art, such as medicine; the experienced
practitioner is better than a man who has theoretical knowledge but no practical experience of disease and remedies. The issue turns, however, upon what
is meant by knowledge. Aristotle's objection ignored the gist of Plato's teaching to the effect that man could not attain a theoretical insight into the good
except as he had passed through years of practical habituation and strenuous
discipline. Knowledge of the good was not a thing to be got either from books
or from others, but was achieved through a prolonged education. It was the
final and culminating grace of a mature experience of life. Irrespective of
Plato's position, it is easy to perceive that the term knowledge is used to denote
things as far apart as intimate and vital personal realization,—a conviction
gained and tested in experience,—and a second-handed, largely symbolic,
recognition that persons in general believe so and so—a devitalized remote
information. That the latter does not guarantee conduct, that it does not
profoundly affect character, goes without saying. But if knowledge means
something of the same sort as our conviction gained by trying and testing that
sugar is sweet and quinine bitter, the case stands otherwise. Every time a man

sits on a chair rather than on a stove, carries an umbrella when it rains, consults a doctor when ill—or in short performs any of the thousand acts which make up his daily life, he proves that knowledge of a certain kind finds direct issue in conduct. There is every reason to suppose that the same sort of knowledge of good has a like expression; in fact "good" is an empty term unless it includes the satisfactions experienced in such situations as those mentioned. Knowledge that other persons are supposed to know something might lead one to act so as to win the approbation others attach to certain actions, or at least so as to give others the impression that one agrees with them; there is no reason why it should lead to personal initiative and loyalty in behalf of the beliefs attributed to them.

It is not necessary, accordingly, to dispute about the proper meaning of the term knowledge. It is enough for educational purposes to note the different qualities covered by the one name, to realize that it is knowledge gained at first hand through the exigencies of experience which affects conduct in significant ways. If a pupil learns things from books simply in connection with school lessons and for the sake of reciting what he has learned when called upon, then knowledge will have effect upon *some* conduct—namely upon that of reproducing statements at the demand of others. There is nothing surprising that such "knowledge" should not have much influence in the life out of school. But this is not a reason for making a divorce between knowledge and conduct, but for holding in low esteem this kind of knowledge. The same thing may be said of knowledge which relates merely to an isolated and technical specialty; it modifies action but only in its own narrow line. In truth, the problem of moral education in the schools is one with the problem of securing knowledge—the knowledge connected with the system of impulses and habits. For the use to which any known fact is put depends upon its connections. The knowledge of dynamite of a safecracker may be identical in verbal form with that of a chemist; in fact, it is different, for it is knit into connection with different aims and habits, and thus has a different import.

Our prior discussion of subject-matter as proceeding from direct activity having an immediate aim, to the enlargement of meaning found in geography and history, and then to scientifically organized knowledge, was based upon the idea of maintaining a vital connection between knowledge and activity. What is learned and employed in an occupation having an aim and involving coöperation with others is moral knowledge, whether consciously so regarded or not. For it builds up a social interest and confers the intelligence needed to make that interest effective in practice. Just because the studies of the curriculum represent standard factors in social life, they are organs of initiation into social values. As mere school studies, their acquisition has only a technical worth. Acquired under conditions where their social significance is realized, they feed moral interest and develop moral insight. Moreover, the qualities of mind discussed under the topic of method of learning are all of them intrinsically moral qualities. Open-mindedness, singlemindedness, sincerity, breadth of outlook, thoroughness, assumption of responsibility for developing the consequences of ideas which are accepted, are moral traits. The habit of identifying moral characteristics with external conformity to authoritative prescriptions may lead us to ignore the ethical value of these intellectual attitudes, but the same habit tends to reduce morals to a dead and machine-like routine. Consequently while such an attitude has moral results, the results are morally undesirable—above all in a democratic society where so much depends upon personal disposition.

4. THE SOCIAL AND THE MORAL

All of the separations which we have been criticizing—and which the idea of education set forth in the previous chapters is designed to avoid—come from taking morals too narrowly—by giving them, on one side, a sentimental goody-goody turn without reference to effective ability to do what is socially needed, and, on the other side, by overemphasis of convention and tradition which limits morals to a list of definitely stated acts. As matter of fact, morals are as broad as acts which concern our relationships with others. And potentially this includes all our acts, even though their social bearing may not be thought of at the time of performance. For every act, by the principle of habit, modifies disposition—it sets up a certain kind of inclination and desire. And it is impossible to tell when the habit thus strengthened may have a direct and perceptible influence on our association with others. Certain traits of character have such an obvious connection with our social relationships that we call them "moral" in an emphatic sense—truthfulness, honesty, chastity, amiability, etc. But this only means that they are, as compared with some other attitudes, central:—that they carry other attitudes with them. They are moral in an emphatic sense not because they are isolated and exclusive, but because they are so intimately connected with thousands of other attitudes which we do not explicitly recognize—which perhaps we have not even names for. To call them virtues in their isolation is like taking the skeleton for the living body. The bones are certainly important, but their importance lies in the fact that they support other organs of the body in such a way as to make them capable of integrated effective activity. And the same is true of the qualities of character which we specifically designate virtues. Morals concern nothing less than the whole character, and the whole character is identical with the man in all his concrete make-up and manifestations. To possess virtue does not signify to have cultivated a few nameable and exclusive traits; it means to be fully and adequately what one is capable of becoming through association with others in all the offices of life.

The moral and the social quality of conduct are, in the last analysis, identical with each other. It is then but to restate explicitly the import of our earlier chapters regarding the social function of education to say that the measure of the worth of the administration, curriculum, and methods of instruction of the school is the extent to which they are animated by a social spirit. And the great danger which threatens school work is the absence of conditions which make possible a permeating social spirit; this is the great enemy of effective moral training. For this spirit can be actively present only when certain conditions are met.

(i) In the first place, the school must itself be a community life in all which that implies. Social perceptions and interests can be developed only in a genuinely social medium—one where there is give and take in the building up of a common experience. Informational statements about things can be acquired in relative isolation by any one who previously has had enough intercourse with others to have learned language. But realization of the *meaning* of the linguistic signs is quite another matter. That involves a context of work and play in association with others. The plea which has been made for education through continued constructive activities in this book rests upon the fact that they afford an opportunity for a social atmosphere. In place of a school set apart from life as a place for learning lessons, we have a miniature social group in which study and growth are incidents of present shared experience. Playgrounds, shops, workrooms, laboratories not only direct the natural active tendencies of youth, but they involve intercourse, communication, and coöperation,—all extending the perception of connections.

(ii) The learning in school should be continuous with that out of school. There should be a free interplay between the two. This is possible only when there are numerous points of contact between the social interests of the one and of the other. A school is conceivable in which there should be a spirit of companionship and shared activity, but where its social life would no more represent or typify that of the world beyond the school walls than that of a monastery. Social concern and understanding would be developed, but they would not be available outside; they would not carry over. The proverbial separation of town and gown, the cultivation of academic seclusion, operate in this direction. So does such adherence to the culture of the past as generates a reminiscent social spirit, for this makes an individual feel more at home in the life of other days than in his own. A professedly cultural education is peculiarly exposed to this danger. An idealized past becomes the refuge and solace of the spirit; present-day concerns are found sordid, and unworthy of attention. But as a rule, the absence of a social environment in connection with which learning is a need and a reward is the chief reason for the isolation of the school; and this isolation renders school knowledge inapplicable to life and so infertile in character.

A narrow and moralistic view of morals is responsible for the failure to recognize that all the aims and values which are desirable in education are themselves moral. Discipline, natural development, culture, social efficiency, are moral traits—marks of a person who is a worthy member of that society which it is the business of education to further. There is an old saying to the effect that it is not enough for a man to be good; he must be good for something. The something for which a man must be good is capacity to live as a social member so that what he gets from living with others balances with what he contributes. What he gets and gives as a human being, a being with desires, emotions, and ideas, is not external possessions, but a widening and deepening of conscious life—a more intense, disciplined, and expanding realization of meanings. What he *materially* receives and gives is at most opportunities and means for the evolution of conscious life. Otherwise, it is neither giving nor taking, but a shifting about of the position of things in space, like the stirring of water and sand with a stick. Discipline, culture, social efficiency, personal refinement, improvement of character are but phases of the growth of capacity nobly to share in such a balanced experience. And education is not a mere means to such a life. Education is such a life. To maintain capacity for such education is the essence of morals. For conscious life is a continual beginning afresh.

.   .   .

EXPERIENCE
AND EDUCATION

PREFACE

All social movements involve conflicts which are reflected intellectually in controversies. It would not be a sign of health if such an important social interest as education were not also an arena of struggles, practical and theoretical. But for theory, at least for the theory that forms a philosophy of education, the practical conflicts and the controversies that are conducted upon the level of these conflicts, only set a problem. It is the business of an intelligent theory of education to ascertain the causes for the conflicts that exist and then, instead of taking one side or the other, to indicate a plan of operations proceeding from a level deeper and more inclusive than is represented by the practices and ideas of the contending parties.

This formulation of the business of the philosophy of education does not mean that the latter should attempt to bring about a compromise between opposed schools of thought, to find a *via media*, nor yet make an eclectic combination of points picked out hither and yon from all schools. It means the necessity of the introduction of a new order of conceptions leading to new modes of practice. It is for this reason that it is so difficult to develop a philosophy of education, the moment tradition and custom are departed from. It is for this reason that the conduct of schools, based upon a new order of conceptions, is so much more difficult than is the management of schools which walk in beaten paths. Hence, every movement in the direction of a new order of ideas and of activities directed by them calls out, sooner or later, a return to what appear to be simpler and more fundamental ideas and practices of the past—as is exemplified at present in education in the attempt to revive the principles of ancient Greece and of the middle ages.

It is in this context that I have suggested at the close of this little volume that those who are looking ahead to a new movement in education, adapted to the existing need for a new social order, should think in terms of Education itself rather than in terms of some 'ism about education, even such an 'ism as "progressivism." For in spite of itself any movement that thinks and acts in terms of an 'ism becomes so involved in reaction against other 'isms that it is unwittingly controlled by them. For it then forms its principles by reaction against them instead of by a comprehensive, constructive survey of actual needs, problems, and possibilities. Whatever value is possessed by the essay presented in this little volume resides in its attempt to call attention to the larger and deeper issues of Education so as to suggest their proper frame of reference.

CHAPTER I
TRADITIONAL VS. PROGRESSIVE EDUCATION

Mankind likes to think in terms of extreme opposites. It is given to formulating its beliefs in terms of *Either-Ors*, between which it recognizes no intermediate possibilities. When forced to recognize that the extremes cannot be acted upon, it is still inclined to hold that they are all right in theory but that when it comes to practical matters circumstances compel us to compromise. Educational philosophy is no exception. The history of educational theory is marked by opposition between the idea that education is development from within and that it is formation from without; that it is based upon natural endowments and that education is a process of overcoming natural inclination and substituting in its place habits acquired under external pressure.

At present, the opposition, so far as practical affairs of the school are concerned, tends to take the form of contrast between traditional and progressive education. If the underlying ideas of the former are formulated broadly, without the qualifications required for accurate statement, they are found to be about as follows: The subject-matter of education consists of bodies of information and of skills that have been worked out in the past; therefore, the chief business of the school is to transmit them to the new generation. In the past, there have also been developed standards and rules of conduct; moral training consists in forming habits of action in conformity with these rules and standards. Finally, the general pattern of school organization (by which I mean the relations of pupils to one another and to the teachers) constitutes the school a kind of institution sharply marked off from other social institutions. Call up in imagination the ordinary schoolroom, its time-schedules, schemes of classification, of examination and promotion, of rules of order, and I think you will grasp what is meant by "pattern of organization." If then you contrast this scene with what goes on in the family, for example, you will appreciate what is meant by the school being a kind of institution sharply marked off from any other form of social organization.

The three characteristics just mentioned fix the aims and methods of instruction and discipline. The main purpose or objective is to prepare the young for future responsibilities and for success in life, by means of acquisition of the organized bodies of information and prepared forms of skill which comprehend the material of instruction. Since the subject-matter as well as standards of proper conduct are handed down from the past, the attitude of pupils must, upon the whole, be one of docility, receptivity, and obedience. Books, especially textbooks, are the chief representatives of the lore and wisdom of the past, while teachers are the organs through which pupils are brought into effective connection with the material. Teachers are the agents through which knowledge and skills are communicated and rules of conduct enforced.

I have not made this brief summary for the purpose of criticizing the underlying philosophy. The rise of what is called new education and progressive schools is of itself a product of discontent with traditional education. In effect it is a criticism of the latter. When the implied criticism is made explicit it reads somewhat as follows: The traditional scheme is, in essence, one of imposition from above and from outside. It imposes adult standards, subject-matter, and methods upon those who are only growing slowly toward maturity. The gap is so great that the required subject-matter, the methods of learning and of behaving are foreign to the existing capacities of the young. They are beyond the reach of the experience the young learners already possess. Consequently, they must be imposed; even though good teachers will use devices of art to cover up the imposition so as to relieve it of obviously brutal features.

But the gulf between the mature or adult products and the experience and abilities of the young is so wide that the very situation forbids much active participation by pupils in the development of what is taught. Theirs is to do —and learn, as it was the part of the six hundred to do and die. Learning here means acquisition of what already is incorporated in books and in the heads of the elders. Moreover, that which is taught is thought of as essentially static. It is taught as a finished product, with little regard either to the ways in which it was originally built up or to changes that will surely occur in the future. It is to a large extent the cultural product of societies that assumed the future would be much like the past, and yet it is used as educational food in a society where change is the rule, not the exception.

If one attempts to formulate the philosophy of education implicit in the practices of the new education, we may, I think, discover certain common principles amid the variety of progressive schools now existing. To imposition from above is opposed expression and cultivation of individuality; to external discipline is opposed free activity; to learning from texts and teachers, learning through experience; to acquisition of isolated skills and techniques by drill is opposed acquisition of them as means of attaining ends which make direct vital appeal; to preparation for a more or less remote future is opposed making the most of all the opportunities of present life; to static aims and materials is opposed acquaintance with a changing world.

Now, all principles by themselves are abstract. They become concrete only in the consequences which result from their application. Just because the principles set forth are so fundamental and far-reaching, everything depends upon the interpretation given them as they are put into practice in the school and the home. It is at this point that the reference made earlier to *Either-Or* philosophies becomes peculiarly pertinent. The general philosophy of the new education may be sound, and yet the difference in abstract principles will not decide the way in which the moral and intellectual preference involved shall be worked out in practice. There is always the danger in a new movement that in rejecting the aims and methods of that which it would supplant, it may develop its principles negatively rather than positively and constructively. Then it takes its clew in practice from that which is rejected instead of from the constructive development of its own philosophy.

I take it that the fundamental unity of the newer philosophy is found in the idea that there is an intimate and necessary relation between the processes of actual experience and education. If this be true, then a positive and constructive development of its own basic idea depends upon having a correct idea of experience. Take, for example, the question of organized subject-matter—which will be discussed in some detail later. The problem for progressive education is: What is the place and meaning of subject-matter and of organization *within* experience? How does subject-matter function? Is there anything inherent in experience which tends towards progressive organization of its contents? What results follow when the materials of experience are not progressively organized? A philosophy which proceeds on the basis of rejection, of sheer opposition, will neglect these questions. It will tend to suppose that because the old education was based on ready-made organization, therefore it suffices to reject the principle of organization *in toto*, instead of striving to discover what it means and how it is to be attained on the basis of experience. We might go through all the points of difference between the new and the old education and reach similar conclusions. When external control is rejected, the problem becomes that of finding the factors of control that are inherent within experience. When external authority is rejected, it does not follow that all authority should be rejected, but rather that there is need to search for a more effective source of authority. Because the older education imposed the knowledge, methods, and the rules of conduct of the mature person upon the young, it does not follow, except upon the basis of the extreme *Either-Or* philosophy, that the knowledge and skill of the mature person has no directive value for the experience of the immature. On the contrary, basing education upon personal experience may mean more multiplied and more intimate contacts between the mature and the immature than ever existed in the traditional school, and consequently more, rather than less, guidance by others. The problem, then, is: how these contacts can be established without violating the principle of learning through personal experience. The solution of this problem requires a well thought-out philosophy of the social factors that operate in the constitution of individual experience.

What is indicated in the foregoing remarks is that the general principles of the new education do not of themselves solve any of the problems of the actual or practical conduct and management of progressive schools. Rather, they set new problems which have to be worked out on the basis of a new philosophy of experience. The problems are not even recognized, to say nothing of being solved, when it is assumed that it suffices to reject the ideas and practices of the old education and then go to the opposite extreme. Yet I am sure that you will appreciate what is meant when I say that many of the newer schools tend to make little or nothing of organized subject-matter of study; to proceed as if any form of direction and guidance by adults were an invasion of individual freedom, and as if the idea that education should be concerned with the present and future meant that acquaintance with the past has little or no role to play in education. Without pressing these defects to the point of exaggeration, they at least illustrate what is meant by a theory and practice of education which proceeds negatively or by reaction against what has been current in education rather than by a positive and constructive development of purposes, methods, and subject-matter on the foundation of a theory of experience and its educational potentialities.

It is not too much to say that an educational philosophy which professes to be based on the idea of freedom may become as dogmatic as ever was the traditional education which is reacted against. For any theory and set of practices is dogmatic which is not based upon critical examination of its own underlying principles. Let us say that the new education emphasizes the freedom of the learner. Very well. A problem is now set. What does freedom mean and what are the conditions under which it is capable of realization? Let us say that the kind of external imposition which was so common in the traditional school limited rather than promoted the intellectual and moral development of the young. Again, very well. Recognition of this serious defect sets a problem. Just what is the role of the teacher and of books in promoting the educational development of the immature? Admit that traditional education employed as the subject-matter for study facts and ideas so bound up with the past as to give little help in dealing with the issues of the present and future. Very well. Now we have the problem of discovering the connection which actually exists *within* experience between the achievements of the past and the issues of the present. We have the problem of ascertaining how acquaintance with the past may be translated into a potent instrumentality for dealing effectively with the future. We may reject knowledge of the past as the *end* of education and thereby only emphasize its importance as a *means*. When we do that we have a problem that is new in the story of education: How shall the young become acquainted with the past in such a way that the acquaintance is a potent agent in appreciation of the living present?

CHAPTER II
THE NEED OF A THEORY OF EXPERIENCE

In short, the point I am making is that rejection of the philosophy and practice of traditional education sets a new type of difficult educational problem for those who believe in the new type of education. We shall operate blindly and in confusion until we recognize this fact; until we thoroughly appreciate that departure from the old solves no problems. What is said in the following pages is, accordingly, intended to indicate some of the main problems with which the newer education is confronted and to suggest the main lines along which their solution is to be sought. I assume that amid all uncertainties there is one permanent frame of reference: namely, the organic connection between education and personal experience; or, that the new philosophy of education is committed to some kind of empirical and experimental philosophy. But experience and experiment are not self-explanatory ideas. Rather, their meaning is part of the problem to be explored. To know the meaning of empiricism we need to understand what experience is.

The belief that all genuine education comes about through experience does not mean that all experiences are genuinely or equally educative. Experience and education cannot be directly equated to each other. For some experiences are mis-educative. Any experience is mis-educative that has the effect of arresting or distorting the growth of further experience. An experience may be such as to engender callousness; it may produce lack of sensitivity and of responsiveness. Then the possibilities of having richer experience in the future are restricted. Again, a given experience may increase a person's automatic skill in a particular direction and yet tend to land him in a groove or rut; the effect again is to narrow the field of further experience. An experience may be immediately enjoyable and yet promote the formation of a slack and careless attitude; this attitude then operates to modify the quality of subsequent experiences so as to prevent a person from getting out of them what they have to give. Again, experiences may be so disconnected from one another that, while each is agreeable or even exciting in itself, they are not linked cumulatively to one another. Energy is then dissipated and a person becomes scatterbrained. Each experience may be lively, vivid, and "interesting," and yet their disconnectedness may artificially generate dispersive, disintegrated, centrifugal habits. The consequence of formation of such habits is inability to control future experiences. They are then taken, either by way of enjoyment or of discontent and revolt, just as they come. Under such circumstances, it is idle to talk of self-control.

Traditional education offers a plethora of examples of experiences of the kinds just mentioned. It is a great mistake to suppose, even tacitly, that the traditional schoolroom was not a place in which pupils had experiences. Yet this is tacitly assumed when progressive education as a plan of learning by experience is placed in sharp opposition to the old. The proper line of attack is that the experiences which were had, by pupils and teachers alike, were largely of a wrong kind. How many students, for example, were rendered callous to ideas, and how many lost the impetus to learn because of the way in which learning was experienced by them? How many acquired special skills by means of automatic drill so that their power of judgment and capacity to act intelligently in new situations was limited? How many came to associate the learning process with ennui and boredom? How many found what they did learn so foreign to the situations of life outside the school as to give them no power of control over the latter? How many came to associate books with dull drudgery, so that they were "conditioned" to all but flashy reading matter?

If I ask these questions, it is not for the sake of wholesale condemnation of the old education. It is for quite another purpose. It is to emphasize the fact, first, that young people in traditional schools do have experiences; and, secondly, that the trouble is not the absence of experiences, but their defective and wrong character—wrong and defective from the standpoint of connection with further experience. The positive side of this point is even more important in connection with progressive education. It is not enough to insist upon the necessity of experience, nor even of activity in experience. Everything depends upon the *quality* of the experience which is had. The quality of any experience has two aspects. There is an immediate aspect of agreeableness or disagreeableness, and there is its influence upon later experiences. The first is obvious and easy to judge. The *effect* of an experience is not borne on its face. It sets a problem to the educator. It is his business to arrange for the kind of experiences which, while they do not repel the student, but rather engage his activities are, nevertheless, more than immediately enjoyable since they promote having desirable future experiences. Just as no man lives or dies to himself, so no experience lives and dies to itself. Wholly independent of desire or intent, every experience lives on in further experiences. Hence the central problem of an education based upon experience is to select the kind of present experiences that live fruitfully and creatively in subsequent experiences.

Later, I shall discuss in more detail the principle of the continuity of experience or what may be called the experiential continuum. Here I wish simply to emphasize the importance of this principle for the philosophy of educative experience. A philosophy of education, like any theory, has to be stated in words, in symbols. But so far as it is more than verbal it is a plan for conducting education. Like any plan, it must be framed with reference to what is to be done and how it is to be done. The more definitely and sincerely it is held that education is a development within, by, and for experience, the more important it is that there shall be clear conceptions of what experience is. Unless experience is so conceived that the result is a plan for deciding upon subject-matter, upon methods of instruction and discipline, and upon material equipment and social organization of the school, it is wholly in the air. It is reduced to a form of words which may be emotionally stirring but for which any other set of words might equally well be substituted unless they indicate operations to be initiated and executed. Just because traditional education was a matter of routine in which the plans and programs were handed down from the past, it does not follow that progressive education is a matter of planless improvisation.

The traditional school could get along without any consistently developed philosophy of education. About all it required in that line was a set of abstract words like culture, discipline, our great cultural heritage, etc., actual guidance being derived not from them but from custom and established routines. Just because progressive schools cannot rely upon established traditions and institutional habits, they must either proceed more or less haphazardly or be directed by ideas which, when they are made articulate and coherent, form a philosophy of education. Revolt against the kind of organization characteristic of the traditional school constitutes a demand for a kind of organization based upon ideas. I think that only slight acquaintance with the history of education is needed to prove that educational reformers and innovators alone have felt the need for a philosophy of education. Those who adhered to the established system needed merely a few fine-sounding words to justify existing practices. The real work was done by habits which were so fixed as to be institutional. The lesson for progressive education is that it requires in an urgent degree, a degree more pressing than was incumbent upon former innovators, a philosophy of education based upon a philosophy of experience.

I remarked incidentally that the philosophy in question is, to paraphrase the saying of Lincoln about democracy, one of education of, by, and for experience. No one of these words, *of, by,* or *for,* names anything which is self-evident. Each of them is a challenge to discover and put into operation a principle of order and organization which follows from understanding what educative experience signifies.

It is, accordingly, a much more difficult task to work out the kinds of materials, of methods, and of social relationships that are appropriate to the new education than is the case with traditional education. I think many of the difficulties experienced in the conduct of progressive schools and many of the criticisms leveled against them arise from this source. The difficulties are aggravated and the criticisms are increased when it is supposed that the new education is somehow easier than the old. This belief is, I imagine, more or less current. Perhaps it illustrates again the *Either-Or* philosophy, springing from the idea that about all which is required is *not* to do what is done in traditional schools.

I admit gladly that the new education is *simpler* in principle than the old. It is in harmony with principles of growth, while there is very much which is artificial in the old selection and arrangement of subjects and methods, and artificiality always leads to unnecessary complexity. But the easy and the simple are not identical. To discover what is really simple and to act upon the discovery is an exceedingly difficult task. After the artificial and complex is once institutionally established and ingrained in custom and routine, it is easier to walk in the paths that have been beaten than it is, after taking a new point of view, to work out what is practically involved in the new point of view. The old Ptolemaic astronomical system was more complicated with its cycles and epicycles than the Copernican system. But until organization of actual astronomical phenomena on the ground of the latter principle had been effected the easiest course was to follow the line of least resistance provided by the old intellectual habit. So we come back to the idea that a coherent *theory* of experience, affording positive direction to selection and organization of appropriate educational methods and materials, is required by the attempt to give new direction to the work of the schools. The process is a slow and arduous one. It is a matter of growth, and there are many obstacles which tend to obstruct growth and to deflect it into wrong lines.

I shall have something to say later about organization. All that is needed, perhaps, at this point is to say that we must escape from the tendency to think of organization in terms of the *kind* of organization, whether of content (or subject-matter), or of methods and social relations, that mark traditional education. I think that a good deal of the current opposition to the idea of organization is due to the fact that it is so hard to get away from the picture of the studies of the old school. The moment "organization" is mentioned imagination goes almost automatically to the kind of organization that is familiar, and in revolting against that we are led to shrink from the very idea of any organization. On the other hand, educational reactionaries, who are now gathering force, use the absence of adequate intellectual and moral organization in the newer type of school as proof not only of the need of organization, but to identify any and every kind of organization with that instituted before the rise of experimental science. Failure to develop a conception of organization upon the empirical and experimental basis gives reactionaries a too easy victory. But the fact that the empirical sciences now offer the best type of intellectual organization which can be found in any field shows that there is no reason why we, who call ourselves empiricists, should be "pushovers" in the matter of order and organization.

CHAPTER III
CRITERIA OF EXPERIENCE

If there is any truth in what has been said about the need of forming a theory of experience in order that education may be intelligently conducted upon the basis of experience, it is clear that the next thing in order in this discussion is to present the principles that are most significant in framing this theory. I shall not, therefore, apologize for engaging in a certain amount of philosophical analysis, which otherwise might be out of place. I may, however, reassure you to some degree by saying that this analysis is not an end in itself but is engaged in for the sake of obtaining criteria to be applied later in discussion of a number of concrete and, to most persons, more interesting issues.

I have already mentioned what I called the category of continuity, or the experiential continuum. This principle is involved, as I pointed out, in every attempt to discriminate between experiences that are worth while education-ally and those that are not. It may seem superfluous to argue that this discrimi-nation is necessary not only in criticizing the traditional type of education but also in initiating and conducting a different type. Nevertheless, it is advisable to pursue for a little while the idea that it is necessary. One may safely assume, I suppose, that one thing which has recommended the progressive movement is that it seems more in accord with the democratic ideal to which our people is committed than do the procedures of the traditional school, since the latter have so much of the autocratic about them. Another thing which has con-tributed to its favorable reception is that its methods are humane in compari-son with the harshness so often attending the policies of the traditional school.

The question I would raise concerns why we prefer democratic and humane arrangements to those which are autocratic and harsh. And by "why," I mean the *reason* for preferring them, not just the *causes* which lead us to the prefer-ence. One *cause* may be that we have been taught not only in the schools but by the press, the pulpit, the platform, and our laws and law-making bodies that democracy is the best of all social institutions. We may have so assimilated this idea from our surroundings that it has become an habitual part of our mental and moral make-up. But similar causes have led other persons in different surroundings to widely varying conclusions—to prefer fascism, for example. The cause for our preference is not the same thing as the reason why we *should* prefer it.

It is not my purpose here to go in detail into the reason. But I would ask a single question: Can we find any reason that does not ultimately come down to the belief that democratic social arrangements promote a better quality of human experience, one which is more widely accessible and enjoyed, than do non-democratic and anti-democratic forms of social life? Does not the princi-ple of regard for individual freedom and for decency and kindliness of human relations come back in the end to the conviction that these things are tributary to a higher quality of experience on the part of a greater number than are methods of repression and coercion or force? Is it not the reason for our preference that we believe that mutual consultation and convictions reached through persuasion, make possible a better quality of experience than can otherwise be provided on any wide scale?

If the answer to these questions is in the affirmative (and personally I do not see how we can justify our preference for democracy and humanity on any other ground), the ultimate reason for hospitality to progressive education, because of its reliance upon and use of humane methods and its kinship to democracy, goes back to the fact that discrimination is made between the inherent values of different experiences. So I come back to the principle of continuity of experience as a criterion of discrimination.

At bottom, this principle rests upon the fact of habit, when *habit* is interpreted biologically. The basic characteristic of habit is that every experience enacted and undergone modifies the one who acts and undergoes, while this modification affects, whether we wish it or not, the quality of subsequent experiences. For it is a somewhat different person who enters into them. The principle of habit so understood obviously goes deeper than the ordinary conception of *a* habit as a more or less fixed way of doing things, although it includes the latter as one of its special cases. It covers the formation of attitudes, attitudes that are emotional and intellectual; it covers our basic sensitivities and ways of meeting and responding to all the conditions which we meet in living. From this point of view, the principle of continuity of experience means that every experience both takes up something from those which have gone before and modifies in some way the quality of those which come after. As the poet states it,

> . . . all experience is an arch wherethro'
> Gleams that untraveled world, whose margin fades
> For ever and for ever when I move.

So far, however, we have no ground for discrimination among experiences. For the principle is of universal application. There is *some* kind of continuity in every case. It is when we note the different forms in which continuity of experience operates that we get the basis of discriminating among experiences. I may illustrate what is meant by an objection which has been brought against an idea which I once put forth—namely, that the educative process can be identified with growth when that is understood in terms of the active participle, *growing.*

Growth, or growing as developing, not only physically but intellectually and morally, is one exemplification of the principle of continuity. The objection made is that growth might take many different directions: a man, for example, who starts out on a career of burglary may grow in that direction, and by practice may grow into a highly expert burglar. Hence it is argued that "growth" is not enough; we must also specify the direction in which growth takes place, the end towards which it tends. Before, however, we decide that the objection is conclusive we must analyze the case a little further.

That a man may grow in efficiency as a burglar, as a gangster, or as a corrupt politician, cannot be doubted. But from the standpoint of growth as education and education as growth the question is whether growth in this direction promotes or retards growth in general. Does this form of growth create conditions for further growth, or does it set up conditions that shut off the person who has grown in this particular direction from the occasions, stimuli, and opportunities for continuing growth in new directions? What is the effect of growth in a special direction upon the attitudes and habits which alone open up avenues for development in other lines? I shall leave you to answer these questions, saying simply that when and *only* when development in a particular line conduces to continuing growth does it answer to the criterion of education as growing. For the conception is one that must find universal and not special-ized limited application.

I return now to the question of continuity as a criterion by which to discrimi-nate between experiences which are educative and those which are mis-educa-tive. As we have seen, there is some kind of continuity in any case since every experience affects for better or worse the attitudes which help decide the quality of further experiences, by setting up certain preference and aversion, and making it easier or harder to act for this or that end. Moreover, every experience influences in some degree the objective conditions under which further experiences are had. For example, a child who learns to speak has a new facility and new desire. But he has also widened the external conditions of subsequent learning. When he learns to read, he similarly opens up a new environment. If a person decides to become a teacher, lawyer, physician, or stockbroker, when he executes his intention he thereby necessarily determines to some extent the environment in which he will act in the future. He has rendered himself more sensitive and responsive to certain conditions, and relatively immune to those things about him that would have been stimuli if he had made another choice.

But, while the principle of continuity applies in some way in every case, the quality of the present experience influences the *way* in which the principle applies. We speak of spoiling a child and of the spoilt child. The effect of over-indulging a child is a continuing one. It sets up an attitude which operates as an automatic demand that persons and objects cater to his desires and caprices in the future. It makes him seek the kind of situation that will enable him to do what he feels like doing at the time. It renders him averse to and comparatively incompetent in situations which require effort and perseverance in overcoming obstacles. There is no paradox in the fact that the principle of the continuity of experience may operate so as to leave a person arrested on a low plane of development, in a way which limits later capacity for growth.

On the other hand, if an experience arouses curiosity, strengthens initiative, and sets up desires and purposes that are sufficiently intense to carry a person over dead places in the future, continuity works in a very different way. Every experience is a moving force. Its value can be judged only on the ground of what it moves toward and into. The greater maturity of experience which should belong to the adult as educator puts him in a position to evaluate each experience of the young in a way in which the one having the less mature experience cannot do. It is then the business of the educator to see in what direction an experience is heading. There is no point in his being more mature if, instead of using his greater insight to help organize the conditions of the experience of the immature, he throws away his insight. Failure to take the moving force of an experience into account so as to judge and direct it on the ground of what it is moving into means disloyalty to the principle of experience itself. The disloyalty operates in two directions. The educator is false to the understanding that he should have obtained from his own past experience. He is also unfaithful to the fact that all human experience is ultimately social: that it involves contact and communication. The mature person, to put it in moral terms, has no right to withhold from the young on given occasions whatever capacity for sympathetic understanding his own experience has given him.

No sooner, however, are such things said than there is a tendency to react to the other extreme and take what has been said as a plea for some sort of disguised imposition from outside. It is worth while, accordingly, to say something about the way in which the adult can exercise the wisdom his own wider experience gives him without imposing a merely external control. On one side, it is his business to be on the alert to see what attitudes and habitual tendencies are being created. In this direction he must, if he is an educator, be able to judge what attitudes are actually conducive to continued growth and what are detrimental. He must, in addition, have that sympathetic understanding of individuals as individuals which gives him an idea of what is actually going on in the minds of those who are learning. It is, among other things, the need for these abilities on the part of the parent and teacher which makes a system of education based upon living experience a more difficult affair to conduct successfully than it is to follow the patterns of traditional education.

But there is another aspect of the matter. Experience does not go on simply inside a person. It does go on there, for it influences the formation of attitudes of desire and purpose. But this is not the whole of the story. Every genuine experience has an active side which changes in some degree the objective conditions under which experiences are had. The difference between civilization and savagery, to take an example on a large scale, is found in the degree in which previous experiences have changed the objective conditions under which subsequent experiences take place. The existence of roads, of means of rapid movement and transportation, tools, implements, furniture, electric light and power, are illustrations. Destroy the external conditions of present civilized experience, and for a time our experience would relapse into that of barbaric peoples.

In a word, we live from birth to death in a world of persons and things which in large measure is what it is because of what has been done and transmitted from previous human activities. When this fact is ignored, experience is treated as if it were something which goes on exclusively inside an individual's body and mind. It ought not to be necessary to say that experience does not occur in a vacuum. There are sources outside an individual which give rise to experience. It is constantly fed from these springs. No one would question that a child in a slum tenement has a different experience from that of a child in a cultured home; that the country lad has a different kind of experience from the city boy, or a boy on the seashore one different from the lad who is brought up on inland prairies. Ordinarily we take such facts for granted as too commonplace to record. But when their educational import is recognized, they indicate the second way in which the educator can direct the experience of the young without engaging in imposition. A primary responsibility of educators is that they not only be aware of the general principle of the shaping of actual experience by environing conditions, but that they also recognize in the concrete what surroundings are conducive to having experiences that lead to growth. Above all, they should know how to utilize the surroundings, physical and social, that exist so as to extract from them all that they have to contribute to building up experiences that are worth while.

Traditional education did not have to face this problem; it could systematically dodge this responsibility. The school environment of desks, blackboards, a small school yard, was supposed to suffice. There was no demand that the teacher should become intimately acquainted with the conditions of the local community, physical, historical, economic, occupational, etc., in order to utilize them as educational resources. A system of education based upon the necessary connection of education with experience must, on the contrary, if faithful to its principle, take these things constantly into account. This tax upon the educator is another reason why progressive education is more difficult to carry on than was ever the traditional system.

It is possible to frame schemes of education that pretty systematically subordinate objective conditions to those which reside in the individuals being educated. This happens whenever the place and function of the teacher, of books, of apparatus and equipment, of everything which represents the products of the more mature experience of elders, is systematically subordinated to the immediate inclinations and feelings of the young. Every theory which assumes that importance can be attached to these objective factors only at the expense of imposing external control and of limiting the freedom of individuals rests finally upon the notion that experience is truly experience only when objective conditions are subordinated to what goes on within the individuals having the experience.

I do not mean that it is supposed that objective conditions can be shut out. It is recognized that they must enter in: so much concession is made to the inescapable fact that we live in a world of things and persons. But I think that observation of what goes on in some families and some schools would disclose that some parents and some teachers are acting upon the idea of *subordinating* objective conditions to internal ones. In that case, it is assumed not only that the latter are primary, which in one sense they are, but that just as they temporarily exist they fix the whole educational process.

Let me illustrate from the case of an infant. The needs of a baby for food, rest, and activity are certainly primary and decisive in one respect. Nourishment must be provided; provision must be made for comfortable sleep, and so on. But these facts do not mean that a parent shall feed the baby at any time when the baby is cross or irritable, that there shall not be a program of regular hours of feeding and sleeping, etc. The wise mother takes account of the needs of the infant but not in a way which dispenses with her own responsibility for regulating the objective conditions under which the needs are satisfied. And if she is a wise mother in this respect, she draws upon past experiences of experts as well as her own for the light that these shed upon what experiences are in general most conducive to the normal development of infants. Instead of these conditions being subordinated to the immediate internal condition of the baby, they are definitely ordered so that a particular kind of *interaction* with these immediate internal states may be brought about.

The word "interaction," which has just been used, expresses the second chief principle for interpreting an experience in its educational function and force. It assigns equal rights to both factors in experience—objective and internal conditions. Any normal experience is an interplay of these two sets of conditions. Taken together, or in their interaction, they form what we call a *situation*. The trouble with traditional education was not that it emphasized the external conditions that enter into the control of the experiences but that it paid so little attention to the internal factors which also decide what kind of experience is had. It violated the principle of interaction from one side. But this violation is no reason why the new education should violate the principle from the other side—except upon the basis of the extreme *Either-Or* educational philosophy which has been mentioned.

The illustration drawn from the need for regulation of the objective conditions of a baby's development indicates, first, that the parent has responsibility for arranging the conditions under which an infant's experience of food, sleep, etc., occurs, and, secondly, that the responsibility is fulfilled by utilizing the funded experience of the past, as this is represented, say, by the advice of competent physicians and others who have made a special study of normal physical growth. Does it limit the freedom of the mother when she uses the body of knowledge thus provided to regulate the objective conditions of nourishment and sleep? Or does the enlargement of her intelligence in fulfilling her parental function widen her freedom? Doubtless if a fetish were made of the advice and directions so that they came to be inflexible dictates to be followed under every possible condition, then restriction of freedom of both parent and child would occur. But this restriction would also be a limitation of the intelligence that is exercised in personal judgment.

In what respect does regulation of objective conditions limit the freedom of the baby? Some limitation is certainly placed upon its immediate movements and inclinations when it is put in its crib, at a time when it wants to continue playing, or does not get food at the moment it would like it, or when it isn't picked up and dandled when it cries for attention. Restriction also occurs when mother or nurse snatches a child away from an open fire into which it is about to fall. I shall have more to say later about freedom. Here it is enough to ask whether freedom is to be thought of and adjudged on the basis of relatively momentary incidents or whether its meaning is found in the continuity of developing experience.

The statement that individuals live in a world means, in the concrete, that they live in a series of situations. And when it is said that they live *in* these situations, the meaning of the word "in" is different from its meaning when it is said that pennies are "in" a pocket or paint is "in" a can. It means, once more, that interaction is going on between an individual and objects and other persons. The conceptions of *situation* and of *interaction* are inseparable from each other. An experience is always what it is because of a transaction taking place between an individual and what, at the time, constitutes his environment, whether the latter consists of persons with whom he is talking about some topic or event, the subject talked about being also a part of the situation; or the toys with which he is playing; the book he is reading (in which his environing conditions at the time may be England or ancient Greece or an imaginary region); or the materials of an experiment he is performing. The environment, in other words, is whatever conditions interact with personal needs, desires, purposes, and capacities to create the experience which is had. Even when a person builds a castle in the air he is interacting with the objects which he constructs in fancy.

The two principles of continuity and interaction are not separate from each other. They intercept and unite. They are, so to speak, the longitudinal and lateral aspects of experience. Different situations succeed one another. But because of the principle of continuity something is carried over from the earlier to the later ones. As an individual passes from one situation to another, his world, his environment, expands or contracts. He does not find himself living in another world but in a different part or aspect of one and the same world. What he has learned in the way of knowledge and skill in one situation becomes an instrument of understanding and dealing effectively with the situations which follow. The process goes on as long as life and learning continue. Otherwise the course of experience is disorderly, since the individual factor that enters into making an experience is split. A divided world, a world whose parts and aspects do not hang together, is at once a sign and a cause of a divided personality. When the splitting-up reaches a certain point we call the person insane. A fully integrated personality, on the other hand, exists only when successive experiences are integrated with one another. It can be built up only as a world of related objects is constructed.

Continuity and interaction in their active union with each other provide the measure of the educative significance and value of an experience. The immediate and direct concern of an educator is then with the situations in which interaction takes place. The individual, who enters as a factor into it, is what he is at a given time. It is the other factor, that of objective conditions, which lies to some extent within the possibility of regulation by the educator. As has already been noted, the phrase "objective conditions" covers a wide range. It includes what is done by the educator and the way in which it is done, not only words spoken but the tone of voice in which they are spoken. It includes equipment, books, apparatus, toys, games played. It includes the materials with which an individual interacts, and, most important of all, the total *social* set-up of the situations in which a person is engaged.

When it is said that the objective conditions are those which are within the power of the educator to regulate, it is meant, of course, that his ability to influence directly the experience of others and thereby the education they obtain places upon him the duty of determining that environment which will interact with the existing capacities and needs of those taught to create a worth-while experience. The trouble with traditional education was not that educators took upon themselves the responsibility for providing an environment. The trouble was that they did not consider the other factor in creating an experience; namely, the powers and purposes of those taught. It was assumed that a certain set of conditions was intrinsically desirable, apart from its ability to evoke a certain quality of response in individuals. This lack of mutual adaptation made the process of teaching and learning accidental. Those to whom the provided conditions were suitable managed to learn. Others got on as best they could. Responsibility for selecting objective conditions carries with it, then, the responsibility for understanding the needs and capacities of the individuals who are learning at a given time. It is not enough that certain materials and methods have proved effective with other individuals at other times. There must be a reason for thinking that they will function in generating an experience that has educative quality with particular individuals at a particular time.

It is no reflection upon the nutritive quality of beefsteak that it is not fed to infants. It is not an invidious reflection upon trigonometry that we do not teach it in the first or fifth grade of school. It is not the subject *per se* that is educative or that is conducive to growth. There is no subject that is in and of itself, or without regard to the stage of growth attained by the learner, such that inherent educational value can be attributed to it. Failure to take into account adaptation to the needs and capacities of individuals was the source of the idea that certain subjects and certain methods are intrinsically cultural or intrinsically good for mental discipline. There is no such thing as educational value in the abstract. The notion that some subjects and methods and that acquaintance with certain facts and truths possess educational value in and of themselves is the reason why traditional education reduced the material of education so largely to a diet of predigested materials. According to this notion, it was enough to regulate the quantity and difficulty of the material provided, in a scheme of quantitative grading, from month to month and from year to year. Otherwise a pupil was expected to take it in the doses that were prescribed from without. If the pupil left it instead of taking it, if he engaged in physical truancy, or in the mental truancy of mind-wandering and finally built up an emotional revulsion against the subject, he was held to be at fault. No question was raised as to whether the trouble might not lie in the subject-matter or in the way in which it was offered. The principle of interaction makes it clear that failure of adaptation of material to needs and capacities of individuals may cause an experience to be non-educative quite as much as failure of an individual to adapt himself to the material.

The principle of continuity in its educational application means, nevertheless, that the future has to be taken into account at every stage of the educational process. This idea is easily misunderstood and is badly distorted in traditional education. Its assumption is, that by acquiring certain skills and by learning certain subjects which would be needed later (perhaps in college or perhaps in adult life) pupils are as a matter of course made ready for the needs and circumstances of the future. Now "preparation" is a treacherous idea. In a certain sense every experience should do something to prepare a person for later experiences of a deeper and more expansive quality. That is the very meaning of growth, continuity, reconstruction of experience. But it is a mistake to suppose that the mere acquisition of a certain amount of arithmetic, geography, history, etc., which is taught and studied because it may be useful at some time in the future, has this effect, and it is a mistake to suppose that acquisition of skills in reading and figuring will automatically constitute preparation for their right and effective use under conditions very unlike those in which they were acquired.

Almost everyone has had occasion to look back upon his school days and wonder what has become of the knowledge he was supposed to have amassed during his years of schooling, and why it is that the technical skills he acquired have to be learned over again in changed form in order to stand him in good stead. Indeed, he is lucky who does not find that in order to make progress, in order to go ahead intellectually, he does not have to unlearn much of what he learned in school. These questions cannot be disposed of by saying that the subjects were not actually learned, for they were learned at least sufficiently to enable a pupil to pass examinations in them. One trouble is that the subject-matter in question was learned in isolation; it was put, as it were, in a water-tight compartment. When the question is asked, then, what has become of it, where has it gone to, the right answer is that it is still there in the special compartment in which it was originally stowed away. If exactly the same conditions recurred as those under which it was acquired, it would also recur and be available. But it was segregated when it was acquired and hence is so disconnected from the rest of experience that it is not available under the actual conditions of life. It is contrary to the laws of experience that learning of this kind, no matter how thoroughly engrained at the time, should give genuine preparation.

Nor does failure in preparation end at this point. Perhaps the greatest of all pedagogical fallacies is the notion that a person learns only the particular thing he is studying at the time. Collateral learning in the way of formation of enduring attitudes, of likes and dislikes, may be and often is much more important than the spelling lesson or lesson in geography or history that is learned. For these attitudes are fundamentally what count in the future. The most important attitude that can be formed is that of desire to go on learning. If impetus in this direction is weakened instead of being intensified, something much more than mere lack of preparation takes place. The pupil is actually robbed of native capacities which otherwise would enable him to cope with the circumstances that he meets in the course of his life. We often see persons who have had little schooling and in whose case the absence of set schooling proves to be a positive asset. They have at least retained their native common sense and power of judgment, and its exercise in the actual conditions of living has given them the precious gift of ability to learn from the experiences they have. What avail is it to win prescribed amounts of information about geography and history, to win ability to read and write, if in the process the individual loses his own soul: loses his appreciation of things worth while, of the values to which these things are relative; if he loses desire to apply what he has learned and, above all, loses the ability to extract meaning from his future experiences as they occur?

What, then, is the true meaning of preparation in the educational scheme? In the first place, it means that a person, young or old, gets out of his present experience all that there is in it for him at the time in which he has it. When preparation is made the controlling end, then the potentialities of the present are sacrificed to a suppositious future. When this happens, the actual preparation for the future is missed or distorted. The ideal of using the present simply to get ready for the future contradicts itself. It omits, and even shuts out, the very conditions by which a person can be prepared for his future. We always live at the time we live and not at some other time, and only by extracting at each present time the full meaning of each present experience are we prepared for doing the same thing in the future. This is the only preparation which in the long run amounts to anything.

All this means that attentive care must be devoted to the conditions which give each present experience a worth-while meaning. Instead of inferring that it doesn't make much difference what the present experience is as long as it is enjoyed, the conclusion is the exact opposite. Here is another matter where it is easy to react from one extreme to the other. Because traditional schools tended to sacrifice the present to a remote and more or less unknown future, therefore it comes to be believed that the educator has little responsibility for the kind of present experiences the young undergo. But the relation of the present and the future is not an *Either-Or* affair. The present affects the future anyway. The persons who should have some idea of the connection between the two are those who have achieved maturity. Accordingly, upon them devolves the responsibility for instituting the conditions for the kind of present experience which has a favorable effect upon the future. Education as growth or maturity should be an ever-present process.

CHAPTER IV
SOCIAL CONTROL

I have said that educational plans and projects, seeing education in terms of life-experience, are thereby committed to framing and adopting an intelligent theory or, if you please, philosophy of experience. Otherwise they are at the mercy of every intellectual breeze that happens to blow. I have tried to illustrate the need for such a theory by calling attention to two principles which are fundamental in the constitution of experience: the principles of interaction and of continuity. If, then, I am asked why I have spent so much time on expounding a rather abstract philosophy, it is because practical attempts to develop schools based upon the idea that education is found in life-experience are bound to exhibit inconsistencies and confusions unless they are guided by some conception of what experience is, and what marks off educative experience from non-educative and mis-educative experience. I now come to a group of actual educational questions the discussion of which will, I hope, provide topics and material that are more concrete than the discussion up to this point.

The two principles of continuity and interaction as criteria of the value of experience are so intimately connected that it is not easy to tell just what special educational problem to take up first. Even the convenient division into problems of subject-matter or studies and of methods of teaching and learning is likely to fail us in selection and organization of topics to discuss. Consequently, the beginning and sequence of topics is somewhat arbitrary. I shall commence, however, with the old question of individual freedom and social control and pass on to the questions that grow naturally out of it.

It is often well in considering educational problems to get a start by temporarily ignoring the school and thinking of other human situations. I take it that no one would deny that the ordinary good citizen is as a matter of fact subject to a great deal of social control and that a considerable part of this control is not felt to involve restriction of personal freedom. Even the theoretical anarchist, whose philosophy commits him to the idea that state or government control is an unmitigated evil, believes that with abolition of the political state other forms of social control would operate: indeed, his opposition to governmental regulation springs from his belief that other and to him more normal modes of control would operate with abolition of the state.

Without taking up this extreme position, let us note some examples of social control that operate in everyday life, and then look for the principle underlying them. Let us begin with the young people themselves. Children at recess or after school play games, from tag and one-old-cat to baseball and football. The games involve rules, and these rules order their conduct. The games do not go on haphazardly or by a succession of improvisations. Without rules there is no game. If disputes arise there is an umpire to appeal to, or discussion and a kind of arbitration are means to a decision; otherwise the game is broken up and comes to an end.

There are certain fairly obvious controlling features of such situations to which I want to call attention. The first is that the rules are a part of the game. They are not outside of it. No rules, then no game; different rules, then a different game. As long as the game goes on with a reasonable smoothness, the players do not feel that they are submitting to external imposition but that they are playing the game. In the second place an individual may at times feel that a decision isn't fair and he may even get angry. But he is not objecting to a rule but to what he claims is a violation of it, to some one-sided and unfair action. In the third place, the rules, and hence the conduct of the game, are fairly standardized. There are recognized ways of counting out, of selection of sides, as well as for positions to be taken, movements to be made, etc. These rules have the sanction of tradition and precedent. Those playing the game have seen, perhaps, professional matches and they want to emulate their elders. An element that is conventional is pretty strong. Usually, a group of youngsters change the rules by which they play only when the adult group to which they look for models have themselves made a change in the rules, while the change made by the elders is at least supposed to conduce to making the game more skillful or more interesting to spectators.

Now, the general conclusion I would draw is that control of individual actions is effected by the whole situation in which individuals are involved, in which they share and of which they are co-operative or interacting parts. For even in a competitive game there is a certain kind of participation, of sharing in a common experience. Stated the other way around, those who take part do not feel that they are bossed by an individual person or are being subjected to the will of some outside superior person. When violent disputes do arise, it is usually on the alleged ground that the umpire or some person on the other side is being unfair; in other words, that in such cases some individual is trying to impose his individual will on someone else.

It may seem to be putting too heavy a load upon a single case to argue that this instance illustrates the general principle of social control of individuals without the violation of freedom. But if the matter were followed out through a number of cases, I think the conclusion that this particular instance does illustrate a general principle would be justified. Games are generally competitive. If we took instances of co-operative activities in which all members of a group take part, as for example in well-ordered family life in which there is mutual confidence, the point would be even clearer. In all such cases it is not the will or desire of any one person which establishes order but the moving spirit of the whole group. The control is social, but individuals are parts of a community, not outside of it.

I do not mean by this that there are no occasions upon which the authority of, say, the parent does not have to intervene and exercise fairly direct control. But I do say that, in the first place, the number of these occasions is slight in comparison with the number of those in which the control is exercised by situations in which all take part. And what is even more important, the authority in question when exercised in a well-regulated household or other community group is not a manifestation of merely personal will; the parent or teacher exercises it as the representative and agent of the interests of the group as a whole. With respect to the first point, in a well-ordered school the main reliance for control of this and that individual is upon the activities carried on and upon the situations in which these activities are maintained. The teacher reduces to a minimum the occasions in which he or she has to exercise authority in a personal way. When it is necessary, in the second place, to speak and act firmly, it is done in behalf of the interest of the group, not as an exhibition of personal power. This makes the difference between action which is arbitrary and that which is just and fair.

Moreover, it is not necessary that the difference should be formulated in words, by either teacher or the young, in order to be felt in experience. The number of children who do not feel the difference (even if they cannot articulate it and reduce it to an intellectual principle) between action that is motivated by personal power and desire to dictate and action that is fair, because in the interest of all, is small. I should even be willing to say that upon the whole children are more sensitive to the signs and symptoms of this difference than are adults. Children learn the difference when playing with one another. They are willing, often too willing if anything, to take suggestions from one child and let him be a leader if his conduct adds to the experienced value of what they are doing, while they resent the attempt at dictation. Then they often withdraw and when asked why, say that it is because so-and-so "is too bossy."

I do not wish to refer to the traditional school in ways which set up a caricature in lieu of a picture. But I think it is fair to say that one reason the personal commands of the teacher so often played an undue role and a reason why the order which existed was so much a matter of sheer obedience to the will of an adult was because the situation almost forced it upon the teacher. The school was not a group or community held together by participation in common activities. Consequently, the normal, proper conditions of control were lacking. Their absence was made up for, and to a considerable extent had to be made up for, by the direct intervention of the teacher, who, as the saying went, "*kept* order." He kept it because order was in the teacher's keeping, instead of residing in the shared work being done.

The conclusion is that in what are called the new schools, the primary source of social control resides in the very nature of the work done as a social enterprise in which all individuals have an opportunity to contribute and to which all feel a responsibility. Most children are naturally "sociable." Isolation is even more irksome to them than to adults. A genuine community life has its ground in this natural sociability. But community life does not organize itself in an enduring way purely spontaneously. It requires thought and planning ahead. The educator is responsible for a knowledge of individuals and for a knowledge of subject-matter that will enable activities to be selected which lend themselves to social organization, an organization in which all individuals have an opportunity to contribute something, and in which the activities in which all participate are the chief carrier of control.

I am not romantic enough about the young to suppose that every pupil will respond or that any child of normally strong impulses will respond on every occasion. There are likely to be some who, when they come to school, are already victims of injurious conditions outside of the school and who have become so passive and unduly docile that they fail to contribute. There will be others who, because of previous experience, are bumptious and unruly and perhaps downright rebellious. But it is certain that the general principle of social control cannot be predicated upon such cases. It is also true that no general rule can be laid down for dealing with such cases. The teacher has to deal with them individually. They fall into general classes, but no two are exactly alike. The educator has to discover as best he or she can the causes for the recalcitrant attitudes. He or she cannot, if the educational process is to go on, make it a question of pitting one will against another in order to see which is strongest, nor yet allow the unruly and non-participating pupils to stand permanently in the way of the educative activities of others. Exclusion perhaps is the only available measure at a given juncture, but it is no solution. For it may strengthen the very causes which have brought about the undesirable anti-social attitude, such as desire for attention or to show off.

Exceptions rarely prove a rule or give a clue to what the rule should be. I would not, therefore, attach too much importance to these exceptional cases, although it is true at present that progressive schools are likely often to have more than their fair share of these cases, since parents may send children to such schools as a last resort. I do not think weakness in control when it is found in progressive schools arises in any event from these exceptional cases. It is much more likely to arise from failure to arrange in advance for the kind of work (by which I mean all kinds of activities engaged in) which will create situations that of themselves tend to exercise control over what this, that, and the other pupil does and how he does it. This failure most often goes back to lack of sufficiently thoughtful planning in advance. The causes for such lack are varied. The one which is peculiarly important to mention in this connection is the idea that such advance planning is unnecessary and even that it is inherently hostile to the legitimate freedom of those being instructed.

Now, of course, it is quite possible to have preparatory planning by the teacher done in such a rigid and intellectually inflexible fashion that it does result in adult imposition, which is none the less external because executed with tact and the semblance of respect for individual freedom. But this kind of planning does not follow inherently from the principle involved. I do not know what the greater maturity of the teacher and the teacher's greater knowledge of the world, of subject-matters and of individuals, is for unless the teacher can arrange conditions that are conducive to community activity and to organization which exercises control over individual impulses by the mere fact that all are engaged in communal projects. Because the kind of advance planning heretofore engaged in has been so routine as to leave little room for the free play of individual thinking or for contributions due to distinctive individual experience, it does not follow that all planning must be rejected. On the contrary, there is incumbent upon the educator the duty of instituting a much more intelligent, and consequently more difficult, kind of planning. He must survey the capacities and needs of the particular set of individuals with whom he is dealing and must at the same time arrange the conditions which provide the subject-matter or content for experiences that satisfy these needs and develop these capacities. The planning must be flexible enough to permit free play for individuality of experience and yet firm enough to give direction towards continuous development of power.

The present occasion is a suitable one to say something about the province and office of the teacher. The principle that development of experience comes about through interaction means that education is essentially a social process. This quality is realized in the degree in which individuals form a community group. It is absurd to exclude the teacher from membership in the group. As the most mature member of the group he has a peculiar responsibility for the conduct of the interactions and intercommunications which are the very life of the group as a community. That children are individuals whose freedom should be respected while the more mature person should have no freedom as an individual is an idea too absurd to require refutation. The tendency to exclude the teacher from a positive and leading share in the direction of the activities of the community of which he is a member is another instance of reaction from one extreme to another. When pupils were a class rather than a social group, the teacher necessarily acted largely from the outside, not as a director of processes of exchange in which all had a share. When education is based upon experience and educative experience is seen to be a social process, the situation changes radically. The teacher loses the position of external boss or dictator but takes on that of leader of group activities.

In discussing the conduct of games as an example of normal social control, reference was made to the presence of a standardized conventional factor. The counterpart of this factor in school life is found in the question of manners, especially of good manners in the manifestations of politeness and courtesy. The more we know about customs in different parts of the world at different times in the history of mankind, the more we learn how much manners differ from place to place and time to time. This fact proves that there is a large conventional factor involved. But there is no group at any time or place which does not have some code of manners as, for example, with respect to proper ways of greeting other persons. The particular form a convention takes has nothing fixed and absolute about it. But the existence of some form of convention is not itself a convention. It is a uniform attendant of all social relationships. At the very least, it is the oil which prevents or reduces friction.

It is possible, of course, for these social forms to become, as we say, "mere formalities." They may become merely outward show with no meaning behind them. But the avoidance of empty ritualistic forms of social intercourse does not mean the rejection of every formal element. It rather indicates the need for development of forms of intercourse that are inherently appropriate to social situations. Visitors to some progressive schools are shocked by the lack of manners they come across. One who knows the situation better is aware that to some extent their absence is due to the eager interest of children to go on with what they are doing. In their eagerness they may, for example, bump into each other and into visitors with no word of apology. One might say that this condition is better than a display of merely external punctilio accompanying intellectual and emotional lack of interest in school work. But it also represents a failure in education, a failure to learn one of the most important lessons of life, that of mutual accommodation and adaptation. Education is going on in a one-sided way, for attitudes and habits are in process of formation that stand in the way of the future learning that springs from easy and ready contact and communication with others.

CHAPTER V
THE NATURE OF FREEDOM

At the risk of repeating what has been often said by me I want to say something about the other side of the problem of social control, namely, the nature of freedom. The only freedom that is of enduring importance is freedom of intelligence, that is to say, freedom of observation and of judgment exercised in behalf of purposes that are intrinsically worth while. The commonest mistake made about freedom is, I think, to identify it with freedom of movement, or with the external or physical side of activity. Now, this external and physical side of activity cannot be separated from the internal side of activity; from freedom of thought, desire, and purpose. The limitation that was put upon outward action by the fixed arrangements of the typical traditional schoolroom, with its fixed rows of desks and its military regimen of pupils who were permitted to move only at certain fixed signals, put a great restriction upon intellectual and moral freedom. Strait-jacket and chain-gang procedures had to be done away with if there was to be a chance for growth of individuals in the intellectual springs of freedom without which there is no assurance of genuine and continued normal growth.

But the fact still remains that an increased measure of freedom of outer movement is a *means*, not an end. The educational problem is not solved when this aspect of freedom is obtained. Everything then depends, so far as education is concerned, upon what is done with this added liberty. What end does it serve? What consequences flow from it? Let me speak first of the advantages which reside potentially in increase of outward freedom. In the first place, without its existence it is practically impossible for a teacher to gain knowledge of the individuals with whom he is concerned. Enforced quiet and acquiescence prevent pupils from disclosing their real natures. They enforce artificial uniformity. They put seeming before being. They place a premium upon preserving the outward appearance of attention, decorum, and obedience. And everyone who is acquainted with schools in which this system prevailed well knows that thoughts, imaginations, desires, and sly activities ran their own unchecked course behind this façade. They were disclosed to the teacher only when some untoward act led to their detection. One has only to contrast this highly artificial situation with normal human relations outside the schoolroom, say in a well-conducted home, to appreciate how fatal it is to the teacher's acquaintance with and understanding of the individuals who are, supposedly, being educated. Yet without this insight there is only an accidental chance that the material of study and the methods used in instruction will so come home to an individual that his development of mind and character is actually directed. There is a vicious circle. Mechanical uniformity of studies and methods creates a kind of uniform immobility and this reacts to perpetuate uniformity of studies and of recitations, while behind this enforced uniformity individual tendencies operate in irregular and more or less forbidden ways.

The other important advantage of increased outward freedom is found in the very nature of the learning process. That the older methods set a premium upon passivity and receptivity has been pointed out. Physical quiescence puts a tremendous premium upon these traits. The only escape from them in the standardized school is an activity which is irregular and perhaps disobedient. There cannot be complete quietude in a laboratory or workshop. The nonsocial character of the traditional school is seen in the fact that it erected silence into one of its prime virtues. There is, of course, such a thing as intense intellectual activity without overt bodily activity. But capacity for such intellectual activity marks a comparatively late achievement when it is continued for a long period. There should be brief intervals of time for quiet reflection provided for even the young. But they are periods of genuine reflection only when they follow after times of more overt action and are used to organize what has been gained in periods of activity in which the hands and other parts of the body beside the brain are used. Freedom of movement is also important as a means of maintaining normal physical and mental health. We have still to learn from the example of the Greeks who saw clearly the relation between a sound body and a sound mind. But in all the respects mentioned freedom of outward action is a means to freedom of judgment and of power to carry deliberately chosen ends into execution. The amount of external freedom which is needed varies from individual to individual. It naturally tends to decrease with increasing maturity, though its complete absence prevents even a mature individual from having the contacts which will provide him with new materials upon which his intelligence may exercise itself. The amount and the quality of this kind of free activity as a means of growth is a problem that must engage the thought of the educator at every stage of development.

There can be no greater mistake, however, than to treat such freedom as an end in itself. It then tends to be destructive of the shared co-operative activities which are the normal source of order. But, on the other hand, it turns freedom which should be positive into something negative. For freedom from restriction, the negative side, is to be prized only as a means to a freedom which is power: power to frame purposes, to judge wisely, to evaluate desires by the consequences which will result from acting upon them; power to select and order means to carry chosen ends into operation.

Natural impulses and desires constitute in any case the starting point. But there is no intellectual growth without some reconstruction, some remaking, of impulses and desires in the form in which they first show themselves. This remaking involves inhibition of impulse in its first estate. The alternative to externally imposed inhibition is inhibition through an individual's own reflection and judgment. The old phrase "stop and think" is sound psychology. For thinking is stoppage of the immediate manifestation of impulse until that impulse has been brought into connection with other possible tendencies to action so that a more comprehensive and coherent plan of activity is formed. Some of the other tendencies to action lead to use of eye, ear, and hand to observe objective conditions; others result in recall of what has happened in the past. Thinking is thus a postponement of immediate action, while it effects internal control of impulse through a union of observation and memory, this union being the heart of reflection. What has been said explains the meaning of the well-worn phrase "self-control." The ideal aim of education is creation of power of self-control. But the mere removal of external control is no guarantee for the production of self-control. It is easy to jump out of the frying-pan into the fire. It is easy, in other words, to escape one form of external control only to find oneself in another and more dangerous form of external control. Impulses and desires that are not ordered by intelligence are under the control of accidental circumstances. It may be a loss rather than a gain to escape from the control of another person only to find one's conduct dictated by immediate whim and caprice; that is, at the mercy of impulses into whose formation intelligent judgment has not entered. A person whose conduct is controlled in this way has at most only the illusion of freedom. Actually he is directed by forces over which he has no command.

CHAPTER VI
THE MEANING OF PURPOSE

It is, then, a sound instinct which identifies freedom with power to frame purposes and to execute or carry into effect purposes so framed. Such freedom is in turn identical with self-control; for the formation of purposes and the organization of means to execute them are the work of intelligence. Plato once defined a slave as the person who executes the purposes of another, and, as has just been said, a person is also a slave who is enslaved to his own blind desires. There is, I think, no point in the philosophy of progressive education which is sounder than its emphasis upon the importance of the participation of the learner in the formation of the purposes which direct his activities in the learning process, just as there is no defect in traditional education greater than its failure to secure the active co-operation of the pupil in construction of the purposes involved in his studying. But the meaning of purposes and ends is not self-evident and self-explanatory. The more their educational importance is emphasized, the more important it is to understand what a purpose is; how it arises and how it functions in experience.

A genuine purpose always starts with an impulse. Obstruction of the immediate execution of an impulse converts it into a desire. Nevertheless neither impulse nor desire is itself a purpose. A purpose is an end-view. That is, it involves foresight of the consequences which will result from acting upon impulse. Foresight of consequences involves the operation of intelligence. It demands, in the first place, observation of objective conditions and circumstances. For impulse and desire produce consequences not by themselves alone but through their interaction or co-operation with surrounding conditions. The impulse for such a simple action as walking is executed only in active conjunction with the ground on which one stands. Under ordinary circumstances, we do not have to pay much attention to the ground. In a ticklish situation we have to observe very carefully just what the conditions are, as in climbing a steep and rough mountain where no trail has been laid out. Exercise of observation is, then, one condition of transformation of impulse into a purpose. As in the sign by a railway crossing, we have to stop, look, listen.

But observation alone is not enough. We have to understand the *significance* of what we see, hear, and touch. This significance consists of the consequences that will result when what is seen is acted upon. A baby may *see* the brightness of a flame and be attracted thereby to reach for it. The significance of the flame is then not its brightness but its power to burn, as the consequence that will result from touching it. We can be aware of consequences only because of previous experiences. In cases that are familiar because of many prior experiences we do not have to stop to remember just what those experiences were. A flame comes to signify light and heat without our having expressly to think of previous experiences of heat and burning. But in unfamiliar cases, we can not tell just what the consequences of observed conditions will be unless we go over past experences in our mind, unless we reflect upon them and by seeing what is similar in them to those now present, go on to form a judgment of what may be expected in the present situation.

The formation of purposes is, then, a rather complex intellectual operation. It involves (1) observation of surrounding conditions; (2) knowledge of what has happened in similar situations in the past, a knowledge obtained partly by recollection and partly from the information, advice, and warning of those who have had a wider experience; and (3) judgment which puts together what is observed and what is recalled to see what they signify. A purpose differs from an original impulse and desire through its translation into a plan and method of action based upon foresight of the consequences of acting under given observed conditions in a certain way. "If wishes were horses, beggars would ride." Desire for something may be intense. It may be so strong as to override estimation of the consequences that will follow acting upon it. Such occurrences do not provide the model for education. The crucial educational problem is that of procuring the postponement of immediate action upon desire until observation and judgment have intervened. Unless I am mistaken, this point is definitely relevant to the conduct of progressive schools. Overemphasis upon activity as an end, instead of upon *intelligent* activity, leads to identification of freedom with immediate execution of impulses and desires. This identification is justified by a confusion of impulse with purpose; although, as has just been said, there is no purpose unless overt action is postponed until there is foresight of the consequences of carrying the impulse into execution —a foresight that is impossible without observation, information, and judgment. Mere foresight, even if it takes the form of accurate prediction, is not, of course, enough. The intellectual anticipation, the idea of consequence , must blend with desire and impulse to acquire moving force. It then gives direction to what otherwise is blind, while desire gives ideas impetus and momentum. An idea then becomes a plan in and for an activity to be carried out. Suppose a man has a desire to secure a new home, say by building a house. No matter how strong his desire, it cannot be directly executed. The man must form an idea of what kind of house he wants, including the number and arrangement of rooms, etc. He has to draw a plan, and have blue prints and specifications made. All this might be an idle amusement for spare time unless he also took stock of his resources. He must consider the relation of his funds and available credit to the execution of the plan. He has to investigate available sites, their price, their nearness to his place of business, to a congenial neighborhood, to school facilities, and so on and so on. All of the things reckoned with: his ability to pay, size and needs of family, possible locations, etc., etc., are objective facts. They are no part of the original desire. But they have to be viewed and judged in order that a desire may be converted into a purpose and a purpose into a plan of action.

All of us have desires, all at least who have not become so pathological that they are completely apathetic. These desires are the ultimate moving springs of action. A professional businessman wishes to succeed in his career; a general wishes to win the battle; a parent to have a comfortable home for his family, and to educate his children, and so on indefinitely. The intensity of the desire measures the strength of the efforts that will be put forth. But the wishes are empty castles in the air unless they are translated into the means by which they may be realized. The question of *how soon* or of means takes the place of a projected imaginative end, and, since means are objective, they have to be studied and understood if a genuine purpose is to be formed.

Traditional education tended to ignore the importance of personal impulse and desire as moving springs. But this is no reason why progressive education should identify impulse and desire with purpose and thereby pass lightly over the need for careful observation, for wide range of information, and for judgment if students are to share in the formation of the purposes which activate them. In an *educational* scheme, the occurrence of a desire and impulse is not the final end. It is an occasion and a demand for the formation of a plan and method of activity. Such a plan, to repeat, can be formed only by study of conditions and by securing all relevant information.

The teacher's business is to see that the occasion is taken advantage of. Since freedom resides in the operations of intelligent observation and judgment by which a purpose is developed, guidance given by the teacher to the exercise of the pupils' intelligence is an aid to freedom, not a restriction upon it. Sometimes teachers seem to be afraid even to make suggestions to the members of a group as to what they should do. I have heard of cases in which children are surrounded with objects and materials and then left entirely to themselves, the teacher being loath to suggest even what might be done with the materials lest freedom be infringed upon. Why, then, even supply materials, since they are a source of some suggestion or other? But what is more important is that the suggestion upon which pupils act must in any case come from somewhere. It is impossible to understand why a suggestion from one who has a larger experience and a wider horizon should not be at least as valid as a suggestion arising from some more or less accidental source.

It is possible of course to abuse the office, and to force the activity of the young into channels which express the teacher's purpose rather than that of the pupils. But the way to avoid this danger is not for the adult to withdraw entirely. The way is, first, for the teacher to be intelligently aware of the capacities, needs, and past experiences of those under instruction, and, secondly, to allow the suggestion made to develop into a plan and project by means of the further suggestions contributed and organized into a whole by the members of the group. The plan, in other words, is a co-operative enterprise, not a dictation. The teacher's suggestion is not a mold for a cast-iron result but is a starting point to be developed into a plan through contributions from the experience of all engaged in the learning process. The development occurs through reciprocal give-and-take, the teacher taking but not being afraid also to give. The essential point is that the purpose grow and take shape through the process of social intelligence.

CHAPTER VII
PROGRESSIVE ORGANIZATION
OF SUBJECT-MATTER

Allusion has been made in passing a number of times to objective conditions involved in experience and to their function in promoting or failing to promote the enriched growth of further experience. By implication, these objective conditions, whether those of observation, of memory, of information procured from others, or of imagination, have been identified with the subject-matter of study and learning; or, speaking more generally, with the stuff of the course of study. Nothing, however, has been said explicitly so far about subject-matter as such. That topic will now be discussed. One consideration stands out clearly when education is conceived in terms of experience. Anything which can be called a study, whether arithmetic, history, geography, or one of the natural sciences, must be derived from materials which at the outset fall within the scope of ordinary life-experience. In this respect the newer education contrasts sharply with procedures which start with facts and truths that are outside the range of the experience of those taught, and which, therefore, have the problem of discovering ways and means of bringing them within experience. Undoubtedly one chief cause for the great success of newer methods in early elementary education has been its observance of the contrary principle.

But finding the material for learning within experience is only the first step. The next step is the progressive development of what is already experienced into a fuller and richer and also more organized form, a form that gradually approximates that in which subject-matter is presented to the skilled, mature person. That this change is possible without departing from the organic connection of education with experience is shown by the fact that this change takes place outside of the school and apart from formal education. The infant, for example, begins with an environment of objects that is very restricted in space and time. That environment steadily expands by the momentum inherent in experience itself without aid from scholastic instruction. As the infant learns to reach, creep, walk, and talk, the intrinsic subject-matter of its experience widens and deepens. It comes into connection with new objects and events which call out new powers, while the exercise of these powers refines and enlarges the content of its experience. Life-space and life-durations are expanded. The environment, the world of experience, constantly grows larger and, so to speak, thicker. The educator who receives the child at the end of this period has to find ways for doing consciously and deliberately what "nature" accomplishes in the earlier years.

It is hardly necessary to insist upon the first of the two conditions which have been specified. It is a cardinal precept of the newer school of education that the beginning of instruction shall be made with the experience learners already have; that this experience and the capacities that have been developed during its course provide the starting point for all further learning. I am not so sure that the other condition, that of orderly development toward expansion and organization of subject-matter through growth of experience, receives as much attention. Yet the principle of continuity of educative experience requires that equal thought and attention be given to solution of this aspect of the educational problem. Undoubtedly this phase of the problem is more difficult than the other. Those who deal with the pre-school child, with the kindergarten child, and with the boy and girl of the early primary years do not have much difficulty in determining the range of past experience or in finding activities that connect in vital ways with it. With older children both factors of the problem offer increased difficulties to the educator. It is harder to find out the background of the experience of individuals and harder to find out just how the subject-matters already contained in that experience shall be directed so as to lead out to larger and better organized fields.

It is a mistake to suppose that the principle of the leading on of experience to something different is adequately satisfied simply by giving pupils some new experiences any more than it is by seeing to it that they have greater skill and ease in dealing with things with which they are already familiar. It is also essential that the new objects and events be related intellectually to those of earlier experiences, and this means that there be some advance made in conscious articulation of facts and ideas. It thus becomes the office of the educator to select those things within the range of existing experience that have the promise and potentiality of presenting new problems which by stimulating new ways of observation and judgment will expand the area of further experience. He must constantly regard what is already won not as a fixed possession but as an agency and instrumentality for opening new fields which make new demands upon existing powers of observation and of intelligent use of memory. Connectedness in growth must be his constant watchword.

The educator more than the member of any other profession is concerned to have a long look ahead. The physician may feel his job done when he has restored a patient to health. He has undoubtedly the obligation of advising him how to live so as to avoid similar troubles in the future. But, after all, the conduct of his life is his own affair, not the physician's; and what is more important for the present point is that as far as the physician does occupy himself with instruction and advice as to the future of his patient he takes upon himself the function of an educator. The lawyer is occupied with winning a suit for his client or getting the latter out of some complication into which he has got himself. If it goes beyond the case presented to him he too becomes an educator. The educator by the very nature of his work is obliged to see his present work in terms of what it accomplishes, or fails to accomplish, for a future whose objects are linked with those of the present.

Here, again, the problem for the progressive educator is more difficult than for the teacher in the traditional school. The latter had indeed to look ahead. But unless his personality and enthusiasm took him beyond the limits that hedged in the traditional school, he could content himself with thinking of the next examination period or the promotion to the next class. He could envisage the future in terms of factors that lay within the requirements of the school system as that conventionally existed. There is incumbent upon the teacher who links education and actual experience together a more serious and a harder business. He must be aware of the potentialities for leading students into new fields which belong to experiences already had, and must use this knowledge as his criterion for selection and arrangement of the conditions that influence their present experience.

Because the studies of the traditional school consisted of subject-matter that was selected and arranged on the basis of the judgment of adults as to what would be useful for the young sometime in the future, the material to be learned was settled upon outside the present life-experience of the learner. In consequence, it had to do with the past; it was such as had proved useful to men in past ages. By reaction to an opposite extreme, as unfortunate as it was probably natural under the circumstances, the sound idea that education should derive its materials from present experience and should enable the learner to cope with the problems of the present and future has often been converted into the idea that progressive schools can to a very large extent ignore the past. If the present could be cut off from the past, this conclusion would be sound. But the achievements of the past provide the only means at command for understanding the present. Just as the individual has to draw in memory upon his own past to understand the conditions in which he individually finds himself, so the issues and problems of present *social* life are in such intimate and direct connection with the past that students cannot be prepared to understand either these problems or the best way of dealing with them without delving into their roots in the past. In other words, the sound principle that the objectives of learning are in the future and its immediate materials are in present experience can be carried into effect only in the degree that present experience is stretched, as it were, backward. It can expand into the future only as it is also enlarged to take in the past.

If time permitted, discussion of the political and economic issues which the present generation will be compelled to face in the future would render this general statement definite and concrete. The nature of the issues cannot be understood save as we know how they came about. The institutions and customs that exist in the present and that give rise to present social ills and dislocations did not arise overnight. They have a long history behind them. Attempt to deal with them simply on the basis of what is obvious in the present is bound to result in adoption of superficial measures which in the end will only render existing problems more acute and more difficult to solve. Policies framed simply upon the ground of knowledge of the present cut off from the past is the counterpart of heedless carelessness in individual conduct. The way out of scholastic systems that made the past an end in itself is to make acquaintance with the past a *means* of understanding the present. Until this problem is worked out, the present clash of educational ideas and practices will continue. On the one hand, there will be reactionaries that claim that the main, if not the sole, business of education is transmission of the cultural heritage. On the other hand, there will be those who hold that we should ignore the past and deal only with the present and future.

That up to the present time the weakest point in progressive schools is in the matter of selection and organization of intellectual subject-matter is, I think, inevitable under the circumstances. It is as inevitable as it is right and proper that they should break loose from the cut and dried material which formed the staple of the old education. In addition, the field of experience is very wide and it varies in its contents from place to place and from time to time. A single course of studies for all progressive schools is out of the question; it would mean abandoning the fundamental principle of connection with life-experiences. Moreover, progressive schools are new. They have had hardly more than a generation in which to develop. A certain amount of uncertainty and of laxity in choice and organization of subject-matter is, therefore, what was to be expected. It is no ground for fundamental criticism or complaint.

It is a ground for legitimate criticism, however, when the ongoing movement of progressive education fails to recognize that the problem of selection and organization of subject-matter for study and learning is fundamental. Improvisation that takes advantage of special occasions prevents teaching and learning from being stereotyped and dead. But the basic material of study cannot be picked up in a cursory manner. Occasions which are not and cannot be foreseen are bound to arise wherever there is intellectual freedom. They should be utilized. But there is a decided difference between using them in the development of a continuing line of activity and trusting to them to provide the chief material of learning.

Unless a given experience leads out into a field previously unfamiliar no problems arise, while problems are the stimulus to thinking. That the conditions found in present experience should be used as sources of problems is a characteristic which differentiates education based upon experience from traditional education. For in the latter, problems were set from outside. Nonetheless, growth depends upon the presence of difficulty to be overcome by the exercise of intelligence. Once more, it is part of the educator's responsibility to see equally to two things: First, that the problem grows out of the conditions of the experience being had in the present, and that it is within the range of the capacity of students; and, secondly, that it is such that it arouses in the learner an active quest for information and for production of new ideas. The new facts and new ideas thus obtained become the ground for further experiences in which new problems are presented. The process is a continuous spiral. The inescapable linkage of the present with the past is a principle whose application is not restricted to a study of history. Take natural science, for example. Contemporary social life is what it is in very large measure because of the results of application of physical science. The experience of every child and youth, in the country and the city, is what it is in its present actuality because of appliances which utilize electricity, heat, and chemical processes. A child does not eat a meal that does not involve in its preparation and assimilation chemical and physiological principles. He does not read by artificial light or take a ride in a motor car or on a train without coming into contact with operations and processes which science has engendered.

It is a sound educational principle that students should be introduced to scientific subject-matter and be initiated into its facts and laws through acquaintance with everyday social applications. Adherence to this method is not only the most direct avenue to understanding of science itself but as the pupils grow more mature it is also the surest road to the understanding of the economic and industrial problems of present society. For they are the products to a very large extent of the application of science in production and distribution of commodities and services, while the latter processes are the most important factor in determining the present relations of human beings and social groups to one another. It is absurd, then, to argue that processes similar to those studied in laboratories and institutes of research are not a part of the daily life-experience of the young and hence do not come within the scope of education based upon experience. That the immature cannot study scientific facts and principles in the way in which mature experts study them goes without saying. But this fact, instead of exempting the educator from responsibility for using present experiences so that learners may gradually be led, through extraction of facts and laws, to experience of a scientific order, sets one of his main problems.

For if it is true that existing experience in detail and also on a wide scale is what it is because of the application of science, first, to processes of production and distribution of goods and services, and then to the relations which human beings sustain socially to one another, it is impossible to obtain an understanding of present social forces (without which they cannot be mastered and directed) apart from an education which leads learners into knowledge of the very same facts and principles which in their final organization constitute the sciences. Nor does the importance of the principle that learners should be led to acquaintance with scientific subject-matter cease with the insight thereby given into present social issues. The methods of science also point the way to the measures and policies by means of which a better social order can be brought into existence. The applications of science which have produced in large measure the social conditions which now exist do not exhaust the possible field of their application. For so far science has been applied more or less casually and under the influence of ends, such as private advantage and power, which are a heritage from the institutions of a prescientific age.

We are told almost daily and from many sources that it is impossible for human beings to direct their common life intelligently. We are told, on one hand, that the complexity of human relations, domestic and international, and on the other hand, the fact that human beings are so largely creatures of emotion and habit, make impossible large-scale social planning and direction by intelligence. This view would be more credible if any systematic effort, beginning with early education and carried on through the continuous study and learning of the young, had ever been undertaken with a view to making the method of intelligence, exemplified in science, supreme in education. There is nothing in the inherent nature of habit that prevents intelligent method from becoming itself habitual; and there is nothing in the nature of emotion to prevent the development of intense emotional allegiance to the method.

The case of science is here employed as an illustration of progressive selection of subject-matter resident in present experience towards organization: an organization which is free, not externally imposed, because it is in accord with the growth of experience itself. The utilization of subject-matter found in the present life-experience of the learner towards science is perhaps the best illustration that can be found of the basic principle of using existing experience as the means of carrying learners on to a wider, more refined, and better organized environing world, physical and human, than is found in the experiences from which educative growth sets out. Hogben's recent work, *Mathematics for the Million*, shows how mathematics, if it is treated as a mirror of civilization and as a main agency in its progress, can contribute to the desired goal as surely as can the physical sciences. The underlying ideal in any case is that of progressive organization of knowledge. It is with reference to organization of knowledge that we are likely to find *Either-Or* philosophies most acutely active. In practice, if not in so many words, it is often held that since traditional education rested upon a conception of organization of knowledge that was almost completely contemptuous of living present experience, therefore education based upon living experience should be contemptuous of the organization of facts and ideas.

When a moment ago I called this organization an *ideal*, I meant, on the negative side, that the educator cannot start with knowledge already organized and proceed to ladle it out in doses. But as an ideal the active process of organizing facts and ideas is an ever-present educational process. No experience is educative that does not tend both to knowledge of more facts and entertaining of more ideas and to a better, a more orderly, arrangement of them. It is not true that organization is a principle foreign to experience. Otherwise experience would be so dispersive as to be chaotic. The experience of young children centers about persons and the home. Disturbance of the normal order of relationships in the family is now known by psychiatrists to be a fertile source of later mental and emotional troubles—a fact which testifies to the reality of this kind of organization. One of the great advances in early school education, in the kindergarten and early grades, is that it preserves the social and human center of the organization of experience, instead of the older violent shift of the center of gravity. But one of the outstanding problems of education, as of music, is modulation. In the case of education, modulation means movement from a social and human center toward a more objective intellectual scheme of organization, always bearing in mind, however, that intellectual organization is not an end in itself but is the means by which social relations, distinctively human ties and bonds, may be understood and more intelligently ordered.

When education is based in theory and practice upon experience, it goes without saying that the organized subject-matter of the adult and the specialist cannot provide the starting point. Nevertheless, it represents the goal toward which education should continuously move. It is hardly necessary to say that one of the most fundamental principles of the scientific organization of knowledge is the principle of cause and effect. The way in which this principle is grasped and formulated by the scientific specialist is certainly very different from the way in which it can be approached in the experience of the young. But neither the relation nor grasp of its meaning is foreign to the experience of even the young child. When a child two or three years of age learns not to approach a flame too closely and yet to draw near enough a stove to get its warmth he is grasping and using the causal relation. There is no intelligent activity that does not conform to the requirements of the relation, and it is intelligent in the degree in which it is not only conformed to but consciously borne in mind.

In the earlier forms of experience the causal relation does not offer itself in the abstract but in the form of the relation of means employed to ends attained; of the relation of means and consequences. Growth in judgment and understanding is essentially growth in ability to form purposes and to select and arrange means for their realization. The most elementary experiences of the young are filled with cases of the means-consequence relation. There is not a meal cooked nor a source of illumination employed that does not exemplify this relation. The trouble with education is not the absence of situations in which the causal relation is exemplified in the relation of means and consequences. Failure to utilize the situations so as to lead the learner on to grasp the relation in the given cases of experience is, however, only too common. The logician gives the names "analysis and synthesis" to the operations by which means are selected and organized in relation to a purpose.

This principle determines the ultimate foundation for the utilization of *activities* in school. Nothing can be more absurd educationally than to make a plea for a variety of active occupations in the school while decrying the need for progressive organization of information and ideas. Intelligent activity is distinguished from aimless activity by the fact that it involves selection of means—analysis—out of the variety of conditions that are present, and their arrangement—synthesis—to reach an intended aim or purpose. That the more immature the learner is, the simpler must be the ends held in view and the more rudimentary the means employed, is obvious. But the principle of organization of activity in terms of some perception of the relation of consequences to means applies even with the very young. Otherwise an activity ceases to be educative because it is blind. With increased maturity, the problem of interrelation of means becomes more urgent. In the degree in which intelligent observation is transferred from the relation of means to ends to the more complex question of the relation of means to one another, the idea of cause and effect becomes prominent and explicit. The final justification of shops, kitchens, and so on in the school is not just that they afford opportunity for activity, but that they provide opportunity for the *kind* of activity or for the acquisition of mechanical skills which leads students to attend to the relation of means and ends, and then to consideration of the way things interact with one another to produce definite effects. It is the same in principle as the ground for laboratories in scientific research.

Unless the problem of intellectual organization can be worked out on the ground of experience, reaction is sure to occur toward externally imposed methods of organization. There are signs of this reaction already in evidence. We are told that our schools, old and new, are failing in the main task. They do not develop, it is said, the capacity for critical discrimination and the ability to reason. The ability to think is smothered, we are told, by accumulation of miscellaneous ill-digested information, and by the attempt to acquire forms of skill which will be immediately useful in the business and commercial world. We are told that these evils spring from the influence of science and from the magnification of present requirements at the expense of the tested cultural heritage from the past. It is argued that science and its method must be subordinated; that we must return to the logic of ultimate first principles expressed in the logic of Aristotle and St. Thomas, in order that the young may have sure anchorage in their intellectual and moral life, and not be at the mercy of every passing breeze that blows.

If the method of science had ever been consistently and continuously applied throughout the day-by-day work of the school in all subjects, I should be more impressed by this emotional appeal than I am. I see at bottom but two alternatives between which education must choose if it is not to drift aimlessly. One of them is expressed by the attempt to induce educators to return to the intellectual methods and ideals that arose centuries before scientific method was developed. The appeal may be temporarily successful in a period when general insecurity, emotional and intellectual as well as economic, is rife. For under these conditions the desire to lean on fixed authority is active. Nevertheless, it is so out of touch with all the conditions of modern life that I believe it is folly to seek salvation in this direction. The other alternative is systematic utilization of scientific method as the pattern and ideal of intelligent exploration and exploitation of the potentialities inherent in experience.

The problem involved comes home with peculiar force to progressive schools. Failure to give constant attention to development of the intellectual content of experiences and to obtain ever-increasing organization of facts and ideas may in the end merely strengthen the tendency toward a reactionary return to intellectual and moral authoritarianism. The present is not the time nor place for a disquisition upon scientific method. But certain features of it are so closely connected with any educational scheme based upon experience that they should be noted.

In the first place, the experimental method of science attaches more importance, not less, to ideas as ideas than do other methods. There is no such thing as experiment in the scientific sense unless action is directed by some leading idea. The fact that the ideas employed are hypotheses, not final truths, is the reason why ideas are more jealously guarded and tested in science than anywhere else. The moment they are taken to be first truths in themselves there ceases to be any reason for scrupulous examination of them. As fixed truths they must be accepted and that is the end of the matter. But as hypotheses, they must be continuously tested and revised, a requirement that demands they be accurately formulated.

In the second place, ideas or hypotheses are tested by the consequences which they produce when they are acted upon. This fact means that the consequences of action must be carefully and discriminatingly observed. Activity that is not checked by observation of what follows from it may be temporarily enjoyed. But intellectually it leads nowhere. It does not provide knowledge about the situations in which action occurs nor does it lead to clarification and expansion of ideas.

In the third place, the method of intelligence manifested in the experimental method demands keeping track of ideas, activities, and observed consequences. Keeping track is a matter of reflective review and summarizing, in which there is both discrimination and record of the significant features of a developing experience. To reflect is to look back over what has been done so as to extract the net meanings which are the capital stock for intelligent dealing with further experiences. It is the heart of intellectual organization and of the disciplined mind.

I have been forced to speak in general and often abstract language. But what has been said is organically connected with the requirement that experiences in order to be educative must lead out into an expanding world of subject-matter, a subject-matter of facts or information and of ideas. This condition is satisfied only as the educator views teaching and learning as a continuous process of reconstruction of experience. This condition in turn can be satisfied only as the educator has a long look ahead, and views every present experience as a moving force in influencing what future experiences will be. I am aware that the emphasis I have placed upon scientific method may be misleading, for it may result only in calling up the special technique of laboratory research as that is conducted by specialists. But the meaning of the emphasis placed upon scientific method has little to do with specialized techniques. It means that scientific method is the only authentic means at our command for getting at the significance of our everyday experiences of the world in which we live. It means that scientific method provides a working pattern of the way in which and the conditions under which experiences are used to lead ever onward and outward. Adaptation of the method to individuals of various degrees of maturity is a problem for the educator, and the constant factors in the problem are the formation of ideas, acting upon ideas, observation of the conditions which result, and organization of facts and ideas for future use. Neither the ideas, nor the activities, nor the observations, nor the organization are the same for a person six years old as they are for one twelve or eighteen years old, to say nothing of the adult scientist. But at every level there is an expanding development of experience if experience is educative in effect. Consequently, whatever the level of experience, we have no choice but either to operate in accord with the pattern it provides or else to neglect the place of intelligence in the development and control of a living and moving experience.

CHAPTER VIII
EXPERIENCE—THE MEANS AND GOAL
OF EDUCATION

In what I have said I have taken for granted the soundness of the principle that education in order to accomplish its ends both for the individual learner and for society must be based upon experience—which is always the actual life-experience of some individual. I have not argued for the acceptance of this principle nor attempted to justify it. Conservatives as well as radicals in education are profoundly discontented with the present educational situation taken as a whole. There is at least this much agreement among intelligent persons of both schools of educational thought. The educational system must move one way or another, either backward to the intellectual and moral standards of a pre-scientific age or forward to ever greater utilization of scientific method in the development of the possibilities of growing, expanding experience. I have but endeavored to point out some of the conditions which must be satisfactorily fulfilled if education takes the latter course.

For I am so confident of the potentialities of education when it is treated as intelligently directed development of the possibilities inherent in ordinary experience that I do not feel it necessary to criticize here the other route nor to advance arguments in favor of taking the route of experience. The only ground for anticipating failure in taking this path resides to my mind in the danger that experience and the experimental method will not be adequately conceived. There is no discipline in the world so severe as the discipline of experience subjected to the tests of intelligent development and direction. Hence the only ground I can see for even a temporary reaction against the standards, aims, and methods of the newer education is the failure of educators who professedly adopt them to be faithful to them in practice. As I have emphasized more than once, the road of the new education is not an easier one to follow than the old road but a more strenuous and difficult one. It will remain so until it has attained its majority and that attainment will require many years of serious co-operative work on the part of its adherents. The greatest danger that attends its future is, I believe, the idea that it is an easy way to follow, so easy that its course may be improvised, if not in an impromptu fashion, at least almost from day to day or from week to week. It is for this reason that instead of extolling its principles, I have confined myself to showing certain conditions which must be fulfilled if it is to have the successful career which by right belongs to it.

I have used frequently in what precedes the words "progressive" and "new" education. I do not wish to close, however, without recording my firm belief that the fundamental issue is not of new versus old education nor of progressive against traditional education but a question of what anything whatever must be to be worthy of the name *education*. I am not, I hope and believe, in favor of any ends or any methods simply because the name progressive may be applied to them. The basic question concerns the nature of education with no qualifying adjectives prefixed. What we want and need is education pure and simple, and we shall make surer and faster progress when we devote ourselves to finding out just what education is and what conditions have to be satisfied in order that education may be a reality and not a name or a slogan. It is for this reason alone that I have emphasized the need for a sound philosophy of experience.

Alfred North Whitehead

(1861-1947)

WHITEHEAD never wrote a comprehensive work in philosophy of education, but on a number of occasions he delivered lectures concerned with various aspects of educational policy. These incisive lectures are collected in his book *The Aims of Education and Other Essays.*

It is interesting to compare his views with those of Dewey, for the two men were contemporaries, and their ideas are in some respects quite similar. Like Dewey, Whitehead stresses the importance of the utilization of knowledge, the need to interest students in their work, and the dangers of undiscriminating discipline. On occasion even the language they employ is similar. For instance, Whitehead argues that "the only use of a knowledge of the past is to equip us for the present." Dewey remarked that "knowledge of the past is the key to understanding the present."

It is difficult to determine, however, to what extent Whitehead's emphasis on the concept of "style" and the theory of "The Rhythm of Education" are consistent with Dewey's general position. There are certainly differences in approach between these two thinkers, which are to some extent accounted for by their diverse social and academic backgrounds. Whitehead was an Englishman who was educated and taught at the University of Cambridge. Dewey was born in Vermont, was educated at the University of Vermont, and taught high school in Pennsylvania before embarking upon his career in graduate education.

Among Whitehead's most compelling thoughts is that "one secret of a successful teacher is that he has formulated quite clearly in his mind what the pupil has got to know in precise fashion." An inexperienced teacher often hesitates to present material in a clear, easily understandable fashion for fear that this may rob his students of their initiative or creativity. Such a teacher soon learns that the presentation of material in a disorganized, confusing manner results in disorganized, confused students. As Whitehead notes, "a certain ruthless definiteness is essential in education."

One further point should be kept in mind. Whitehead expresses the view that "a merely well-informed man is the most useless bore on God's earth." He does not say, nor does he believe, that it is useless to be well-informed. Whitehead was himself one of the best-informed men of his time.

THE AIMS
OF EDUCATION

Culture is activity of thought, and receptiveness to beauty and humane feeling. Scraps of information have nothing to do with it. A merely well-informed man is the most useless bore on God's earth. What we should aim at producing is men who possess both culture and expert knowledge in some special direction. Their expert knowledge will give them the ground to start from, and their culture will lead them as deep as philosophy and as high as art. We have to remember that the valuable intellectual development is self-development, and that it mostly takes place between the ages of sixteen and thirty. As to training, the most important part is given by mothers before the age of twelve. A saying due to Archbishop Temple illustrates my meaning. Surprise was expressed at the success in after-life of a man, who as a boy at Rugby had been somewhat undistinguished. He answered, "It is not what they are at eighteen, it is what they become afterwards that matters."

In training a child to activity of thought, above all things we must beware of what I will call "inert ideas"—that is to say, ideas that are merely received into the mind without being utilized, or tested, or thrown into fresh combinations.

In the history of education, the most striking phenomenon is that schools of learning, which at one epoch are alive with a ferment of genius, in a succeeding generation exhibit merely pedantry and routine. The reason is, that they are overladen with inert ideas. Education with inert ideas is not only useless: it is, above all things, harmful—*Corruptio optimi, pessima.* Except at rare intervals of intellectual ferment, education in the past has been radically infected with inert ideas. That is the reason why uneducated clever women, who have seen much of the world, are in middle life so much the most cultured part of the community. They have been saved from this horrible burden of inert ideas. Every intellectual revolution which has ever stirred humanity into greatness has been a passionate protest against inert ideas. Then, alas, with pathetic ignorance of human psychology, it has proceeded by some educational scheme to bind humanity afresh with inert ideas of its own fashioning.

Let us now ask how in our system of education we are to guard against this mental dryrot. We enunciate two educational commandments, "Do not teach too many subjects," and again, "What you teach, teach thoroughly."

The result of teaching small parts of a large number of subjects is the passive reception of disconnected ideas, not illumined with any spark of vitality. Let the main ideas which are introduced into a child's education be few and important, and let them be thrown into every combination possible. The child should make them his own, and should understand their application here and now in the circumstances of his actual life. From the very beginning of his education, the child should experience the joy of discovery. The discovery which he has to make, is that general ideas give an understanding of that stream of events which pours through his life, which is his life. By understanding I mean more than a mere logical analysis, though that is included. I mean "understanding" in the sense in which it is used in the French proverb, "To understand all, is to forgive all." Pedants sneer at an education which is useful. But if education is not useful, what is it? Is it a talent, to be hidden away in a napkin? Of course, education should be useful, whatever your aim in life. It was useful to Saint Augustine and it was useful to Napoleon. It is useful, because understanding is useful.

I pass lightly over that understanding which should be given by the literary side of education. Nor do I wish to be supposed to pronounce on the relative merits of a classical or a modern curriculum. I would only remark that the understanding which we want is an understanding of an insistent present. The only use of a knowledge of the past is to equip us for the present. No more deadly harm can be done to young minds than by depreciation of the present. The present contains all that there is. It is holy ground; for it is the past, and it is the future. At the same time it must be observed that an age is no less past if it existed two hundred years ago than if it existed two thousand years ago. Do not be deceived by the pedantry of dates. The ages of Shakespeare and of Molière are no less past than are the ages of Sophocles and of Virgil. The communion of saints is a great and inspiring assemblage, but it has only one possible hall of meeting, and that is, the present; and the mere lapse of time through which any particular group of saints must travel to reach that meeting-place, makes very little difference.

Passing now to the scientific and logical side of education, we remember that here also ideas which are not utilized are positively harmful. By utilizing an idea, I mean relating it to that stream, compounded of sense perceptions, feelings, hopes, desires, and of mental activities adjusting thought to thought, which forms our life. I can imagine a set of beings which might fortify their souls by passively reviewing disconnected ideas. Humanity is not built that way—except perhaps some editors of newspapers.

In scientific training, the first thing to do with an idea is to prove it. But allow me for one moment to extend the meaning of "prove"; I mean—to prove its worth. Now an idea is not worth much unless the propositions in which it is embodied are true. Accordingly an essential part of the proof of an idea is the proof, either by experiment or by logic, of the truth of the propositions. But it is not essential that this proof of the truth should constitute the first introduction to the idea. After all, its assertion by the authority of respectable teachers is sufficient evidence to begin with. In our first contact with a set of propositions, we commence by appreciating their importance. That is what we all do in after-life. We do not attempt, in the strict sense, to prove or to disprove anything, unless its importance makes it worthy of that honour. These two processes of proof, in the narrow sense, and of appreciation, do not require a rigid separation in time. Both can be proceeded with nearly concurrently. But in so far as either process must have the priority, it should be that of appreciation by use.

Furthermore, we should not endeavour to use propositions in isolation. Emphatically I do not mean, a neat little set of experiments to illustrate Proposition I and then the proof of Proposition I, a neat little set of experiments to illustrate Proposition II and then the proof of Proposition II, and so on to the end of the book. Nothing could be more boring. Interrelated truths are utilized *en bloc*, and the various propositions are employed in any order, and with any reiteration. Choose some important applications of your theoretical subject; and study them concurrently with the systematic theoretical exposition. Keep the theoretical exposition short and simple, but let it be strict and rigid so far as it goes. It should not be too long for it to be easily known with thoroughness and accuracy. The consequences of a plethora of half-digested theoretical knowledge are deplorable. Also the theory should not be muddled up with the practice. The child should have no doubt when it is proving and when it is utilizing. My point is that what is proved should be utilized, and that what is utilized should—so far as is practicable—be proved. I am far from asserting that proof and utilization are the same thing.

At this point of my discourse, I can most directly carry forward my argument in the outward form of a digression. We are only just realizing that the art and science of education require a genius and a study of their own; and that this genius and this science are more than a bare knowledge of some branch of science or of literature. This truth was partially perceived in the past generation; and headmasters, somewhat crudely, were apt to supersede learning in their colleagues by requiring left-hand bowling and a taste for football. But culture is more than cricket, and more than football, and more than extent of knowledge.

Education is the acquisition of the art of the utilization of knowledge. This is an art very difficult to impart. Whenever a text-book is written of real educational worth, you may be quite certain that some reviewer will say that it will be difficult to teach from it. Of course it will be difficult to teach from it. If it were easy, the book ought to be burned; for it cannot be educational. In education, as elsewhere, the broad primrose path leads to a nasty place. . . .

We now return to my previous point, that theoretical ideas should always find important applications within the pupil's curriculum. This is not an easy doctrine to apply, but a very hard one. It contains within itself the problem of keeping knowledge alive, of preventing it from becoming inert, which is the central problem of all education.

The best procedure will depend on several factors, none of which can be neglected, namely, the genius of the teacher, the intellectual type of the pupils, their prospects in life, the opportunities offered by the immediate surroundings of the school, and allied factors of this sort. It is for this reason that the uniform external examination is so deadly. We do not denounce it because we are cranks, and like denouncing established things. We are not so childish. Also, of course, such examinations have their use in testing slackness. Our reason of dislike is very definite and very practical. It kills the best part of culture. When you analyze in the light of experience the central task of education, you find that its successful accomplishment depends on a delicate adjustment of many variable factors. The reason is that we are dealing with human minds, and not with dead matter. The evocation of curiosity, of judgment, of the power of mastering a complicated tangle of circumstances, the use of theory in giving foresight in special cases—all these powers are not to be imparted by a set rule embodied in one schedule of examination subjects.

I appeal to you, as practical teachers. With good discipline, it is always possible to pump into the minds of a class a certain quantity of inert knowledge. You take a text-book and make them learn it. So far, so good. The child then knows how to solve a quadratic equation. But what is the point of teaching a child to solve a quadratic equation? There is a traditional answer to this question. It runs thus: The mind is an instrument, you first sharpen it, and then use it; the acquisition of the power of solving a quadratic equation is part of the process of sharpening the mind. Now there is just enough truth in this answer to have made it live through the ages. But for all its half-truth, it embodies a radical error which bids fair to stifle the genius of the modern world. I do not know who was first responsible for this analogy of the mind to a dead instrument. For aught I know, it may have been one of the seven wise men of Greece, or a committee of the whole lot of them. Whoever was the originator, there can be no doubt of the authority which it has acquired by the continuous approval bestowed upon it by eminent persons. But whatever its weight of authority, whatever the high approval which it can quote, I have no hesitation in denouncing it as one of the most fatal, erroneous, and dangerous conceptions ever introduced into the theory of education. The mind is never passive; it is a perpetual activity, delicate, receptive, responsive to stimulus. You cannot postpone its life until you have sharpened it. Whatever interest attaches to your subject-matter must be evoked here and now; whatever powers you are strengthening in the pupil, must be exercised here and now; whatever possibilities of mental life your teaching should impart, must be exhibited here and now. That is the golden rule of education, and a very difficult rule to follow.

The difficulty is just this: the apprehension of general ideas, intellectual habits of mind, and pleasurable interest in mental achievement can be evoked by no form of words however accurately adjusted. All practical teachers know that education is a patient process of the mastery of details, minute by minute, hour by hour, day by day. There is no royal road to learning through an airy path of brilliant generalizations. There is a proverb about the difficulty of seeing the wood because of the trees. That difficulty is exactly the point which I am enforcing. The problem of education is to make the pupil see the wood by means of the trees.

The solution which I am urging, is to eradicate the fatal disconnection of subjects which kills the vitality of our modern curriculum. There is only one subject-matter for education, and that is Life in all its manifestations. Instead of this single unity, we offer children—Algebra, from which nothing follows; Geometry, from which nothing follows; Science, from which nothing follows; History, from which nothing follows; a Couple of Languages, never mastered; and lastly, most dreary of all, Literature, represented by plays of Shakespeare, with philological notes and short analyses of plot and character to be in substance committed to memory. Can such a list be said to represent Life, as it is known in the midst of the living of it? The best that can be said of it is, that it is a rapid table of contents which a deity might run over in his mind while he was thinking of creating a world, and has not yet determined how to put it together.

Let us now return to quadratic equations. We still have on hand the unanswered question. Why should children be taught their solution? Unless quadratic equations fit into a connected curriculum, of course there is no reason to teach anything about them. Furthermore, extensive as should be the place of mathematics in a complete culture, I am a little doubtful whether for many types of boys algebraic solutions of quadratic equations do not lie on the specialist side of mathematics. I may here remind you that as yet I have not said anything of the psychology or the content of the specialism, which is so necessary a part of an ideal education. But all that is an evasion of our real question, and I merely state it in order to avoid being misunderstood in my answer.

Quadratic equations are part of algebra, and algebra is the intellectual instrument which has been created for rendering clear the quantitative aspects of the world. There is no getting out of it. Through and through the world is infected with quantity. To talk sense, is to talk in quantities. It is no use saying that the nation is large,—How large? It is no use saying that radium is scarce,—How scarce? You cannot evade quantity. You may fly to poetry and to music, and quantity and number will face you in your rhythms and your octaves. Elegant intellects which despise the theory of quantity, are but half developed. They are more to be pitied than blamed. The scraps of gibberish, which in their school-days were taught to them in the name of algebra, deserve some contempt.

This question of the degeneration of algebra into gibberish, both in word and in fact, affords a pathetic instance of the uselessness of reforming educational schedules without a clear conception of the attributes which you wish to evoke in the living minds of the children. A few years ago there was an outcry that school algebra was in need of reform, but there was a general agreement that graphs would put everything right. So all sorts of things were extruded, and graphs were introduced. So far as I can see, with no sort of idea behind them, but just graphs. Now every examination paper has one or two questions on graphs. Personally I am an enthusiastic adherent of graphs. But I wonder whether as yet we have gained very much. You cannot put life into any schedule of general education unless you succeed in exhibiting its relation to some essential characteristic of all intelligent or emotional perception. It is a hard saying, but it is true; and I do not see how to make it any easier. In making these little formal alterations you are beaten by the very nature of things. You are pitted against too skilful an adversary, who will see to it that the pea is always under the other thimble.

Reformation must begin at the other end. First, you must make up your mind as to those quantitative aspects of the world which are simple enough to be introduced into general education; then a schedule of algebra should be framed which will about find its exemplification in these applications. We need not fear for our pet graphs, they will be there in plenty when we once begin to treat algebra as a serious means of studying the world. Some of the simplest applications will be found in the quantities which occur in the simplest study of society. The curves of history are more vivid and more informing than the dry catalogues of names and dates which comprise the greater part of that arid school study. What purpose is effected by a catalogue of undistinguished kings and queens? Tom, Dick, or Harry, they are all dead. General resurrections are failures, and are better postponed. The quantitative flux of the forces of modern society is capable of very simple exhibition. Meanwhile, the idea of the variable, of the function, of rate of change, of equations and their solution, of elimination, are being studied as an abstract science for their own sake. Not, of course, in the pompous phrases with which I am alluding to them here, but with that iteration of simple special cases proper to teaching.

If this course be followed, the route from Chaucer to the Black Death, from the Black Death to modern Labour troubles, will connect the tales of the mediaeval pilgrims with the abstract science of algebra, both yielding diverse aspects of that single theme, Life. . . .

But in considering this description, I must beg you to remember what I have been insisting on above. In the first place, one train of thought will not suit all groups of children. For example, I should expect that artisan children will want something more concrete and, in a sense, swifter than I have set down here. Perhaps I am wrong, but that is what I should guess. In the second place, I am not contemplating one beautiful lecture stimulating, once and for all, an admiring class. That is not the way in which education proceeds. No; all the time the pupils are hard at work solving examples, drawing graphs, and making experiments, until they have a thorough hold on the whole subject. I am describing the interspersed explanations, the directions which should be given to their thoughts. The pupils have got to be made to feel that they are studying something, and are not merely executing intellectual minuets.

Finally, if you are teaching pupils for some general examination, the problem of sound teaching is greatly complicated. Have you ever noticed the zig-zag moulding round a Norman arch? The ancient work is beautiful, the modern work is hideous. The reason is, that the modern work is done to exact measure, the ancient work is varied according to the idiosyncrasy of the workman. Here it is crowded, and there it is expanded. Now the essence of getting pupils through examinations is to give equal weight to all parts of the schedule. But mankind is naturally specialist. One man sees a whole subject, where another can find only a few detached examples. I know that it seems contradictory to allow for specialism in a curriculum especially designed for a broad culture. Without contradictions the world would be simpler, and perhaps duller. But I am certain that in education wherever you exclude specialism you destroy life.

We now come to the other great branch of a general mathematical education, namely Geometry. The same principles apply. The theoretical part should be clear-cut, rigid, short, and important. Every proposition not absolutely necessary to exhibit the main connection of ideas should be cut out, but the great fundamental ideas should be all there. No omission of concepts, such as those of Similarity and Proportion. We must remember that, owing to the aid rendered by the visual presence of a figure, Geometry is a field of unequalled excellence for the exercise of the deductive faculties of reasoning. Then, of course, there follows Geometrical Drawing, with its training for the hand and eye.

But, like Algebra, Geometry and Geometrical Drawing must be extended beyond the mere circle of geometrical ideas. In an industrial neighbourhood, machinery and workshop practice form the appropriate extension. For example, in the London Polytechnics this has been achieved with conspicuous success. For many secondary schools I suggest that surveying and maps are the natural applications. In particular, plane-table surveying should lead pupils to a vivid apprehension of the immediate application of geometric truths. Simple drawing apparatus, a surveyor's chain, and a surveyor's compass, should enable the pupils to rise from the survey and mensuration of a field to the construction of the map of a small district. The best education is to be found in gaining the utmost information from the simplest apparatus. The provision of elaborate instruments is greatly to be deprecated. To have constructed the map of a small district, to have considered its roads, its contours, its geology, its climate, its relation to other districts, the effects on the status of its inhabitants, will teach more history and geography than any knowledge of Perkin Warbeck or of Behren's Straits. I mean not a nebulous lecture on the subject, but a serious investigation in which the real facts are definitely ascertained by the aid of accurate theoretical knowledge. A typical mathematical problem should be: Survey such and such a field, draw a plan of it to such and such a scale, and find the area. It would be quite a good procedure to impart the necessary geometrical propositions without their proofs. Then, concurrently in the same term, the proofs of the propositions would be learnt while the survey was being made.

Fortunately, the specialist side of education presents an easier problem than does the provision of a general culture. For this there are many reasons. One is that many of the principles of procedure to be observed are the same in both cases, and it is unnecessary to recapitulate. Another reason is that specialist training takes place—or should take place—at a more advanced stage of the pupil's course, and thus there is easier material to work upon. But undoubtedly the chief reason is that the specialist study is normally a study of peculiar interest to the student. He is studying it because, for some reason, he wants to know it. This makes all the difference. The general culture is designed to foster an activity of mind; the specialist course utilizes this activity. But it does not do to lay too much stress on these neat antitheses. As we have already seen, in the general course foci of special interest will arise; and similarly in the special study, the external connections of the subject drag thought outwards.

Again, there is not one course of study which merely gives general culture, and another which gives special knowledge. The subjects pursued for the sake of a general education are special subjects specially studied; and, on the other hand, one of the ways of encouraging general mental activity is to foster a special devotion. You may not divide the seamless coat of learning. What education has to impart is an intimate sense for the power of ideas, for the beauty of ideas, and for the structure of ideas, together with a particular body of knowledge which has peculiar reference to the life of the being possessing it.

The appreciation of the structure of ideas is that side of a cultured mind which can only grow under the influence of a special study. I mean that eye for the whole chess-board, for the bearing of one set of ideas on another. Nothing but a special study can give any appreciation for the exact formulation of general ideas, for their relations when formulated, for their service in the comprehension of life. A mind so disciplined should be both more abstract and more concrete. It has been trained in the comprehension of abstract thought and in the analysis of facts.

Finally, there should grow the most austere of all mental qualities; I mean the sense for style. It is an aesthetic sense, based on admiration for the direct attainment of a foreseen end, simply and without waste. Style in art, style in literature, style in science, style in logic, style in practical execution have fundamentally the same aesthetic qualities, namely, attainment and restraint. The love of a subject in itself and for itself, where it is not the sleepy pleasure of pacing a mental quarter-deck, is the love of style as manifested in that study.

Here we are brought back to the position from which we started, the utility of education. Style, in its finest sense, is the last acquirement of the educated mind; it is also the most useful. It pervades the whole being. The administrator with a sense for style hates waste; the engineer with a sense for style economizes his material; the artisan with a sense for style prefers good work. Style is the ultimate morality of mind.

But above style, and above knowledge, there is something, a vague shape like fate above the Greek gods. That something is Power. Style is the fashioning of power, the restraining of power. But, after all, the power of attainment of the desired end is fundamental. The first thing is to get there. Do not bother about your style, but solve your problem, justify the ways of God to man, administer your province, or do whatever else is set before you.

Where, then, does style help? In this, with style the end is attained without side issues, without raising undesirable inflammations. With style you attain your end and nothing but your end. With style the effect of your activity is calculable, and foresight is the last gift of gods to men. With style your power is increased, for your mind is not distracted with irrelevancies, and you are more likely to attain your object. Now style is the exclusive privilege of the expert. Whoever heard of the style of an amateur painter, of the style of an amateur poet? Style is always the product of specialist study, the peculiar contribution of specialism to culture.

English education in its present phase suffers from a lack of definite aim, and from an external machinery which kills its vitality. Hitherto in this address I have been considering the aims which should govern education. In this respect England halts between two opinions. It has not decided whether to produce amateurs or experts. The profound change in the world which the nineteenth century has produced is that the growth of knowledge has given foresight. The amateur is essentially a man with appreciation and with immense versatility in mastering a given routine. But he lacks the foresight which comes from special knowledge. The object of this address is to suggest how to produce the expert without loss of the essential virtues of the amateur. . . .

When one considers in its length and in its breadth the importance of this question of the education of a nation's young, the broken lives, the defeated hopes, the national failures, which result from the frivolous inertia with which it is treated, it is difficult to restrain within oneself a savage rage. In the conditions of modern life the rule is absolute, the race which does not value trained intelligence is doomed. Not all your heroism, not all your social charm, not all your wit, not all your victories on land or at sea, can move back the finger of fate. To-day we maintain ourselves. To-morrow science will have moved forward yet one more step, and there will be no appeal from the judgment which will then be pronounced on the uneducated.

We can be content with no less than the old summary of educational ideal which has been current at any time from the dawn of our civilization. The essence of education is that it be religious.

Pray, what is religious education?

A religious education is an education which inculcates duty and reverence. Duty arises from our potential control over the course of events. Where attainable knowledge could have changed the issue, ignorance has the guilt of vice. And the foundation of reverence is this perception, that the present holds within itself the complete sum of existence, backwards and forwards, that whole amplitude of time, which is eternity.

THE RHYTHMIC CLAIMS
OF FREEDOM AND DISCIPLINE

The fading of ideals is sad evidence of the defeat of human endeavour. In the schools of antiquity philosophers aspired to impart wisdom, in modern colleges our humbler aim is to teach subjects. The drop from the divine wisdom, which was the goal of the ancients, to text-book knowledge of subjects, which is achieved by the moderns, marks an educational failure, sustained through the ages. I am not maintaining that in the practice of education the ancients were more successful than ourselves. You have only to read Lucian, and to note his satiric dramatizations of the pretentious claims of philosophers, to see that in this respect the ancients can boast over us no superiority. My point is that, at the dawn of our European civilization, men started with the full ideals which should inspire education, and that gradually our ideals have sunk to square with our practice.

But when ideals have sunk to the level of practice, the result is stagnation. In particular, so long as we conceive intellectual education as merely consisting in the acquirement of mechanical mental aptitudes, and of formulated statements of useful truths, there can be no progress; though there will be much activity, amid aimless re-arrangement of syllabuses, in the fruitless endeavour to dodge the inevitable lack of time. We must take it as an unavoidable fact, that God has so made the world that there are more topics desirable for knowledge than any one person can possibly acquire. It is hopeless to approach the problem by the way of the enumeration of subjects which every one ought to have mastered. There are too many of them, all with excellent title-deeds. Perhaps, after all, this plethora of material is fortunate; for the world is made interesting by a delightful ignorance of important truths. What I am anxious to impress on you is that though knowledge is one chief aim of intellectual education, there is another ingredient, vaguer but greater, and more dominating in its importance. The ancients called it "wisdom." You cannot be wise without some basis of knowledge; but you may easily acquire knowledge and remain bare of wisdom.

Now wisdom is the way in which knowledge is held. It concerns the handling of knowledge, its selection for the determination of relevant issues, its employment to add value to our immediate experience. This mastery of knowledge, which is wisdom, is the most intimate freedom obtainable. The ancients saw clearly—more clearly than we do—the necessity for dominating knowledge by wisdom. But, in the pursuit of wisdom in the region of practical education, they erred sadly. To put the matter simply, their popular practice assumed that wisdom could be imparted to the young by procuring philosophers to spout at them. Hence the crop of shady philosophers in the schools of the ancient world. The only avenue towards wisdom is by freedom in the presence of knowledge. But the only avenue towards knowledge is by discipline in the acquirement of ordered fact. Freedom and discipline are the two essentials of education, and hence the title of my discourse to-day, "The Rhythmic Claims of Freedom and Discipline."

The antithesis in education between freedom and discipline is not so sharp as a logical analysis of the meanings of the terms might lead us to imagine. The pupil's mind is a growing organism. On the one hand, it is not a box to be ruthlessly packed with alien ideas: and, on the other hand, the ordered acquirement of knowledge is the natural food for a developing intelligence. Accordingly, it should be the aim of an ideally constructed education that the discipline should be the voluntary issue of free choice, and that the freedom should gain an enrichment of possibility as the issue of discipline. The two principles, freedom and discipline, are not antagonists, but should be so adjusted in the child's life that they correspond to a natural sway, to and fro, of the developing personality. It is this adaptation of freedom and discipline to the natural sway of development that I have elsewhere called The Rhythm of Education. I am convinced that much disappointing failure in the past has been due to neglect of attention to the importance of this rhythm. My main position is that the dominant note of education at its beginning and at its end is freedom, but that there is an intermediate stage of discipline with freedom in subordination: Furthermore, that there is not one unique threefold cycle of freedom, discipline, and freedom; but that all mental development is composed of such cycles, and of cycles of such cycles. Such a cycle is a unit cell, or brick; and the complete stage of growth is an organic structure of such cells. In analyzing any one such cell, I call the first period of freedom the "stage of Romance," the intermediate period of discipline I call the "stage of Precision," and the final period of freedom is the "stage of Generalization."

Let me now explain myself in more detail. There can be no mental development without interest. Interest is the *sine qua non* for attention and apprehension. You may endeavour to excite interest by means of birch rods, or you may coax it by the incitement of pleasurable activity. But without interest there will be no progress. Now the natural mode by which living organisms are excited towards suitable self-development is enjoyment. The infant is lured to adapt itself to its environment by its love of its mother and its nurse; we eat because we like a good dinner: we subdue the forces of nature because we have been lured to discovery by an insatiable curiosity: we enjoy exercise: and we enjoy the unchristian passion of hating our dangerous enemies. Undoubtedly pain is one subordinate means of arousing an organism to action. But it only supervenes on the failure of pleasure. Joy is the normal healthy spur for the *élan vital.* I am not maintaining that we can safely abandon ourselves to the allurement of the greater immediate joys. What I do mean is that we should seek to arrange the development of character along a path of natural activity, in itself pleasurable. The subordinate stiffening of discipline must be directed to secure some long-time good; although an adequate object must not be too far below the horizon, if the necessary interest is to be retained.

The second preliminary point which I wish to make, is the unimportance—indeed the evil—of barren knowledge. The importance of knowledge lies in its use, in our active mastery of it—that is to say, it lies in wisdom. It is a convention to speak of mere knowledge, apart from wisdom, as of itself imparting a peculiar dignity to its possessor. I do not share in this reverence for knowledge as such. It all depends on who has the knowledge and what he does with it. That knowledge which adds greatness to character is knowledge so handled as to transform every phase of immediate experience. It is in respect to the activity of knowledge that an over-vigorous discipline in education is so harmful. The habit of active thought, with freshness, can only be generated by adequate freedom. Undiscriminating discipline defeats its own object by dulling the mind. If you have much to do with the young as they emerge from school and from the university, you soon note the dulled minds of those whose education has consisted in the acquirement of inert knowledge. Also the deplorable tone of English society in respect to learning is a tribute to our educational failure. Furthermore, this overhaste to impart mere knowledge defeats itself. The human mind rejects knowledge imparted in this way. The craving for expansion, for activity, inherent in youth is disgusted by a dry imposition of disciplined knowledge. The discipline, when it comes, should satisfy a natural craving for the wisdom which adds value to bare experience.

But let us now examine more closely the rhythm of these natural cravings of the human intelligence. The first procedure of the mind in a new environment is a somewhat discursive activity amid a welter of ideas and experience. It is a process of discovery, a process of becoming used to curious thoughts, of shaping questions, of seeking for answers, of devising new experiences, of noticing what happens as the result of new ventures. This general process is both natural and of absorbing interest. We must often have noticed children between the ages of eight and thirteen absorbed in its ferment. It is dominated by wonder, and cursed be the dullard who destroys wonder. Now undoubtedly this stage of development requires help, and even discipline. The environment within which the mind is working must be carefully selected. It must, of course, be chosen to suit the child's stage of growth, and must be adapted to individual needs. In a sense it is an imposition from without; but in a deeper sense it answers to the call of life within the child. In the teacher's consciousness the child has been sent to his telescope to look at the stars, in the child's consciousness he has been given free access to the glory of the heavens. Unless, working somewhere, however obscurely, even in the dullest child, there is this transfiguration of imposed routine, the child's nature will refuse to assimilate the alien material. It must never be forgotten that education is not a process of packing articles in a trunk. Such a simile is entirely inapplicable. It is, of course, a process completely of its own peculiar genus. Its nearest analogue is the assimilation of food by a living organism: and we all know how necessary to health is palatable food under suitable conditions. When you have put your boots in a trunk, they will stay there till you take them out again; but this is not at all the case if you feed a child with the wrong food.

This initial stage of romance requires guidance in another way. After all the child is the heir to long ages of civilisation, and it is absurd to let him wander in the intellectual maze of men in the Glacial Epoch. Accordingly, a certain pointing out of important facts, and of simplifying ideas, and of usual names, really strengthens the natural impetus of the pupil. In no part of education can you do without discipline or can you do without freedom; but in the stage of romance the emphasis must always be on freedom, to allow the child to see for itself and to act for itself. My point is that a block in the assimilation of ideas inevitably arises when a discipline of precision is imposed before a stage of romance has run its course in the growing mind. There is no comprehension apart from romance. It is my strong belief that the cause of so much failure in the past has been due to the lack of careful study of the due place of romance. Without the adventure of romance, at the best you get inert knowledge without initiative, and at the worst you get contempt of ideas—without knowledge.

But when this stage of romance has been properly guided another craving grows. The freshness of inexperience has worn off; there is general knowledge of the groundwork of fact and theory: and, above all, there has been plenty of independent browsing amid first-hand experiences, involving adventures of thought and of action. The enlightenment which comes from precise knowledge can now be understood. It corresponds to the obvious requirements of common sense, and deals with familiar material. Now is the time for pushing on, for knowing the subject exactly, and for retaining in the memory its salient features. This is the stage of precision. This stage is the sole stage of learning in the traditional scheme of education, either at school or university. You had to learn your subject, and there was nothing more to be said on the topic of education. The result of such an undue extension of a most necessary period of development was the production of a plentiful array of dunces, and of a few scholars whose natural interest had survived the car of Juggernaut. There is, indeed, always the temptation to teach pupils a little more of fact and of precise theory than at that stage they are fitted to assimilate. If only they could, it would be so useful. We—I am talking of schoolmasters and of university dons —are apt to forget that we are only subordinate elements in the education of a grown man; and that, in their own good time, in later life our pupils will learn for themselves. The phenomena of growth cannot be hurried beyond certain very narrow limits. But an unskilful practitioner can easily damage a sensitive organism. Yet, when all has been said in the way of caution, there is such a thing as pushing on, of getting to know the fundamental details and the main exact generalisations, and of acquiring an easy mastery of technique. There is no getting away from the fact that things have been found out, and that to be effective in the modern world you must have a store of definite acquirement of the best practice. To write poetry you must study metre; and to build bridges you must be learned in the strength of material. Even the Hebrew prophets had learned to write, probably in those days requiring no mean effort. The untutored art of genius is—in the words of the Prayer Book—a vain thing, fondly invented.

During the stage of precision, romance is the background. The stage is dominated by the inescapable fact that there are right ways and wrong ways, and definite truths to be known. But romance is not dead, and it is the art of teaching to foster it amidst definite application to appointed task. It must be fostered for one reason, because romance is after all a necessary ingredient of that balanced wisdom which is the goal to be attained. But there is another reason: The organism will not absorb the fruits of the task unless its powers of apprehension are kept fresh by romance. The real point is to discover in practice that exact balance between freedom and discipline which will give the greatest rate of progress over the things to be known. I do not believe that there is any abstract formula which will give information applicable to all subjects, to all types of pupils, or to each individual pupil; except indeed the formula of rhythmic sway which I have been insisting on, namely, that in the earlier stage the progress requires that the emphasis be laid on freedom, and that in the later middle stage the emphasis be laid on the definite acquirement of allotted tasks. I freely admit that if the stage of romance has been properly managed, the discipline of the second stage is much less apparent, that the children know how to go about their work, want to make a good job of it, and can be safely trusted with the details. Furthermore, I hold that the only discipline, important for its own sake, is self-discipline, and that this can only be acquired by a wide use of freedom. But yet—so many are the delicate points to be considered in education—it is necessary in life to have acquired the habit of cheerfully undertaking imposed tasks. The conditions can be satisfied if the tasks correspond to the natural cravings of the pupil at his stage of progress, if they keep his powers at full stretch, and if they attain an obviously sensible result, and if reasonable freedom is allowed in the mode of execution.

The difficulty of speaking about the way a skilful teacher will keep romance alive in his pupils arises from the fact that what takes a long time to describe, takes a short time to do. The beauty of a passage of Virgil may be rendered by insisting on beauty of verbal enunciation, taking no longer than prosy utterance. The emphasis on the beauty of a mathematical argument, in its marshalling of general considerations to unravel complex fact, is the speediest mode of procedure. The responsibility of the teacher at this stage is immense. To speak the truth, except in the rare case of genius in the teacher, I do not think that it is possible to take a whole class very far along the road of precision without some dulling of the interest. It is the unfortunate dilemma that initiative and training are both necessary, and that training is apt to kill initiative.

But this admission is not to condone a brutal ignorance of methods of mitigating this untoward fact. It is not a theoretical necessity, but arises because perfect tact is unattainable in the treatment of each individual case. In the past the methods employed assassinated interest; we are discussing how to reduce the evil to its smallest dimensions. I merely utter the warning that education is a difficult problem, to be solved by no one simple formula.

In this connection there is, however, one practical consideration which is largely neglected. The territory of romantic interest is large, ill-defined, and not to be controlled by any explicit boundary. It depends on the chance flashes of insight. But the area of precise knowledge, as exacted in any general educational system, can be, and should be, definitely determined. If you make it too wide you will kill interest and defeat your own object: if you make it too narrow your pupils will lack effective grip. Surely, in every subject in each type of curriculum, the precise knowledge required should be determined after the most anxious inquiry. This does not now seem to be the case in any effective way. For example, in the classical studies of boys destined for a scientific career —a class of pupils in whom I am greatly interested—What is the Latin vocabulary which they ought definitely to know? Also what are the grammatical rules and constructions which they ought to have mastered? Why not determine these once and for all, and then bend every exercise to impress just these·on the memory, and to understand their derivatives, both in Latin and also in French and English. Then, as to other constructions and words which occur in the reading of texts, supply full information in the easiest manner. A certain ruthless definiteness is essential in education. I am sure that one secret of a successful teacher is that he has formulated quite clearly in his mind what the pupil has got to know in precise fashion. He will then cease from half-hearted attempts to worry his pupils with memorising a lot of irrelevant stuff of inferior importance. The secret of success is pace, and the secret of pace is concentration. But, in respect to precise knowledge, the watchword is pace, pace, pace. Get your knowledge quickly, and then use it. If you can use it, you will retain it.

We have now come to the third stage of the rhythmic cycle, the stage of generalisation. There is here a reaction towards romance. Something definite is now known; aptitudes have been acquired; and general rules and laws are clearly apprehended both in their formulation and their detailed exemplification. The pupil now wants to use his new weapons. He is an effective individual, and it is effects that he wants to produce. He relapses into the discursive adventures of the romantic stage, with the advantage that his mind is now a disciplined regiment instead of a rabble. In this sense, education should begin in research and end in research. After all, the whole affair is merely a preparation for battling with the immediate experiences of life, a preparation by which to qualify each immediate moment with relevant ideas and appropriate actions. An education which does not begin by evoking initiative and end by encouraging it must be wrong. For its whole aim is the production of active wisdom.

In my own work at universities I have been much struck by the paralysis of thought induced in pupils by the aimless accumulation of precise knowledge, inert and unutilised. It should be the chief aim of a university professor to exhibit himself in his own true character—that is, as an ignorant man thinking, actively utilising his small share of knowledge. In a sense, knowledge shrinks as wisdom grows: for details are swallowed up in principles. The details of knowledge which are important will be picked up *ad hoc* in each avocation of life, but the habit of the active utilisation of well-understood principles is the final possession of wisdom. The stage of precision is the stage of growing into the apprehension of principles by the acquisition of a precise knowledge of details. The stage of generalisations is the stage of shedding details in favour of the active application of principles, the details retreating into subconscious habits. We don't go about explicitly retaining in our own minds that two and two make four, though once we had to learn it by heart. We trust to habit for our elementary arithmetic. But the essence of this stage is the emergence from the comparative passivity of being trained into the active freedom of application. Of course, during this stage, precise knowledge will grow, and more actively than ever before, because the mind has experienced the power of definiteness, and responds to the acquisition of general truth, and of richness of illustration. But the growth of knowledge becomes progressively unconscious, as being an incident derived from some active adventure of thought.

So much for the three stages of the rhythmic unit of development. In a general way the whole period of education is dominated by this threefold rhythm. Till the age of thirteen or fourteen there is the romantic stage, from fourteen to eighteen the stage of precision, and from eighteen to two and twenty the stage of generalisation. But these are only average characters, tinging the mode of development as a whole. I do not think that any pupil completes his stages simultaneously in all subjects. For example, I should plead that while language is initiating its stage of precision in the way of acquisition of vocabulary and of grammar, science should be in its full romantic stage. The romantic stage of language begins in infancy with the acquisition of speech, so that it passes early towards a stage of precision; while science is a late comer. Accordingly a precise inculcation of science at an early age wipes out initiative and interest, and destroys any chance of the topic having any richness of content in the child's apprehension. Thus, the romantic stage of science should persist for years after the precise study of language has commenced.

There are minor eddies, each in itself a threefold cycle, running its course in each day, in each week, and in each term. There is the general apprehension of some topic in its vague possibilities, the mastery of the relevant details, and finally the putting of the whole subject together in the light of the relevant knowledge. Unless the pupils are continually sustained by the evocation of interest, the acquirement of technique, and the excitement of success, they can never make progress, and will certainly lose heart. Speaking generally, during the last thirty years the schools of England have been sending up to the universities a disheartened crowd of young folk, inoculated against any outbreak of intellectual zeal. The universities have seconded the efforts of the schools and emphasised the failure. Accordingly, the cheerful gaiety of the young turns to other topics, and thus educated England is not hospitable to ideas. When we can point to some great achievement of our nation—let us hope that it may be something other than a war—which has been won in the class-room of our schools, and not in their playing-fields, then we may feel content with our modes of education.

So far I have been discussing intellectual education, and my argument has been cramped on too narrow a basis. After all, our pupils are alive, and cannot be chopped into separate bits, like the pieces of a jig-saw puzzle. In the production of a mechanism the constructive energy lies outside it, and adds discrete parts to discrete parts. The case is far different for a living organism which grows by its own impulse towards self-development. This impulse can be stimulated and guided from outside the organism, and it can also be killed. But for all your stimulation and guidance the creative impulse towards growth comes from within, and is intensely characteristic of the individual. Education is the guidance of the individual towards a comprehension of the art of life; and by the art of life I mean the most complete achievement of varied activity expressing the potentialities of that living creature in the face of its actual environment. This completeness of achievement involves an artistic sense, subordinating the lower to the higher possibilities of the indivisible personality. Science, art, religion, morality, take their rise from this sense of values within the structure of being. Each individual embodies an adventure of existence. The art of life is the guidance of this adventure. The great religions of civilisation include among their original elements revolts against the inculcation of morals as a set of isolated prohibitions. Morality, in the petty negative sense of the term, is the deadly enemy of religion. Paul denounces the Law, and the Gospels are vehement against the Pharisees. Every outbreak of religion exhibits the same intensity of antagonism—an antagonism diminishing as religion fades. No part of education has more to gain from attention to the rhythmic law of growth than has moral and religious education. Whatever be the right way to formulate religious truths, it is death to religion to insist on a premature stage of precision. The vitality of religion is shown by the way in which the religious spirit has survived the ordeal of religious education.

The problem of religion in education is too large to be discussed at this stage of my address. I have referred to it to guard against the suspicion that the principles here advocated are to be conceived in a narrow sense. We are analysing the general law of rhythmic progress in the higher stages of life, embodying the initial awakening, the discipline, and the fruition on the higher plane. What I am now insisting is that the principle of progress is from within:

the discovery is made by ourselves, the discipline is self-discipline, and the fruition is the outcome of our own initiative. The teacher has a double function. It is for him to elicit the enthusiasm by resonance from his own personality, and to create the environment of a larger knowledge and a firmer purpose. He is there to avoid the waste, which in the lower stages of existence is nature's way of evolution. The ultimate motive power, alike in science, in morality, and in religion, is the sense of value, the sense of importance. It takes the various forms of wonder, of curiosity, of reverence, or worship, of tumultuous desire for merging personality in something beyond itself. This sense of value imposes on life incredible labours, and apart from it life sinks back into the passivity of its lower types. The most penetrating exhibition of this force is the sense of beauty, the aesthetic sense of realised perfection. This thought leads me to ask, whether in our modern education we emphasise sufficiently the functions of art.

. . . You cannot, without loss, ignore in the life of the spirit so great a factor as art. Our aesthetic emotions provide us with vivid apprehensions of value. If you maim these, you weaken the force of the whole system of spiritual apprehensions. The claim for freedom in education carries with it the corollary that the development of the whole personality must be attended to. You must not arbitrarily refuse its urgent demands. . . . History shows us that an efflorescence of art is the first activity of nations on the road to civilisation. Yet, in the face of this plain fact, we practically shut out art from the masses of the population. Can we wonder that such an education, evoking and defeating cravings, leads to failure and discontent? The stupidity of the whole procedure is, that art in simple popular forms is just what we can give to the nation without undue strain on our resources. . . . It would . . . require no very great effort to use our schools to produce a population with some love of music, some enjoyment of drama, and some joy in beauty of form and colour. We could also provide means for the satisfaction of these emotions in the general life of the population. . . .

Shakespeare wrote his plays for English people reared in the beauty of the country, amid the pageant of life as the Middle Age merged into the Renaissance, and with a new world across the ocean to make vivid the call of romance. To-day we deal with herded town populations, reared in a scientific age. I have no doubt that unless we can meet the new age with new methods, to sustain for our populations the life of the spirit, sooner or later, amid some savage outbreak of defeated longings, the fate of Russia will be the fate of England. Historians will write as her epitaph that her fall issued from the spiritual blindness of her governing classes, from their dull materialism, and from their Pharisaic attachment to petty formulae of statesmanship.

Bertrand Russell

(1872-   )

RUSSELL'S reflections on education are wide-ranging and provocative. In the following selection he considers the influence of democracy on education, the sense in which education should be useful, the nature of discipline, and the importance of educational psychology.

His discussion of discipline is of special importance, since it is such a common fallacy to assume that discipline is necessarily a burden which oppresses the student rather than an ability which liberates him. Russell notes that "the right discipline consists, not in external compulsion, but in habits of mind which lead spontaneously to desirable rather than undesirable activities." Locke remarked similarly that discipline is "a power of denying ourselves the satisfaction of our own desires, where reason does not authorize them," and Dewey described discipline as "power at command . . . a power to endure in an intelligently chosen course in face of distraction, confusion, and difficulty." Each of these men was aware of how difficult it is to obtain this power, but all knew that its possession is a prime requisite for the achievement of worthwhile goals.

In Russell's discussion of those characteristics that educators ought to imbue in the young, the close relationship between a thinker's moral views and his educational views is again apparent. Russell believes that people ought to possess the traits of vitality, courage, sensitiveness, and intelligence. He thus commits himself to defend those educational policies that most effectively instill these characteristics in students. It is not sufficient, however, merely to list the traits that one believes to be desirable. What is crucial, and what Russell provides, is a detailed account of the precise nature of each of these traits.

He considers at some length, for instance, the extent to which a person ought to be dominated by the "herd instinct" or, as we might say, the extent to which one ought to be a conformist. Russell points out that there is a time for conformity and a time for nonconformity. An individual ought to have the courage to defend his convictions regardless of how many others may happen to disagree with him. On the other hand, to drive on the wrong side of the road in order to assert one's independence is mere foolishness.

ON EDUCATION

CHAPTER I
POSTULATES OF MODERN
EDUCATIONAL THEORY

In reading even the best treatises on education written in former times, one becomes aware of certain changes that have come over educational theory. The two great reformers of educational theory before the nineteenth century were Locke and Rousseau. Both deserved their reputation, for both repudiated many errors which were widespread when they wrote. But neither went as far in his own direction as almost all modern educationists go. Both, for example, belong to the tendency which led to liberalism and democracy; yet both consider only the education of an aristocratic boy, to which one man's whole time is devoted. However excellent might be the results of such a system, no man with a modern outlook would give it serious consideration, because it is arithmetically impossible for every child to absorb the whole time of an adult tutor. The system is therefore one which can only be employed by a privileged caste; in a just world, its existence would be impossible. The modern man, though he may seek special advantages for his own children in practice, does not consider the theoretical problem solved except by some method of education which could be open to all, or at least to all whose capacities render them capable of profiting by it. I do not mean that the well-to-do should, here and now, forgo educational opportunities which, in the existing world, are not open to all. To do that would be to sacrifice civilization to justice. What I do mean is that the educational system we must aim at producing in the future is one which gives to every boy and girl an opportunity for the best that exists. The ideal system of education must be democratic, although that ideal is not immediately attainable. This, I think, would, nowadays, be pretty generally conceded. In this sense, I shall keep democracy in view. Whatever I shall advocate will be capable of being universal, though the individual should not meantime sacrifice his children to the badness of what is common, if he has the intelligence and the opportunity to secure something better. Even this very attenuated form of democratic principle is absent from the treatises of Locke and Rousseau. Although the latter was a disbeliever in aristocracy, he never

From *On Education* by Bertrand Russell, London, George Allen & Unwin, Ltd., 1926, pp. 15–65 (with omissions as indicated in the text). Also appears as *Education and the Good Life* by Bertrand Russell, New York, Liveright, Publishers, pp. 13–50. Copyright 1954 by Bertrand Russell. Reprinted by permission of both publishers.

perceived the implications of his disbelief where education was concerned.

This matter of democracy and education is one as to which clarity is important. It would be disastrous to insist upon a dead level of uniformity. Some boys and girls are cleverer than others, and can derive more benefit from higher education. Some teachers have been better trained or have more native aptitude than others, but it is impossible that everybody should be taught by the few best teachers. Even if the highest education were desirable for all, which I doubt, it is impossible that all should have it at present, and therefore a crude application of democratic principles might lead to the conclusion that none should have it. Such a view, if adopted, would be fatal to scientific progress, and would make the general level of education a hundred years hence needlessly low. Progress should not be sacrificed to a mechanical equality at the present moment; we must approach educational democracy carefully, so as to destroy in the process as little as possible of the valuable products that happen to have been associated with social injustice.

.   .   .

There is another modern tendency in education, which is connected with democracy, but perhaps somewhat more open to question—I mean the tendency to make education useful rather than ornamental. . . .

Many separate controversies, in all of which other questions arise, are in part dependent upon our present question. Should boys learn mainly classics or mainly science? Among other considerations, one is that the classics are ornamental and science is useful. Should education as soon as possible become technical instruction for some trade or profession? Again the controversy between the useful and the ornamental is relevant, though not decisive. Should children be taught to enunciate correctly and to have pleasant manners, or are these mere relics of aristocracy? Is appreciation of art a thing of any value except in the artist? Should spelling be phonetic? All these and many other controversies are argued in part in terms of the controversy between the useful and the ornamental.

Nevertheless, I believe the whole controversy to be unreal. As soon as the terms are defined, it melts away. If we interpret "useful" broadly and "ornamental" narrowly, the one side has it; in the contrary interpretation the other side has it. In the widest and most correct sense of the word, an activity is "useful" when it has good results. And these results must be "good" in some other sense than merely "useful," or else we have no true definition. We cannot say that a useful activity is one which has useful results. The essence of what is "useful" is that it ministers to some result which is not merely useful. Sometimes a long chain of results is necessary before the final result is reached which can be called simply "good." A plough is useful because it breaks up the ground. But breaking up the ground is not good on its own account: it is in turn merely useful because it enables seed to be sown. This is useful because it produces grain, which is useful because it produces bread, which is useful because it preserves life. But life must be capable of some intrinsic value: if life were merely useful as a means to other life, it would not be useful at all. Life may be good or bad according to circumstances; it may therefore also be useful, when it is a means to good life. Somewhere we must get beyond the chain of successive utilities, and find a peg from which the chain is to hang; if not, there is no real usefulness in any link of the chain. When "useful" is defined in this way, there can be no question whether education should be useful. Of course it should, since the process of educating is a means to an end, not an end in itself. But that is not quite what the advocates of utility in education have in mind. What they are urging is that the *result* of education should be useful: put crudely, they would say that an educated man is a man who knows how to make machines. If we ask what is the use of machines, the answer is ultimately that they produce necessaries and comforts for the body—food, clothing, houses, etc. Thus we find that the advocate of utility, in the sense in which his view is questionable, is a man who attaches intrinsic value only to physical satisfactions: the "useful," for him, is that which helps us to gratify the needs and desires of the body. When this is what is really meant, the advocate of utility is certainly in the wrong if he is enunciating an ultimate philosophy, though in a world where many people are starving he may be right as a politician, since the satisfaction of physical needs may be at the moment more urgent than anything else.

Much the same sort of dissection is necessary in considering the other side of this controversy. To call the other side "ornamental" is, of course, to concede a point to the advocate of utility, since "ornament" is understood to be more or less trivial. The epithet "ornamental" is quite justified as applied to the traditional conception of a "gentleman" or a "lady." The eighteenth-century gentleman spoke with a refined accent, quoted the classics on appropriate occasions, dressed in the fashion, understood punctilio, and knew when a duel would advance his reputation. . . . No one nowadays would advocate an ornamental education in this narrow sense.

But that is not the real issue. The real issue is: should we, in education, aim at filling the mind with knowledge which has direct practical utility, or should we try to give our pupils mental possessions which are good on their own account? It is useful to know that there are twelve inches in a foot, and three feet in a yard, but this knowledge has no intrinsic value; to those who live where the metric system is in use it is utterly worthless. To appreciate *Hamlet*, on the other hand, will not be much use in practical life, except in those rare cases where a man is called upon to kill his uncle; but it gives a man a mental possession which he would be sorry to be without, and makes him in some sense a more excellent human being. It is this latter sort of knowledge that is preferred by the man who argues that utility is not the sole aim of education.

There appear to be three different substantial issues wrapped up in the debate between advocates of a utilitarian education and their opponents. There is first a form of the debate between aristocrats and democrats, the former holding that the privileged class should be taught to employ its leisure in ways that are agreeable to itself, while the subordinate class should be taught to employ its labour in ways that are useful to others. The opposition of the democrats to this view tends to be somewhat confused: they dislike the teaching of what is useless to the aristocrat, and at the same time argue that the wage-earner's education should not be confined to what is useful. Thus we find a democratic opposition to the old-fashioned classical education in the public schools, combined with a democratic demand that working men should have opportunities for learning Latin and Greek. This attitude, even though it may imply some lack of theoretical clarity, is on the whole right in practice. The democrat does not wish to divide the community into two sections, one useful and one ornamental; he will therefore give more merely useful knowledge to the hitherto merely ornamental classes, and more merely delightful knowledge to the hitherto merely useful classes. But democracy, *per se*, does not decide the proportions in which these ingredients should be mixed.

The second issue is between men who aim only at material goods and men who care for mental delights. Most modern well-to-do Englishmen and Americans, if they were transported by magic into the age of Elizabeth, would wish themselves back in the modern world. The society of Shakespeare and Raleigh and Sir Philip Sydney, the exquisite music, the beauty of the architecture, would not console them for the absence of bath-rooms, tea and coffee, motor-cars, and other material comforts of which that age was ignorant. Such men, except in so far as they are influenced by conservative tradition, tend to think that the main purpose of education is to increase the number and variety of commodities produced. They may include medicine and hygiene, but they will not feel any enthusiasm for literature or art or philosophy. Undoubtedly such men have provided a great part of the driving force for the attack upon the classical curriculum established at the Renaissance.

I do not think it would be fair to meet this attitude by the mere assertion that mental goods are of more value than such as are purely physical. I believe this assertion to be true, but not the whole truth. For, while physical goods have no very high value, physical evils may be so bad as to outweigh a great deal of mental excellence. Starvation and disease, and the ever-present fear of them, have overshadowed the lives of the great majority of mankind since foresight first became possible. Most birds die of starvation, but they are happy when food is abundant, because they do not think about the future. Peasants who have survived a famine will be perpetually haunted by memory and apprehension.

Men are willing to toil long hours for a pittance rather than die, while animals prefer to snatch pleasure when it is available, even if death is the penalty. It has thus come about that most men have put up with a life almost wholly devoid of pleasure, because on any other terms life would be brief. For the first time in history, it is now possible, owing to the industrial revolution and its by-products, to create a world where everybody shall have a reasonable chance of happiness. Physical evil can, if we choose, be reduced to very small proportions. It would be possible, by organization and science, to feed and house the whole population of the world, not luxuriously, but sufficiently to prevent great suffering. It would be possible to combat disease, and to make chronic ill-health very rare. It would be possible to prevent the increase of population from outrunning improvements in the food supply. The great terrors which have darkened the sub-conscious mind of the race, bringing cruelty, oppression, and war in their train, could be so much diminished as to be no longer important. All this is of such immeasurable value to human life that we dare not oppose the sort of education which will tend to bring it about. In such an education, applied science will have to be the chief ingredient. Without physics and physiology and psychology, we cannot build the new world. We can build it without Latin and Greek, without Dante and Shakespeare, without Bach and Mozart. That is the great argument in favour of a utilitarian education. I have stated it strongly, because I feel it strongly. Nevertheless, there is another side to the question. What will be the good of the conquest of leisure and health, if no one remembers how to use them? The war against physical evil, like every other war, must not be conducted with such fury as to render men incapable of the arts of peace. What the world possesses of ultimate good must not be allowed to perish in the struggle against evil.

This brings me to the third issue involved in our controversy. Is it true that only useless knowledge is intrinsically valuable? Is it true that any intrinsically valuable knowledge is useless? For my part, I spent in youth a considerable proportion of my time upon Latin and Greek, which I now consider to have been almost completely wasted. Classical knowledge afforded me no help whatever in any of the problems with which I was concerned in later life. Like 99 per cent. of those who are taught the classics, I never acquired sufficient proficiency to read them for pleasure. I learned such things as the genitive of "supellex," which I have never been able to forget. This knowledge has no more intrinsic value than the knowledge that there are three feet to a yard, and its utility, to me, has been strictly confined to affording me the present illustration. On the other hand, what I learned of mathematics and science has been not only of immense utility, but also of great intrinsic value, as affording subjects of contemplation and reflection, and touch-stones of truth in a deceitful world. This is, of course, in part a personal idiosyncrasy; but I am sure that a capacity to profit by the classics is a still rarer idiosyncrasy among modern men. France and Germany also have valuable literatures; their languages are easily learnt, and are useful in many practical ways. The case for French and German, as against Latin and Greek, is therefore overwhelming. Without belittling the importance of the sort of knowledge which has no immediate practical utility, I think we may fairly demand that, except in the education of specialists, such knowledge shall be given in ways that do not demand an immense expenditure of time and energy on technical apparatus such as grammar. The sum of human knowledge and the complexity of human problems are perpetually increasing; therefore every generation must overhaul its educational methods if time is to be found for what is new. We must preserve the balance by means of compromises. The humanistic elements in education must remain, but they must be sufficiently simplified to leave room for the other elements without which the new world rendered possible by science can never be created.

I do not wish to suggest that the humanistic elements in education are less important than the utilitarian elements. To know something of great literature, something of world history, something of music and painting and architecture, is essential if the life of imagination is to be fully developed. And it is only through imagination that men become aware of what the world might be; without it, "progress" would become mechanical and trivial. But science, also, can stimulate the imagination. When I was a boy, astronomy and geology did more for me in this respect than the literatures of England, France, and Germany, many of whose masterpieces I read under compulsion without the faintest interest. This is a personal matter: one boy or girl will derive stimulus from one source, another from another. What I suggest is that, where a difficult technique is indispensable to the mastering of a subject, it is better, except in training specialists, that the subject should be useful. . . .

So far, we have been considering what sort of knowledge should be imparted. I come now to a different set of problems, concerned partly with methods of teaching, partly with moral education and the training of character. Here we are no longer concerned with politics, but with psychology and ethics. Psychology was, until fairly lately, a merely academic study, with very little application to practical affairs. This is all changed now. We have, for instance, industrial psychology, clinical psychology, educational psychology, all of the greatest practical importance. We may hope and expect that the influence of psychology upon our institutions will rapidly increase in the near future. In education, at any rate, its effect has already been great and beneficent.

Let us take first the question of "discipline." The old idea of discipline was simple. A child or boy was ordered to do something he disliked, or abstain from something he liked. When he disobeyed, he suffered physical chastisement, or, in extreme cases, solitary confinement on bread and water. . . .

But the modern educationist does not simply eschew discipline; he secures it by new methods. On this subject, those who have not studied the new methods are apt to have mistaken ideas. I had always understood that Madame Montessori dispensed with discipline, and I had wondered how she managed a roomful of children. On reading her own account of her methods, I found that discipline still held an important place, and that there was no attempt to dispense with it. On sending my little boy of three to spend his mornings in a Montessori school, I found that he quickly became a more disciplined human being, and that he cheerfully acquiesced in the rules of the school. But he had no feeling whatever of external compulsion: the rules were like the rules of a game, and were obeyed as a means of enjoyment. The old idea was that children could not possibly *wish* to learn, and could only be compelled to learn by terror. It has been found that this was entirely due to lack of skill in pedagogy. By dividing what has to be learnt—for instance, reading and writing —into suitable stages, every stage can be made agreeable to the average child. And when children are doing what they like, there is, of course, no reason for external discipline. A few simple rules—no child must interfere with another child, no child must have more than one sort of apparatus at a time—are easily apprehended, and felt to be reasonable, so that there is no difficulty in getting them observed. The child thus acquires self-discipline, which consists partly of good habits, partly of the realization, in concrete instances, that it is sometimes worth while to resist an impulse for the sake of some ultimate gain. Everybody has always known that it is easy to obtain this self-discipline in games, but no one had supposed that the acquisition of knowledge could be made sufficiently interesting to bring the same motives into operation. We now know that this is possible, and it will come to be done, not only in the education of infants, but at all stages. I do not pretend that it is easy. The pedagogical discoveries involved here required genius, but the teachers who are to apply them do not require genius. They require only the right sort of training, together with a degree of sympathy and patience which is by no means unusual. The fundamental idea is simple: that the right discipline consists, not in external compulsion, but in habits of mind which lead spontaneously to desirable rather than undesirable activities. What is astonishing is the great success in finding technical methods of embodying this idea in education. For this, Madame Montessori deserves the highest praise.

The change in educational methods has been very much influenced by the decay of the belief in original sin. The traditional view, now nearly extinct, was that we are all born Children of Wrath, with a nature full of wickedness; before there can be any good in us we have to become Children of Grace, a process much accelerated by frequent castigation. Most moderns can hardly believe how much this theory influenced the education of our fathers and grandfathers. . . .

There is an opposite error . . . and that is the belief that children are naturally virtuous, and are only corrupted by the spectacle of their elders' vices. This view is traditionally associated with Rousseau; perhaps he held it in the abstract, but when one reads *Emile* one finds that the pupil stood in need of much moral training before he became the paragon that the system was designed to produce. The fact is that children are not naturally either "good" or "bad." They are born with only reflexes and a few instincts; out of these, by the action of the environment, habits are produced, which may be either healthy or morbid. Which they are to be depends chiefly upon the wisdom of mothers or nurses, the child's nature being, at first, almost incredibly malleable. In the immense majority of children there is the raw material of a good citizen, and also the raw material of a criminal. Scientific psychology shows that flogging on week-days and sermons on Sundays do not constitute the ideal technique for the production of virtue. But it is not to be inferred that there is no technique for this purpose. It is difficult to resist Samuel Butler's view that the educators of former times took a pleasure in torturing children; otherwise it is hard to see how they can have persisted so long in inflicting useless misery. It is not difficult to make a healthy child happy, and most children will be healthy if their minds and bodies are properly tended. . . . The spontaneous wish to learn, which every normal child possesses, as shown in its efforts to walk and talk, should be the driving-force in education. The substitution of this driving-force for the rod is one of the great advances of our time.

This brings me to the last point which I wish to notice in this . . . survey of modern tendencies—I mean the greater attention paid to infancy. This is closely connected with the change in our ideas as to the training of character. The old idea was that virtue depends essentially upon *will:* we were supposed to be full of bad desires, which we controlled by an abstract faculty of volition. It was apparently regarded as impossible to root out bad desires: all we could do was to control them. The situation was exactly analogous to that of the criminal and the police. No one supposed that a society without would-be criminals was possible; the most that could be done was to have such an efficient police force that most people would be afraid to commit crimes, and the few exceptions would be caught and punished. The modern psychological criminologist is not content with this view; he believes that the impulse to crime could, in most cases, be prevented from developing by suitable education. And what applies to society applies also to the individual. Children, especially, wish to be liked by their elders and their companions; they have, as a rule, impulses which can be developed in good or bad directions according to the situations in which they find themselves. Moreover, they are at an age at which the formation of new habits is still easy; and good habits can make a great part of virtue almost automatic. On the other hand, the older type of virtue, which left bad desires rampant, and merely used will-power to check their manifestations, has been found to afford a far from satisfactory method of controlling bad conduct. The bad desires, like a river which has been dammed, find some other outlet which has escaped the watchful eye of the will. The man who, in youth, would have liked to murder his father, finds satisfaction later on in flogging his son, under the impression that he is chastising "moral evil." Theories which justify cruelty almost always have their source in some desire diverted by the will from its natural channel, driven underground, and at last emerging unrecognized as hatred of sin or something equally respectable. The control of bad desires by the will, therefore, though necessary on occasion, is inadequate as a technique of virtue.

These considerations bring us to the province of psycho-analysis. There is much in the detail of psycho-analysis which I find fantastic, and not supported by adequate evidence. But the general method appears to me very important, and essential to the creation of right methods of moral training. The importance which many psycho-analysts attach to early infancy appears to me exaggerated; they sometimes talk as if character were irrevocably fixed by the time a child is three years old. This, I am sure, is not the case. But the fault is a fault on the right side. . . . This whole study is still in its infancy, but its importance is already very great, and almost sure to become greater. It is clear that education of character must begin at birth, and requires a reversal of much of the practice of nurses and ignorant mothers. It is also clear that definite instruction can begin earlier than was formerly thought, because it can be made pleasant and no strain upon the infant's powers of attention. In both these respects educational theory has been radically transformed in recent years, with beneficent effects which are likely to become more and more evident as the years go by. . . .

CHAPTER II
THE AIMS OF EDUCATION

Before considering how to educate, it is well to be clear as to the sort of result which we wish to achieve. . . . We must have some conception of the kind of person we wish to produce, before we can have any definite opinion as to the education which we consider best.

. . .

I will take four characteristics which seem to me jointly to form the basis of an ideal character: vitality, courage, sensitiveness, and intelligence. I do not suggest that this list is complete, but I think it carries us a good way. Moreover, I firmly believe that, by proper physical, emotional, and intellectual care of the young, these qualities could all be made very common. I shall consider each in turn.

Vitality is rather a physiological than a mental characteristic; it is presumably always present where there is perfect health but it tends to ebb with advancing years, and gradually dwindles to nothing in old age. In vigorous children it quickly rises to a maximum before they reach school age, and then tends to be diminished by education. Where it exists, there is pleasure in feeling alive, quite apart from any specific pleasant circumstance. It heightens pleasures and diminishes pains. It makes it easy to take an interest in whatever occurs, and thus promotes objectivity, which is an essential of sanity. Human beings are prone to become absorbed in themselves, unable to be interested in what they see and hear or in anything outside their own skins. This is a great misfortune to themselves, since it entails at best boredom and at worst melancholia; it is also a fatal barrier to usefulness, except in very exceptional cases. Vitality promotes interest in the outside world; it also promotes the power of hard work. Moreover, it is a safeguard against envy, because it makes one's own existence pleasant. As envy is one of the great sources of human misery, this is a very important merit in vitality. . . .

Courage—the second quality on our list— . . . is a combination of self-respect with an impersonal outlook on life. To begin with self-respect: some men live from within, while others are mere mirrors of what is felt and said by their neighbours. The latter can never have true courage: they must have admiration, and are haunted by the fear of losing it. The teaching of "humility," which used to be thought desirable, was the means of producing a perverted form of this same vice. "Humility" suppressed self-respect, but not the desire for the respect of others; it merely made nominal self-abasement the means of acquiring credit. Thus it produced hypocrisy and falsification of instinct. Children were taught unreasoning submission, and proceeded to exact it when they grew up; it was said that only those who have learned to obey know how to command. What I suggest is that no one should learn how to obey, and no one should attempt to command. I do not mean, of course, that there should not be leaders in co-operative enterprises; but their authority should be like that of a captain of a football team, which is suffered voluntarily in order to achieve a common purpose. Our purposes should be our own, not the result of external authority; and our purposes should never be forcibly imposed upon others. This is what I mean when I say no one should command and no one should obey.

There is one thing more required for the highest courage, and that is what I called just now an impersonal outlook on life. The man whose hopes and fears are all centered upon himself can hardly view death with equanimity, since it extinguishes his whole emotional universe. Here, again, we are met by a tradition urging the cheap and easy way of repression: the saint must learn to renounce Self, must mortify the flesh and forgo instinctive joys. This can be done, but its consequences are bad. Having renounced pleasure for himself, the ascetic saint renounces it for others also, which is easier. Envy persists under-ground, and leads him to the view that suffering is ennobling, and may there-fore be legitimately inflicted. Hence arises a complete inversion of values: what is good is thought bad, and what is bad is thought good. The source of all the harm is that the good life has been sought in obedience to a negative impera-tive, not in broadening and developing natural desires and instincts. There are certain things in human nature which take us beyond Self without effort. The commonest of these is love, more particularly parental love, which in some is so generalized as to embrace the whole human race. Another is knowledge. There is no reason to suppose that Galileo was particularly benevolent, yet he lived for an end which was not defeated by his death. Another is art. But in fact every interest in something outside a man's own body makes his life to that degree impersonal. For this reason, paradoxical as it may seem, a man of wide and vivid interests finds less difficulty in leaving life than is experienced by some miserable hypochondriac whose interests are bounded by his own ailments. Thus the perfection of courage is found in the man of many interests, who *feels* his ego to be but a small part of the world, not through despising himself, but through valuing much that is not himself. This can hardly happen except where instinct is free and intelligence is active. From the union of the two grows a comprehensiveness of outlook unknown both to the voluptuary and to the ascetic; and to such an outlook personal death appears a trivial matter. . . . It is courage in this . . . sense that I regard as one of the major ingredients in a perfect character.

Sensitiveness, the third quality in our list, is in a sense a corrective of mere courage. Courageous behaviour is easier for a man who fails to apprehend dangers, but such courage may often be foolish. We cannot regard as satisfactory any way of acting which is dependent upon ignorance or forgetfulness: the fullest possible knowledge and realization are an essential part of what is desirable. The cognitive aspect, however, comes under the head of intelligence; sensitiveness, in the sense in which I am using the term, belongs to the emotions. A purely theoretical definition would be that a person is emotionally sensitive when many stimuli produce emotions in him; but taken thus broadly the quality is not necessarily a good one. If sensitiveness is to be good, the emotional reaction must be in some sense *appropriate:* mere intensity is not what is needed. The quality I have in mind is that of being affected pleasurably or the reverse by many things, and by the right things. What are the right things, I shall try to explain. The first step, which most children take at the age of about five months, is to pass beyond mere pleasures of sensation, such as food and warmth, to the pleasure of social approbation. This pleasure, as soon as it has arisen, develops very rapidly: every child loves praise and hates blame. Usually the wish to be thought well of remains one of the dominant motives throughout life. It is certainly very valuable as a stimulus to pleasant behaviour, and as a restraint upon impulses of greed. If we were wiser in our admirations, it might be much more valuable. But so long as the most admired heroes are those who have killed the greatest number of people, love of admiration cannot alone be adequate to the good life.

The next stage in the development of a desirable form of sensitiveness is sympathy. There is a purely physical sympathy: a very young child will cry because a brother or sister is crying. This, I suppose, affords the basis for the further developments. The two enlargements that are needed are: first, to feel sympathy even when the sufferer is not an object of special affection; secondly, to feel it when the suffering is merely known to be occurring, not sensibly present. The second of these enlargements depends largely upon intelligence. It may only go so far as sympathy with suffering which is portrayed vividly and touchingly, as in a good novel; it may, on the other hand, go so far as to enable a man to be moved emotionally by statistics. This capacity for abstract sympathy is as rare as it is important. Almost everybody is deeply affected when someone he loves suffers from cancer. Most people are moved when they see the sufferings of unknown patients in hospitals. Yet when they read that the death-rate from cancer is such-and-such, they are as a rule only moved to momentary personal fear lest they or someone dear to them should acquire the disease. The same is true of war: people think it dreadful when their son or brother is mutilated, but they do not think it a million times as dreadful that a million people should be mutilated. A man who is full of kindliness in all personal dealings may derive his income from incitement to war or from the torture of children in "backward" countries. All these familiar phenomena are due to the fact that sympathy is not stirred, in most people, by a merely abstract stimulus. A large proportion of the evils in the modern world would cease if this could be remedied. . . .

Cognitive sensitiveness, which should also be included, is practically the same thing as a habit of observation, and this is more naturally considered in connection with intelligence. . . . I will therefore pass on to the last of the four qualities we enumerated, namely, intelligence.

One of the great defects of traditional morality has been the low estimate it placed upon intelligence. The Greeks did not err in this respect, but the Church led men to think that nothing matters except virtue, and virtue consists in abstinence from a certain list of actions arbitrarily labelled "sin." So long as this attitude persists, it is impossible to make men realize that intelligence does more good than an artificial conventional "virtue." When I speak of intelligence, I include both actual knowledge and receptivity to knowledge. The two are, in fact, closely connected. Ignorant adults are unteachable; on such matters as hygiene or diet, for example, they are totally incapable of believing what science has to say. The more a man has learnt, the easier it is for him to learn still more—always assuming that he has not been taught in a spirit of dogmatism. Ignorant people have never been compelled to change their mental habits, and have stiffened into an unchangeable attitude. It is not only that they are credulous where they should be sceptical; it is just as much that they are incredulous where they should be receptive. No doubt the word "intelligence" properly signifies rather an aptitude for acquiring knowledge than knowledge already acquired; but I do not think this aptitude is acquired except by exercise, any more than the aptitude of a pianist or an acrobat. It is, of course, possible to impart information in ways that do not train intelligence; it is not only possible, but easy, and frequently done. But I do not believe that it is possible to train intelligence without imparting information, or at any rate causing knowledge to be acquired. And without intelligence our complex modern world cannot subsist; still less can it make progress. I regard the cultivation of intelligence, therefore, as one of the major purposes of education. This might seem a commonplace, but in fact it is not. The desire to instil what are regarded as correct beliefs has made educationists too often indifferent to the training of intelligence. To make this clear, it is necessary to define intelligence a little more closely so as to discover the mental habits which it requires. For this purpose I shall consider only the aptitude for acquiring knowledge, not the store of actual knowledge which might legitimately be included in the definition of intelligence.

The instinctive foundation of the intellectual life is curiosity, which is found among animals in its elementary forms. Intelligence demands an alert curiosity, but it must be of a certain kind. The sort that leads village neighbours to try to peer through curtains after dark has no very high value. The widespread interest in gossip is inspired, not by a love of knowledge, but by malice: no one gossips about other people's secret virtues, but only about their secret vices. Accordingly most gossip is untrue, but care is taken not to verify it. Our neighbour's sins, like the consolations of religion, are so agreeable that we do not stop to scrutinize the evidence closely. Curiosity properly so-called, on the other hand, is inspired by a genuine love of knowledge. You may see this impulse, in a moderately pure form, at work in a cat which has been brought to a strange room, and proceeds to smell every corner and every piece of furniture. You will see it also in children, who are passionately interested when a drawer or cupboard, usually closed, is open for their inspection. Animals, machines, thunderstorms, and all forms of manual work, arouse the curiosity of children, whose thirst for knowledge puts the most intelligent adult to shame. This impulse grows weaker with advancing years, until at last what is unfamiliar inspires only disgust, with no desire for a closer acquaintance. This is the stage at which people announce that the country is going to the dogs, and that "things are not what they were in my young days." The thing which is not the same as it was in that far-off time is the speaker's curiosity. And with the death of curiosity we may reckon that active intelligence, also, has died.

But although curiosity lessens in intensity and in extent after childhood, it may for a long time improve in quality. Curiosity about general propositions shows a higher level of intelligence than curiosity about particular facts; broadly speaking, the higher the order of generality, the greater is the intelligence involved. (This rule, however, must not be taken too strictly.) Curiosity dissociated from personal advantage shows a higher development than curiosity connected (say) with a chance of food. The cat that sniffs in a new room is not a wholly disinterested scientific inquirer, but probably also wants to find out whether there are mice about. Perhaps it is not quite correct to say that curiosity is best when it is disinterested, but rather that it is best when the connection with other interests is not direct and obvious, but discoverable only by means of a certain degree of intelligence. This point, however, it is not necessary for us to decide.

If curiosity is to be fruitful, it must be associated with a certain technique for the acquisition of knowledge. There must be habits of observation, belief in the possibility of knowledge, patience, and industry. These things will develop of themselves, given the original fund of curiosity and the proper intellectual education. But since our intellectual life is only a part of our activity, and since curiosity is perpetually coming into conflict with other passions, there is need of certain intellectual virtues, such as open-mindedness. We become impervious to new truth both from habit and from desire; we find it hard to disbelieve what we have emphatically believed for a number of years, and also what ministers to self-esteem or any other fundamental passion. Open-mindedness should therefore be one of the qualities that education aims at producing. . . .

Courage is essential to intellectual probity, as well as to physical heroism. The real world is more unknown than we like to think; from the first day of life we practise precarious inductions, and confound our mental habits with laws of external nature. All sorts of intellectual systems—Christianity, Socialism, Patriotism, etc.—are ready, like orphan asylums, to give safety in return for servitude. A free mental life cannot be as warm and comfortable and sociable as a life enveloped in a creed: only a creed can give the feeling of a cosy fireside while the winter storms are raging without.

This brings us to a somewhat difficult question: to what extent should the good life be emancipated from the herd? I hesitate to use the phrase "herd instinct," because there are controversies as to its correctness. But, however interpreted, the phenomena which it describes are familiar. We like to stand well with those whom we feel to be the group with which we wish to co-operate —our family, our neighbours, our colleagues, our political party, or our nation. This is natural, because we cannot obtain any of the pleasures of life without co-operation. Moreover, emotions are infectious, especially when they are felt by many people at once. Very few people can be present at an excited meeting without getting excited: if they are opponents, their opposition becomes excited. And to most people such opposition is only possible if they can derive support from the thought of a different crowd in which they will win approbation. That is why the Communion of Saints has afforded such comfort to the persecuted. Are we to acquiesce in this desire for co-operation with a crowd, or shall our education try to weaken it? There are arguments on both sides, and the right answer must consist in finding a just proportion, not in a wholehearted decision for either party.

I think myself that the desire to please and to co-operate should be strong and normal, but should be capable of being overcome by other desires on certain important occasions. The desirability of a wish to please has already been considered in connection with sensitiveness. Without it, we should all be boors, and all social groups, from the family upwards, would be impossible. Education of young children would be very difficult if they did not desire the good opinion of their parents. The contagious character of emotions also has its uses, when the contagion is from a wiser person to a more foolish one. But in the case of panic fear and panic rage it is of course the very reverse of useful. Thus the question of emotional receptivity is by no means simple. Even in purely intellectual matters, the issue is not clear. The great discoverers have had to withstand the herd, and incur hostility by their independence. But the average man's opinions are much less foolish than they would be if he thought for himself: in science, at least, his respect for authority is on the whole beneficial.

I think that in the life of a man whose circumstances are not very exceptional there should be a large sphere where what is vaguely termed herd instinct dominates, and a small sphere into which it does not penetrate. The small sphere should contain the region of his special competence. We think ill of a man who cannot admire a woman unless everybody else also admires her: we think that, in the choice of a wife a man should be guided by his own independent feelings, not by a reflection of the feelings of his society. It is no matter if his judgments of people in general agree with those of his neighbours, but when he falls in love he ought to be guided by his own independent feelings. Much the same thing applies in other directions. A farmer should follow his own judgment as to the capacities of the fields which he cultivates himself, though his judgment should be formed after acquiring a knowledge of scientific agriculture. An economist should form an independent judgment on currency questions, but an ordinary mortal had better follow authority. Wherever there is special competence, there should be independence. But a man should not make himself into a kind of hedgehog, all bristles to keep the world at a distance. The bulk of our ordinary activities must be co-operative, and co-operation must have an instinctive basis. Nevertheless, we should all learn to be able to think for ourselves about matters that are particularly well known to us, and we ought all to have acquired the courage to proclaim unpopular opinions when we believe them to be important. The application of these broad principles in special cases may, of course, be difficult. But it will be less difficult than it is at present in a world where men commonly have the virtues we have been considering in this chapter. The persecuted saint, for instance, would not exist in such a world. The good man would have no occasion to bristle and become self-conscious; his goodness would result from following his impulses, and would be combined with instinctive happiness. His neighbours would not hate him, because they would not fear him; the hatred of pioneers is due to the terror they inspire, and this terror would not exist among men who had acquired courage. Only a man dominated by fear would join the Ku Klux Klan or the Fascisti. In a world of brave men, such persecuting organizations could not exist, and the good life would involve far less resistance to instinct than it does at present. The good world can only be created and sustained by fearless men, but the more they succeed in their task the fewer occasions there will be for the exercise of their courage.

.   .   .

Jacques Maritain

(1882-   )

MARITAIN'S philosophy of education is a prime example of the ways in which metaphysical considerations can influence decisions concerning educational policy. Maritain is a Roman Catholic, and he commits himself to what he terms "the Christian idea of man." He warns against acceptance of the claim that man's knowledge is limited to what is discovered by the utilization of the scientific method, and he stresses the importance of recognizing the existence and nature of the human soul.

Views such as these lead him to establish "contemplation and self-perfection" as the proper aims of education and to defend the thesis that "the ultimate end of education concerns the human person in his personal life and spiritual progress, not in his relationship to the social environment." His position is clearly opposed to that of a philosopher such as Dewey, and Maritain explicitly contrasts his ideas with those which he describes as "pragmatic."

On occasion, however, Maritain's attacks against "pragmatism" seem misdirected. He states, for instance, that thinking "ends up in insights which are made true by rational proving or experimental verifying, not by pragmatic sanction." But it was Dewey, so often referred to as a "pragmatist," who observed that knowledge is acquired only through "experimentation carried out under conditions of deliberate control."

One especially intriguing aspect of Maritain's carefully developed educational philosophy is his approach to moral education. He does not believe that the school ought directly to develop moral virtues in the young. Rather, he emphasizes the need "to enlighten and strengthen reason."

It is customary to assume that orthodox religious believers defend the policy of indoctrinating youth in morality, whereas those opposed to orthodox religion oppose such a policy. Surprisingly enough, it was Aristotle and Dewey, neither of them defenders of orthodox religion, who emphasized the importance of developing the proper habits of moral virtue in children, while it is Maritain who emphasizes the importance of developing a child's intellectual virtue.

No doubt Maritain's position on this issue is related to his belief that moral principles must be taught "as grounded on truth rather than as suitable to social convenience." This is a distinction that neither Aristotle nor Dewey recognized. Aristotle argued that "the end of politics is the good for man," and Dewey remarked that "every quality . . . is judged to be good according as it contributes to amelioration of existing ills." In other words Aristotle and Dewey believed that moral principles which would contribute to the betterment of the human condition are, by virtue of that fact, true.

EDUCATION AT THE CROSSROADS

CHAPTER I
THE AIMS OF EDUCATION

1. THE NATURE OF MAN AND EDUCATION

Education is an art, and an especially difficult one. Yet it belongs by its nature to the sphere of ethics and practical wisdom. Education is an *ethical* art (or rather a practical wisdom in which a determinate art is embodied). Now every art is a dynamic trend toward an object to be achieved, which is the aim of this art. There is no art without ends, art's very vitality is the energy with which it tends toward its end, without stopping at any intermediary step.

Here we see from the outset the two most general misconceptions against which education must guard itself. The first misconception is a lack or disregard of ends. If means are liked and cultivated for the sake of their own perfection, and not as means alone, to that very extent they cease to lead to the end, and art loses its practicality; its vital efficiency is replaced by a process of infinite multiplication, each means developing and spreading for its own sake. This supremacy of means over end and the consequent collapse of all sure purpose and real efficiency seem to be the main reproach to contemporary education. The means are not bad. On the contrary, they are generally much better than those of the old pedagogy. The misfortune is precisely that they are so good that we lose sight of the end. Hence the surprising weakness of education today, which proceeds from our attachment to the very perfection of our modern educational means and methods and our failure to bend them toward the end. The child is so well tested and observed, his needs so well detailed, his psychology so clearly cut out, the methods for making it easy for him everywhere so perfected, that the end of all these commendable improvements runs the risk of being forgotten or disregarded. Thus modern medicine is often hampered by the very excellence of its means: for instance, when a doctor makes the examination of the patient's reactions so perfectly and carefully in his laboratory that he forgets the cure; in the meantime the patient may die, for having been too well tended, or rather analyzed. The scientific improvement of the pedagogical means and methods is in itself outstanding progress. But the more it takes on importance, the more it requires a parallel

From *Education at the Crossroads* by Jacques Maritain, New Haven, Yale University Press, 1943, pp. 2–63 (with omissions as indicated in the text). Copyright 1943 by Yale University Press. Reprinted by permission of the publishers.

strengthening of practical wisdom and of the dynamic trend toward the goal.

The second general error or misconception of education does not consist of an actual dearth of appreciation of the end but false or incomplete ideas concerning the nature of this end. The educational task is both greater and more mysterious and, in a sense, humbler than many imagine. If the aim of education is the helping and guiding of man toward his own human achievement, education cannot escape the problems and entanglements of philosophy, for it supposes by its very nature a philosophy of man, and from the outset it is obliged to answer the question: "What is man?" which the philosophical sphinx is asking.

I should like to observe at this point that, definitely speaking, there are only two classes or categories of notions concerning man which play fair, so to speak: the purely scientific idea of man and the philosophical-religious one. According to its genuine methodological type, the scientific idea of man, like every idea recast by strictly experimental science, gets rid as far as possible of any ontological content, so that it may be entirely verifiable in sense-experience. On this point the most recent theorists of science, the neopositivists of the school of Vienna, are quite right. The purely scientific idea of man tends only to link together measurable and observable data taken as such, and is determined from the very start not to consider anything like being or essence, not to answer any question like: Is there a soul or isn't there? Does the spirit exist or only matter? Is there freedom or determinism? Purpose or chance? Value or simple fact? For such questions are out of the realm of science. The purely scientific idea of man is, and must be, a phenomenalized idea without reference to ultimate reality.

The philosophical-religious idea of man, on the contrary, is an ontological idea. It is not entirely verifiable in sense-experience, though it possesses criteria and proofs of its own, and it deals with the essential and intrinsic though not visible or tangible characters, and with the intelligible density of that being which we call man.

Now it is obvious that the purely scientific idea of man can provide us with invaluable and ever-growing information concerning the means and tools of education, but by itself it can neither primarily found nor primarily guide education, for education needs primarily to know what man *is*, what is the nature of man and the scale of values it essentially involves; and the purely scientific idea of man, because it ignores "being-as-such," does not know such things, but only what emerges from the human being in the realm of sense observation and measurement. Young Tom, Dick, or Harry, who are the subjects of education, are not only a set of physical, biological, and psychological phenomena, the knowledge of which is moreover thoroughly needed and necessary; they are the children of man—this very name "man" designating for the common sense of parents, educators, and society the same ontological mystery as is recognized in the rational knowledge of philosophers and theologians.

It should be pointed out that if we tried to build education on the single pattern of the scientific idea of man and carry it out accordingly, we could only do so by distorting or warping this idea: for we should have to ask what is the nature and destiny of man, and we should be pressing the only idea at our disposal, that is the scientific one, for an answer to our question. Then we would try, contrary to its type, to draw from it a kind of metaphysics. From the logical point of view, we would have a spurious metaphysics disguised as science and yet deprived of any really philosophical insight; and from the practical point of view, we would have a denial or misconception of those very realities and values without which education loses all human sense or becomes the training of an animal for the utility of the state.

Thus the fact remains that the complete and integral idea of man which is the prerequisite of education can only be a philosophical and religious idea of man. I say philosophical, because this idea pertains to the nature or essence of man; I say religious, because of the existential status of this human nature in relation to God and the special gifts and trials and vocation involved.

.   .   .

In answer to our question, then, "What is man?" we may give the Greek, Jewish, and Christian idea of man: man as an animal endowed with reason, whose supreme dignity is in the intellect; and man as a free individual in personal relation with God, whose supreme righteousness consists in voluntarily obeying the law of God; and man as a sinful and wounded creature called to divine life and to the freedom of grace, whose supreme perfection consists of love.

.   .   .

. . . Thus what is of most importance in educators themselves is a respect for the soul as well as for the body of the child, the sense of his innermost essence and his internal resources, the a sort of sacred and loving attention to his mysterious identity, which is a hidden thing that no techniques can reach. And what matters most in the educational enterprise is a perpetual appeal to intelligence and free will in the young. Such an appeal, fittingly proportioned to age and circumstances, can and should begin with the first educational steps. Each field of training, each school activity—physical training as well as elementary reading or the rudiments of childhood etiquette and morals—can be intrinsically improved and can outstrip its own immediate practical value through being *humanized* in this way by understanding. Nothing should be required of the child without an explanation and without making sure that the child has understood.

2. CONCERNING THE AIMS OF EDUCATION

We may now define in a more precise manner the aim of education. It is to guide man in the evolving dynamism through which he shapes himself as a human person—armed with knowledge, strength of judgment, and moral virtues—while at the same time conveying to him the spiritual heritage of the nation and the civilization in which he is involved, and preserving in this way the century-old achievements of generations. The utilitarian aspect of education—which enables the youth to get a job and make a living—must surely not be disregarded, for the children of man are not made for aristocratic leisure. But this practical aim is best provided by the general human capacities developed. And the ulterior specialized training which may be required must never imperil the essential aim of education.

Now in order to get a complete idea of the aim of education, it is necessary to take into closer consideration the human person and his deep natural aspirations.

The chief aspirations of a person are aspirations to freedom—I do not mean that freedom which is free will and which is a gift of nature in each of us, I mean that freedom which is spontaneity, expansion, or autonomy, and which we have to gain through constant effort and struggle. And what is the more profound and essential form of such a desire? It is the desire for inner and spiritual freedom. In this sense Greek philosophy, especially Aristotle, spoke of the independence which is granted to men by intellect and wisdom as the perfection of the human being. And the Gospel was to lift up human perfection to a higher level—a truly divine one—by stating that it consists of the perfection of love and, as St. Paul put it, of the freedom of those who are moved by the divine Spirit. In any case it is by the activities that the philosophers call "immanent"—because they perfect the very subject which exerts them, and are within it the supreme activities of internal achievement and superabundance—that the full freedom of independence is won. Thus the prime goal of education is the conquest of internal and spiritual freedom to be achieved by the individual person, or, in other words, his liberation through knowledge and wisdom, good will, and love.

At this point we must observe that the freedom of which we are speaking is not a mere unfolding of potentialities without any object to be grasped, or a mere movement for the sake of movement, without aim or objective to be attained. It is sheer nonsense to offer such a movement to man as constituting his glory. A movement without aim is just running around in circles and getting nowhere. The aim, here on earth, will always be grasped in a partial and imperfect manner, and in this sense, indeed, the movement is to be pursued without end. Yet the aim will somehow be grasped, even though partially. Moreover the spiritual activities of the human being are *intentional* activities, they tend by nature toward an object, an objective aim, which will measure and rule them, not materially and by means of bondage, but spiritually and by means of liberty, for the object of knowledge or of love is internalized by the activity itself of the intelligence and the will, and becomes within them the very fire of their perfect spontaneity. Truth—which does not depend on us but on *what is*—truth is not a set of ready-made formulas to be passively recorded, so as to have the mind closed and enclosed by them. Truth is an infinite realm —as infinite as being—whose wholeness transcends infinitely our powers of perception, and each fragment of which must be grasped through vital and purified internal activity. This conquest of being, this progressive attainment of new truths, or the progressive realization of the ever-growing and ever-renewed significance of truths already attained, opens and enlarges our mind and life, and really situates them in freedom and autonomy. And speaking of will and love rather than knowledge, no one is freer, or more independent, than the one who gives himself for a cause or a real being worthy of the gift.

Here we find ourselves confronted with the inappropriateness of the pragmatic overemphasis in education—a third error or misconception that we meet on our path. Many things are excellent in the emphasis on action and "praxis," for life consists of action. But action and praxis aim at an object, a determining end without which they lose direction and vitality. And life exists, too, for an end which makes it worthy of being lived. Contemplation and self-perfection, in which human life aspires to flower forth, escape the purview of the pragmatic mind.

It is an unfortunate mistake to define human thought as an organ of response to the actual stimuli and situations of the environment, that is to say, to define it in terms of animal knowledge and reaction, for such a definition exactly covers the way of "thinking" proper only to animals without reason. On the contrary, it is because every human idea, to have a meaning, must attain in some measure (be it even in the symbols of a mathematical interpretation of phenomena), what things *are* or consist of unto themselves; it is because human thought is an instrument or rather a vital energy of knowledge or spiritual intuition (I don't mean "knowledge about," I mean "knowledge into"); it is because thinking begins, not only with difficulties but with *insights*, and ends up in insights which are made true by rational proving or experimental verifying, not by pragmatic sanction, that human thought is able to illumine experience, to realize desires which are human because they are rooted in the prime desire for unlimited good, and to dominate, control, and refashion the world. At the beginning of human action, insofar as it is human, there is truth, grasped or believed to be grasped for the sake of truth. Without trust in truth, there is no human effectiveness. Such is, to my mind, the chief criticism to be made of the pragmatic and instrumentalist theory of knowledge.

In the field of education, this pragmatic theory of knowledge, passing from philosophy to upbringing, can hardly produce in the youth anything but a scholarly skepticism equipped with the best techniques of mental training and the best scientific methods, which will be unnaturally used against the very grain of intelligence, so as to cause minds to distrust the very idea of truth and wisdom, and to give up any hope of inner dynamic unity. Moreover, by dint of insisting that in order to teach John mathematics it is more important to know John than to know mathematics—which is true enough in one sense— the teacher will so perfectly succeed in knowing John that John will never succeed in knowing mathematics. Modern pedagogy has made invaluable progress in stressing the necessity of carefully analyzing and fixing its gaze on the human subject. The wrong begins when *the object to be taught* and *the primacy of the object* are forgotten, and when the cult of the means—not to an end, but without an end—only ends up in a psychological worship of the subject.

I have spoken of the aspiration of the human person to freedom, and, first of all, to inner and spiritual freedom. The second essential form of this desire is the desire for freedom externally manifested, and this freedom is linked to social life and lies at its very root. For society is "natural" to man in terms not only of animal or instinctive nature but of human nature, that is, of reason and freedom. If man is a naturally political animal, this is so in the sense that society, required by nature, is achieved through free consent, and because the human person demands the communications of social life through the openness and generosity proper to intelligence and love as well as through the needs of a human individual born naked and destitute. Thus it is that social life tends to emancipate man from the bondage of material nature. It subordinates the individual to the common good, but always in order that the common good flow back upon the individuals, and that they enjoy that freedom of expansion or independence which is insured by the economic guarantees of labor and ownership, political rights, civil virtues, and the cultivation of the mind.

As a result, it is obvious that man's education must be concerned with the social group and prepare him to play his part in it. Shaping man to lead a normal, useful and coöperative life in the community, or guiding the development of the human person in the social sphere, awakening and strengthening both his sense of freedom and his sense of obligation and responsibility, is an essential aim. But it is not the primary, it is the secondary essential aim. The ultimate end of education concerns the human person in his personal life and spiritual progress, not in his relationship to the social environment. Moreover, with regard to the secondary aim itself of which I am speaking, we must never forget that personal freedom itself is as the core of social life, and that a human society is veritably a group of human freedoms which accept obedience and self-sacrifice and a common law for the general welfare, in order to enable each of these freedoms to reach in everyone a truly human fulfillment. The man and the group are intermingled with each other and they surpass each other in different respects. Man finds himself by subordinating himself to the group, and the group attains its goal only by serving man and by realizing that man has secrets which escape the group and a vocation which is not included in the group.

Here we are confronted with a fourth error of misconception akin to the third one, which derives the supreme rule and standard of education from social conditioning. The essence of education does not consist in adapting a potential citizen to the conditions and interactions of social life, but first in *making a man*, and by this very fact in preparing a citizen. Not only is it nonsense to oppose education for the person and education for the commonwealth, but the latter supposes the former as a prerequisite, and in return the former is impossible without the latter, for one does not make a man except in the bosom of social ties where there is an awakening of civic understanding and civic virtues.

The old education is to be reproached for its abstract and bookish individualism. To have made education more experiential, closer to concrete life and permeated with social concerns from the very start is an achievement of which modern education is justly proud. Yet in order to reach completion such a necessary reform must understand, too, that to be a good citizen and a man of civilization what matters above all is the inner center, the living source of personal conscience in which originate idealism and generosity, the sense of law and the sense of friendship, respect for others, but at the same time deep-rooted independence with regard to common opinion. We must also understand that without abstract insight and intellectual enlightenment the more striking experiences are of no use to man, like beautiful colors in darkness; that the best way not to be bookish is to avoid textbooks as a plague, even textbooks in experientialism, but to read books, I mean to read them avidly; and to understand also that, in a more general way, the pursuit of concrete life becomes a decoy if it scatters the attention of man or child among practical trifles, psychotechnical recipes, and the infinity of utilitarian activities, while disregarding the genuine concrete life of the intellect and the soul. The sense of concrete reality is made blunt by utilitarianism; it develops and flowers forth through those activities which are all the more needed by human life since they are not at the service of any practical utility, because they are in themselves, freedom, fruit, and joy. Unfortunate is a youth who does not know the pleasure of the spirit and is not exalted in the joy of knowing and the joy of beauty, and enthusiasm for ideas, and quickening experience in the first love, delight and luxury of wisdom and poetry. Boredom and weariness with human affairs will come early enough indeed; to deal with them is the job of the grown-up.

To discuss the matter in a more specific manner, I should like to make the following observations: that conception which makes education itself a constantly renewed experiment, starting from the pupil's present purposes and developing in one way or another according to the success of his problem-solving activity with regard to these purposes and to new purposes arising from broadened experience in unforeseen directions, such a pragmatist conception has its own merits when it comes to the necessity of adapting educational methods to the natural interests of the pupil. But what are the standards for judging the purposes and values thus successively emerging in the pupil's mind? If the teacher himself has no general aim, nor final values to which all this process is related; if education itself is to grow "in whatever direction a novelly emerging future renders most feasible";[1] in other words, if the pragmatist theory requires a perpetual experimental reconstruction of the ends of the educator himself (and not only of the experience of the pupil), then it teaches educational recipes but gets away from any real art of education: for an education which does not have any goal of its own and tends only to growth itself without "end beyond further growth"[2] is no more an art than an art of architecture which would not have any idea of what is to be built, and would only tend to the growth of the construction in whatever direction a new addition of materials is feasible. In nature itself, biological growth is nothing but a morphological process, or the progressive acquisition of a definite form. And finally the pragmatist theory can only subordinate and enslave education to the trends which may develop in collective life and society, for in the last analysis the aims newly arising in such a "reconstruction of ends" will only be determined by the precarious factors of the environment to be controlled and the values made at each moment predominant by given social conditions or tendencies or by the state.

The element of truth which must be preserved in the conception I have just discussed, is the fact that the final end of education—the fulfillment of man as a human person—is infinitely higher and broader than the aim of architectural art or even the aim of medical art, for it deals with our very freedom and spirit, whose boundless potentialities can be led to full human stature only by means of constant creative renewal. As a result, the vital spontaneity of the one to be educated plays a major part in the progress toward this final end, as well as the steady widening of the pupil's experience; and the need for constantly renewed adaptation of methods, means, and approaches is much greater in educational art than in any art dealing only with some material achievement.

With regard to the powers of the human soul I should like now to indicate as briefly as possible two other errors which oppose one another and which come from overemphasis: intellectualism, the fifth error or misconception on our list; the other, voluntarism.

Intellectualism takes on two principal forms: a certain form of intellectualism seeks the supreme achievements of education in sheer dialectical or rhetorical skill—such was the case of classical pedagogy, especially in the bourgeois era, in which education was a privilege of privileged classes.

[1] John S. Brubacher, *Modern Philosophies of Education* (New York and London, 1939), p. 329.
[2] *Ibid.*

Another form of intellectualism, a modern one, gives up universal values and insists upon the working and experiential functions of intelligence. It seeks the supreme achievements of education in scientific and technical specialization. Now specialization is more and more needed by the technical organization of modern life, yet it should be compensated for by a more vigorous general training, especially during youth. If we remember that the animal is a specialist, and a perfect one, all of its knowing-power being fixed upon a single task to be done, we ought to conclude that an educational program which would only aim at forming specialists ever more perfect in ever more specialized fields, and unable to pass judgment on any matter that goes beyond their specialized competence, would lead indeed to a progressive animalization of the human mind and life. Finally as the life of bees consists of producing honey, the real life of man would consist of producing in a perfectly pigeonholed manner economic values and scientific discoveries, while some cheap pleasure or social entertainment would occupy leisure time, and a vague religious feeling, without any content of thought and reality, would make existence a little less flat, perhaps a little more dramatic and stimulating, like a happy dream. The overwhelming cult of specialization dehumanizes man's life.

Fortunately, nowhere in the world has any educational system been set up solely on this basis. Yet there exists everywhere a trend toward such a conception of education, following a more or less conscious materialistic philosophy of life. This represents a great peril for the democracies, because the democratic ideal more than any other requires faith in and the development of spiritual energies—a field which is over and above any specialization—and because a complete division of the human mind and activities into specialized compartments would make impossible the very "government of the people, by the people, and for the people." How could the common man be capable of judging about the good of the people if he felt able to pass judgment only in the field of his own specialized vocational competence? Political activity and political judgment would become the exclusive job of specialized experts in the matter—a kind of state technocracy which does not open particularly felicitous perspectives either for the good of the people or for liberty. As for education —complemented by some imperative vocational guidance—it would become the regular process of differentiation of the bees in the human beehive. In reality, the democratic way of life demands primarily liberal education for all and a general humanistic development throughout society. Even as to industrial achievements, man's free ingenuity strengthened by an education which liberates and broadens the mind is of as great import as technical specialization, for out of these free resources of human intelligence there arises, in managers and workers, the power of adapting themselves to new circumstances and mastering them.

Voluntarism, also, has two principal forms. In reaction against the first form of intellectualism, a voluntarist trend, developed since the time of Schopenhauer, has contributed to upset the internal order of human nature, by making intelligence subservient to the will and by appealing to the virtue of irrational forces. Accordingly, education was intended to concentrate either on the will which was to be disciplined according to some national pattern or on the free expansion of nature and natural potentialities. The merit of the best and wisest forms of voluntarism in the educational field[3] has been to call attention again to the essential importance of the voluntary functions, disregarded by intellectualist pedagogy, and to the primacy of morality, virtue, and generosity in the upbringing of man. For the main point is surely to be a good man rather than to be a learned man. As Rabelais put it, science without conscience is the ruin of the soul. Such was the ideal but in actual fact the pedagogic achievements of voluntarism have been strangely disappointing, at least from the point of view of the good. From the point of view of evil, they have had plenty of success—I mean in the effectiveness of Nazi training, schools, and youth organizations, in smashing all sense of truth in human minds and in perverting the very function of language and morally devastating the youth and making the intellect only an organ of the technical equipment of the state.

For the voluntarist trend in education combines very well with technical training. We find such a combination not only in the totalitarian corruption of education but elsewhere also, and there to some good purpose. As we see it in democratic countries, this peculiar form of educational voluntarism may be described as an effort to compensate for the inconveniences of the second form of intellectualism—overspecialized technical training—by what is known as education of will, education of feeling, formation of character, etc. Yet the misfortune is that this commendable effort has yielded, as a rule, the same disappointing result of which I spoke a moment ago. Character is something easily warped or debased, difficult to shape. All the pedagogical hammering of nails into the shoe doesn't make the shoe more comfortable to the foot. The methods which change the school into a hospital for refitting and vitalizing the wills, suggesting altruistic behavior or infusing good citizenship, may be well conceived and psychologically suitable, but they are for the most part dishearteningly ineffective.

We believe that intelligence is in and by itself nobler than the will of man, for its activity is more immaterial and universal. But we believe also that, in regard to the things or the very objects on which this activity bears, it is better to will and love the good than simply to know it. Moreover it is through man's will, when it is good, not through his intelligence, be it ever so perfect, that man is made good and right. A similar intermingling of roles is to be found in education, taken in its broadest sense. The upbringing of the human being must lead both intelligence and will toward achievement, and the shaping of the will is throughout more important to man than the shaping of the intellect. Yet, whereas the educational system of schools and colleges succeeds as a rule

---

[3] I am thinking for instance of the work of F. W. Foerster, whose influence has been great in many European pedagogical circles.

in equipping man's intellect for knowledge, it seems to be missing its main achievement, the equipping of man's will. What an infelicity!

3. THE PARADOXES OF EDUCATION

. . . We must here stress some characteristics of school and college education which are often insufficiently taken into account. School and college education is only a part of education. It pertains only to the beginnings and the completed *preparation* of the upbringing of man, and no illusion is more harmful than to try to push back into the microcosm of school education the entire process of shaping the human being, as if the system of schools and universities were a big factory through the back door of which the young child enters like a raw material, and from the front door of which the youth in his brilliant twenties will go out as a successfully manufactured man. Our education goes on until our death. Further, even in this preparatory field, school education itself has only a partial task, and this task is primarily concerned with knowledge and intelligence.

Teaching's domain is the domain of truth—I mean speculative as well as practical truth. The only dominating influence in the school and the college must be that of truth, and of the intelligible realities whose illuminating power obtains by its own virtue, not by virtue of the human authority of the master's say-so, the assent of an "open mind," intending to pronounce one way or another "according to the worth of evidence." No doubt the child's "open mind" is still unarmed, and unable to judge "according to the worth of evidence"; the child must believe his teacher. But from the very start the teacher must respect in the child the dignity of the mind, must appeal to the child's power of understanding, and conceive of his own effort as preparing a human mind to think for itself. The one who does not yet know must believe a master, but only in order to know, and maybe to reject at this very moment the opinions of the master; and he believes him provisionally, only because of the truth which the teacher is supposed to convey.

Thus it is chiefly through the instrumentality of intelligence and truth that the school and the college may affect the powers of desire, will, and love in the youth, and help him gain control of his tendential dynamism. Moral education plays an essential part in school and college education, and this part must be more and more emphasized. But it is essentially and above all by way of knowledge and teaching that school education must perform this moral task, that is to say, not by exercising and giving rectitude to the will—nor by merely illuminating and giving rectitude to speculative reason—but by illuminating and giving rectitude to practical reason. The forgetting of this distinction between *will* and *practical reason* explains the above-mentioned failure of school pedagogy in its attempts to "educate the will."

Now as concerns the will itself, and the so-called "education of the will" or character-building (let us say, more accurately, with regard to the attainment of moral virtues and spiritual freedom), the specific task of school education amounts essentially to the two following points: first, the teacher must be solidly instructed in and deeply aware of the psychology of the child, less in order to form the latter's will and feelings than in order to avoid deforming or wounding them by pedagogical blunders to which unfortunately adults seem naturally inclined (here all of the modern psychological research may afford great help). Second, school and school life have to do, in an especially important manner, with what I would suggest calling "premoral" training, a point which deals not with morality strictly speaking, but with the preparation and first tilling of the soil thereof. Yet the main duty in the educational spheres of the school as well as of the state is not to shape the will and directly to develop moral virtues in the youth, but to enlighten and strengthen reason; so it is that an indirect influence is exerted on the will, by a sound equipment of knowledge and a sound development of the powers of thinking.

Thus the paradox of which I have spoken at such length comes to a solution: what is most important in the upbringing of man, that is, the uprightness of the will and the attainment of spiritual freedom, as well as the achievement of a sound relationship with society, is truly the main objective of education in its broadest sense. Concerning *direct* action on the will and the shaping of character, this objective chiefly depends on educational spheres other than school and college education—not to speak of the role which the extra-educational sphere plays in this matter. On the contrary, concerning *indirect* action on the will and the character, school and college education provides a basis and necessary preparation for the main objective in question by concentrating on knowledge and the intellect, not on the will and direct moral training, and by keeping sight, above all, of the development and uprightness of speculative and practical reason. School and college education has indeed its own world, which essentially consists of the dignity and achievements of knowledge and the intellect, that is, of the human being's root faculty. And of this world itself that knowledge which is wisdom is the ultimate goal.

CHAPTER II
THE DYNAMICS OF EDUCATION

1. THE DYNAMIC FACTORS

In order to discuss the dynamic factors in education, we must naturally reckon first with the Platonic conception: that all learning is in the learner, not in the teacher. Every reader of the *Phaedo* recalls that according to Plato knowledge preëxists from the very start in human souls, which before descending into the body have contemplated the eternal Ideas; but when these souls are bound to a body, they are prevented from freely considering those truths of which they already possess knowledge. The student, in this way, does not acquire knowledge from the teacher, who has no real causal influence and who is at best only an occasional agent: the teacher only awakens the attention of the student to those things which he already knows, so that to learn is nothing else than to remember.

There are great truths in these exaggerated views of Plato. And one cannot but wonder at the nobility and delicacy of his Socratic way of teaching which so ennobles the one who is taught—surely—since it deals with him as with an angel, asleep indeed, but nevertheless an angel. These educational views have been taken up afresh by many modern educators, though from quite different philosophical standpoints. In reality, however, things are not as Plato saw them who, after all, when treating of education from the political point of view in his *Laws* was to overemphasize so surprisingly the authoritative aspect of education. The teacher does possess a knowledge which the student does not have. He actually communicates knowledge to the student whose soul has *not* previously contemplated the divine Ideas before being united to his body; and whose intellect, before being fecundated by sense-perception and sense-experience, is but a *tabula rasa*, as Aristotle put it.

Yet what is the kind of causality or dynamic action exerted by the teacher? Teaching is an art; the teacher is an artist. Is the teacher, then, like a sculptor, a powerful Michelangelo who belabors the marble or despotically imposes the form he has conceived on the passive clay? Such a conception was not infrequent in the education of old. It is a coarse and disastrous conception, contrary to the nature of things. For if the one who is being taught is not an angel, neither is he inanimate clay.

It is rather with the art of medicine that the art of education must be compared. Medicine deals with a living being that possesses inner vitality and the internal principle of health. The doctor exerts real causality in healing a sick man, yes, but in a very particular manner: by imitating the ways of nature herself in her operations, and by helping nature, by providing appropriate diet and remedies that nature herself uses, according to her own dynamism, toward a biological equilibrium. In other words, medicine is *ars cooperativa naturae*, an art of ministering, an art subservient to nature. And so is education. The implications of this are far-reaching indeed.

Ready-made knowledge does not, as Plato believed, exist in human souls. But the vital and active principle of knowledge does exist in each of us. The inner seeing power of intelligence, which naturally and from the very start perceives through sense-experience the primary notions on which all knowledge depends, is thereby able to proceed from what it already knows to what it does not yet know. An example of this is a Pascal discovering without any teacher and by virtue of his own ingenuity the first thirty-two propositions of the first book of Euclid. This inner vital principle the teacher must respect above all; his art consists in imitating the ways of the intellectual nature in its own operations. Thus the teacher has to offer to the mind either examples from experience or particular statements which the pupil is able to judge by virtue of what he already knows and from which he will go on to discover broader horizons. The teacher has further to comfort the mind of the pupil by putting before his eyes the logical connections between ideas which the analytical or deductive power of the pupil's mind is perhaps not strong enough to establish by itself.

All this boils down to the fact that the mind's natural activity on the part of the learner and the intellectual guidance on the part of the teacher are both dynamic factors in education, but that the principal agent in education, the primary dynamic factor or propelling force, is the internal vital principle in the one to be educated; the educator or teacher is only the secondary—though a genuinely effective—dynamic factor and a ministerial agent.

Here, we teachers and professors may sometimes find consolation for our failures—we can think of them as due to the defect of the principal agent, the inner principle within the student, and not to our own deficiencies. And such an excuse is often valid. Yet quite apart from this kind of solace to teachers, the very simple considerations which I have just laid down in paraphrasing Thomas Aquinas, are, to my mind, of great import to the philosophy of education. I think that they illuminate the whole conflict between the old form of education by the rod and progressive education, which centers upon and stresses the freedom and the inner natural vitality of the child.

Education by the rod is positively bad education. If from a love of paradox I were to say something on its behalf, I should only observe that it has been able, actually, to produce some strong personalities, because it is difficult to kill the internal principle of spontaneity in living beings, and because this principle occasionally develops more powerfully when it reacts and sometimes revolts against constraint, fear, and punishment than when everything is made easy, lenient, and psychotechnically compliant to it. Strangely enough, we may wonder whether an education which yields itself entirely to the sovereignty of the child, and which suppresses any obstacle to be overcome, does not result in making students both indifferent and too docile, too passively permeable to anything the teacher is saying. However that may be, it is still true that birch and taws are bad educational measures, and that any education which considers the teacher as the principal agent perverts the very nature of the educational task.

The actual merit of modern conceptions in education since Pestalozzi, Rousseau, and Kant, has been the rediscovery of the fundamental truth that the principal agent and dynamic factor is not the art of the teacher but the inner principle of activity, the inner dynamism of nature and of the mind. If there were time we could insist, in this connection, that the search for new methods and inspiration, as emphasized by progressive education and what is called in Europe the "active school," should be valued, developed, and expanded—on condition that progressive education gives up its out-of-date rationalistic prejudices and utopian philosophy of life and does not forget that the teacher, too, is a real cause and agent—though only coöperating with nature—a real giver whose own dynamism, moral authority, and positive guidance are indispensable. If this complementary aspect is forgotten, the finest endeavors which arise from the mere cult of the freedom of the child will be washed away in the sands.

The freedom of the child is not the spontaneity of animal nature, moving right from the start along the fixed determinate paths of instinct (at least we usually think of animal instinct in this form, which is really too simplified, for animal instinct has a first period of progressive fixation). The freedom of the child is the spontaneity of a human and rational nature, and this largely *undetermined* spontaneity has its inner principle of final determination only in reason, which is not yet developed in the child.

The plastic and suggestible freedom of the child is harmed and led astray if it is not helped and guided. An education which consisted in making the child responsible for acquiring information about that of which he does not know he is ignorant, an education which only contemplated a blossoming forth of the child's instincts, and which rendered the teacher a tractable and useless attendant, is but a bankruptcy of education and of the responsibility of adults toward the youth. The right of the child to be educated requires that the educator shall have moral authority over him, and this authority is nothing else than the duty of the adult to the freedom of the youth.

·   ·   ·

2. THE FUNDAMENTAL DISPOSITIONS TO BE FOSTERED

We have had a view of the being who is to be formed into a true human person, perfecting himself by knowledge and by love, and capable of giving himself; and we have seen that to achieve rationality and freedom this being must have knowledge taught and discipline, and these require the office of the teacher. I now come to the second general topic, the basic dispositions of human nature.

If the nature and spirit of the child are the principal agent in education, then, obviously, the fundamental dispositions to be fostered in this principal agent are the very basis of the task of education. They are rooted in nature but they may be warped, and they need to be carefully cultivated. Without pretending to a complete enumeration, I should say that the fundamental dispositions are the five following ones:

First, the love of truth, which is the primary tendency of any intellectual nature. (That children tell lies is obvious, yet most often the lies of children are not lies but only a spontaneous mythology of the imagination. Besides I am not thinking now of a love of telling the truth but of the love for knowing the truth.)

Second, the love of good and justice, and even the love of heroic feats, and this too is natural to the children of man.

Third, that disposition which might be called simplicity and openness with regard to existence. A disposition which is natural, though often thwarted by egotism or pride or unhappy experiences, and which is so elemental that we cannot easily express it in terms of psychology. For nothing is more basic and elemental than that to which it refers, that is, existence. I would describe this disposition as the attitude of a being who *exists* gladly, is unashamed of existing, stands upright in existence, and for whom to be and to accept the natural limitations of existence are matters of equally simple assent. Trees and animals are like this, though only in a physical way. In man this has to pass over and be drawn into the sphere of psychic life. We can interpret in this way the saying of Emerson: "Be first a good animal." Such a disposition is still far from the human virtues of magnanimity and humility, but it constitutes their natural soil; and it is so deeply and elementarily vital that the wounds it happens to undergo in many children, often very early, from family life and social life—spoken of today as an inferiority complex with its manifold morbid "compensations"—are especially grievous and difficult to cure. "Fear and trembling," undoubtedly, are part of the great experiences of the human soul, when it has become mature and enters the mysterious avenues of the spirit, but they are bad beginnings in education. At the dawn of our history the misfortune of mankind was that it was bound to begin its education under their shadow.

The fourth fundamental disposition concerns the sense of a job well done, for next to the attitude toward existence there is nothing more basic in man's psychic life than the attitude toward work. I do not mean by this the habit of being hard working. I am aware that laziness, as well as pride, is natural to us. Moreover laziness in children is often not real laziness but only an absorption of the mind with the workings of vegetative growth or psychophysical hardships. I am speaking of something deeper and more human, a respect for the job to be done, a feeling of faithfulness and responsibility regarding it. A lazy man, a poet if you will, may display, when he happens to work, the most passionate attachment to the inner requirements of his work. I am convinced that when this fundamental disposition, which is the first natural move toward self-discipline, this probity in regard to work is marred, an essential basis of human morality is lacking.

The fifth fundamental disposition is the sense of coöperation, which is as natural in us, and as thwarted too, as the tendency to social and political life.

3. THE FUNDAMENTAL NORMS OF EDUCATION

Now I arrive at my third section: the fundamental rules of education for the teacher or the ministerial agent. Assuredly, the primary rule is to foster those fundamental dispositions which enable the principal agent to grow in the life of the mind. It is clear, in this connection, that the task of the teacher is above all one of liberation. To liberate the good energies is the best way of repressing the bad ones, though repression is also needed, but only as a secondary means, as dealing particularly with that part of animal training in human education of which I spoke in my first chapter, and even so it is useful only on condition that the repression of bad tendencies will always be bound up with enlightenment and encouragement. Encouragement is as fundamentally necessary as humiliation is harmful. A mere prohibition of evil-doing is less efficacious than illumination about the good that this evil-doing will spoil. The real art is to make the child heedful of his own resources and potentialities for the beauty of well-doing.

The second fundamental norm is to center attention on the inner depths of personality and its preconscious spiritual dynamism, in other words, to lay stress on inwardness and the internalization of the educational influence.

. . . Here we see that important and helpful changes might take place in our educational methods. Here it is not a question of techniques, nor of a training of the subconscious. It is rather a question of liberating the vital preconscious sources of the spirit's activity. Using Bergsonian language, I would say that in the education of the mind the emphasis should be shifted from that which is *pressure* (which, of course, remains somewhat necessary, but secondary) to that which awakens and frees the *aspirations* of spiritual nature in us. Thus creative imagination, and the very life of the intellect, would not be sacrificed to cramming memorization or to conventional rules of skill in making use of concepts or words, or to the honest and conscientious but mechanical and hopeless cultivation of overspecialized fields of learning.

·   ·   ·

What matters most in the life of reason is intellectual insight or intuition. There is no training or learning for that. Yet if the teacher keeps in view above all the inner center of vitality at work in the preconscious depths of the life of the intelligence, he may center the acquisition of knowledge and solid formation of the mind on the freeing of the child's and the youth's intuitive power. By what means? By moving forward along the paths of spontaneous interest and natural curiosity, by grounding the exercise of memory in intelligence, and primarily by giving courage, by listening a great deal, and by causing the youth to trust and give expression to those spontaneous poetic or noetic impulses of his own which seem to him fragile and bizarre, because they are not assured by any social sanction—and in fact any awkward gesture or rebuff or untimely advice on the part of the teacher can crush such timid sproutings and push them back into the shell of the unconscious.

I should like, moreover, to suggest that, in order to set free creative and perceptive intellectual intuition, the path through which it is naturally awakened, the path of sense-perception and sense-experience and imagination, should be respected and followed as far as possible by the teacher. Above all the liberation of which we are speaking depends essentially on the free adhesion of the mind to the objective reality to be seen. Let us never deceive or rebuke the thirst for seeing in youth's intelligence! The freeing of the intuitive power is achieved in the soul through the object grasped, the intelligible grasping toward which this power naturally tends. The germ of insight starts within a preconscious intellectual cloud, arising from experience, imagination, and a kind of spiritual feeling, but it is from the outset a tending toward an object to be grasped. And to the extent that this tendency is set free and the intellect becomes accustomed to grasping, seeing, expressing the objects toward which it tends, to that very extent its intuitive power is liberated and strengthened. Before giving a youth the rules of good style, let us tell him first never to write anything which does not seem to him really beautiful, whatever the result may be. In the first approach to mathematics, physics, or philosophy, let us see to it that the student actually grasps each step of the simplest mathematical demonstration, however slow this may be—that he actually understands in the laboratory how logically the statement of the physicist emerges from the experiment—that he becomes intensely involved, through the very anxiety of his mind, in the first great philosophical problems, and after that, that he really sees the solution. In asking a youth to read a book, let us get him to undertake a real spiritual adventure and meet and struggle with the internal world of a given man, instead of glancing over a collection of bits of thought and dead opinions, looked upon from without and with sheer indifference, according to the horrible custom of so many victims of what they call "being informed." Perhaps with such methods the curriculum will lose a little in scope, which will be all to the good.[4]

Finally the very mood of the teaching is here of crucial import. If a teacher himself is concerned with discerning and seeing, with getting vision, rather than with collecting facts and opinions, and if he handles his burden of knowledge so as to see through it into the reality of things, then in the mind of the student the power of intuition will be awakened and strengthened unawares, by the very intuitivity traversing such teaching.

I come now to the third fundamental rule, which I shall try to express as

---

[4]With such methods, in any case, we would give up that peculiar procedure in examinations, which consists in asking the student to check as true or false a certain number of ready-made sentences, astutely prepared by the teachers, and which seems calculated to kill any personal effort of thought and expression.

follows: the whole work of education and teaching must tend to unify, not to spread out; it must strive to foster internal unity in man.

This means that from the very start, and, as far as possible, all through the years of youth, hands and mind should be at work together. This point has been made particularly clear by modern pedagogy as regards childhood. It is also valid for youth. The importance of manual work accompanying the education of the mind during the high school and college training is more and more recognized. There is no place closer to man than a workshop, and the intelligence of a man is not only in his head, but in his fingers too. Not only does manual work further psychological equilibrium, but it also furthers ingenuity and accuracy of the mind, and is the prime basis of artistic activity. . . .

A second implication of the rule we are discussing is that education and teaching must start with experience, but in order to complete themselves with reason. This is obvious and needs no elucidation, save perhaps that special stress should be laid upon the second part of the statement, in an age where an empiricist philosophy often makes capital out of experience, and the highest functions of reason and the insights of abstract thought are disregarded. To be sure, sense-experience is the very origin of all our knowledge, and education must follow the course of nature. Modern methods are perfectly aware of that, especially with children. The point, however, is to disengage from experience the rational and necessary connections with which that experience is pregnant, and which become visible only by means of abstraction and universal concepts, and in the light of the intuitive first principles of reason. Thus knowledge and science arise from experience. Neither those empiricists who despise abstract reason, logic, and the conceptual insights of intelligence, nor those rationalists who ignore experience, are integrated minds. Education must inspire eagerness both for experience and for reason, teach reason to base itself on facts and experience to realize itself in rational knowledge, grounded on principles, looking at the *raisons d'être*, causes and ends, and grasping reality in terms of how and why.

Yet what the present rule means basically is that education and teaching should never lose sight of the organic unity of the task to be performed, and of the essential need and aspiration of the mind to be freed in unity. If a man does not overcome the inner multiplicity of his drives and especially of the diverse currents of knowledge and belief and the diverse vital energies at play in his mind, he will always remain more a slave than a free man. Tears, sweat, and blood are needed for this all too difficult task of unifying our internal world. The school should help us in this effort, and not impair it and make it hopeless. The dispersion and atomization of human life are in our day the great distress of the adult world. Instead of opening itself more and more to this devastating dispersion, the school system at least should prepare us to surmount it, and provide our youth with a more fortunate world of its own, fitted to our spiritual demand and centered on unity.

Undoubtedly the tremendous multiplicity of the fields of knowledge, due to the very progress of modern science, makes the work of unification more difficult than ever. Yet a great symphony can and must have internal unity as well as a piece of chamber music. What is wanted here is nothing less than inspiration and vision.

In order to establish an organic and architectonic ordering of teaching, the prerequisite background is a sound philosophy of knowledge and of the degrees of knowledge, but the inspiring motive force is the vision embracing the whole practical dynamism of teaching. And toward what can such a vision be directed, except the very goal of this dynamism? And what is this very goal but wisdom? That knowledge we call wisdom, which penetrates and embraces things with the deepest, most universal, and most united insights. Such a knowledge, which lives not only by supreme science, but also by human and spiritual experience, is over and above any field of specialization, for it has to do with realities which permeate each and every being and with aspirations which call to the very nature and freedom of man. It is in itself the highest value for the human mind. Education and teaching can only achieve their internal unity if the manifold parts of their whole work are organized and quickened by a vision of wisdom as the supreme goal, so as progressively to make youth capable of sharing to some degree in the intellectual and moral fruits of wisdom.

The purpose of elementary and higher education is not to make of the youth a truly wise man, but to equip his mind with an ordered knowledge which will enable him to advance toward wisdom in his manhood. Its specific aim is to provide him with the foundations of real wisdom, and with a universal and articulate comprehension of human achievements in science and culture, before he enters upon the definite and limited tasks of adult life in the civil community, and even while he is preparing himself for these tasks through a specialized scientific, technical, or vocational training.

Such a universal and articulate comprehension of human achievements in science and culture, such a "music" of the wit, as Plato put it, takes shape in profoundly different ways on the several levels of education. In each of the great educational divisions which correspond to the main periods of the youth's life, from the years of childhood to the years of university and graduate study, we have to face a mental world of comprehensive universality which has only a proportional similarity with the mental worlds of other levels. The universality adapted to the young readers of fairy tales and *Alice in Wonderland* is of quite another nature than that fitted to the students reading Kant or Spinoza. Yet each educational stage deals with a comprehensive universality of its own, approaching little by little that of maturity, and at each stage education should be guided by the vision of the appropriate mental world of comprehensive or "symphonic" universality. And this vision should be communicated in some way to the ones who are taught, in order to make them realize the vital interest of their task and to give them inspiration and energy.

What are known in this country as "orientation courses" are stimulating beginnings and attempts in this direction, although they are still, it seems to me, in the nature of a compensation and palliative rather than a token of a general recasting of the educational scheme.

Finally there is a fourth fundamental rule, which demands that teaching liberate intelligence instead of burdening it, in other words, that teaching result in the freeing of the mind through the mastery of reason over the things learned.

. . . The rule of Thomas Aquinas, in his own studies, was "never to leave behind him any difficulty unsolved." "Always make sure," he warned students, "that you actually understand what you read or listen to," and "avoid speechifying on anything whatsoever." He also warned teachers—this advice was already necessary for the educators of his time—"never to dig," in front of the steps of the student, "never to dig a ditch that you fail to fill up." He knew that to raise clever doubts, to prefer searching to finding, and perpetually to pose problems without ever solving them are the great enemies of education.

To summarize: What is learned should never be passively or mechanically received, as dead information which weighs down and dulls the mind. It must rather be actively transformed by understanding into the very life of the mind, and thus strengthen the latter, as wood thrown into fire and transformed into flame makes the fire stronger. But a big mass of damp wood thrown into the fire only puts it out. Reason which receives knowledge in a servile manner does not really know and is only depressed by a knowledge which is not its own but that of others. On the contrary, reason which receives knowledge by assimilating it vitally, that is, in a free and liberating manner, really knows, and is exalted in its very activity by this knowledge which henceforth is its own. Then it is that reason really masters the things learned.

We are confronted here with the notion of mental training which at the time of John Locke was already emphasized by the adversaries of the liberal arts, and with the opposition so frequently aired between knowledge-value and training-value. Does the liberation of the mind mean that what essentially matters is not the possession of knowledge but only the development of the strength, skill, and accuracy of man's mental powers, whatever the thing to be learned may be? This question is of tremendous significance, and the wrong answer has probably gone a long way to water down contemporary education.

. . . The knowledge which is "of most worth"—I don't mean which has the most practical value, I mean which makes the mind penetrate into those things which are the richest in truth and intelligibility—such knowledge affords by itself the best mental training, for it is by grasping the object and having itself seized and vitalized by truth that the human mind gains both its strength and its freedom. It is not by the gymnastics of its faculties, it is by truth that it is set free, when truth is really known, that is, vitally assimilated by the insatiable

activity which is rooted in the depths of self. The opposition between knowledge-value and training-value comes from an ignorance of what knowledge is,
from the assumption that knowledge is a cramming of materials into a bag, and
not the most vital action by means of which things are spiritualized in order
to become one with the spirit. In the knowledge which is "of most worth,"
notably in the liberal arts, to give the upper hand to mental training, or to the
mere dialectical disquisition of how great works are made or how great
thoughts go on, to give such training the upper hand over beauty to be delighted in or the truth to be apprehended and assented to, would be to turn
upside down the natural and vital tendency of the mind and drift toward
dilettantism—and a dilettante has certainly a weak and not a well-trained
mind.

There are people who think that it is wonderful to have a mind that is quick,
clever, ready to see pros and cons, eager to discuss, and to discuss anything,
and who believe that such a mind is that to which university education must
give scope—regardless of *what* is thought about, *what* is discussed, and *how
important* the matter is. These people are unaware that if they succeeded in
making such a conception prevail, they would at best transform universities
into schools of sophistry. In fact, they would not even produce sophists, who
have some force, but rather disarmed and talkative minds, that believe they
are well informed but live by words and opinions. Such persons are afraid to
face reality, especially when reality is intellectually difficult and stringent, deep
or dire, and they replace the personal effort to grasp things as they are with
a ceaseless comparison of opinions. Youth taught according to this pattern
may furnish excellent specialists in the field of technique and the sciences of
matter, precisely because in this field such educational patterns cannot be
applied. For the rest, in all that has regard to the understanding of man and
culture and the highest and the most urgent human problems, not only do they
develop a helpless nominalistic timidity, but they are absolutely lost in the
midst of matters of knowledge and discussion the inner value and the respective importance of which they cannot and do not want to discern and recognize. For if we begin by denying that any subject matter is in itself and by
reason of truth more important than another, then we deny in reality that any
subject matter has any importance in itself, and everything vanishes into
futility.

. . . We are facing there a result of the fact that too often contemporary
education has deemed it suitable to substitute training-value for knowledge-
value—in other words, mental gymnastics for truth, and being in fine fettle, for
wisdom.

Yet the opposition between knowledge-value and training-value may be
understood in another way and help us to make useful discrimination in the
field of teaching and school exercises. There are school subjects—those whose

knowledge is "of most worth"—the main value of which is knowledge-value. And there are subjects—those whose knowledge is "of least worth"—the main value of which (I don't say the only value) is that of training. I should like to place the latter in the category of play—in broadening, of course, the sense of this word—and the former in the category of learning. Play has an essential part, though secondary, in school life; it possesses a value and worth of its own, being the activity of free expansion and a gleam of poetry in the very field of those energies which tend by nature toward utility. In the category of play thus broadly understood, I should like to see many things which are taught in elementary and secondary education—not only games, sports, and physical training, but first of all that handicraft work and dexterity in mechanics of which I spoke earlier, and, moreover, everything that the school can fancy to give training in, gardening, beekeeping, rustic lore, even cooking, jam-making, home economics, and so forth, and what is known as artistic training insofar as the "arts" involved are what is called in French *les arts d'agrément*, and in English, if I am not mistaken, "accomplishments." All of these things are dignified if they are dealt with as play activity, not with too much seriousness or too many frowns, but with some free and poetical cheerfulness. They lose educational meaning and make the school ever so slightly absurd if they are dealt with as an activity of learning, and put on the same level as genuine learning.

Above the category of play comes the category of learning, devoted to those matters whose main value is knowledge-value. Here too I think it would be best to trace a line of demarcation. In a first division we would place those matters the knowledge of which concerns the intellectual instruments and logical discipline required for the achievements of reason, as well as the treasure of factual and experiential information which must be gathered in memory. In a second division should be placed those matters the knowledge of which refers directly to the creative or perceptive intuition of the intellect and to that thirst for seeing of which we spoke previously.

In the first division I should like to place grammar, with a view to comparative grammar and philology, logic, and languages, on the other hand history, national history as well as the history of man and civilization and especially the history of the sciences, with connected subjects such as geography; all this I should call the field of the preliberal arts. And I should like to see the second division as the field of liberal arts, by recasting the old sevenfold listing of the Middle Ages according to a strictly educational outlook and to the modern progress of knowledge. Our *trivium* would concern the creative activity of the mind, and beauty to be perceived and delighted in. To begin with, it would comprise that *Eloquence* represented by Calliope, the first Muse and the mother of Orpheus, that is to say, the art of thought-expression or creative-expression which is the very art of making the mind actually able to set free and manifest its creative insight and making it really master of its power of expression—an art the neglect of which is so harmful to modern youth, who often lose their sense of the worthiness and accuracy of words, and become unable even to compose, when they enter upon practical life, a clear and articulate report on commercial or industrial matters. Then we would have, as the second of the liberal arts, *Literature and Poetry*, and as the third one, *Music and Fine Arts.*

Our *quadrivium* would concern the knowing and rational activity, the intuitive and judicative activity of the mind—truth to be perceived and assented to "according to the worth of evidence." It would comprise first, *Mathematics*, second, *Physics and the Natural Sciences*, third, *Philosophy*—I mean not only psychology, but also the philosophy of nature, metaphysics, and the theory of knowledge—and fourth, *Ethics and Political and Social Philosophy*, and connected studies.

CHAPTER III
THE HUMANITIES
AND LIBERAL EDUCATION

1. THE RUDIMENTS

As to the principal stages in education, let us note that there are three great periods in education. I should like to designate them as the rudiments (or elementary education), the humanities (comprising both secondary and college education), and advanced studies (comprising graduate schools and higher specialized learning). And these periods correspond not only to three natural chronological periods in the growth of the youth but also to three naturally distinct and qualitatively determinate spheres of psychological development, and, accordingly, of knowledge.

The physical structure of the child is not that of the adult, shortened and abridged. The child is not a dwarf man. Nor is the adolescent. And this is much truer and much more crucial as regards the psychological than the physical structure of the youth. In the realm of physical training, of psychophysical conditioning, of animal and experimental psychology, contemporary education has understood more and more perfectly that a child of man is not just a diminutive man. It has not yet understood this in the spiritual realm of knowing: because, indeed, it is not interested in the psychology of spiritual activities. How, therefore, could it do anything but ignore that realm? The error is twofold. First we have forgotten that science and knowledge are not a self-sufficient set of notions, existing for their own sakes, abstracted and separate from man. Science and knowledge don't exist in books, they do exist in minds, they are vital and internal energies and must develop therefore according to the inner spiritual structure of the mind in which they have their being.

Secondly, we act as if the task of education were to infuse into the child or the adolescent, only abridging and concentrating it, the very science or knowledge of the adult—that is to say, of the philologist, the historian, the grammarian, the scientist, etc., the most specialized experts. So we try to cram young people with a chaos of summarized adult notions which have been either condensed, dogmatized, and textbookishly cut up or else made so easy that they are reduced to the vanishing point. As a result, we run the risk of producing either an instructed, bewildered intellectual dwarf, or an ignorant intellectual dwarf playing at dolls with our science. In a recent essay Professor Douglas Bush recalls "the classic anecdote of the young woman who was asked if she could teach English history. 'Oh yes,' she replied brightly, 'I've had it twice, once in clay and once in sand.' "[5]

The knowledge to be given to youth *is not* the same knowledge as that of adults, it is an intrinsically and basically different knowledge, which is not knowledge in the state of science, such as that possessed by the mind of the adult, but the specific knowledge fitted to quicken and perfect the original world of thought of the child and the adolescent. Consequently I should like to emphasize that at each stage the knowledge must be of a sort fitted to the learners and conceived as reaching its perfection within their universe of thought during a distinct period of their development, instead of laying the foundations of a single sphere of knowledge which would grow in a continuous and uniform way until it became the science of the adult, where alone it would attain perfection.

The universe of a child is the universe of imagination—of an imagination which evolves little by little into reason. The knowledge which has to be given to the child is knowledge in a state of story, an imaginative grasp of the things and values of the world. The child's mentality may be compared in some ways with that of primitive man, and this mentality tends by itself toward magic, and whatever effort the teacher may make, his teaching always runs the risk of being caught and engulfed in a magic ocean. In his task of civilizing the child's mind, therefore, he must progressively tame the imagination to the rule of reason, whilst ever remembering that the proportionally tremendous work of the child's intellect, endeavoring to grasp the external world, is accomplished under the vital and perfectly normal rule of imagination.

I should like to add that beauty is the mental atmosphere and the inspiring power fitted to a child's education, and should be, so to speak, the continuous quickening and spiritualizing contrapuntal base of that education. Beauty

[5]Douglas Bush, *Science, Philosophy and Religion*, Second Symposium (New York, 1942), p. 325.

makes intelligibility pass unawares through sense-awareness. It is by virtue of the allure of beautiful things and deeds and ideas that the child is to be led and awakened to intellectual and moral life.

On the other hand the vitality and intuitiveness of the spirit are quick in the young child and sometimes pierce the world of his imaginative thought with the purest and most surprising flashes, as if his spirit, being not yet both strengthened and organized by the exercise of reason, enjoyed a kind of bounding temperamental, and lucid freedom. At the same time, however, the immature workings of instinct and the violence of nature make him capable of intense resentment, wickedness, and manifold perversion. This vitality of the spirit should be relied upon as an invaluable factor in the first stages of education. Even from a purely naturalistic point of view it is a pity to see the child's mysterious expectant gravity and his resources as regards spiritual life neglected or trampled upon by his elders, either from some positivist bias or because they think it is their duty, when they deal with children, to make themselves childish.

2. THE HUMANITIES

The universe of the adolescent is a transition state on the way to the universe of man. Judgment and intellectual strength are developing but are not yet really acquired. Such a mobile and anxious universe evolves under the rule of the natural impulses and tendencies of intelligence—an intelligence which is not yet matured and strengthened by those inner living energies, the sciences, arts, and wisdom, but which is sharp and fresh, eager to pass judgment on everything, and both trustful and exacting, and which craves intuitive sight. The knowledge which has to develop in the adolescent is knowledge appealing to the natural powers and gifts of the mind, knowledge as tending toward all things by the natural instinct of intelligence. The mental atmosphere for adolescence should be one of truth to be embraced. Truth is the inspiring force needed in the education of the youth—truth rather than erudition and self-consciousness—all-pervading truth rather than the objectively isolated truth at which each of the diverse sciences aims. Here we are confronted with a natural and instinctive impulse toward some all-embracing truth, which must be shaped little by little to critical reflection, but which I should like to compare primarily to the trend of the first thinkers of ancient Greece toward an undifferentiated world of science, wisdom, and poetry. Common sense and the spontaneous pervasiveness of natural insight and reasoning constitute the dynamic unity of the adolescent's universe of thought, before wisdom may achieve in man a stabler unity. Just as imagination was the mental heaven of childhood, so now ascending reason, natural reason with its freshness, boldness, and first sparkling ambitions, is the mental heaven of adolescence; it is with reasoning that adolescence happens to be intoxicated. Here is a natural impulse to be turned to account by education, both by stimulating and by disciplining reason.

Such are, to my mind, the considerations which should guide the teachers of youth in the most important and difficult part of their task, which consists in determining the *mode* in which the instruments of thought and the liberal arts are to be taught. The quality of the mode or style is of much greater moment than the quantity of things taught, it constitutes the very soul of teaching and preserves its unity and makes it alive and buoyant. If we seek to characterize the general objective of instruction at the stage of college education, we might say the objective is less the acquisition of science itself or art itself than the grasp of their meaning and the comprehension of the truth or beauty they yield. It is less a question of sharing in the very activity of the scientist or the poet than of nourishing oneself intellectually on the results of their achievement. Still less is it a question of developing one's own mental skill and taste in the fashion of the dilettante by gaining a superficial outlook on scientific or artistic procedures or the ways and means, the grammar, logic, methodology thereof. What I call the *meaning* of a science or art is contained in the specific truth or beauty it offers us. The objective of education is to see to it that the youth grasps this truth or beauty by the natural power and gifts of his mind and the natural intuitive energy of his reason backed up by his whole sensuous, imaginative, and emotional dynamism. In doing that a liberal education will cause his natural intelligence to follow in the footsteps of those intellectual virtues which are the eminent merit of the real scientist or artist. The practical condition for all that is to strive to penetrate as deeply as possible into the great achievements of the human mind rather than to tend toward material erudition and atomized memorization. So I should say that the youth is to learn and know music in order to understand the meaning of music rather than in order to become a composer. He must learn and know physics in order to understand the meaning of physics rather than to become a physicist. Thus college education can keep its necessary character of comprehensive universality and at the same time till and cultivate the whole mind, made available and alive, for the tasks of man. . . .

Sidney Hook

(1902-   )

SIDNEY HOOK is a leading contemporary philosopher who has defended and developed the views of his teacher, John Dewey. In the past thirty years opposition to Dewey's educational philosophy has come not only from Maritain but also from such individuals as Robert Hutchins, Mortimer Adler, and Mark van Doren, all of whom subscribe in great measure to the sort of educational philosophy propounded by Maritain.

In his book *Education for Modern Man* Hook elaborates Dewey's position and replies to those who have criticized it. Hook argues against the views that democracy in education encourages mediocrity, that man's nature does not change, and that tradition by itself determines the content of education.

He also presents a classic account of the qualities that make for good teaching. His claim that "the bane of much college teaching is improvisation" is reminiscent of Whitehead's emphasis on the need for a teacher to have clearly in mind precisely what it is that he wishes the students to learn.

Hook's comments concerning the poor quality of much college teaching serve to remind us that a passion for the acquisition of knowledge does not necessarily result in a passion for the transmission of knowledge. One cannot be an outstanding teacher without a thorough knowledge of subject matter, but to possess a thorough knowledge of subject matter is no guarantee that one possesses the ability to communicate this subject matter to a student. And it is this ability, by no means easy to acquire, that is the *sine qua non* of good teaching.

EDUCATION FOR MODERN MAN

CHAPTER I
THE CONTEMPORARY SCENE
IN EDUCATION

For many years the phrases "democracy in education" and "education for democracy" have been shibboleths bandied about by writers more interested in declaring their allegiance than in clarifying ideas. Today these phrases are at a discount. As the swing toward the revival of traditional positions acquires momentum, many critics contend that the meaning given to these phrases in the writings of Dewey, and still more in the practices of progressive education which received his blessing, encourages, even if it does not explicitly approve, the habits of adjustment and conformity to existing mores, the cult of mediocrity, the fetish of equality, and the systematic denigration of intellectual excellence.

... [W]e can hardly do better than to restate what "democracy in education" means in the educational writings of John Dewey and its bearing on current practices.

The essence of Dewey's view is that democracy is committed to an equality of concern for each individual in the community to develop himself as a person. Education is the chief means by which those personal capacities are to be discovered and liberated. Education should enable human beings to achieve their maximum *distinctive* growth in harmony with their fellows. Equality of concern is not the same thing as equal treatment. It is compatible with unequal treatment, provided this treatment is required by the necessities of intellectual and emotional growth in each case. "Moral equality," he says, "means incommensurability, the inapplicability of common and quantitative standards. It means intrinsic qualities which require *unique* opportunities and *differential* manifestation ..." The principle of moral equality or ideal democracy is the most revolutionary principle in the world because its scope embraces all social institutions.

Even a half-careful reading of Dewey reveals that individuals for him come first in the order of concern, and that to be an individual is to be different in some distinctive and important way from others even though many things are

From *Education for Modern Man: A New Perspective* by Sidney Hook, New York, Alfred A. Knopf, Inc., 1963, pp. 28–235 (with omissions as indicated in the text). Copyright 1946, 1963 by Sidney Hook. Reprinted by permission of the publisher.

shared in common with others. Conceptually, it is very difficult to express this union of equality of concern with difference of treatment in a formal rule. But we may illustrate it by reference to another institution. In a healthy and happy family where children vary in age, strength, and intellectual gifts, it would be absurd for parents to treat them equally in specific situations—absurd precisely because they are considered equally, valued equally. A family, of course, cannot be taken as a literal model for a complex society—there are no parents in society—but ethically it illustrates the principle which Dewey believed should be exhibited in the functioning of social institutions in a democracy, or which should be its controlling and guiding spirit. And it is striking to observe how often Dewey uses the family for analogical purposes to make an educational recommendation. Consider, for example, his well-known words: "What the best and wisest parent wants for his own child, that must the community want for all its children. Any other ideal for our schools is narrow and unlovely; acted upon, it destroys our democracy."

The significance of this observation is all the more important as an indicator of Dewey's meaning because the words are such an obvious overstatement. We have never acted on this ideal and have not destroyed our democracy, because democracy so conceived has never really existed. But these words do express in the most emphatic way an entire complex of values, values which must guide our action if we are to approach closer to the democratic ideal. And this ideal rests on the primacy of freedom, on the right to be different, on the right to be an individual—so much so that, although social institutions are recognized as the indispensable means by which personality is aided in coming to development, all social institutions must nevertheless be criticized and reformed in the light of the qualities of human experience to which they give rise. The individual person comes first in the order of significance, not of time.

The educational corollaries which follow from such a democratic philosophy are fantastically different from those drawn by critics who see in it the prolegomenon to an ideological justification for mediocrity. The very contrary is true. Mediocrity is the consequence of imposing one uniform pattern on individual differences, of the attempt to make everyone talk and sing and think alike about the same things at the same time. How can Dewey's philosophy be interpreted as advocating that the gifted child be denied the special attention which would bring his gifts to fruition? Historically, the earliest concern with providing appropriate educational opportunities for gifted children was manifested by educators and psychologists strongly influenced by Dewey. By all means, education must aim at excellence! But is there only one kind of excellence? Must one excellence be sacrificed to another? Must, as Ernest Renan asks, whatever is unfit for the altar of the gods be thrown to the dogs? Or, put more concretely, does it follow that, because we should exert our efforts to provide the educational stimulation that will generate the most fruitful results for students of the highest IQ, we should therefore not exert ourselves to generate the most fruitful results for students of lower IQs? If this is what it means, where is our equality of concern?

We must distinguish between standards of achievement that individuals must meet before certain professions are open to them—and from which, both in their own personal interests and in those of society, they can be legitimately barred—and the standard of growth and progress that is applicable to each individual. It is the latter which concerns the teacher, insofar as he accepts responsibility for the education of the person. And this means not the elimination or the dilution of subject matter, not the substitution of play for study, not a cafeteria of snap courses—but holding up ever higher goals to be reached by every student until he has attained *his* best. Such an approach is perfectly compatible with prescribed courses and studies. For if all needs are individual, many of them are at the same time common needs in a common world of common dangers and opportunities. There are some things everyone needs to know. Not everything, however, needs to be known by everybody.

What this democratic conception of education involves is better grasped by contrasting it with the view that would discriminate not merely *between* capacities but *against* them. Such a view advocates a kind of elite system in which the prizes and the power are to go to those who by natural endowment or social preferment (the two are often hard to separate) reach the head of their class. It not only differentiates but subtly demeans, by suggesting that the hierarchy of intelligence is the key to the hierarchy of human value, and that this hierarchy sooner or later determines position in a hierarchy of social standing and political power. Sometimes this view also calls itself democratic, but its spirit as well as its recommendations are altogether opposed to democracy as Dewey understood it.

Let us examine, for example, the view of Professor William Hocking, who has written widely on education. For him genuine democracy consists in *"the democracy of identical standard"* to be applied to all, irrespective of capacities. And he explains his meaning by an analogy:

> We do not, in our athletic contests, trim the length of the mile to the convenience of the runners: The democracy of the race does not consist in the assumption that everybody must get a prize; it consists in the identity of the spacing and timing for all entrants. This is what democracy must mean in higher education, and to retain this integrity, there must be losers, and a thinning out of the mass trend to the colleges.[1]

What this means in practice is indicated by the question: "But where is the college which is willing to flunk 50 per cent of its graduating class?"

Hocking does not explain why democracy means this only in higher education and not in secondary or even primary education. If "every man has a right and duty to be a whole man," as he puts it, why has not every individual a right

[1]William Hocking: *Experiment in Education* (Chicago: Henry Regnery Co.; 1954), p. 275.

to that kind of education which will carry him further to that wholeness at any level? And what has all this to do with degrees or certification of professional competence, which are fundamentally socially protective devices? And above all, what has the process of education to do with a race? And even in a race, we do not expect, unless we are Nietzschean, the halt, the blind, the crippled to start from scratch. And if the course of study is to be considered a race course, who ever heard of fifty per cent of the runners winning the prize? Why not flunk ninety per cent of the graduating class—indeed, why not all except the man who wins by coming in first?

The analogy reveals the unconscious, anti-democratic, almost Prussian conception underlying this view of education. Education is not a race or a combat or a competition, although, properly implemented, these may be pedagogic devices to add zest to learning. If we must use language of this sort, it is better to have the individual run a race against his own potentialities; which means, since they grow with achievement, that the race, like the process of education and self-education, is never finished.

Allied to the conception of education as the process by which prizes and power are won is the view of society as a graded and hierarchically organized system, in which intelligence—not birth, social status, or wealth—is the principle of differentiation. No matter what the principle of differentiation is, if it involves hierarchy, official or unofficial, it involves the likelihood of exploitation. It is well to realize that we do not owe the great movements for social justice and political freedom to the educated classes of hierarchically ordered European societies. On the whole, these classes sided with church and king and the social status quo during the centuries of struggle for the extension of human rights. Higher intelligence and specialized education give both the duty and right to exercise specific functions in a complex society, but so does not-so-high intelligence and more general education. Unless there is a mutuality of esteem and a recognition that there are many kinds of desirable distinctions, the entire principle of distinction becomes invidious, a badge of social snobbery and an instrument by which special interests are furthered. A society in which there are class struggles between the better educated and the less well educated, between the more intelligent and the less intelligent, not only violates the principles of moral equality, but is one in which the best educated are likely to lose.

.   .   .

In a democracy we can have education for expertness of any kind, including education for civil service officials as well as generals and physicians. We cannot, strictly speaking, have education for political leadership, as distinct from the political education of all the citizens of the community. It was the political education of the whole people that Jefferson was most concerned with, of a kind that would immunize them against the usurpations of power.

This squares with his reiterated belief that political freedom "can never be safe except in the hands of the people themselves," rather than in any aristocracy of talent or virtue, and that ultimate political authority must rest with them. This faith may be mistaken but without it there can be no reasoned defense of democracy. Nonetheless Jefferson was aware that to entrust political power to the people was not a sufficient guarantee of the perpetuation of political freedom. Without proper education, a people could not long remain free. The abiding political function of education in a democracy, therefore, is to impart the knowledge, develop the skills, and strengthen the values which are required to enable men to make a success of the experiment of self-government. Everything else is a matter of relative curricular detail for him in this respect.

· · · ·

CHAPTER II
THE ENDS OF EDUCATION

There are two generic ways of reaching what are sometimes called "the ultimate" ends of education. One relies on an immediate, self-certifying *intuition* of the nature of man; the other on the observation of the consequences of different proposals of treating man. The first is essentially theological and metaphysical; the second is experimental and scientific.

When they are intelligently formulated both approaches recognize that the ends of education are relevant to the nature of man. But a world of difference separates their conception of the nature of man. The religious or metaphysical approach seeks to deduce what men *should be* from what they *are*. And what they are can only be grasped by an intuition of their "essential" nature. Whatever the differences between Aristotle, Aquinas, and Rousseau on other points —and they are vast—all assert that from the true nature of man the true nature of education follows logically. If we know what man is, then we can lay down the essentials of an adequate education for all men, everywhere, always. The scientific approach, on the other hand, is interested in discovering what the nature of man is, not in terms of an absolute essence, but *in terms of a developing career in time* and in relation to the world of things, culture, and history of which he is an inseparable part. It recognizes man's nature not as a premise from which to deduce the aims of education, but as a set of *conditions* which limit the range of *possible* educational aims in order to select the best or most *desirable* from among those for which man's nature provides a ground. An education should not be what it cannot be; it can be what it should not be; it may be what it should be.

In this chapter I shall briefly indicate an experimental approach to the question of educational ends and their relation to human nature. In the next, I shall consider the opposing claims made for a currently fashionable metaphysical view.

There are at least three distinguishable, but not separable, aspects of man's nature that are relevant to the formulation of valid educational ideals. (a) First, man is a biological organism subject to definite laws of growth. Certain powers and capacities mature, flourish, and decline according to a definite cycle. (b) Second, man is a member of society, heir to a cultural heritage and social organization that determine the forms in which his biological needs and impulses find expression. (c) Third, man as a personality or character exhibits a distinctive pattern of behavior, rooted in biological variation and influenced by the dominant norms of his culture, which he gradually develops through a series of successive choices.

Given these threefold aspects of man's powers, what ends of education should be stressed, and why? We say ends, rather than end, because an education that is relevant to at least these three aspects of human nature will have plural, even if related, ends.

(a) In relation to the development of the human organism, physical and mental, a desirable education takes as its end *growth*. By "growth" I mean the maturation of man's natural powers toward the highest desirable point which his body, his mind, and his culture make possible. It is a process which results physically in a state of health, and intellectually in a continuing activity of self-education.

The maturation of body and mind is natural; but so is stunting and retardation. Therefore, in selecting growth as an end, we are not *deducing* what should be from what is but are choosing the preferred consequences of one mode of action rather than another. There are many societies in which the development of certain features of the body and powers of the mind is not encouraged. For the same reason, since there are multiple possibilities of development, in selecting growth we are selecting a certain type or kind of development.

Growth, as everyone knows, has been emphasized by John Dewey as one of the central aims of education. But, as soon as one speaks of growth, critics who approach this end as if it were being urged in isolation from others are sure to inquire: growth in what direction? There is criminal growth, fascist growth, cancerous growth. From the fact that a thing is, it doesn't follow that it must or should grow. From the belief that a thing should grow, we do not yet know what direction the potentialities of growth should be encouraged to take. The necessity for a social frame of reference is clearly indicated as soon as we select growth as an educational end.

No one has seen this more clearly nor stressed it more insistently than John Dewey. From the very outset the end of personal growth has been allied with the social end of democracy in his educational philosophy.

This idea [that the object and reward of learning is continued capacity for growth] cannot be applied to *all* the members of a society except where intercourse of man with man is mutual, and except where there is adequate provision for the reconstruction of social habits and institutions by means of wide stimulation arising from equitably distributed interests. And this means a democratic society.[2]

Education for growth, then, goes hand in hand with education for democracy and a justification of one is tantamount to a justification of the other. But why continuous growth even if democracy is accepted as a social goal? There are at least two reasons. One flows from the nature of the democratic ideal, which is incompatible with fixed social divisions. It cannot function properly where individuals are trained independently of their maturing powers and possibilities of development. The second is that a world in which continuous growth is encouraged is more likely to make for the diversification and enrichment of experience than a world where individuals remain at the same level they have reached at the close of their schooling, learning nothing new even if they forget nothing old.

(b) We have already seen that every choice we make in selecting and fortifying certain tendencies among the plurality of potentialities in the individual must be undertaken from the standpoint of some social philosophy, or some ideal of social organization. What, then, are the grounds for our choice of the democratic social philosophy? Here, also, as in the case of the justification of ends, there are two generic approaches open to those who recognize the validity of the question—a metaphysical or religious "demonstration" ultimately based on absolute intuitions, and an empirical approach which regards the test of consequences as decisive.

The metaphysical and theological premises from which the validity of democracy has been allegedly derived are of the most heterogeneous variety. Many of them are mutually incompatible. They have been offered by polytheists, monotheists, atheists; Jews, Mohammedans, and Christians; Catholics, Lutherans, and Unitarians; and by philosophers of diverse schools. This suggests that the conviction with which the democratic ideal is held rests not so much on alleged metaphysical presuppositions that are beyond the test of experience, but on the actual or anticipated values of democracy in experience as contrasted with nondemocratic alternatives. It is interesting to observe that these *nondemocratic* alternatives historically have been justified by the identical metaphysical and theological presuppositions which have been advanced as the alleged premises on which democracy rests. And since these premises are compatible with social philosophies that are mutually contradictory, the latter cannot be derived from the former.

The existence of democratic communities in which individuals of conflicting religious faiths and metaphysical beliefs sincerely co-operate in democracy's

[2]John Dewey: *Democracy and Education* (New York: The Macmillan Company; 1916), p. 117.

support indicates that it is possible to find criteria for accepting democracy that do not depend on revelation or intuition. Indeed, to claim that democracy is uniquely entailed by only one set of theological or metaphysical intuitions, and that no one can sincerely or consistently be a democrat who does not embrace them, is not only logically false—it imperils the very existence of a democratic community. For the nonempirical character of these intuitions makes it impossible to find a workable method by which conflicts among them may be resolved and uncoerced agreements reached. In matters of faith, each sect regards itself as illumined and all others as blind.

The empirical method which regards democracy as an hypothesis, warranted by its consequences for weal and woe, holds out some promise of reaching agreement provided human beings can be induced to follow its lead in social affairs as in physical affairs. If we ask, then, why we should treat individuals of unequal talents and endowments as persons who are equally entitled to relevant consideration and care—the central idea underlying democratic institutions—we can point to consequences of the following *type:* it makes for greater tranquillity, justice, freedom, security, creative diversity, reasonableness, and less cruelty, insensitiveness, and intellectual intolerance than any other social system that has so far been devised or proposed.[3] There are more widespread commitments among men to these values, and a greater agreement on the methods by which evidence is reached concerning whether or not they are present in any situation, than to any metaphysical or theological system which allegedly underlies them. Any one of these values has been or can be challenged in the course of experience. Its rejection or vindication depends on whether or not it furthers other values. There is no last resting point, nor is there a circle. We rest at each problem, until a new one arises.

This may be and has been contested by those who assert that there are ultimate values which are inarbitrable and that in the end only a radically ungrounded choice can be made when these ultimate values conflict. Existentialism is one of a variety of philosophical positions which stress the alleged fact of these ultimate values as a reason for denying or limiting the relevance of rational, scientific inquiry to problems of moral conflict.

Whether there are "ultimate" values for which we can offer no further justification or good reason is something which cannot be settled by fiat. It is a question of fact, not of definition. If there are such ultimate values, they may all be equally objective even if not universal. And if there are such ultimate values, it is clear from the complex chains of justification which are offered in defense of myriads of policies and decisions, that they are very few in number. An overwhelming number of value conflicts would be still arbitrable in the light of some shared ultimate or terminal value.

[3]For an amplification of this point, cf. my essay, "Naturalism and Democracy," in *Naturalism and the Human Spirit,* ed. Y. H. Krikorian (New York: Columbia University Press; 1944), pp. 40–64.

Further, when we analyze judgments of value in the problematic contexts in which they are made, we invariably find in the structure of the situation a reference to what is the case or might very well be the case that has a bearing upon the validity of the judgment. Taken out of context, out of a real situation of danger and choice, the answer to the question: Should I live or not? may seem ultimate or arbitrary in the sense that no further justification can be given. Examined in the actual, living context in which a genuine problem arises whether one should live or die, a thousand good or bad reasons may suggest themselves for doing one or the other. Theoretically, it is *possible* that those who differ in their judgments of value in any specific situation may agree about all the facts involved and all the consequences for themselves and others likely to follow from the envisaged alternatives. If and when this is the case, we may speak of the difference in value judgment as ultimate. So far, I have never found a situation of strong value conflict in which this *is* the case. Conflicts over values seem always associated with conflicting assessments of causes and consequences. As far as the justification of democracy is concerned against its communist or fascist critics, I have always found that the argument seems to depend directly or indirectly upon judgments of fact. This would seem to indicate that the conflict of values is here not ultimate but penultimate.

(c) On the level of character and personality, the aim of education should be the development of intelligence. Here we reach the key value in the sense that it is both an end and the means of testing the validity of all other ends —moral, social, and educational. How is it to be justified? Why should we educate for intelligence? Once again, the answers divide into those which reply in terms of the antecedent nature of man, and those which point to the consequences of intelligence in use. These consequences are many and desirable. Intelligence enables us to break the blind routines of habit when confronted by new difficulties, to discover alternatives when uninformed impulse would thrust us into action, to foresee what cannot be avoided and to control what can. Intelligence helps us to discern the means by which to instate possibilities; to reckon costs before they are brought home; to order our community, our household, and our own moral economy. All this and more, in addition to the joys of understanding.

Whether man is intelligent, and how intelligent, and what conditions his intelligence, are empirical questions on which considerable evidence has accumulated. One might, of course, ask: What must the nature of man be in order for him to become intelligent? And if anyone can derive from the answer more illumination than he had before, we can reply: Man must potentially have the nature of a rational creature in order to *become* intelligent. How little this tells us is apparent when we reflect that it is tautological, except possibly for cases of mutation, to assert that a thing possesses potentially the qualities and relations it actually exhibits in the course of its development. Potentialities may not all be realized but, in a certain sense, everything realized may be regarded as potential prior to the moment of its actualization. Men are and may become unintelligent, too. Unintelligence (or stupidity) is therefore also an antecedent potentiality. But since, potentially, man is both intelligent *and* unintelligent, what we select as the trait to encourage depends not merely on its potentiality but rather on its desirability. And desirability is an affair of fruits, not of origins.

.   .   .

CHAPTER III
THE NATURE OF MAN

We have been attempting to justify the ends of education by their consequences in experience. There is another approach which rules out all reference to consequences as irrelevant. This declares that we are dealing with a metaphysical question, which requires an answer based on the true metaphysics. Its chief exponents in America are Robert M. Hutchins, Monsignor Fulton Sheen, and Mortimer Adler. They hold that the appropriate end of education can be *deduced* from the true nature of man. The true nature of man is that which differentiates him from animals, on the one hand, and angels, on the other. It is expressed in the proposition: "Man is a rational animal." From which it is inferred that the end of human education should be the cultivation of reason.

We shall have occasion to see that the term "reason" does not mean the same thing as the term "intelligence"—that it designates something that has a different origin, nature, and function. But for present purposes, we shall ignore the differences in the meanings of the terms "reason" and "intelligence." The main point is that a patent fallacy is involved in the presumed deduction of the ends of education from what uniquely differentiates man from other animals.

First of all, if what we have previously said is true, from what man *is* we can at best reach conclusions only about what human education is, not what it *should be.* What man should be is undoubtedly related to what he is, for no man should be what he cannot be. Yet a proposition about what he is no more uniquely entails what he should be than the recognition of the nature of an egg necessitates our concluding that the egg should become a chicken rather than an egg sandwich.

A further assumption of the argument is the Aristotelian doctrine that the good of anything is the performance of its specific virtue or the realization of its potentiality. The "good" egg is one that becomes a chicken, the "good" man is one who realizes his natural capacity to think. This overlooks the fact that the natural capacities of a thing limit the range of its fulfillments but do not determine any specific fulfillment. Not every natural power of man has only one natural end; and not every power which has one end achieves it by one mode of development. Thinking is no more or no less natural to man than eating and singing. But what, when, and how a man should eat; what, when, and how a man should sing; about what and when he should think—all this depends not so much upon the natural powers of eating, singing, or thinking as upon an ideal of fitness, appropriateness, or goodness, that is *not* given with natural powers but brought to bear *upon* them in social, historical, and personal experience. When we assert that men *should* be rational, we are not talking biology or metaphysics but voicing a social directive that selectively modifies the natural exercise of human powers in the light of preferred consequences among possible alternate uses.

Second, granted for the sake of the argument that animals other than man are incapable of any rationality. The question is an old and difficult one, handled satirically by Plutarch and experimentally by Köhler, both of whom disagree with the airy dogmatism of the neo-Thomists. Nonetheless, rationality is not the only feature which differentiates man from other animals. Man can be defined, and has been by Benjamin Franklin and Karl Marx, as a "tool-making animal." By the same reasoning employed by neo-Thomists, we can "deduce" that man's proper education should be vocational! Man is also the only animal that can will to commit suicide. Does it follow that education should therefore be a preparation for death? Man is also the only animal that ruts all year round. What educational corollary does this unique trait entail?

Thirdly, even if man is a rational animal, he is not only that. He has many other traits—needs, feelings, emotions, desires, whose nobility or ignobility depend upon their social context. An education appropriate to man would not necessarily limit itself to one aspect of his nature even if that aspect were regarded as more valuable than any other. It is a queer view of the nature of any organism that limits itself to a concern only with its differentia. The notion that the education of reason can or should be carried out independently of the education of the emotions has been called by Whitehead "one of the most fatal, erroneous and dangerous conceptions ever introduced into the theory of education."[4] At any rate what is clear is that we can go from the nature of man to the conclusion that we should educate for reason only because some selective principle has been introduced. The basic educational issues, like the basic ethical issues, pose problems of choice. The nature of man is always relevant; but just as relevant is our decision as to what we want to make of it, what we want men to become. At this point no metaphysical deduction, whether proceeding from materialistic or spiritualistic premises concerning the nature of "reality," can guide us.

[4] Alfred North Whitehead: *The Aims of Education and Other Essays* (New York: The Macmillan Company; 1929), p. 9 [p. 268 in this book].

What, after all, is meant by "*the* nature of man" whenever we speak of relating educational ends to it? The phrase masks a certain ambiguity that makes it difficult to tell whether its reference is empirical or metaphysical. A great deal of philosophical profundity consists in shifting back and forth between these two references and not being found out. When the neo-Thomists speak of *the* nature of man as a basis for educational ideals, their concern is not primarily with biological, psychological, historical, and social features of human behavior. For since these items designate specific processes of *interaction* between an organism and its environment, it would be risky to choose any set of traits as fixing forever *the* nature of human nature, and therefore *the* nature of education. But the position we are examining is concerned precisely with a conception of human nature which will permit the deduction that, in the words of Mr. Hutchins, "education should everywhere be the same." Everywhere and at every time? Everywhere and at every time. In a weakened form, Mr. Adler repeats this: "If man is a rational animal, constant in nature through history, there must be certain constant features in every sound educational program regardless of culture and epoch."[5] And Mr. Mark van Doren, who carries all of his teacher's ideas to recognizable absurdity, adds that because education and democracy have the same end—the making of men— they are one and the same. "So education is democracy and democracy is education."[6] From man's nature we can apparently deduce not only that education should everywhere be the same, but the social system, too.

If education is determined by human nature, may not human nature change, and with it the nature of education? *"We must insist,"* writes Mr. Hutchins, *"that no matter how environments differ human nature is, always has been, and always will be the same everywhere."*[7]

This is truly a remarkable assertion. Before we inquire on what evidence Mr. Hutchins knows this to be true, let us see what it implies. For one thing, it implies that human nature is completely independent of changes in the world of physical nature with which the human organism is in constant interaction. Now, certainly, Mr. Hutchins cannot know that the world of nature "is, always has been, and always will be the same everywhere." He therefore must believe that no transformation of the physical basis of human life can possibly affect human nature. His assertion further implies that man's nature is completely independent of changes in the human body, particularly the brain and nervous system. At one stroke this calls into question the whole evolutionary approach to the origin and development of the human species. Finally, it implies that the habitation of man's nature in a human body is unaffected by changes in society and social nurture. The enormous range of variation in social behavior, which testifies to the plasticity of the simplest physiological response under cultural conditioning, leaves the essence of human nature unaltered. In short,

[5]Mortimer Adler: "The Crisis in Contemporary Education," *Social Frontier*, Vol. 5, No. 42 (February 1939), p. 140.
[6]Mark van Doren: *Liberal Education* (New York: Henry Holt & Company; 1943), p. 38.
[7]Robert M. Hutchins: "Towards a Durable Society," *Fortune*, Vol. 27, No. 6 (June, 1943), p. 158. My italics.

human nature is taken out of the world altogether. It is removed from any verifiable context in experience which would permit us to identify it and observe its operations. For anything which operates in the world does so in *interaction* with other things that help shape its character.

There is only one entity that satisfies all these conditions. It is the supernatural soul as conceived by theologians of the orthodox Christian tradition. It is not the Aristotelian concept of the soul because, for Aristotle, the soul was the form of the body, all forms were incarnate in matter, and the nature of man was construed from his behavior. The constancy of human nature in Aristotle was predicated on the notion of the constancy of the natural order as well. Were he, in the light of modern science, to abandon the latter notion, he would have surrendered the belief in the constancy of human nature, since it was integrally related to the behavior of the body in nature and society. For Aristotle man can become a rational animal only because he is also a social and physical animal. But Mr. Hutchins admits all the facts of physical and biological change as well as historical and social development in man's *environment*, yet insists that man's nature cannot change or develop. It is only when we realize that he is not talking about empirical, historical, suffering man but about a mystical, supernatural entity, which has a temporary abode in the human body, that the peculiarities and ambiguities of his language are understandable.

This is the secret behind the talk of man's true and constant nature that defies all change. Bishop Sheen and M. Maritain are more frank with us than their epigoni at Chicago and elsewhere. But all of them owe us a proof that the immortal soul, as defined by them, exists. So far not a shred of valid experimental evidence has been adduced to warrant belief in its existence. In fact, the achievements of genuine knowledge about human nature in medicine, biology, psychology, and history have been largely won by a bitter struggle against obstacles set in the path of scientific inquiry by believers in a supernatural soul.

When it is understood that by "human nature" Hutchins really means the human soul, whose study involves rational theology, and whose goal cannot be adequately grasped without the deliverances of sacred theology and revealed religion, another article of his educational faith becomes clear. The true education of man must include the education of his soul by the one true metaphysics and theology. In the writings of Mr. Hutchins this conclusion is obliquely expressed, but it is explicitly drawn in those of his mentor, Mr. Adler.

> Sacred theology is superior to philosophy, both theoretically and practically. . . . Just as there are no systems of philosophy but only philosophical knowledge less or more adequately possessed by different men, so there is only one true religion, less or more adequately embodied in the existing diversity of creeds.[8]

To this he adds the claim that anyone who does not accept the truth of these

[8]Mortimer Adler: "God and the Professors," in *Proceedings of the Conference on Science, Philosophy and Religion* (ed. Louis Finkelstein; New York: Harper & Brothers; 1940), p. 131.

propositions has no logical right to call himself, or be regarded, as a democrat, together with the urgent recommendation that all teachers who do not subscribe to these truths should be purged ("liquidated" is his word) from our culture.

Since the central problem of education is for Mr. Hutchins a metaphysical problem, all the basic issues depend for their solution upon finding *the* true metaphysical answer. Consequently, metaphysics, including rational theology, occupies the chief place in the recommended curriculum of studies as the only discipline that can impart to students a rational view of the world.

> By way of metaphysics, . . . students on their part may recover a rational view of the universe and of their role in it. If you deny this proposition you take the responsibility of asserting that a rational view of the universe and one's place in it is no better than an irrational one or none at all.[9]

The philosophic presumption of this passage vies with its atrocious logic. To deny the proposition "by way of metaphysics students may recover a rational view of the universe" is certainly *not* to assert that "a rational view of the universe . . . is no better than an irrational one or none at all." The denial of the first proposition implies that students cannot get a rational view of the universe by way of metaphysics; it leaves open the possibility that they may get a rational view of the universe by the study of *other* disciplines, e.g., the sciences, social studies, literature, and history. It emphatically does not imply that a rational conception of the universe is worthless or worth no more than an irrational one. I pass over the additional confusion of identifying a rational conception of the world with the conception that men are rational and the world rationally ordered. A rational conception is one warranted by evidence and a conception of the world may be rational *if* the evidence points to the fact that men are irrational and the world chaotic. I am not saying they are, but contesting the relevance of an a priori metaphysical deduction to these questions. Nor am I denying that the study of philosophy has an important place in the liberal arts curriculum. It has many justifications—among them the achievement of a methodological sophistication that may immunize students against the confusion of definitions or linguistic resolutions with empirical hypotheses of varying degrees of generality, which constitutes so much of traditional and popular metaphysics.

It is important to know what men are in order intelligently to determine what they should become. Educational aims merely restate what we believe men should become insofar as they can be influenced by the processes of learning and teaching. The comparative study of cultures shows how diverse men may become; it also shows certain similarities and identities. The vital physiological sequences are the same in every culture. A social organization,

---

[9] Robert M. Hutchins: *Education for Freedom* (Baton Rouge: Louisiana State University Press; 1943), pp. 26-27.

a form of mating, and other institutions are also everywhere observable where men live together. But there are all types and degrees of cultural institutions. And these institutions, in turn, give varied meanings to identical physiological acts. These meanings enter so integrally into the performance of the physiological action that it requires an abstract science like biology to distinguish between what is attributable to the unlearned behavior of the organism and what is learned from the culture.

> It would be idle . . . to disregard the fact that the impulse leading to the simplest physiological performance is as highly plastic and determined by tradition as it is ineluctable in the long run because determined by physiological necessities.[10]

Depending upon the particular aspect of human behavior we are interested in, we can establish an empirical case for the constancy or mutability of human nature. Provided we keep the distinctions in mind, there is nothing incompatible in asserting that in certain respects human nature is the same, in others different. What is apparent is that those aspects of human nature which appear constant are a set of unconscious processes that are a condition of life. Although these are taken note of in every sensible educational program, they are far from the center of educational concern, which is understanding the dominant cultural problems of the present in relation to the past out of which they have grown, and to the future whose shape depends in part upon that understanding. Whether men remain the same or different, in the sense in which the question is educationally significant, depends upon whether they choose to retain or transform their culture.

The whole question of the constancy of human nature is sometimes obscured by a simple failure to distinguish between names and things. The name we give anything originally fixes our attention on it and identifies it as the object whose behavior (or nature) we are going to inquire into. After we have discovered its behavior, the name is used not only to identify the thing but as a shorthand indication of selected traits of its behavior. If and when these traits change, it becomes a matter of convention whether we are going to continue using the same name or some other name to designate the new properties. If we decide to use another name, this by no means gainsays the historical fact that the traits which hitherto have constituted the nature of the thing have changed or been modified. This is denied in the following passage which is typical of members of the school we are discussing:

> The most familiar form of the problem [permanence and change] has to do with the nature of man, concerning which the educated person will know what he knows about any nature, namely that insofar as it is a nature, it does not change. For then we should have another nature; meaning that in the case of man he would have another name.[11]

---

[10]Bronislaw Malinowski: *A Scientific Theory of Culture and Other Essays* (ed. Huntington Cairns; Chapel Hill: University of North Carolina Press; 1944), p. 87.

[11]Van Doren: *Liberal Education*, p. 26.

Apparently an educated man cannot distinguish between things and names. Names are intelligently used to communicate knowledge and facilitate the control of things. The names we choose to attach to things have no bearing on how they actually are going to behave; they summarize what our experience has led us to believe they will do. The argument of the passage is equivalent to saying that what comes from a cow's udders can never become material for apparel because, since the first we call "milk" and the second "cloth," their essential natures must be different. Milk *cannot* change into cloth. How can a metaphysical bull, in its triple sense, determine that what comes from a cow's udders must be drunk by human beings, instead, after appropriate treatment, of being turned into cloth for apparel? The whole of modern science would come to a stop if it took this word-magic seriously. Since the changes that men undergo are part of their nature, it is absurd to argue from a definition of the *term* "human nature" that human nature throughout its long historical pilgrimage has not changed and cannot change. For if this be true by definition, it is an analytic statement or tautology that does not tell us anything about the world (except about how a certain writer proposes to use a certain word). But those who write this way set great store by statements of this kind as momentous truths about men.

In conclusion. To speak of *the* nature of man is already a sign that a selective interest is present. What is designated by the term "man" may have many natures depending upon the context and purpose of inquiry. Even if *the* nature of man is defined in terms of what differentiates him from other animals, we can choose any one of a number of diverse traits that will satisfy the formal conditions of the definition. And for many purposes what man has in common with other animals may not be irrelevant to his nature. Once we assign a term to stand for a thing and seek to discover its nature, that nature is disclosed not by a definition and its logical implications, as in mathematics, but in its activity or behavior. The activity or behavior of man depends upon many things within and outside of his body. From the point of view of education, the most important of the forces beyond the skin of a man's body which control his behavior is the culture of which he is a part. It also controls many things that occur beneath his skin. Human history is an eloquent record of cultural change, of continuities and discontinuities, in social institutions, language, values, and ideas. It is therefore the sheerest dogmatism to deny that human nature can change.

Education should be adequate to man. Man's nature does not change. Therefore an education adequate to man will always be the same. So Mr. Hutchins and his fellow-metaphysicians argue.

Education should be adequate to man. Man's nature shows a pattern of development in which both constant and variable elements may be discerned. Therefore an education adequate to man will reveal a pattern that reflects this development. So the experimentalist educator.

Value judgments underlie both positions. But the first can be held only so long as the term "human nature" is an unanalyzable abstraction. Just as soon as an empirical meaning is given it, its falsity is palpable. The fact that certain specific educational proposals—like an identical curriculum for all students— are justified by the alleged universal constancy of "human nature" indicates that the term is being used with systematic ambiguity.

.   .   .

CHAPTER VI
THE CONTENT
OF EDUCATION

All controversies in education start from dissatisfaction with what our children are learning or with what they are not being taught. *What should we teach and why?* is a question that arises on the very threshold of intelligent concern with the process of schooling. It is a sad commentary on the character of contemporary education that few institutions, until the war brought an unsought leisure to liberal arts teachers, stopped to ask themselves this question; and that still fewer were able to answer it when they did. To be sure, it is not the only question that can or should be answered, nor is it unrelated to other questions of great import like: *Whom are we educating?* and *For what are we educating?* But it has a directness and a challenging simplicity that everyone recognizes and which no philosophy of education that seeks to guide practice can evade.

The easiest answer to the question *What should we teach?* is also the most deceptive. We should teach—so runs this answer—those subjects which embody the great truths of our human tradition, the accumulated knowledge, skills, and wisdom which are the inalienable heritage of every child. This answer is deceptive because it assumes that there are educators, or others for that matter, who assert that we should *not* teach these things. If there are any such, they have never given a sign of their presence. To infer that those who believe that *more* than these things should be taught are therefore opposed to including them is to exhibit one of those passionate lapses in thinking which suggest that the issue lies somewhere else. The answer is deceptive because it is an over-all truism through which is insinuated the notion that emphasis upon *present-day problems* involves its rejection or denial. Nothing can be taught which does not at one point or another involve the use of some tradition—let it be no more than language. Nothing can be learned which is not continuous with something already known. Instead of an honest confrontation of the issue: What should be the *relative* place of study of the past and present in our education? the issue is lost in the rhetorical flourishes and overtones of what in Aristotle's day was already recognized as a commonplace.

Nor is the issue fairly stated by those who, like Hutchins and Maritain, charge modern educators with the fallacy of "presentism." According to the former, those who would include a study of modern industrial processes in the education of the American student are adherents of "the cult of immediacy." "In this view the way to comprehend the world is to grapple with the reality you find about you. . . . There is no past."[12] One would imagine that grappling with the realities that surround us is precisely the way to begin to understand the world. One would imagine that through such an effort we would discover not only that there is a past, but that it has an inescapable bearing and importance upon the realities surrounding us. To identify the view that the present world is a legitimate object of study for those who are going to live in it, with the view that the present is nothing but a specious bloom of immediacy with no roots in the past and no fruits in the future, is intellectually cheap. It evades considered argument by caricature, and blocks fruitful discussion of the place of the present *and* past in a desirable educational experience.

.   .   .

To say that the present is sacred ground does not imply that the problems and materials of present-day life are sacred. For the present in this context designates the locus of educational justification, not the nature of educational subject matter. But at the same time it does suggest a criterion which will enable us to evaluate the respective claims of different subject matters. This is the criterion of *relevance*.

To demand that the content of instruction be relevant to the present emphatically does not preclude a study of the past. It only prevents us from getting lost in the past. It enables us to make some intelligent *selection* out of the limitless materials inherited from the past.

. . . If we examine the actual content of courses of study based upon material of the past, we make an interesting discovery. A considerable portion of the classical curriculum is devoted to the social and political questions of antiquity, the medieval period, the Renaissance and post-Renaissance—in short, of every age but our own. Those who fulminate against the degeneration of modern education because some schools pay attention to the bridges, waterways, and sanitation systems of our large cities, together with other great feats of engineering, regard it as perfectly proper to study and glow about the marvels of Roman aqueducts, plumbing, and roads. Those who scoff at concern with unemployment and with the devices of ballyhoo by which modern dictators come to power, claim that there is a great lesson to be learned from the role of "bread and circuses" in Roman history. Study of the First and Second World Wars need not be part of a liberal education: the study of the Peloponne-

---

[12] Robert M. Hutchins: *Education for Freedom* (Baton Rouge: Louisiana State University Press; 1943), p. 32.

sian and Punic Wars must be. The "proper" subject matter of a liberal education, on this view, is not the Russian Revolution but the conspiracy of Cataline; not the state papers of Woodrow Wilson, of Clemenceau, of Lenin, but the orations of Demosthenes and Cicero.

The significance of the fact that the Greeks, the greatest of the ancient peoples, made their history and conducted their education without models, without historical examples, without great books, is lost sight of by those who glorify past times. This does not mean that we can or should imitate the Greeks in this respect. Rather does it suggest that, without denying their legacy, we would do well to add to it in order to leave a still richer patrimony to those who follow us. In education as in life we must learn to look to ourselves as ancestors, not merely descendants.

. . .

TRADITION

It is often alleged that a modern curriculum sins against tradition, and thus violates one of the deepest hungers of man, continuity with the past. But as important as tradition is, reflection makes clear that by itself it cannot determine the content of instruction. No matter what turning in the road we take, it is continuous with the road by which we have come. And there are few things we can do today for which some warrant in past traditions cannot be found. Those who defend tradition in education would be the first to deny that the traditional is synonymous with the dead or obsolete. How, then, do we distinguish between obsolete and living traditions? When traditions are invoked to settle issues, they are always *selections* from the heritage of the past—judgments of comparative worth or value testifying to needs in the present—and are justified by their consequences.

The deepest traditions of a community are those that are so completely taken for granted that they rarely emerge on the level of critical awareness, and still more rarely become subjects of debate—like our language and folkways. But let an issue once force itself on the attention of a community to the point of arousing discussion; then it becomes obvious that what the tradition *has been*, of itself does not decide. It is we who decide what our tradition *should be*. The past is so rich that we can always find an historical paternity to legitimize our current offspring.

Those who appeal to tradition as a bulwark against change are curiously unaware of its actual content. For most traditions represent departures from earlier traditions, and their subsequent history is full of further departures from their original purposes and beginnings. No one can survey the history of American religious practice, for example, without realizing that tolerance to dissenters marked a break with earlier traditions, and that the recognition of equal rights for all religions marked a departure from the tradition of mere tolerance. How much truer is this for the history of Western culture. Those who speak of *the* great tradition of the Western world, and charge "decadent" liberals with attempting to ignore it, betray an insensitiveness to the richness, complexity, and contradictory features of what is summed up by the phrase. The dominant traditions of Greek culture are at least as fundamentally different from those of medieval Christendom as the latter are from the traditions of the Renaissance, the Reformation, and the American, the French, and the industrial Revolutions. In different respects, we are the inheritors of them all. Our indiscriminate allegiance to them testifies to a basic confusion in our purposes and values. It is an evasion of the challenge of our own time and culture.

The function of a liberal education in the modern world is to bring some degree of order to minds that have inherited conflicting traditions. It must weave the problems and materials of the modern world into a recognizable pattern by which individuals may take their bearings for a full and responsible life. In liberating individuals from confusion, such education liberates within them fresh energies to redirect or remake, separately and together, the worlds they live in. If their action is enlightened, it will increase human freedom by extending control of nature; if it is mature, it will enhance the quality of freedom by bringing the control of nature under wise human control.

· · ·

CHAPTER X
THE GOOD TEACHER

All plans for educational reforms depend on the teacher for their proper realization. Unless carried out by a personnel sincerely imbued with the philosophy animating the reforms and trained in the arts of effective teaching, they are doomed to failure. Everyone who remembers his own educational experience remembers teachers, not methods and techniques. The teacher is the kingpin of the educational situation. He makes and breaks programs. . . .

Teaching is an art and like all arts it can be learned with varying degrees of proficiency. Some are so gifted by nature that they can perform as good teachers without learning the arts of teaching, just as some singers can have brilliant musical careers without studying voice culture. On the other hand, there are some individuals who are naturally so handicapped for a teaching career that instruction in the teaching arts can do as little for them as musical study for the tone deaf. Most teachers fall between these two extremes. It is a crime against students to permit individuals of the second kind to enter the ordinary classroom as teachers, no matter how great their gifts may be in other respects or in other fields. Whatever teaching is, it should at least not be an obstruction to learning. But it is certainly no crime, it is not even a hardship, to require of naturally gifted teachers—those who are to the teaching manner born—that they learn the formal rudiments of the art of teaching. They can always improve their skills. An enormous amount of time can be saved by familiarizing oneself with teaching devices and techniques even if one already possesses the educator's insight and an adequate educational philosophy. No one who has not actually attempted to teach the details of a curriculum can properly appreciate the great difference that mastery of specific ways and means can make in motivating interest, facilitating communication, and starting in students a train of thought which run its course to the click of understanding. There are some things that are best learned *not* on the job. And although we can rely on any teacher to learn by trial and error experience, why should the students pay the price for that experience?

. . .

A good teacher is not good for all purposes and in all circumstances. In the army, in the church, in the political party, in the penitentiary, as they are presently constituted, a good teacher as we shall define him cannot be used. What makes a good teacher, like what makes a good education, must be considered in relation to certain values. What we are seeking are the criteria of a good teacher in a democratic society whose educational system has embraced the fundamental aims we have previously outlined.

(a) The first criterion is intellectual competence. By this I mean not only the truism that the teacher should have a mastery of the subject matter he is teaching and that he should keep abreast of important developments in his field, but that he should have some capacity for analysis. Without this capacity, he cannot develop it in his students. There are different levels and types of analysis, but what they have in common is an understanding of how to approach problems, of how to take ideas apart, of how to relate our language habits to our intellectual practices. Capacity for analysis is something different from mere possession of the dry-bones and heaps of knowledge. Insofar as the distinction can be made, it is bound up more with method than content. Whatever information a teacher imparts, he must know (and wherever relevant be able to explain) how it is reached, what its validity depends on, and the role of empirical and conventional elements in the answer.

Another element in intellectual competence is a sense of relevant connection. The good teacher should be well oriented in some other fields besides the one in which he may claim to be a specialist. He should be able to follow the thread of an argument or the ramifications of a problem without concern for what a subject is called or for departmental non-trespass signs. I have heard a professor of political science bitterly complain that the economics department was teaching government, too! If the teaching was good, he should have applauded it. On the other hand, not everything in the world is interrelated;

and if it were, not all of it would be equally relevant to a specific problem. The most obvious evidence of bad teaching is classroom "thinking by association," in which by a series of grasshopper jumps topics are dwelt on that have no logical connection with each other. The usual result is that the original problem, where there is one, is lost sight of.

Related to intellectual competence is the willingness to countenance, if not to encourage, rational opposition and spirited critical dissent by students. The inquiring mind even among youth sometimes probes deeply. Only a teacher unsure of himself will resent embarrassing questions to which the only honest reply must be a confession of ignorance. Intellectual independence is such a rare virtue that the good teacher positively welcomes it, despite the occasional excesses of youthful dogmatism and exuberance. . . .

Some teachers seem to be constitutionally incapable of tolerating disagreement. Most often their views are deeply conservative. But there are also radical teachers, advanced thinkers about all subjects from sex to salvation, who are just as intolerant of disagreement as the most extreme reactionaries. If anything, their unction and hypocrisy makes their failure a more painful experience. Both types have chosen the wrong profession. In the classroom, the crusader must always play a subordinate role to the teacher and the inquirer. Otherwise he becomes a persecutor in behalf of the old gods or the new.

(b) Intellectual competence is necessary but not sufficient for good teaching. It must be accompanied by a quality of patience towards beginners which accepts as natural the first groping steps towards understanding by the uninitiated. The "simple" and the "obvious" are relative to antecedent skills and knowledge. Failure to see and act on this is responsible for intellectual browbeating by otherwise competent teachers and for the air, deliberately only half-concealed, of suffering the hopeless stupidity of those who are stumbling their way forward. The intellectually quick, and all teachers should be quick, have a tendency towards intellectual impatience. The impatience but not the quickness must be curbed. Patience is something that can be learned, except by certain temperaments who should never be entrusted with a class. Good teaching is not found where a star teacher holds forth for the benefit only of his star pupils, but where some participating response is evoked from every normal member of the class. Nothing is easier than to yield to the pleasures of colloquy with the exceptional students of a class—and nothing is more unfair to the rest, in whom this builds up intense resentment, oddly enough not against the teacher but against their exceptional classmates. Special provision should be made for the instruction of superior students, but a good teacher does not let their special needs dominate the class to the exclusion of the legitimate educational needs of the others.

(c) The third characteristic of good teaching is ability to plan a lesson, without mechanically imposing it on the class, in those subjects where basic materials have to be acquired, and to guide the development of discussion to a cumulative result in subjects in which the seminar method is used. The bane of much college teaching is improvisation. Improvisation is not only legitimate but unavoidable in motivating interest and finding points of departure or illustration for principles. But it cannot replace the planful survey of subject matter and problems, nor provide direction to discussion. It is delightful to follow the argument wherever it leads. But it must be an argument. And it should lead somewhere.

Where improvisation is chronic and draws its materials from autobiography, teaching sinks to its lowest level. In my own experience I recall teachers who rarely knew what they were going to talk about before they came to class. Usually they would talk about themselves or their families. Over the years, when members of their successive classes came together, they were able to construct a fairly accurate composite family portrait. The personalities of such teachers rarely possessed a richness or power that might justify taking themselves as subject matter. The contempt in which intelligent students held them was checked only by the teachers' powers to distribute grades—a power which they wielded with a whimsical irresponsibility.

Naturally, the responsibility of the teacher for the progressive organization of subject matter varies with elementary and advanced classes, and he will proceed differently in presenting a lecture and in conducting a tutorial. Nothing I have said suggests the necessity of a detailed lesson plan which is as often a drawback as an aid even in the secondary schools. What the teacher must aim at is to make each class hour an integrated experience with an aesthetic, if possible a dramatic, unity of its own. Without a spontaneity that can point up the give and take of discussion, and a skill in weaving together what the students themselves contribute, preparation will not save the hour from dullness. The pall of dullness which hangs over the memories of school days in the minds of many unfortunately envelops the whole question of education.

(d) Another important quality the good teacher possesses is knowledge of human beings. He is in a sense a practical psychologist. He knows something more about people than the laws of their learning curves, and what he knows he has not found in textbooks on psychology. The more one studies students, the more differences they reveal. These differences need not be relevant to what they are trying to learn; but sometimes they are. A teacher devoid of this knowledge cannot solve the problem of motivation or evoke full participation from his class. Nor can he tell when to temper the wind, when to let it blow, when to build up self-assurance in the pathologically shy, when to deflate the bumptious. Unable to diversify his challenges, he cannot teach with proper justice and discipline in a class of miscellaneous talents. He may have a standard for the group; he should have a standard for each individual in terms of his special needs—whether they be disabilities or advantages.

Except on the frontiers of knowledge, subject matter cannot be continuously fresh. The great bulk of what is taught to students in every institution except the graduate schools of universities is "old stuff" to their teachers. To stay intellectually alive as one traverses familiar ground year in and year out is not easy. It can be done, of course, by rotating assignments, by taking sabbaticals and, most important of all, by strong theoretical interests in one's own field and related fields. But to stay intellectually alive in the classroom is something else again. Yet for the sake of students one must be alive there if nowhere else. The new developments in one's field seldom bear upon the fundamentals of college instruction, and the minutiae of scholarship have meaning only to those who are already well instructed.

The secret of intellectual vitality in the classroom, when a theorem is being derived for the twentieth time or when an elementary point in the grammar of a foreign language is being explained or when the nerve of an old philosophic argument is being laid bare, lies in experiencing the situation as a fresh problem in communication rather than one in personal discovery. Or, putting it a little differently, it consists in getting the students to reach the familiar conclusion with a sense of having made their own discovery. The task is to make as many as possible see as much as possible of what they have not seen before. It is this perennial challenge, which cannot be adequately met without a knowledge of people, that keeps the good teacher alive. If he does not recognize it, he is a pedagogical automaton and almost always a bore.

Where knowledge has not yet been won and the authority of method does not point to inescapable and well-tested conclusions, the love of truth can be relied on to generate its own enthusiasm. But where knowledge is already warranted by methods that are themselves warranted, and where originality is likely to be little more than a craving for attention or an expression of conceit, the love of truth by itself cannot be relied upon to make a lesson exciting. There is something suspicious about any mind that can be thrown into raptures of enthusiasm at stated intervals, and in pretty much the same language too, by the statement of truths he has been purveying to students term in, term out. Such enthusiasm is synthetic and the students know it.[13]

There is a crackle of interest always present in the classroom of a good teacher no matter how trite or timeworn the theme. It is supplied not merely by the teacher's love of truth but by the students' desire to discover the truth, and by the teacher's interest in that desire and in the arts of gratifying it. In the end, the good teacher makes himself superfluous and the good student learns the art of self-education. But it is literally in the end.

(e) He knows man best who loves him best. A teacher cannot love all his students, nor is it wise to love any of them. The knowledge appropriate for good teaching requires an emotion not so strong as love but also not so irrational. This emotion is sympathy. The good teacher must like people and be interested in them as people, and yet he need not like or be interested in

---

[13]There is a story told on the campus of an eastern college of an art teacher, now happily no longer teaching, who used to lecture by what might be called the method of sustained respiration. In treating of a certain figure in the history of art, at a fixed point in his course, he would draw a deep breath and, in a mounting crescendo, declaim the artist's wonders. One day he began as usual. "He had no sense of form, he had no sense of color, he had no sense for religion or morals, he broke all the rules of good drawing . . ." and before he could finish, back chorused the class with his punch-line, "But my God! could that man paint!"

everyone. I am speaking of a general personality trait. It need not find universal expression in every action. But without it an intellectually competent teacher may do more harm than good. There is such a thing as sadism in educational life. Teachers have enormous powers to make students miserable; and, where they are chosen haphazardly, there will always be some who will visit their frustrations and disappointments upon those before them, usually under the guise of being strict disciplinarians. The incidence of insanity is higher among teachers than in any other profession, and the academic community is no freer from phobias like anti-Semitism than the rest of the community. It requires only one teacher to ruin a student's career.

Sympathy is a positive attitude of imaginative concern with the personal needs of others. Benevolent neutrality and mechanical application of rules, no matter how scrupulous, are no substitutes for it. If justice is based on understanding, then without sympathy there cannot be true justice. For understanding is never complete without the sympathy that awakens our organs of perception. Those who teach large numbers and never get to know their students have a tendency to regard all but a brilliant few as a dull, cloddish mass. Reduce the number in each class, shorten the perspective, and no one worthy of being a teacher will fail to see the interesting variety of potentiality in every group. Even outside the classroom it takes two people to make one bore. And, next to ideas, persons are the most interesting things in the world. In each person there is some unique quality of charm, intelligence, or character, some promise and mystery that invites attention and nurture. The teacher who seeks it will find it.

Students respond to sympathy for their special intellectual needs like plants to sunshine and rain. They undertake more and achieve more. A certain danger exists that they may at the beginning undertake tasks in order to please their teacher or not to disappoint him but, if proper guidance is furnished, their own sense of growing mastery of a task and of its increasing significance provides intellectual momentum. The function of the teacher at this point is unobtrusively to raise the stick of achievement higher and to offer criticism without killing self-confidence. Students rarely disappoint teachers who assure them in advance that they are doomed to failure. They do not, of course, always live up to the more optimistic expectations of their teachers but they invariably do the better for it.

It is easy to caricature what I am saying by pretending that this is a demand that the teacher be a nurse or a psychiatrist to his students or that he serve literally *in loco parentis*. It would be helpful, naturally, if a teacher were to know the chief relevant facts about those students who need psychiatrists or nurses, if only to put them in proper professional hands and thus prevent them from serving as a drag on other students. But the teacher should not essay the role of amateur psychiatrist or nurse. His sympathy must be primarily directed to his students as growing intellectual organisms in a growing intellectual community, in the faith that they will become integrated persons capable of responsible choice. He cannot cope with all their emotional needs or assume the responsibilities of family and society, priest or judge. He must be friendly without becoming a friend, although he may pave the way for later friendship, for friendship is a mark of preference and expresses itself in indulgence, favors, and distinctions that unconsciously find an invidious form. There is a certain distance between teacher and student, compatible with sympathy, which should not be broken down—for the sake of the student. A teacher who becomes "just one of the boys," who courts popularity, who builds up personal loyalties in exchange for indulgent treatment, has missed his vocation. He should leave the classroom for professional politics.

What I have said flows from the faith that imaginative sympathy towards the needs of the individual student, based on an intelligent appraisal of his equipment and achievements, will enhance his powers of growth. This faith may appear utopian or romantic. Those who are so impressed usually confuse two things: whom we shall teach and how we shall teach. If, at any level or for a specific purpose, a student is uneducable, a large assumption but sometimes obviously true, he should either be directed to a field in which he is educable or committed to an institution for the feeble-minded, for that is where people who are absolutely uneducable belong. But so long as a teacher finds himself before a class in which there are varied talents, varied capacities for educability, he is under an obligation to help each one develop the best within him. That is what he is there for. If he accepts his obligation gladly and not as a chore, he will find that the results are worth the effort.

What to teach and how to teach must be distinguished from the problem of certification of student competence. Competence is a relation not only to subject matter but to comparative performance and to a set of conditions, far from fixed, defined by the nature of the task for which competence is required. There is also something that may be called a "conventional" element in the determination of competence. This is clearest when, because only a certain number can be certified, all whose achievements fall below this number are failed even though their achievements surpass those of individuals who have been previously certified. Competence established by position on a comparative scale can be ascertained even by those who are not teachers. What the teacher alone can supply is testimony of intellectual and personal qualities which he is uniquely qualified to observe. This testimony together with other data of measurable competence should determine the educational decision to advance, to hold, or to transfer the individual student. The basic consideration should be: what action will educationally most profit the individual without too great a cost to others? Detailed rules cannot wisely be drawn *in abstracto*. For all sorts of factors, sometimes even the state of the nation, may affect their formulation.

To develop the best in each student, therefore, emphatically does not mean that the teacher believes that all students are equally good, or that when he must rate them he should rate them all in the same way, or that he must sacrifice "standards"—a blessed word which is the hardest-worked substitute for thinking on educational matters among college teachers. Those who mouth the word most loudly as soon as any proposal is made to liberalize liberal education do not know what "standards" actually are, their source, their history, and that "standards," too, must face a test which requires other standards. They usually maintain that their own standards are absolute and objective, but no two of them agree with each other. It is notorious that one college's *Pass* student is another's *cum laude*, and that even in the same college one professor's *A* is another's *C.* Time and again it has been experimentally proved that the same teacher, irrespective of subject matter, rates the same paper differently, when he has not identified it as such, depending on matters that have nothing to do with education. Those who talk in absolutes here are only absolutizing their own subjectivity. Those who are militantly self-righteous about the number of students they regularly fail rarely stop to ask whether the fault lies in their own teaching or in the kind of standards they are using. I have heard teachers urge the imposition of standards which would obviously have barred *them* from any possibility of a college education if the proposed standards had been applied in all fields when they were students.

The teacher's working standards in the classroom should be distinct from the rules that determine the next step in the educational career of the student, i.e., whether he is to pass or fail. These working standards cannot be adjudged "high" or "low," for they should be nothing else but the realization of the fundamental ends of the educational process itself through the use of the most appropriate means that will insure the maximum intellectual growth of every student entrusted to him. If these are his working standards, the teacher will never be satisfied that this maximum has been finally reached. For with every intellectual achievement new vistas of knowledge open before us.

(f) The good teacher, to close our inventory of his traits, possesses vision. It is the source of both his intellectual enthusiasm and his detachment in the face of inevitable failures and disappointments. Without vision he may become a kindly technician, useful in a limited way. But he cannot inspire a passion for excellence. The vision may take many forms. It may be a doctrine—but he must not preach it. It may be a dream—but he must not keep talking about it. It may be a hope, an ambition, a work in progress, so long as it is not merely personal and has a scope or sweep of some imaginative appeal. But it must not obtrude itself into the details of instruction. Its presence should be inferrable from the spirit with which the instruction is carried on. It should operate in such a way as to lift up the students' hearts and minds beyond matters of immediate concern and enable them to see the importance of a point of view. Wherever an intellectually stimulating teacher is found, there will also be found some large perspective of interest that lights up the corners of his subject matter. If students catch fire from it, it should not be in order to believe some dogma but to strengthen them in the search for truth and to become more sensitive to visions that express other centers of experience.

The best teacher possesses all of the qualities we have mentioned to a pre-eminent degree. But the best teacher is to be found only in a Platonic heaven. Good teachers, however, who exhibit some or all of these qualities are to be found on earth. They can become, can be helped to become, and can help others to become, better teachers. If a resolute beginning is made by those who educate and select teachers, in time the community will discover that a new spirit and morale is abroad in the teaching profession. It will discover that a good teacher is a *dedicated* person, strong in his faith in what he is doing, worthy not only of honor in a democracy but of a place in its councils.

When educational laymen speak of the non-material rewards of good teaching, only too often their kindly observations are fumbling words of consolation for the presumed deprivation of careers isolated from the dramatic struggles of "real" life. There *are* deprivations entailed by the profession of teaching but these are not among them. Most teachers are not men of action by temperament and self-selection keeps them out of the forays and battles of daily life. And no matter what their temperament, a lifetime of exposure to immature minds unfits them for positions in politics or business in which risks must be run and quick decisions taken before all the evidence is in. Teachers unaware of the limiting effect of the very fact of pedagogic excellence upon their habits of mind tend to take themselves too seriously and to regard the world as a classroom waiting for the proper lessons to solve the problems of adult experience. A sense of humor about themselves is the best assurance of a sense of proportion in these matters—a safeguard against taking themselves too seriously as well as against vain regrets. When a man becomes a teacher it is extremely unlikely that the world has lost a great political leader or prophet.

Every choice among viable alternatives involves a sacrifice of some genuine good. Teachers, like others, make sacrifices in the selection and pursuit of their calling. To the individual who has found himself in teaching these sacrifices are far from galling. For if he has found himself in his calling, in all likelihood he has had a successful career. It is not the emoluments and social status or holiday words of community praise which are criteria of success for him. Rather is it a twofold satisfaction. First, he is aware of being a part of a continuing tradition which, no matter how humble his role in it, connects the great minds of the past with those of the present and future. Second, although the teacher like the actor is a sculptor in snow and can leave no permanent monument of his genius behind, he can reach the minds of those who will survive him, and through them affect the future. The lives of most people would have been pretty much the same no matter who their teachers were. But there are a sufficient number of men and women in the world who can truthfully testify to the determining and redetermining role which some teachers played in their lives. To very few is it given to exercise this influence. The opportunity to do so is a measure both of the power of the teacher and of his responsibility.

PART III

Analytic Philosophy of Education

Steven M. Cahn

STEVEN CAHN is Assistant Professor of Philosophy in the Graduate School of Arts and Science at New York University.

The following selection is intended as an introduction to analytic philosophy of education. The analytic movement is today the prevalent philosophical movement in the United States and England. Unfortunately, far too many of its proponents have not concerned themselves with philosophy of education, for it seems to them that this field is one to which analytic philosophy cannot contribute in any significant way.

This essay attempts to explain what analytic philosophy is and how it can, in fact, be utilized to shed light upon discussion of the proper aims of education.

IS THERE AN ANALYTIC PHILOSOPHY OF EDUCATION?

Philosophy of education has been an area of vital concern for many of the world's most renowned philosophical thinkers. Plato, Aristotle, Locke, Rousseau, Kant, and Dewey all made significant contributions to this field of inquiry. Indeed, for Plato and Dewey philosophy of education occupied a central place in philosophic thought. Dewey, in fact, once suggested that "philosophy may even be defined *as the general theory of education.* "[1]

In view of this traditional interest in philosophy of education it is perhaps surprising to find that the area has been neglected by many contemporary philosophers. And this neglect is especially severe among the large group of philosophers who are broadly described as proponents of "philosophical analysis."

This leading movement of twentieth-century philosophic thought is distinguished, not by its specific philosophical theses, but by its conception of the entire philosophical enterprise. From the standpoint of analytic philosophy a philosopher is not a moralist. It is not the task of the philosopher to suggest how a man ought to live his life or what his moral views ought to be. The philosopher has no special expertise in these areas. He is neither saint nor prophet.

Instead, the philosopher is an analyst, but not in the same sense, for example, as is a scientist. The philosopher does not engage in carefully controlled observation and experimentation, and he does not utilize any special technical equipment. Rather, he seeks to discover the nature of and justification for the basic principles that underlie human inquiry.

For example, it has often been claimed that science rests on the principle of determinism, the thesis that every event has a cause. Suppose a scientist when asked to explain the occurrence of a particular event were to reply that no such explanation could possibly be given since the event in question had no cause. Would not such a reply be scientific heresy, a repudiation of the scientific enterprise itself? It is such a question that brings to the fore important philosophical issues. What exactly is meant by the principle that every event has a cause? Is this principle a scientific law? What, in fact, is a scientific law? How does it differ from a scientific theory? How are such laws and theories proven to be true? Has determinism been proven to be true or has it been assumed to be true? There is a sense in which science can proceed in its task without answers to all of these questions. Nevertheless, if we are fully to

[1]John Dewey, *Democracy and Education* (New York, Macmillan, 1963), p. 328.

understand the scientific enterprise, it is necessary to employ the tools of philosophical analysis in order to answer satisfactorily questions such as these.

Philosophy, however, is not limited to analyzing the basic principles of scientific inquiry. Each of the other major fields of human inquiry has its own basic principles which are in need of clarification and justification. History, mathematics, theology, psychology, political theory, morals, art criticism, and linguistics give rise in turn to philosophy of history, philosophy of mathematics, philosophy of religion, philosophy of mind, political philosophy, ethics, philosophy of art, and philosophy of language. Each of these areas of philosophical inquiry bears the same relation to its central field of concern as philosophy of science bears to science. Moreover, all of the above-mentioned fields of philosophy have themselves certain basic principles which underlie inquiry in these fields. It is the investigation of the nature of and justification for these principles that give rise to the two fundamental fields of philosophical inquiry, metaphysics and epistemology.

This, in brief, is the conception of the philosophical enterprise that is held by proponents of philosophical analysis. Whatever one's ultimate judgment may be concerning the limitations of the tasks that these philosophers have set for themselves, there can be no doubt that the results achieved by analytic philosophy have proved to be an indispensable aid to those who wish to think clearly and precisely about any philosophical issue.

Not all areas of philosophical inquiry, however, have been of equal concern to analytic philosophers. This is due in great part to the special interests of those who led philosophical analysis in its early days. Moore, Wittgenstein, and the logical positivists placed heavy emphasis on philosophy of science, philosophy of mathematics, epistemology, and metaphysics. It was in these crucial areas that analytic philosophy made its earliest contributions. In the past two decades, however, analytic philosophers have turned with ever-increasing frequency to such areas as philosophy of religion, philosophy of art, and philosophy of history. The results have certainly been of great value to those who seek enlightenment on fundamental issues in these fields.

Despite these developments philosophy of education remains a field virtually untouched by analytic philosophers. What is the reason for this? Philosophy of science, philosophy of art, and philosophy of religion all have a legitimate place in the spectrum of analytic philosophy. Why should philosophy of education be omitted?

But this is a deceptively simple analogy. Though philosophy of science, philosophy of art, and philosophy of religion are all considered appropriate areas for philosophical analysis, "philosophy of cooking," "philosophy of baseball," and "philosophy of traffic" are not. Indeed, it is not at all clear just what is meant by these latter phrases. Their oddness lies in the fact that cooking, baseball, and traffic are not inquires. They are simply activities. Since analytic philosophy concerns itself only with the basic principles that underlie any inquiry, the blank in the phrase "philosophy of _____" must be filled in with the name of an inquiry if it is to be meaningful.[2] Thus, if philosophy of education is to be considered a valid field of inquiry for analytic philosophy, the term "education" in this context must refer to some major field of inquiry and not merely to the activity of educating individuals.

This may seem to be an excessively narrow criterion for determining the philosophical relevance of a particular subject. Why is the phrase "philosophy of baseball" a meaningless one? Suppose a baseball manager states the principles on which he bases his strategy: for example, that pitching is seventy-five percent of the game. Is he not providing us with his philosophy of baseball? Furthermore, to take a more important subject, why should the philosopher of art be limited to analyzing the basic principles of art criticism? Why should he not discuss the role of the arts in society and examine the most effective ways of organizing society so as to promote the finest possible artistic achievements? Such an approach to philosophy would also provide a clear-cut place for the philosophy of education. Indeed, this is the place traditionally given to philosophy of education, viz., a discussion of the aims or goals of education.

Such an approach to philosophy, however, is opposed by analytic philosophers. It is not that analytic philosophers consider questions about the place of the arts in society and the aims of education to be unimportant. Quite to the contrary, they believe that these questions are so important that they ought not be answered exclusively by philosophers, since philosophers have no special expertise which would enable them to provide better answers than could be provided by artists, historians, or educators. The philosopher qua philosopher knows no more about the arts in society or about the aims of education than does any other individual. There is nothing wrong with philosophers having opinions on these matters, but these matters do not constitute a distinctive field of inquiry, which, according to analytic philosophers, is what philosophy constitutes.

Thus, if philosophy of education is to be a legitimate part of analytic philosophy, it is necessary to return to the original question as to what sort of inquiry, pertaining to education, might replace the blank in the phrase "philosophy of _____." If no such inquiry can be found, philosophy of education will be of no more concern to analytic philosophers than are "philosophy of baseball" or "philosophy of traffic."

As a matter of fact, however, there is such an inquiry pertaining to education, and, furthermore, this inquiry is badly in need of a critical examination of its basic principles. The inquiry to which I refer is the inquiry into the proper aims of education, the inquiry that results in what is generally referred to as an educational philosophy. Analytic philosophy of education does not propose such an educational philosophy. Rather, it seeks to discover the nature of and justification for the basic principles that underlie such an educational philoso-

[2]Of course, analytic philosophers do not concern themselves specifically with every inquiry, but analyze the presuppositions only of major fields of inquiry. For example, there is no need to have a "philosophy of European history," since there are no basic principles of European history that are not basic principles of history in general.

phy, whatever views that educational philosophy may happen to espouse.

In order to clarify further this conception of analytic philosophy of education, it would be well to contrast it with the conceptions of analytic philosophy of education presented by D. J. O'Connor and Israel Scheffler, two analytic philosophers each of whom has formulated his own approach to this subject.

O'Connor defines the philosophy of education as "those problems of philosophy that are of direct relevance to educational theory."[3] He points out that every educational theory contains moral judgments and that some educational theories rest upon religious claims. This leads him to inquire (1) in what ways, if any, an educational theory is similar to a scientific theory, (2) how ethical judgments can be justified, and (3) whether religious claims are meaningful.

The first of these issues, though it is linked to issues in the philosophy of science, is an issue in analytic philosophy of education as I have outlined this subject. To examine the nature of an educational theory and clarify its constituent parts falls squarely within the task I have set for analytic philosophy of education. The second and third issues O'Connor discusses, however, are central issues in other branches of philosophy, specifically, ethics and philosophy of religion. There seems little point in merely duplicating the subject matter of these other branches, linking it to education, and then referring to this hybrid as "philosophy of education." It may be true that every educational philosophy contains certain moral judgments, but unless these value judgments differ in some significant way from other value judgments (as, for example, aesthetic judgments differ from moral judgments) philosophy of education becomes merely a subbranch of ethics and is not a distinctive field of inquiry deserving of separate philosophical study. It becomes much like "philosophy of physics" or "philosophy of music" or "philosophy of European history," which are not treated as separate fields and are dealt with under the more inclusive areas of philosophy of science, philosophy of art, and philosophy of history.

This objection to O'Connor's approach also applies to the general approach to analytic philosophy of education taken by Israel Scheffler. Since education centers about the transmission of knowledge, Scheffler seems to view philosophy of education as a subbranch of epistemology. In his book *Conditions of Knowledge: An Introduction to Epistemology and Education* he analyzes the concept of knowledge from what he calls "the perspective of education."[4]

Scheffler is justly noted for the excellence of his analysis, but it seems misleading to refer to his study as philosophy of education. It is true that he sometimes utilizes examples such as "the timid student" or "the untutored student" to illustrate his epistemological views. This, however, does not turn

[3]D. J. O'Connor, *An Introduction to the Philosophy of Education* (London, Routledge, 1957), pp. 14–15. O'Connor uses the term "educational theory" to refer to what I have called an "educational philosophy."

[4]Israel Scheffler, *Conditions of Knowledge: An Introduction to Epistemology and Education* (Chicago, Scott, Foresman, 1965), p. 1.

epistemology into philosophy of education any more than the use of examples such as "Paul Revere knew the British were coming" or "Some reporters on election night in 1948 believed that Thomas Dewey had been elected President of the United States" turns epistemology into philosophy of history.[5]

This is not to say that issues in philosophy of education must be totally divorced from other philosophical issues, any more than issues in philosophy of art must be totally divorced from issues in epistemology, ethics, or metaphysics. But just as there are certain central issues in philosophy of art that are not part of another branch of philosophy since they arise specifically from an examination of the nature of art criticism, so, if analytic philosophy of education is to be a distinctive philosophical inquiry, there must be certain central issues that arise specifically from an examination of the nature of educational philosophies.

What are these issues? I would propose the following questions as a representative sample of central issues in analytic philosophy of education. (1) What precisely is an educational philosophy? (2) To what extent does an educational philosophy depend on specific psychological, epistemological, and metaphysical claims? (3) To what extent is an educational philosophy expected to provide us with educational methodology, that is, specific pedagogical techniques? (4) Are the concepts of intelligent action and habitual action incompatible? (5) What are the significant similarities and differences between the various sorts of knowledge that may be acquired in the educational process? (6) Can virtue be taught? (7) How is it possible for a person who has been taught what is right to act contrary to the principles he has learned? These last two issues take us back, of course, to the works of Plato and Aristotle and thereby serve as a reminder that the issues of analytic philosophy have been treated by almost all philosophers of the first rank, whether they be analytic philosophers or not.

I believe that all of the philosophical issues I have just raised are of importance and that the answers would be of value to anyone genuinely interested in the process of education. There are no doubt further issues of this sort. I do not wish to claim, however, that there are as many issues of significance in analytic philosophy of education as there are, for example, in philosophy of science or ethics. Nevertheless, this is no reason for analytic philosophers to abandon philosophy of education; rather it is reason not to overemphasize its fertility as a field for philosophical analysis. Such overemphasis merely results in the discussion of pseudoanalytic problems and the utilization of pseudoanalytic techniques. It is quite unenlightening, for example, to be told that education is a triadic relation in which the teacher *T* teaches the subject matter *M* to a student *S*. This is a parody of philosophical analysis and is of little use to philosophers or educators.

One further point needs to be emphasized. Analytic philosophy of education

---

[5]In all fairness I should note that in another of his books, *The Language of Education* (Springfield, Ill., Charles C Thomas, 1960), Scheffler does to some extent engage in what I would consider analytic philosophy of education.

will not provide us with the proper aims of education, for by its very nature analytic philosophy avoids the positing of normative judgments. An analysis of the concept of knowledge, for example, does not commit us either to seek knowledge or to shun it. This decision is a further step beyond the mere analysis of the concept. It is tempting, however, to try to take this further step without acknowledging the moral and political commitments it involves. Such a move is illegitimate.

To argue, as Scheffler does, that "teaching . . . requires us to reveal our reasons to the student and, by so doing, to submit them to his evaluation and criticism"[6] is not to argue that teaching is the appropriate manner of educating the young. Totalitarian societies, which make extensive use of indoctrination in education, will hardly be convinced that their policy is wrong by being informed that indoctrination is, by definition, not teaching. Their obvious retort would be that if teaching is to be defined in this manner, then they are not interested in teaching. They would simply give Scheffler his word and continue to maintain the justice of their policy.

Moral issues are not settled solely by philosophical analysis and neither are issues of educational policy. This may well be a strong reason for philosophers to go beyond analytic philosophy of education and attempt to formulate educational philosophies, but if they choose to do so it is only fair that they make explicit the moral and political commitments that are necessarily implicit in such philosophies.

[6] *The Language of Education*, p. 57.

Richard S. Peters

RICHARD S. PETERS is Professor of the Philosophy of Education at the University of London Institute of Education.

His adherence to analytic philosophy is clear from the opening paragraphs of this essay. He is not concerned with discussing the proper aims of education. Rather, he sets out to clarify the very concept of an educational aim. He draws an important distinction between an "aim" and a "principle of procedure," and he calls attention to the fact that many disputes that appear to be about the proper aims of education are in fact disputes about the correct principles of educational procedure.

In the course of his article Peters makes a number of references to the views of educators whom he terms "progressives." Such labels are best avoided, since they tend to confuse issues rather than clarify them. Peters groups together Dewey and William Kilpatrick as "progressives," despite the fact that Dewey's booklet, *Experience and Education,* is a criticism of views similar to those of Kilpatrick. According to Peters, "progressives" believe that the teacher should not utilize his authority over a child, that rewards and punishments are unacceptable educational tools, and that art and drama should be the primary subjects of instruction.

But this is a misinterpretation of Dewey's views. Dewey recognized the need for social control in the classroom and pointed out that "the ordinary good citizen is as a matter of fact subject to a great deal of social control." Dewey was not opposed to rewards and punishments in education. What he objected to was the undue emphasis which so many educators placed upon these external factors. As to the content of education, no one was more concerned than Dewey with the importance of science and history in the curriculum.

The irony of Peters' misunderstanding is that his concluding statement, "there is an important sense in which 'life' must be for the sake of education, not education for life" is an echo of Dewey's statement that "the inclination to learn from life itself and to make the conditions of life such that all will learn in the process of living is the finest product of schooling."

MUST AN EDUCATOR
HAVE AN AIM?

Many in recent times have blamed philosophers for neglecting their traditional task in relation to education. For, in the old days, it is argued, philosophers explained what the good life and the good society were; and this provided aims for educationists. But nowadays, as Sir Richard Livingstone put it, we are lacking in a knowledge of the "science of good and evil." I think that most modern philosophers would claim that, in this respect, they had advisedly neglected their traditional task, for the very good reason that they have become clearer about what their task as philosophers is. The so-called "revolution in philosophy" of the twentieth century has been largely a matter of becoming clearer about what philosophy is and is not. And one of the conclusions that has emerged is that it is not a sort of super-science of good and evil.

However, this newly found modesty about providing blueprints for the good life does not altogether either excuse or explain the neglect by modern philosophers of philosophical problems connected with education. I do not think that this neglect springs from the conviction that there *are* no such philosophical problems. Rather it is because philosophers have been so concerned with their "revolution" that they have concentrated more on the central problems of philosophy—those connected with knowledge and belief, appearance and reality, freewill and determinism, mind and body, space and time. Peripheral problems connected with concepts like "education," "authority," and "character" have been crowded out, as Hobbes put it, "no otherwise than the sun deprives the rest of the stars of light, not by hindering their action, but by obscuring and hiding them with his excess of brightness." It is time that philosophers supplemented their sun-worship by a bit of star-gazing—but this, as I shall try to show, does not mean trying to return to the old task of constructing a horoscope of educational aims.

I suppose the conviction that an educator must have aims is generated by the concept of "education" itself; for it is a concept that has a standard or norm, as it were, built into it. To speak of "education," even in contexts quite remote from that of the class-room, is to commit oneself, by implication, to a judgment of value. One might say, for instance, that it was a "real education" for compilers of the Wolfenden Report to wander round Piccadilly at night-time. Some state of mind is here presupposed which is regarded as commenda-

From *Authority, Responsibility, and Education* by R. S. Peters, London, George Allen & Unwin, Ltd.; New York, Paul S. Eriksson, Inc., 1959, pp. 83–95. Reprinted by permission of both publishers.

ble, and some particular experiences are regarded as leading on to or contributing to it. There is thus a wide sense of "education" in which almost anything could be regarded as being part of one's education. Rousseau said that "education comes to us from nature, from men, and from things." And of course he was right; for the concept works in as wide a way as this. But there is a narrower and more usual sense of "education" in which *men* are very much to the fore. For we usually speak of education in contexts where we consciously put ourselves or others in such improving situations.

Given that "education" implies, first, some commendable state of mind and, secondly, some experience that is thought to lead up to or to contribute to it, and given also that people are usually deliberately put in the way of such experiences, it is only too easy to think of the whole business in terms of models like that of building a bridge or going on a journey. The commendable state of mind is thought of as an end to be aimed at, and the experiences which lead up to it are regarded as means to its attainment. For this model of adopting means to premeditated ends is one that haunts all our thinking about the promotion of what is valuable. In the educational sphere we therefore tend to look round for the equivalent of bridges to be built or ports to be steered to. Hence the complaints of lack of direction when obvious candidates do not appear to fill the bill.

It is my conviction that this model misleads us in the sphere of education. We have got the wrong picture of the way in which values must enter into education; and this is what occasions the disillusioned muttering about the absence of agreed aims. But to bring out how we are misled we must look at the contexts where the means-end model *is* appropriate. There is, first of all, that of plans and purposes where we do things in order to put ourselves in the way of other things. We get on a bus in order to get to work; we fill up a form in order to get some spectacles. Our life is not just doing one thing after another, we impose plans and schedules on what we do by treating some as instrumental to others. Some of these we regard as more commendable than others, and what we call our scale of values bears witness to such choices. The second means-end context is that of making or producing things. We mix the flour in order to make a cake or weld steel in order to make a bridge. We speak of the end-product in a factory and of the means of production in an economic system.

In both these contexts we might well ask a person what he was aiming at, what his objective was. But in both cases the answer would usually be in terms of something pretty concrete. He might say something like "getting a better job" or "marrying the girl" in the first context; or something like "producing a soundless aeroplane" in the second. Similarly if a teacher was asked what he was aiming at, he might state a limited objective like "getting at least six children through the eleven-plus." But he might, as it were, lift his eyes a bit from the scene of battle and commit himself to one of the more general aims of education—elusive things like "the self-realization of the individual," "character," "wisdom," or "citizenship." But here the trouble starts; for going to school is not a *means* to these in the way in which getting on a bus is a means to getting to work; and they are not made or produced out of the material of the mind in the way in which a penny is produced out of copper. These very general aims are neither goals nor are they end-products. Like "happiness" they are high-sounding ways of talking about doing some things rather than others and doing them in a certain manner.

It might be objected that education is an art like medicine and that in medicine there is a commonly accepted end-product—physical health. Why should there not be a similar one for education—mental health, for instance? The answer is fairly obvious. Doctors deal mainly with the body and if they agree about what constitutes physical health it is because it can be defined in terms of physical criteria like temperature level and metabolism rate. Also there is little objection to manipulating and tinkering with the body in order to bring about the required result.

In the case of education, however, there are no agreed criteria for defining mental health; for either it designates something purely negative like the absence of unconscious conflicts, or, in so far as it is a positive concept, it has highly disputable personal and social preferences written into it. Also education is not, like medicine or psychiatry, a remedial business. When we are concerned with the minds of men there are objections to bringing about positive results in certain sorts of ways. People make moral objections to prefrontal leucotomy even as a remedial measure. How much more objectionable would it be to promote some more positive state of mind, like a love of peace, in all men by giving them drugs or operating on everyone at birth? Indeed, in my view, disputes between educationists, which take the form of disputes about aims, have largely been disputes about the desirability of a variety of principles involved in such procedures. Values are involved in education not so much as goals or end-products, but as principles implicit in different manners of proceeding or producing.

Of course there can be considerable disagreement about the value of what is to be passed on as well as about the manner of passing it on. At the moment, for instance, there is much disagreement as to whether education should be liberal, technical, or vocational. And this reflects different assessments about the value of what is to be passed on, which is a matter of governmental policies as well as of personal preferences. An educator has an important social function in a community and, however idiosyncratic his individual aims may be, he cannot be completely indifferent to the pressing needs of the community, especially if he is paid by the state. Different weight is attached by different educators to the needs of the community as distinct from those of the individual child. Indeed those who stress "mental health" as an educational aim may well be protesting against the effects of collective pressure on the individual. Instead of trying to interpret this aim positively we might regard it as a timely warning against pushing the individual into socially approved tasks at too great a cost to his stability. It is as if a teacher was insisting that, whilst he was fulfilling his essential social function of passing on information and skills and preparing children for different jobs, it should never be forgotten that children may become unhappy and neurotic, isolates from their group, or sexually unbalanced. And the educator should not disregard these other things that go to make up "the whole man." In the old days talk of "character-training" used to serve as a corrective to undue academic or vocational pressure; or religious ideals were appealed to. But nowadays such a corrective must seem to have scientific authority. So "mental health" enters the field of education—the old Aristotelian "harmony of the soul" in respectable trappings.

But those who stress the importance of a "liberal" education are not merely voicing a protest against an academic or vocational emphasis in education which neglects the individual needs of children. Neither are they claiming merely that there should be arts subjects in the curriculum as well as science and typewriting. Their protest relates to the manner as well as to the matter of education. For both science and arts subjects can be passed on by liberal or illiberal procedures. Literature and science can both be treated as "subjects" and, as it were, stamped in to a student. Or they can be treated as living disciples of critical thought and of the imagination, in which the student can be trained on an apprenticeship system. "Liberal" is a term used of certain types of principles and procedures such as respect for persons and facts, toleration, and deciding matters by discussion rather than by dictat. Its association with the *content* of courses is derivative from the belief that some subjects foster such principles more than others. But this is a naïve view— rather like the strange belief that technical colleges can be made more "liberal" if a certain amount of time is devoted to teaching "the humanities" to supplement science subjects. For it is surely the *manner* in which any course is presented rather than its matter which is crucial in developing a liberal attitude of mind.

To illustrate more clearly the distinction which I am drawing between "aims" and "principles of procedure," let me take a parallel from politics. A man who believes in equality, might, like Godwin, be lured by a positive picture of a society in which differences between people would be minimized. He might want to get rid of differences in wealth and rank, even to breed people in the attempt to iron out innate differences. He might even go so far as to advocate the abolition of institutions like the army or the Church in which some men were given opportunities of lording it over others. Another social reformer, however, might employ the principle of equality in a much more negative sense without any concrete picture to lure him on his journey. He might insist, merely, that whatever social changes were introduced, no one should be treated differently from anyone else unless a good reason could be produced to justify such unequal treatment. The Godwin type of man would rightly be regarded as pursuing equality as a very general aim; the more cautious liberal would have no particular aim connected with equality. He would merely insist that whatever schemes were put forward must not be introduced in a way which would infringe his procedural principle.

I think that this is an illuminating parallel to the point I am trying to make about the aims of education. For, in my view, many disputes about the aims of education are disputes about principles of procedure rather than about "aims" in the sense of objectives to be arrived at by taking appropriate means. The so-called "aims" in part pick out the different valuations which are built into the different procedures like training, conditioning, the use of authority, teaching by example and rational explanation, all of which fall under the general concept of "education."

Consider, for instance, the classic dispute about the aims of education which is so often connected with an argument about the derivation of the word "education." There were those like Sir Percy Nunn who stressed the connection with *educere*—to lead out. For them the aim of education must therefore be the development or realization of individual potentialities. Others, like Sir John Adams, stressed the derivation from *educare*—to train, or mould according to some specification. They might be regarded as people who in fact believed in aims in a proper sense, in moulding boys into Christian gentlemen, for instance. The progressive who protests against this conception of education is not simply jibbing at the end-product of a Christian gentleman. He is also jibbing at the assimilation of education to an art where something is produced out of material. Rousseau, for instance, protested vociferously against treating children as little mannikins, as material to be poured into an adult mould. A child, he argued, should be treated with respect as a person. The progressive, therefore, like Dewey or Kilpatrick, presents another picture of the educational process. The child's interest must be awakened and he must be put into situations where the task rather than the man exerts the discipline. He will thus acquire habits and skills that are useful to him, and, by co-operating with others in common tasks, will develop respect for others and for himself. In the eyes of the progressive the use of authority as a principle of procedure is not only an inefficient way to pass on skills and information; it is also an immoral way to treat a child. It is made even worse in both respects by techniques like the use of reward and punishment.

So at the one end of the family tree generated by the concept of "education" there are procedures involving the use of authority in which the voice and the cane are used to produce a desirable end-product. Education is here thought of after the model of means to ends in the arts. At the other end the model of purpose and planning is stressed; but it is the purpose and planning of the child, not of the adult. As Rousseau put it: "By attempting nothing in the beginning you would have produced an educational prodigy."

But, as any educationist must know, if he reflects on the matter, these are only a limited selection of the procedures that are in fact employed. There is, for instance, the influence exerted by one person on another in some sort of apprenticeship system, when the teacher guides rather than goads. We learn carpentry by doing it with someone who is a bit better at carpentry; we learn to think clearly by talking with someone who thinks a bit more clearly than we do. And this other person need not be a charismatic figure so beloved by the advocates of "impressionism" in the public schools or Boy Scout movement. It may be a person who is not only skilled but who has the additional ability of being able to explain and give an account of what he is up to. Progressives often object to talk and chalk and confuse the use of the voice with one way in which it is used—the authoritative way. But most good teachers use their voices to excite and to explain, not simply to instruct, command, or drill.

My guess is that most of the important things in education are passed on in this manner—by example and explanation. An attitude, a skill, is caught; sensitivity, a critical mind, respect for people and facts develop where an articulate and intelligent exponent is on the job. Yet the model of means to ends is not remotely applicable to the transaction that is taking place. Values, of course, are involved in the transaction; if they were not it would not be called "education." Yet they are not end-products or terminating points of the process. They reside both in the skills and cultural traditions that are passed on and in the procedure for passing them on. As Aristotle put the matter long ago:

> For the things we have to learn before we can do them, we learn by doing them, e.g. men become builders by building, and lyre-players by playing the lyre; so too we become just by doing just acts, temperate by doing temperate acts . . . but it is not the man who does these that is just and temperate but the man who does them *as* just and temperate men do them.

And how can this happen unless we learn them in the company of experienced practitioners—who understand what they are doing and who can explain it to others?

There are all sorts of things that can be passed on that are valuable. Almost anything, as I started off by saying, can be regarded as being of educational value. And, to a large extent, those who favour one type of procedure rather than another choose examples that suit themselves and advocate the practice of things that can be passed on best in accordance with their favourite model. The man who advocates authority and drill is most at home with things like Latin and arithmetic where rules have simply to be learnt defining what is right or wrong and where, in the early stages at any rate, there is little scope for rational explanation or learning by experience. The progressive is most at home with things like art, drama, and environmental studies where projects can develop without too much artificiality. And the man who believes in rational instruction is usually inclined towards things like science, history, and geometry. An intelligent teacher, I suppose, will always first try to interest his pupils. As Whitehead put it, romance must precede precision. But, given the interest, he will adapt his procedure to what he is trying to teach.

In society generally there are those who are prone to view life not as a stream of experience to be enjoyed nor as a series of predicaments to be lived through but as a chain of obstacles to be overcome in the pursuit of goals that stretch out like a chain of oases in a desert, or as recalcitrant material to be moulded into some pleasing social or personal pattern. And, of course, many of the things which we do can be regarded as ways of implementing concrete and limited objectives. But this picture of the pursuit of aims is often exalted into grandiose talk about the purpose of life or the purpose of political activity. Self-realization, the greatest happiness of the greatest number, and the class-less society act as lures to provide a distant destination for the great journey of life.

Such general aims are not just harmless extravagances due to the overwork-ing of a limited model of means to ends, a sort of metaphysical whistle in the dark. For men will do terrible things to other men in order to implement aims like racial purity which are both idiotic and illusory. The crucial question to ask, when men wax enthusiastic on the subject of their aims, is what *procedures* are to be adopted in order to implement them. We then get down to moral brass tacks. Do they in fact favour the model of implementing aims taken from the arts and from technology? There are those who favour the maximum of authoritative regulation such as is necessary in an army; there are those who use other people and mould them for their own purposes; there are those who are determined to live according to rational principles and to extend the maximum of toleration to others who disagree with them; there are those whose preoccupation is the pursuit of private good for whom hell is the other fellow.

These differences of procedure are writ large in the family, in economic affairs, and in political life. In education they are accentuated because the impact of man upon man is more conscious and because people are put into positions of authority where there is great scope for adopting their favoured procedures. My point is that arguments about the aims of education reflect these basic differences in principles of procedure. The Puritan and the Catholic both thought they were promoting God's kingdom, but they thought it had to be promoted in a different manner. And the different manner made it quite a different kingdom.

Of course arguments about general aims do not reflect *only* differences in principles of procedure or disagreements about the relative importance of public needs and individual development. Equally important are valuations of content where the merits of, e.g., art as distinct from those of science or history are under discussion. But the real issues involved in such comparisons are obscured by talk about self-realization, life, happiness, and so on. For what sort of self is to be realized? What quality of life is worth perpetuating? Teachers surely care whether or not poetry rather than push-pin is perpetuated, to use a time-honoured example.The problem of justifying such "higher" activities is one of the most difficult and persistent problems in ethics. But talk about self-realization and other such omnibus "ends" does more than obscure it; it also encourages an *instrumental* way of looking at the problem of justification. For a nebulous end is invented which such activities are supposed to lead up to, because it is erroneously assumed that education must be justified by reference to an end which is extrinsic to it. The truth is much more that there is a quality of life embedded in the activities which constitute education, and that "self-realization" can be explicated only by reference to such activities. Thus, if by "life" is meant what goes on outside schools and universities, there is an important sense in which "life" must be for the sake of education, not education for life.

Israel Scheffler

ISRAEL SCHEFFLER is Victor S. Thomas Professor of
Education and Philosophy at the Harvard Graduate
School of Education.

His essay is an excellent illustration of the scope and
limits of analytic philosophy of education. Scheffler provides a remarkably succinct and clear explication of the
models of teaching implicit in the writings of Plato (and
St. Augustine), Locke, and Kant. He goes on to point
out the strength and weaknesses inherent in each of
these three models. In so far as his evaluations depend
exclusively on metaphysical and epistemological considerations, he does not overstep the bounds of philosophical inquiry established by analytic philosophers.

But Scheffler does not restrict himself in this way.
Implicitly he brings moral and political considerations
to bear on his evaluations. He concludes his essay by
stating that "in teaching, we do not impose our wills on
the student, but introduce him to the many mansions of
the heritage in which we ourselves strive to live, and to
the improvement of which we are ourselves dedicated."
This is no doubt the ideal of teaching possessed by members of a democratic society, but teachers in a
totalitarian society are expected to impose their wills on
the students. Scheffler does not present any arguments
in favor of a democratic political system, but he implicitly relies on such arguments in formulating his views.

There are those societies, referred to by Dewey as
"progressive," in which the citizens "attempt to shape
the experiences of the young so that instead of reproducing current habits, better habits shall be formed, and
thus the future adult society shall be an improvement on
their own." But not all societies are of this sort. Plato,
for example, believed that the just society does not admit of any change. The proper laws, once established,
ought never to be altered. Scheffler does not agree with

383

Plato, but this is a disagreement which rests, in part, on their divergent moral and political beliefs.

In order to adequately defend his views on the nature of teaching, Scheffler would have to introduce his own value judgments. He might well be willing to do this, but, if he did so, he would no longer be merely analyzing concepts. He would, in addition, be engaged in the defense of a philosophy of education, an enterprise that is beyond the scope of analytic philosophy.

PHILOSOPHICAL MODELS
OF TEACHING

1. INTRODUCTION

Teaching may be characterized as an activity aimed at the achievement of learning, and practiced in such manner as to respect the student's intellectual integrity and capacity for independent judgment. Such a characterization is important for at least two reasons: First, it brings out the intentional nature of teaching, the fact that teaching is a distinctive goal-oriented activity, rather than a distinctively patterned sequence of behavioral steps executed by the teacher. Secondly, it differentiates the activity of teaching from such other activities as propaganda, conditioning, suggestion, and indoctrination, which are aimed at modifying the person but strive at all costs to avoid a genuine engagement of his judgment on underlying issues.

This characterization of teaching, which I believe to be correct, fails, nevertheless, to answer certain critical questions of the teacher: What sort of learning shall I aim to achieve? In what does such learning consist? How shall I strive to achieve it? Such questions are, respectively, normative, epistemological, and empirical in import, and the answers that are provided for them give point and substance to the educational enterprise. Rather than trying to separate these questions, however, and deal with each abstractly and explicitly, I should like, on the present occasion, to approach them indirectly and as a group, through a consideration of three influential models of teaching, which provide, or at any rate suggest, certain relevant answers. These models do not so much aim to *describe* teaching as to *orient* it, by weaving a coherent picture out of epistemological, psychological, and normative elements. Like all models, they simplify, but such simplification is a legitimate way of highlighting what are thought to be important features of the subject. The primary issue, in each case, is whether these features are indeed critically important, whether we should allow our educational thinking to be guided by a model which fastens upon them, or whether we should rather reject or revise the model in question. Although I shall mention some historical affiliations of each model, I make no pretense to historical accuracy. My main purpose is, rather, systematic or dialectical, that is, to outline and examine the three models and to

"Philosophical Models of Teaching" by Israel Scheffler, *Harvard Educational Review;* vol. 35, Spring 1965, pp. 131–143. Copyright 1965 by President and Fellows of Harvard College. Reprinted by permission of the author and the *Review.*

see what, if anything, each has to offer us in our own quest for a satisfactory conception of teaching. I turn, then, first to what may be called the "impression model."

2. THE IMPRESSION MODEL

The impression model is perhaps the simplest and most widespread of the three, picturing the mind essentially as sifting and storing the external impressions to which it is receptive. The desired end result of teaching is an accumulation in the learner of basic elements fed in from without, organized and processed in standard ways, but, in any event, not generated by the learner himself. In the empiricist variant of this model generally associated with John Locke, learning involves the input by experience of simple ideas of sensation and reflection, which are clustered, related, generalized, and retained by the mind. Blank at birth, the mind is thus formed by its particular experiences, which it keeps available for its future use. In Locke's words, (Bk. II, Ch. I, Sec. 2 of the *Essay Concerning Human Understanding):*

> Let us then suppose the mind to be, as we say, white paper, void of all characters, without any ideas; how comes it to be furnished? Whence comes it by that vast store, which the busy and boundless fancy of man has painted on it with an almost endless variety? Whence has it all the materials of reason and knowledge? To this I answer, in one word, From experience; in that all our knowledge is founded, and from that it ultimately derives itself. Our observation, employed either about external sensible objects, or about the internal operations of our minds, perceived and reflected on by ourselves, is that which supplies our understandings with all the materials of thinking. These two are the fountains of knowledge, from whence all the ideas we have, or can naturally have, do spring.

Teaching, by implication, should concern itself with exercising the mental powers engaged in receiving and processing incoming ideas, more particularly powers of perception, discrimination, retention, combination, abstraction, and representation. But, more important, teaching needs to strive for the optimum selection and organization of this experiential input. For potentially, the teacher has enormous power; by controlling the input of sensory units, he can, to a large degree, shape the mind. As Dewey remarked,

> Locke's statements . . . seemed to do justice to both mind and matter. . . . One of the two supplied the matter of knowledge and the object upon which the mind should work. The other supplied definite mental powers, which were few in number and which might be trained by specific exercises.[1]

The process of learning in the child was taken as paralleling the growth of knowledge generally, for all knowledge is constructed out of elementary units of experience, which are grouped, related, and generalized. The teacher's

[1]John Dewey, *Democracy and Education.* New York: The Macmillan Company, 1916, p. 62.

object should thus be to provide data not only useful in themselves, but collectively rich enough to support the progressive growth of adult knowledge in the learner's mind.

The impression model, as I have sketched it, has certain obvious strong points. It sets forth the appeal to experience as a general tool of criticism to be employed in the examination of all claims and doctrines, and it demands that they square with it. Surely such a demand is legitimate, for knowledge does rest upon experience in some way or other. Further, the mind is, in a clear sense, as the impression model suggests, a function of its particular experiences, and it is capable of increased growth with experience. The richness and variety of the child's experiences are thus important considerations in the process of educational planning.

The impression model nevertheless suffers from fatal difficulties. The notions of absolutely simple ideas and of abstract mental powers improvable through exercise have been often and rightly criticized as mythological:[2] Simplicity is a relative, not an absolute, concept and reflects a particular way of analyzing experience; it is, in short, not given but made. And mental powers or faculties invariant with subject matter have, as everyone knows, been expunged from psychology on empirical as well as theoretical grounds. A more fundamental criticism, perhaps, is that the implicit conception of the growth of knowledge is false. Knowledge is not achieved through any standard set of operations for the processing of sensory particulars, however conceived. Knowledge is, first and foremost, embodied in language, and involves a conceptual apparatus not derivable from the sensory data but imposed upon them. Nor is such apparatus built into the human mind; it is, at least in good part a product of guesswork and invention, borne along by culture and by custom. Knowledge further involves *theory*, and theory is surely not simply a matter of generalizing the data, even assuming such data organized by a given conceptual apparatus. Theory is a creative and individualistic enterprise that goes beyond the data in distinctive ways, involving not only generalization, but postulation of entities, deployment of analogies, evaluation of relative simplicity, and, indeed, invention of new languages. Experience is relevant to knowledge through providing tests of our theories; it does not automatically generate these theories, even when processed by the human mind. That we have the theories we do is, therefore, a fact, not simply about the human mind, but about our history and our intellectual heritage.

In the process of learning, the child gets not only sense experiences but the language and theory of his heritage in complicated linkages with discriminable contexts. He is heir to the complex culture of belief built up out of innumerable creative acts of intellect of the past, and comprising a patterned view of the world. To give the child even the richest selection of sense data or particular

[2]Dewey, *Ibid.*, "the supposed original faculties of observation, recollection, willing, thinking, etc., are purely mythological. There are no such ready-made powers waiting to be exercised and thereby trained."

facts alone would in no way guarantee his building up anything resembling what we think of as knowledge, much less his developing the ability to retrieve and apply such knowledge in new circumstances.

A *verbal* variant of the impression model of teaching naturally suggests itself, then, as having certain advantages over the *sensory* version we have just considered: What is to be impressed on the mind is not only sense experience but language and, moreover, accepted theory. We need to feed in not only sense data but the correlated verbal patterning of such data, that is, the *statements* about such data which we ourselves accept. The student's knowledge consists in his stored accumulation of these statements, which have application to new cases in the future. He is no longer, as before, assumed capable of generating our conceptual heritage by operating in certain standard ways on his sense data, for part of what *we* are required to feed into his mind is this very heritage itself.

This verbal variant, which has close affinities to contemporary behaviorism, does have certain advantages over its predecessor, but retains grave inadequacies still, as a model of teaching. To *store* all accepted theories is not the same as being able to *use* them properly in context. Nor, even if some practical correlation with sense data is achieved, does it imply an understanding of what is thus stored, nor an appreciation of the theoretical motivation and experimental evidence upon which it rests.

All versions of the impression model, finally, have this defect: They fail to make adequate room for radical *innovation* by the learner. We do not, after all, feed into the learner's mind all that we hope he will have as an end result of our teaching. Nor can we construe the critical surplus as generated in standard ways out of materials we do supply. We do not, indeed cannot, so construe insight, understanding, new applications of our theories, new theories, new achievements in scholarship, history, poetry, philosophy. There is a fundamental gap which teaching cannot bridge simply by expansion or reorganization of the curriculum input. This gap sets *theoretical* limits to the power and control of the teacher; moreover, it is where his control ends that his fondest hopes for education begin.

3. THE INSIGHT MODEL

The next model I shall consider, the "insight model," represents a radically different approach. Where the impression model supposes the teacher to be conveying ideas or bits of knowledge into the student's mental treasury, the insight model denies the very possibility of such conveyance. Knowledge, it insists, is a matter of vision, and vision cannot be dissected into elementary sensory or verbal units that can be conveyed from one person to another. It can, at most, be stimulated or prompted by what the teacher does, and if it indeed occurs, it goes beyond what is thus done. Vision defines and organizes particular experiences, and points up their significance. It is vision, or insight into meaning, which makes the crucial difference between simply storing and reproducing learned sentences, on the one hand, and understanding their basis and application, on the other.

The insight model is due to Plato, but I shall here consider the version of St. Augustine, in his dialogue, "The Teacher,"[3] for it bears precisely on the points we have dealt with. Augustine argues roughly as follows: The teacher is commonly thought to convey knowledge by his use of language. But knowledge, or rather *new* knowledge, is not conveyed simply by words sounding in the ear. Words are mere noises unless they signify realities present in some way to the mind. Hence a paradox: If the student already knows the realities to which the teacher's words refer, the teacher teaches him nothing new. Whereas, if the student does not know these realities, the teacher's words can have no meaning for him, and must be mere noises. Augustine concludes that language must have a function wholly distinct from that of the signification of realities; it is used to *prompt* people in certain ways. The teacher's words, in particular, prompt the student to search for realities not already known by him. Finding these realities, which are illuminated for him by internal vision, he acquires new knowledge for himself, though indirectly as a result of the teacher's prompting activity. To *believe* something simply on the basis of authority or hearsay is indeed possible, on Augustine's view; to *know* it is not. Mere beliefs may, in his opinion, of course, be useful; they are not therefore knowledge. For knowledge, in short, requires the individual himself to have a grasp of the realities lying behind the words.

The insight model is strong where the impression model is weakest. While the latter, in its concern with the conservation of knowledge, fails to do justice to innovation, the former addresses itself from the start to the problem of *new* knowledge resulting from teaching. Where the latter stresses atomic manipulable bits at the expense of understanding, the former stresses primarily the acquisition of insight. Where the latter gives inordinate place to the feeding in of materials from the outside, the former stresses the importance of firsthand inspection of realities by the student, the necessity for the student to earn his knowledge by his own efforts.

I should argue, nevertheless, that the case offered by Augustine for the prompting theory is not, as it stands, satisfactory. If the student does not know the realities behind the teacher's words, these words are, presumably, mere noises and can serve only to prompt the student to inquire for himself. Yet if they *are* mere noises, how can they even serve to prompt? If they are not understood in any way by the student, how can they lead him to search for the appropriate realities which underlie them? Augustine, furthermore, allows that a person may believe, though not know, what he accepts on mere authority, without having confronted the relevant realities. Such a person might,

[3] *Ancient Christian Writers*, No. 9, St. Augustine, "The Teacher," edited by J. Quasten and J. C. Plumpe, translated and annotated by J. M. Colleran, Newman Press, Westminster, Md., 1950.

presumably, pass from the state of belief to that of knowledge, as a result of prompting under certain conditions. But what, we may ask, could have been the content of his initial belief if the formulation of it had been literally unintelligible to him? The prompting theory, it seems, will not do as a way of escaping Augustine's original paradox.

There is, however, an easier escape. For the paradox itself rests on a confusion of the meaning of *words* with that of *sentences.* Let me explain. Augustine holds that words acquire intelligibility only through acquaintance with reality. Now it may perhaps be initially objected that understanding a word does not always require acquaintance with its signified reality, for words may also acquire intelligibility through definition, lacking such direct acquaintance. But let us waive this objection and grant, for the sake of argument, that understanding a word *always* does require such acquaintance; it still does not follow that understanding a true sentence similarly requires acquaintance with the state of affairs which it represents. We understand new sentences all the time, on the basis of an understanding of their constituent words and of the grammar by which they are concatenated. Thus, given a sentence signifying some fact, it is simply not true that, unless the student already knows this fact, the sentence must be mere noise to him. For he can understand its meaning indirectly, by a synthesis of its parts, and be led thereafter to inquire whether it is, in reality, true or false.

If my argument is correct, then Augustine's paradox of teaching can be simply rejected, on the ground that we *can* understand statements before becoming acquainted with their signified realities. It follows that the teacher can indeed *inform* the student of new facts by means of language. And it further seems to follow that the basis for Augustine's prompting theory of teaching wholly collapses. We are back to the impression model, with the teacher using language not to prompt the student to inner vision, but simply to inform him of new facts.

The latter conclusion seems to me, however, mistaken. For it does *not* follow that the student will *know* these new facts simply because he has been *informed;* on this point Augustine seems to me perfectly right. It is knowing, after all, that Augustine is interested in, and knowing requires something more than the receipt and acceptance of true information. It requires that the student earn the right to his assurance of the truth of the information in question. New *information,* in short, can be intelligibly conveyed by statements; new *knowledge* cannot. Augustine, I suggest, confuses the two cases, arguing in effect for the impossibility of conveying new knowledge by words, on the basis of an alleged similar impossibility for information. I have been urging the falsity of the latter premise. But if Augustine's premise is indeed false, his conclusion as regards knowledge seems to me perfectly true: To *know* the proposition expressed by a sentence is more than just to have been told it, to have grasped its meaning, and to have accepted it. It is to have earned the right, through one's own effort or position, to an assurance of its truth.

Augustine puts the matter in terms of an insightful searching of reality, an inquiry carried out by oneself, and resting in no way on authority. Indeed, he is perhaps too austerely individualistic in this regard, rejecting even legitimate arguments from authority as a basis for knowledge. But his main thesis seems to me correct: One cannot convey new knowledge by words alone. For knowledge is not simply a storage of information by the learner.

The teacher does, of course, employ *language*, according to the insight model, but its primary function is not to impress his statements on the student's mind for later reproduction. The teacher's statements are, rather, instrumental to the student's own insight. The reference to such insight seems to explain, at least partially, how the student can be expected to apply his learning to new situations in the future. For, having acquired this learning not merely by external suggestion but through a personal engagement with reality, the student can appreciate the particular fit which his theories have with real circumstances, and, hence, the proper occasions for them to be brought into play.

There is, furthermore, no reason to construe adoption of the insight model as eliminating the impression model altogether. For the impression model, it may be admitted, does reflect something genuine and important, but mislocates it. It reflects the increase of the culture's written lore, the growth of knowledge as a public and recorded possession. Furthermore, it reflects the primary importance of conserving such knowledge, as a collective heritage. But knowledge in this public sense has nothing to do with the process of learning and the activity of teaching, that is, with the growth of knowledge in the individual learner. The public treasury of knowledge constitutes a basic source of materials for the teacher, but he cannot hope to transfer it bit by bit in growing accumulation within the student's mind. In conducting his teaching, he must rather give up the hope of such simple transfer, and strive instead to encourage individual insight into the meaning and use of public knowledge.

Despite the important emphases of the insight model which we have been considering, there are, however, two respects in which it falls short. One concerns the simplicity of its constituent notion of insight, or vision, as a condition of knowing; the other relates to its specifically cognitive bias, which it shares with the impression model earlier considered. First, the notion that what is crucial in knowledge is a vision of underlying realities, a consulting of what is found within the mind, is far too simple. Certainly, as we have seen, the knower must satisfy *some* condition beyond simply being informed, in order to have the right to his assurance on the matter in question. But to construe this condition in terms of an intellectual inspection of reality is not at all satisfactory. It is plausible only if we restrict ourselves to very simple cases of truths accessible to observation or introspection. As soon as we attempt to characterize the knowing of propositions normally encountered in practical affairs, in the sciences, in politics, history, or the law, we realize that the concept of a *vision of reality* is impossibly simple. Vision is just the wrong metaphor. What seems indubitably more appropriate in all these cases of knowing is an emphasis on the processes of deliberation, argument, judgment, appraisal of reasons *pro* and *con*, weighing of evidence, appeal to principles, and decision-making, none of which fits at all well with the insight model. This model, in short, does not make adequate room for principled deliberation in the characterization of knowing. It is in terms of such principled deliberation, or the potentiality for it, rather than in terms of simple vision, that the distinctiveness of knowing is primarily to be understood.

Secondly, the insight model is specifically cognitive in emphasis, and cannot readily be stretched so as to cover important aspects of teaching. We noted above, for example, that the application of truths to new situations is somewhat better off in the insight than in the impression model, since the appropriateness of a truth for new situations is better judged with awareness of underlying realities than without. But a judgment of appropriateness is not all there is to application; habits of proper execution are also required, and insight itself does not necessitate such habits. Insight also fails to cover the concept of character and the related notions of attitude and disposition. Character, it is clear, goes beyond insight as well as beyond the impression of information. For it involves general principles of conduct logically independent of both insight and the accumulation of information. Moreover, what has been said of character can be applied also to the various institutions of civilization, including those which channel cognition itself. Science, for example, is not just a collection of true insights; it is embodied in a living tradition composed of demanding principles of judgment and conduct. Beyond the cognitive insight, lies the fundamental commitment to principles by which insights are to be criticized and assessed, in the light of publicly available evidence or reasons. In sum, then, the shortcoming of the insight model may be said to lie in the fact that it provides no role for the concept of *principles*, and the associated concept of *reasons*. This omission is very serious indeed, for the concept of principles and the concept of reasons together underlie not only the notions of rational deliberation and critical judgment, but also the notions of rational and moral conduct.

4. THE RULE MODEL

The shortcoming of the insight model just discussed is remedied in the "rule model," which I associate with Kant. For Kant, the primary philosophical emphasis is on reason, and reason is always a matter of abiding by general rules or principles. Reason stands always in contrast with inconsistency and with expediency, in the judgment of particular issues. In the cognitive realm, reason is a kind of justice to the evidence, a fair treatment of the merits of the case, in the interests of truth. In the moral realm, reason is action on principle, action which therefore does not bend with the wind, nor lean to the side of advantage or power out of weakness or self-interest. Whether in the cognitive or the moral realm, reason is always a matter of treating equal reasons equally, and of judging the issues in the light of general principles to which one has bound oneself.

In thus binding myself to a set of principles, I act freely; this is my dignity as a being with the power of choice. But my own free commitment obligates me to obey the principles I have adopted, when they rule against me. This is what fairness or consistency in conduct means: if I could judge reasons differently when they bear on my interests, or disregard my principles when they conflict with my own advantage, I should have no principles at all. The concepts of *principles, reasons,* and *consistency* thus go together and they apply both in the cognitive judgment of beliefs and the moral assessment of conduct. In fact, they define a general concept of rationality. A rational man is one who is consistent in thought and in action, abiding by impartial and generalizable principles freely chosen as binding upon himself. Rationality is an essential aspect of human dignity and the rational goal of humanity is to construct a society in which such dignity shall flower, a society so ordered as to adjudicate rationally the affairs of free rational agents, an international and democratic republic. The job of education is to develop character in the broadest sense, that is, principled thought and action, in which the dignity of man is manifest.

In contrast to the insight model, the rule model clearly emphasizes the role of principles in the exercise of cognitive judgment. The strong point of the insight model can thus be preserved: The knower must indeed satisfy a further condition beyond the mere receiving and storing of a bit of information. But this condition need not, as in the insight model, be taken to involve simply the vision of an underlying reality; rather, it generally involves the capacity for a principled assessment of reasons bearing on justification of the belief in question. The knower, in short, must typically earn the right to confidence in his belief by acquiring the capacity to make a reasonable case for the belief in question. Nor is it sufficient for this case to have been explicitly taught. What is generally expected of the knower is that his autonomy be evidenced in the ability to construct and evaluate fresh and alternative arguments, the power to innovate, rather than just the capacity to reproduce stale arguments earlier stored. The emphasis on innovation, which we found to be an advantage of the insight model, is thus capable of being preserved by the rule model as well.

Nor does the rule model in any way deny the psychological phenomenon of insight. It merely stresses that insight itself, wherever it is relevant to decision or judgment, is filtered through a network of background principles. It brings out thereby that insight is not an isolated, momentary, or personal matter, that the growth of knowledge is not to be construed as a personal interaction between teacher and student, but rather as mediated by general principles definitive of rationality.

Furthermore, while the previous models, as we have seen, are peculiarly and narrowly *cognitive* in relevance, the rule model embraces *conduct* as well as cognition, itself broadly conceived as including processes of judgment and deliberation. Teaching, it suggests, should be geared not simply to the transfer of information nor even to the development of insight, but to the inculcation of principled judgment and conduct, the building of autonomous and rational character which underlies the enterprises of science, morality and culture. Such inculcation should not, of course, be construed mechanically. Rational character and critical judgment grow only through increased participation in adult experience and criticism, through treatment which respects the dignity of learner as well as teacher. We have here, again, a radical gap which cannot be closed by the teacher's efforts alone. He must rely on the spirit of rational dialogue and critical reflection for the development of character, acknowledging that this implies the freedom to reject as well as to accept what is taught. Kant himself holds, however, that rational principles are somehow embedded in the structure of the human mind, so that education builds on a solid foundation. In any event, the stakes are high, for on such building by education depends the prospect of humanity as an ideal quality of life.

There is much of value in the rule model, as I have sketched it. Certainly, rationality is a fundamental cognitive and moral virtue and as such should, I believe, form a basic objective of teaching. Nor should the many historical connotations of the term "rationality" here mislead us. There is no intent to suggest a faculty of reason, nor to oppose reason to experience or to the emotions. Nor is rationality being construed as the process of making logical deductions. What is in point here is simply the autonomy of the student's judgment, his right to seek reasons in support of claims upon his credibilities and loyalties, and his correlative obligation to deal with such reasons in a principled manner.

Moreover, adoption of the rule model does not necessarily exclude what is important in the other two models; in fact, it can be construed quite plausibly as supplementing their legitimate emphasis. For, intermediate between the public treasury of accumulated lore mirrored by the impression model, and the personal and intuitive grasp of the student mirrored by the insight model, it places general principles of rational judgment capable of linking them.

Yet, there is something too formal and abstract in the rule model, as I have thus far presented it. For the operative principles of rational judgment at any given time are, after all, much more detailed and specific than a mere requirement of formal consistency. Such consistency is certainly fundamental, but the way its demands are concretely interpreted, elaborated, and supplemented in any field of inquiry or practice, varies with the field, the state of knowledge, and the advance of relevant methodological sophistication. The concrete rules governing inference and procedure in the special sciences, for example, are surely not all embedded in the human mind, even if the demands of formal consistency, as such, *are* universally compelling. These concrete rules and standards, techniques and methodological criteria evolve and grow with the advance of knowledge itself; they form a live tradition of rationality in the realm of science.

Indeed, the notion of tradition is a better guide here, it seems to me, than appeal to the innate structure of the human mind. Rationality in natural inquiry is embodied in the relatively young tradition of science, which defines and redefines those principles by means of which evidence is to be interpreted and meshed with theory. Rational judgment in the realm of science is, consequently, judgment which accords with such principles, as crystallized at the time in question. To teach rationality in science is to interiorize these principles in the student, but furthermore, to introduce him to the live and evolving *tradition* of natural science, which forms their significant context of development and purpose.

Scholarship in history is subject to an analogous interpretation, for beyond the formal demands of reason, in the sense of consistency, there is a concrete tradition of technique and methodology defining the historian's procedure and his assessment of reasons for or against particular historical accounts. To teach rationality in history is, in effect, here also to introduce the student to a live tradition of historical scholarship. Similar remarks might be made also with respect to other areas, e.g., law, philosophy and the politics of democratic society. The fundamental point is that rationality cannot be taken simply as an abstract and general ideal. It is embodied in *multiple evolving traditions*, in which the basic condition holds that issues are resolved by reference to *reasons*, themselves defined by *principles* purporting to be impartial and universal. These traditions should, I believe, provide an important focus for teaching.

5. CONCLUSIONS

I have intimated that I find something important in each of the models we have considered. The impression model reflects, as I have said, the cumulative growth of knowledge in its *public* sense. Our aim in teaching should surely be to preserve and extend this growth. But we cannot do this by storing it piecemeal within the learner. We preserve it, as the insight model stresses, only if we succeed in transmitting the live spark that keeps it growing, the insight which is a product of each learner's efforts to make sense of public knowledge in his own terms, and to confront it with reality. Finally, as the rule model suggests, such confrontation involves deliberation and judgment, and hence presupposes general and impartial principles governing the assessment of reasons bearing on the issues. Without such guiding principles, the very conception of rational deliberation collapses, and the concepts of rational and moral conduct, moreover, lose their meaning. Our teaching needs thus to introduce students to those principles we ourselves acknowledge as fundamental, general, and impartial, in the various departments of thought and action.

We need not pretend that these principles of ours are immutable or innate. It is enough that they are what we ourselves acknowledge, that they are the best we know, and that we are prepared to improve them should the need and occasion arise. Such improvement is possible, however, only if we succeed in passing on, too, the multiple live traditions in which they are embodied, and in which a sense of their history, spirit, and direction may be discerned. Teaching, from this point of view, is clearly not, as the behaviorists would have it, a matter of the teacher's shaping the student's behavior or of controlling his mind. It is a matter of passing on those traditions of principled thought and action which define the rational life for teacher as well as student.

As Professor Richard Peters has recently written,

> The critical procedures by means of which established content is assessed, revised, and adapted to new discoveries have public criteria written into them that stand as impersonal standards to which both teacher and learner must give their allegiance. . . . To liken education to therapy, to conceive of it as imposing a pattern on another person or as fixing the environment so that he "grows," fails to do justice to the shared impersonality both of the content that is handed on and of the criteria by reference to which it is criticized and revised. The teacher is not a detached operator who is bringing about some kind of result in another person which is external to him. His task is to try to get others on the inside of a public form of life that he shares and considers to be worthwhile.[4]

In teaching, we do not impose our wills on the student, but introduce him to the many mansions of the heritage in which we ourselves strive to live, and to the improvement of which we are ourselves dedicated.

[4]*Education as Initiation,* an inaugural lecture delivered at the University of London Institute of Education, 9 December 1963; published for The University of London Institute of Education by Evans Brothers, Ltd., London.

Jane Roland Martin

JANE MARTIN is a Lecturer and Research Associate at the Harvard Graduate School of Education. Her essay is illustrative of the way in which the techniques of analytic philosophy can be successfully employed to clarify a concept that is crucial to any philosophy of education.

In the *Meno* dialogue Socrates defended the view that "on the supposition that virtue is knowledge, there can be no doubt that virtue is taught." But there are different sorts of knowledge, and it is by no means clear that all of them can be taught. Can Heifetz teach anyone to play the violin as well as he does? Could Ghandi teach anyone to respond to situations as he did? Can a soldier teach anyone how it feels to be in battle?

Through careful analysis Professor Martin distinguishes various kinds of knowledge. She suggests that to the extent that these can be taught, they must be taught in different ways. She points out, furthermore, that the type of test which can be utilized to determine effectively whether an individual possesses one sort of knowledge cannot be utilized to determine effectively whether he possesses a different sort of knowledge.

It is important to note that this essay does not propose what knowledge ought to be taught or what the qualifications ought to be for those who teach. Such issues necessarily involve the author's own value judgments, and it is the absence of such value judgments that characterizes analytic philosophy of education.

ON THE REDUCTION
OF "KNOWING THAT"
TO "KNOWING HOW"

The distinction between "knowing how" and "knowing that," which Gilbert Ryle makes in Chapter 2 of *The Concept of Mind*, is the point of departure for this paper. Ryle's object in writing *The Concept of Mind* was to discredit once and for all Cartesian dualism, or what he calls "the Myth of the Ghost in the Machine." The particular aim of Chapter 2 is to show that "there are many activities which directly display qualities of mind, yet are neither themselves intellectual operations nor yet effects of intellectual operations."[1] When we describe such activities, we are not referring to a "second set of shadowy operations."[2] According to Ryle, intelligent practice, that is, "knowing how," is not a "step-child of theory." On the contrary, theorizing, that is, "knowing that," is "one practice amongst others and is itself intelligently or stupidly conducted."[3] In distinguishing between "knowing how" and "knowing that" Ryle hopes to correct the intellectualist doctrine which tended to view all knowing as "knowing that." He strongly opposed the view that intelligent performance must be preceded by an intellectual acknowledgment of rules or criteria, that a person must "preach to himself before he can practice."[4]

Ryle's distinction is clearly relevant to the problems of teaching and learning. For example, the learning of skills need not be preceded by knowledge of rules: men knew how to reason correctly before the rules of correct reasoning were formulated by Aristotle.[5] Knowledge of rules is not sufficient for the performance of a skill: we do not say that a boy knows how to play chess if he can recite the rules but cannot make the required moves.[6] In judging a performance we must look "beyond," not "behind," the performance. This does not mean we seek an occult cause for a skillful performance, but rather that a single sample of behavior is not sufficient to attribute "knowledge how" to an actor; we must take account of past record and subsequent performance as well.[7]

Because of its simplicity and apparent obviousness, the distinction between "knowing how" and "knowing that" has great appeal, but like any dichotomy

[1]Gilbert Ryle, *The Concept of Mind* (London: Hutchinson's University Library, 1949), p. 26.
[2]Ryle, p. 50.
[3]Ryle, p. 26.
[4]Ryle, p. 29.
[5]Ryle, p. 30.
[6]Ryle, p. 41.
[7]Ryle, pp. 45, 51.
From *Language and Concepts in Education* by B. Othanel Smith and Robert H. Ennis (eds), Chicago, Rand McNally Company, 1961, pp. 59–71. Reprinted by permission of the authors and the publisher.

it gives rise to much controversy and perplexity. Hartland-Swann has argued that "knowing that" can be reduced to "knowing how."[8] Let us grant that his reduction holds if "knowing how" and "knowing that" are used to refer to a rather limited range of dispositions. Once "knowing that" is reduced to "knowing how," however, a distinction must be made between two types of dispositions subsumed under "knowing how." In the first section of this paper I hope to point out the types of dispositions to which Ryle, and hence Hartland-Swann, refer when they use the phrases "knowing how" and "knowing that."[9] In the second section I shall discuss the nature of the new distinction which must be made once we grant Hartland-Swann's reduction. In the third section I shall examine certain "knowing how" and "knowing that" sentences which neither Ryle nor Hartland-Swann considers, in order to discover whether or not the dispositions to which they refer can be subsumed under Hartland-Swann's "knowing how." Finally, in the last section some of the implications of this analysis for education will be mentioned.

It is of practical importance to analyze the various types of "knowing how" and "knowing that" sentences in ordinary speech and to make such differentiations as are necessary, even if the simplicity of Ryle's dichotomy or Hartland-Swann's reduction is thereby lost. Just as Ryle has drawn our attention to the dangers to education inherent in the reduction of "knowing how" to "knowing that," one may point out dangers inherent in a reduction of "knowing that" to "knowing how" if analysis is discontinued at that point. It would seem no more desirable to teach mathematical or historical facts as if they were skills like swimming than to teach swimming as if it were Latin or geometry. And an equally grave mistake would be to teach moral judgments and rules of conduct as if they were either Latin or swimming.

1. RYLE'S DISTINCTION

In order to formulate Ryle's distinction between "knowing how" and "knowing that" as clearly as possible, it is necessary to ascertain the meaning of the terms "knowing how" and "knowing that." Ryle calls "know" a capacity verb, and thus it is safe to conclude that he would call both "knowing how" and "knowing that" capacities also.[10] (Ryle differentiates capacities from tendencies, although both are dispositions. A tendency implies not only that some-

---

[8]John Hartland-Swann, "The Logical Status of 'Knowing That,'" *Analysis,* XVI (1956), 111–15, and "'Knowing That'—A Reply to Mr. Ammerman," *Analysis,* XVII(1957), 69–71.

[9]Ryle characterizes dispositional concepts as follows: "When we describe glass as brittle, or sugar as soluble, we are using dispositional concepts, the logical force of which is this. The brittleness of glass does not consist in the fact that it is at a given moment actually being shivered. It may be brittle without ever being shivered. To say that it is brittle is to say that if it ever is, or ever had been, struck or strained, it would fly or have flown, into fragments. To say that sugar is soluble is to say that it would dissolve, or would have dissolved, if immersed in water[p.43]."

[10]To be precise, he states that "knowing how" is a disposition but never makes explicit the "logical status" of "knowing that."

thing *could* be the case, but that it *would* be the case regularly when the appropriate conditions are realized; a capacity implies the ability to do something under specified conditions but does not imply frequency or regularity.) At no time does he say exactly what he means by the two types of knowing. From the examples he adduces and several of his statements, however, it is possible to determine that "knowing how" refers to skills or operations, for example, knowing how to play chess, knowing how to theorize, knowing how to speak Russian; and that "knowing that" refers to one's "cognitive repertoire," that is, to knowledge of factual propositions, as for instance, knowing that Sussex is a county in England, knowing that *Messer* is the German word for knife.

It is essential to note that Ryle assimilates all "knowing how" to the model "knowing how to perform a task" and all "knowing that" to the model "knowing that such and such is the case," for we then realize that his distinction is of a more limited nature than we might at first have thought. In ordinary language the phrase "knowing how" is often used when performances are not involved, and the phrase "knowing that" is found in sentences which do not refer to knowing factual propositions. For example, we say, "Johnny knows how a motor works," "I know how Eisenhower felt on election night," and "Jones knows how the accident happened." We also say, "Smith knows that he ought to be honest," "The child knows that he should be quiet when someone is speaking," and "Johnny knows that stealing is bad." None of these examples fits Ryle's paradigms for "knowing how" or "knowing that."

To summarize, Ryle's distinction between "knowing how" and "knowing that" is really a distinction between "knowing how to perform skills" and "knowing propositions of a factual nature." When Hartland-Swann discusses the question of the reducibility of "knowing that" to "knowing how," he too, I believe, is viewing "knowing how" and "knowing that" in this way. Thus in discussing his reduction one must not assume that it holds for all "knowing that" sentences. In fact, I think we will find that such sentences as "Johnny knows that he ought to be quiet" and "Jones knows that he should be honest" cannot be reduced to Ryle's and Hartland-Swann's "knowing how." This problem will be discussed in Section 3. First those sentences to which Hartland-Swann's reduction applies will be analyzed.

2. TWO KINDS OF "KNOWING HOW"

Hartland-Swann maintains that Ryle's distinction between "knowing how" and "knowing that"[11] proves to be unstable when subjected to analysis. Every case of "knowing that," he says, is a case of "knowing how." This follows from

[11]In this section "knowing that" and "knowing how" will be used in the narrow sense discussed above; i.e., "knowing that" will refer to knowing factual propositions, and "knowing how" will refer to knowing how to do something.

the fact that "know" is a dispositional term. If I understand him correctly, what he means is that if we call the statement "Johnny knows that Columbus discovered America" dispositional, then it must be translatable into some such form as "Johnny knows how to answer the question 'Who discovered America?' or 'What did Columbus discover?' correctly." The only alternative to this inclusion of "knowing that" in the "knowing how" category, Hartland-Swann feels, would be to give up the dispositional analysis of "know."

I think one must agree with Hartland-Swann that a dispositional analysis of "knowing that" entails a translation of a "knowing that" sentence into a "knowing how" sentence of the type illustrated above, that is, knowing how to answer a question or to state a fact. It would be a mistake, however, to end the analysis of "knowing" with this reduction, for granted that "knowing that" can be reduced to "knowing how," there is still a fundamental distinction to be made within Hartland-Swann's new, expanded "knowing how" category. The basis for this distinction lies in the fact that two very different sorts of dispositions are subsumed under "knowing how."

Let us consider for a moment the case of Jones who was witness to the murder of Y. Without doubt Jones knows that X murdered Y, and this, in turn, means he knows how to state that X murdered Y and knows how to answer the question "Who murdered Y?" Yet it seems intuitively obvious that there is an essential difference between his knowing how to answer the question "Who murdered Y?" and his knowing how to swim or speak French. That is to say, the difference between the capacity involved in knowing how to state that X murdered Y and the capacity involved in knowing how to swim is more basic than the difference between the capacities involved in knowing how to swim and knowing how to do logic, or in knowing how to ice skate and knowing how to play the violin.

I would like to suggest that the feature which distinguishes these two kinds of capacities from each other is *practice*. That is, "knowing how to swim" is a capacity which implies having learned how to swim through practice; "knowing how to answer the question 'Who murdered Y?'" is a capacity which does not imply having learned how to answer the question through practice. When Jones was a witness to the murder, he knew immediately that X murdered Y and did not need to practice stating facts or answering questions. Similarly, when Jones looks out his window and sees rain falling, he knows that it is raining without any sort of practice in saying "It is raining" or answering the question "What is the weather like right now?" To be sure, if he knows that it is raining, he *is able* to state certain facts and answer certain questions, but his capacity to do so does not imply that he has practiced doing so. On the other hand, Jones could not know how to swim or speak French unless he had at some time practiced swimming or tried to speak French. If Jones tells us he knows how to swim we are justified in asking him if he has ever tried to swim. If he answers "No" to our query, his assertion will be discredited. But if Jones tells us that he knows that X murdered Y, it surely would be nonsensical for us to ask him if he has practiced that assertion or tried to answer questions on the subject before.[12]

If, as I propose, the difference between the two types of capacities subsumed under "knowing how" is based on the notion of practice, some interesting consequences follow. If knowing how to swim requires learning to swim through practice, then we usually would not consider the practice itself to be swimming. The practice may consist in kicking and arm waving and, if all goes well, these will gradually approach swimming. Although the point at which the practice in swimming becomes swimming is not for us to determine, it is interesting to consider the case of the individual who practices just up to the point where he actually swims and then gets out of the water. I think we could say of him that he knows how to swim even though he has not yet actualized this capacity by swimming.[13]

Just as there may be cases of knowing how to swim which are not cases of swimming, so there may be cases of swimming which are not cases of knowing how to swim. For example, it is conceivable that Jones falls into the water one day and swims to shore although he has never practiced or tried to swim before. We cannot deny that he is swimming, but we might well wish to deny that he knows how to swim. In the case of swimming, of course, it is logically possible but in fact unlikely that there would be a performance of the skill which had not been preceded by practice. If, however, we think of a skill such as hitting the target, we realize that it is not too unusual for a novice to hit the bull's-eye without any previous practice. In such a situation we would maintain that although he hit his mark he does not "know how" to hit it. For we would expect someone who knows how to hit the target to hit it again. In other words, hitting a target is an occurrence which may be due to accident or luck; knowing how to hit a target is a capacity, and we would be right to look for a certain degree of consistency of behavior.[14]

"Practice," of course, is a vague term. Although I do not think its limits need be set here, it is important to realize that many skills are related and that practice for one skill may thus serve as practice for another. Hence, on those occasions when it appears that we know how to do something without having

[12]With regard to the notion of practice, a possible misinterpretation must be forestalled. I do not mean to say that knowledge of factual propositions is always learned instantaneously. Very often exposure to a variety of experiences and a protracted period of drill is needed before an individual knows that such and such is the case. However, the effort involved in learning and hence knowing that such and such is the case cannot be considered practice in *stating* that particular fact or *answering* a particular question. Moreover, to make the point that knowing factual propositions does not imply having learned to answer questions about them through practice, one case in which practice does not occur is sufficient; the example of Jones knowing that *X* murdered *Y* is surely such a case.

[13]It should be noted that there can also be cases of knowing factual propositions (i.e., knowing how to state certain facts or answer certain questions) which are never actualized. For example, Jones may know that *X* murdered *Y* but never reveals his knowledge to a soul. Thus he has the capacity to state that *X* murdered *Y*, although he never actualizes it.

[14]It should also be noted that there may be cases of *stating* factual propositions which are not cases of *knowing* them. Thus, Johnny may state that *X* murdered *Y* because he has made a lucky guess and not because he knows that *X* murdered *Y*.

practiced it, upon reflection we will discover that we have had practice in a related skill. It is possible, also, for the accidental or lucky occurrence to serve as practice for a skill. For example, if Jones swims to shore although he has never had practice in swimming, this very swimming may provide him with practice.

It is not denied here that we do exhibit some patterns of behavior with consistency although we have not practiced them. Yawning, crying, sneezing are examples. We call these reflexes, not skills, however, and do not speak of "knowing how" to yawn, cry, or sneeze. The exception is the case of the actor who is able to perform these behaviors at will. We might actually say of him that he "knows how" to yawn, cry, or sneeze, but it is clear that he has learned to do so through practice.

It appears, then, that although Hartland-Swann's reduction of "knowing that" to "knowing how" is legitimate for those "knowing that" sentences which are cases of knowing factual propositions, there is still a basic distinction between these sentences and the kinds of "knowing how" sentences which are cases of knowing how to perform an operation. Whether or not it is agreed that the basis for the distinction is practice, I do not think the distinction itself can be denied.

3. A CLASSIFICATION OF "KNOW" DISPOSITIONS

In this section I would like to suggest the beginnings of a classification of "know" dispositions. I have proposed that Hartland-Swann's expanded "knowing how" category be divided into two distinct types of dispositions. I would now like to examine the two types of sentences mentioned in Section 1, examples of which are "Jones knows how the accident happened" and "Johnny knows that he ought to be honest," in order to discover whether or not these represent dispositions which can also be subsumed under Hartland-Swann's "knowing how" category.

Once we perform Hartland-Swann's reduction, we have a "knowing how" category which includes two distinct types of capacities. One type implies that the capacity has been learned through practice whereas the other does not. Let us call the capacities which require practice Type A, and the capacities which do not require practice Type B. Capacities of Type A, then, are skills or competences such as cooking, doing logic, playing tennis, and hitting targets. Although knowing how to perform each skill is, of course, quite different, I think these capacities can be classified together by virtue of the fact that they all require practice. Capacities of Type B are the capacities to state certain facts or answer certain questions correctly, that is, knowing in the sense of knowing factual propositions. These, I have argued, do not require practice.

Let us now examine sentences of the type "Jones knows how the accident happened" and "Johnny knows how Williams hit the ball so hard." Do they fit into the expanded "knowing how" category? From a linguistic standpoint these sentences surely belong under "knowing how." A linguistic criterion is not sufficient, however, for "knowing how the accident happened" must be a capacity if it is to be subsumed under Hartland-Swann's "knowing how."[15]

Since "knowing how the accident happened" is a case of "knowing," there can be no doubt that it is a disposition. Since it implies the ability to do something and does not imply frequency or regularity, it must be a capacity and not a tendency. But what type of capacity is it? "Knowing how the accident happened" is not a case of "knowing how to perform an operation." Moreover, it is a capacity which need not be learned through practice. Certainly if Johnny sees the car skid on the ice and crash into a tree he will not need to practice anything at all in order to know how the accident happened. It would seem, then, that "knowing how the accident happened" is a disposition which does not belong to Type A. Perhaps it belongs to Type B. To be sure, "knowing how the accident happened" appears to involve knowing factual propositions. Indeed, this is why practice is not required. However, the statement "Johnny knows how the accident happened" is less informative than a statement of the Type B variety. Its very broadness renders it uninformative. We know only that Johnny has certain knowledge which presumably could be elicited from him upon demand. But we do not know the specific details of his knowledge, which in turn means that we are not given the specific details of the way the accident happened. A Type B sentence, whether it be "Johnny knows that X murdered Y," "Johnny knows that Columbus discovered America," or "Johnny knows that the road was slippery and the car skidded," gives us a greater amount of information because it is more specific and thus excludes a greater number of alternatives. Moreover, it gives us information about two things at once: about what Johnny knows and about the factual proposition which he knows.

We must conclude then that dispositions such as "knowing how the accident happened," "knowing how Eisenhower felt on election night," and "knowing how the motor works" belong in the "knowing how" category, but are distinct from Types A and B. That is, there is a third type of capacity, which we will call Type C, which is subsumed under "knowing how."

Let us turn now to the last type of sentence to be discussed here, sentences which refer to knowing moral judgments or rules of conduct. Linguistically, sentences which refer to knowing rules of conduct are "knowing that" sentences, for we say "Johnny knows that he ought to be honest" and "Johnny knows that he should be quiet when someone else is talking." There seems to be a difference, however, between these "knowing that" sentences and the "knowing that" sentences which refer to knowing factual propositions. For

[15] It might be argued that "Johnny knows how the accident happened" can be translated into "Johnny knows that the road was slippery, that the car skidded," and so on, and that in this translated form the sentence is an instance of Type B. That is, it is an instance of knowing a factual proposition which, in turn, is reducible to knowing how to state a fact or answer a question. Whether or not such a translation is legitimate, however, I think we must consider the untranslated sentence on its own merits.

although a response at a verbal level informs us that Johnny knows that Columbus discovered America, on one important interpretation of "he knows that he should" it does not inform us that Johnny knows that he should be quiet: the evidence of Johnny's knowledge that he should be quiet, on this interpretation, must be presented at the level of action or conduct.[16]

Since we do not believe that Johnny knows he should be quiet unless he behaves in certain ways, it is evident that "knowing that he should be quiet when someone else is talking" cannot be reduced to "knowing how to state a fact" or "knowing how to answer a question." Perhaps it is reducible to "knowing how to perform an operation" and belongs with capacities such as "knowing how to swim" and "knowing how to do logic." I do not think so, because I believe that "know," in the case of moral judgments and rules of conduct, acts as a tendency word rather than a capacity word. Thus the sentence "Johnny knows that he should be quiet when someone else is talking" is different from "Johnny knows how to swim" because Johnny must be quiet quite regularly when someone else is talking before we will attribute the disposition to him.

An analysis of sentences of the type "Johnny knows that he ought to be honest" or "Johnny knows that he should be quiet in class" as tendencies may give rise to sharp disagreement. It will be argued that we often say "Johnny knows that he should be quiet while someone is speaking but often he is not," and that this is incompatible with the position that the sentence expresses a tendency. We would not, for instance, say, "The dog has a tendency to howl when the moon shines but he almost never does." We would consider this a contradiction. To be sure, we would, in attributing a tendency, permit a small number of lapses. That is, we could say, "Johnny knows he should be quiet while someone is talking but he interrupted the teacher today," just as we could say "Fido has a tendency to howl when the moon shines but last night he didn't." In either case we would seek out the factor which prevented the actualization of the tendency. We might find that Johnny interrupted the teacher because he smelled smoke, and that Fido did not howl because he had become engrossed in a juicy steak bone. Neither lapse would cause us to disbelieve in the tendency. But this does not solve our problem. The fact remains that we do say "Johnny knows he should be quiet, but usually isn't." How then can we call sentences of this sort statements of tendency?

I think this problem can be solved and that the root of it lies in the fact that our language is ambiguous. When we say "he knows that he should" we sometimes mean one thing and sometimes another. We may mean by "he knows that he should" that he knows he is supposed to, or is expected to, or

---

[16]Whether "knowing that" functions in the same way in the sentence "Johnny knows that Columbus discovered America" and in the sentence "Johnny knows that he ought to be honest" depends, perhaps, on one's view of "ought" and other value words. However, I think it is important to differentiate between the use of "knowing that" in factual propositions and in moral judgments or rules of conduct, or else we would be committed to the view that Johnny knows he ought to be honest even if he never does an honest act in his life.

will be whipped if he does not. In this sense I think that "should" is used to express a factual statement. Thus, "Johnny knows that he should be quiet" may mean "Johnny knows that his teacher expects him to be quiet" or "Johnny knows that the rules say he is supposed to be quiet," and so forth. These are statements that rightfully belong under "Knowing how, Type B." If we view them as instances of Type B, we find it not at all surprising that Johnny knows that he should be quiet but is not. For knowing, in the sense of Type B, is a capacity which may be exhibited in behavior at the verbal level only, that is, by answering a question or stating a fact correctly. It would be a mistake indeed to expect Johnny to be quiet if his knowledge of this rule of conduct were of the Type B variety.

Although by "he knows that he should" we sometimes mean "he knows that such and such is the case," we can also mean something quite different. We may use "Johnny knows that he should" to indicate that Johnny has internalized a certain rule of conduct or moral code. When we use "he knows that he should" in this sense, we expect that the behavior will, quite generally, be exhibited. This sense of "he knows that he should" is a statement of tendency and it would be a contradiction to say "he knows that he should but he usually isn't." Thus, whether or not "he knows that he should be quiet but usually isn't" is contradictory depends on what is meant by "he knows that he should." On the one hand, if the phrase is to be taken in the sense of Type B, then we have no contradiction. That is why the phrase sounds so natural to us. But if the phrase is to be taken as an attribution of a tendency, then there is a contradiction.

To summarize the discussion of knowing rules of conduct, it would appear that since in one important sense of "he knows that he should" this type of disposition is a tendency it cannot be subsumed under the "knowing how" category. For that category as set up by Ryle, expanded by Hartland-Swann, and subdivided here contains capacities and not tendencies. Thus another category of "knowing" is needed, a category which contains tendencies. What the name of this new category should be I will leave an open question. For although "Johnny knows that he should be quiet" is a "knowing that" statement of tendency on the surface, it might well turn out that it can be reduced to a "knowing how" statement of tendency. In that event we would have two, completely distinct, "knowing how" categories—one of capacities and one of tendencies.

4. SOME IMPLICATIONS FOR TEACHING AND LEARNING

The analysis of "know" dispositions presented above is in no sense intended to be exhaustive. My purpose has been merely to discuss four types of "knowing how" and "knowing that" sentences and to classify them in a way that seems both precise and useful. One test of the utility of our classification lies in its relevance to education. From our analysis we can see, for example, that the learning of moral judgments and rules of conduct cannot be considered merely to be verbal learning. Thus a verbal test, no matter how ingeniously devised, will only warrant our saying that Johnny knows that he should be kind in the narrow sense of "knowing that he should" which falls under "Knowing how, Type B." In terms of the broad sense of "knowing that he should" which refers to conduct, a verbal test is insufficient. On the other hand, learning moral judgments and rules of conduct cannot be viewed solely in terms of practice in certain behaviors. Since knowledge in these cases consists in a tendency to behave and not simply a capacity, something more than practice is involved. A child who knows how ("Knowing how, Type A") to be kind may act kind in a special situation (e.g., when a visitor comes to the classroom) and unkind at other times. That is, he may be able to perform certain behaviors at will yet not exhibit these behaviors whenever an appropriate occasion arises. We would say he has a tendency to be kind only if whenever the occasion arose he exhibited these behaviors. A test for knowledge of moral judgments and rules of conduct in the broad sense must differ then from a test of skills.

We have seen that from a single performance of, say, hitting a target we are not warranted in inferring a capacity of knowing how to hit a target. A test of skills, therefore, must sample more than one performance of an operation; it must be designed to distinguish the lucky or accidental from the skillful hit. Furthermore, the consistency in performance which licenses us to attribute a capacity should not be confused with the regularity of behavior which allows us to attribute a tendency. After teaching a child how to read, we test him to see if he knows how ("Knowing how, Type A") to read. We often assume, wrongly, that once he has acquired the capacity to read, he will spend his leisure time reading. Before we can expect this, however, we must ensure that he has acquired a tendency to read. We can judge whether a child has acquired a tendency to read by observing the child's daily behavior over a long period of time or by devising special tests of tendencies. It might well be that such tests would require that the subject be unaware that he is being examined lest he display, for the examiner's benefit, his capacity which the examiner mistakes for a tendency.

To infer the presence of a skill in hitting a target or in handling laboratory materials from the results of a verbal test is as much an error as to infer a tendency to read from the results of a test of knowing how to read ("Knowing how, Type A"). By the same token, if we test skills through performance, we are by no means warranted in inferring from the fact that the person knows how to perform an operation that he knows the rules ("Knowing how, Type B") in accordance with which he has acted. Knowing how to answer the question "What are the rules of chess?" is quite different from knowing how to play chess and, conversely, one may know how to play chess yet not be able to state the rules of chess in an acceptable form.

E. C. Moore has argued that the sciences be renamed: ethics, logic, history, and mathematics are to be called, respectively, "the study of doing or behaving," "the study of thinking," "the searching, substantiating, or constructing the outline of the past," and "mathematizing."[17] His point is that school subjects are usually viewed as ready-made bodies of knowledge whereas their value "does not lie in their factual side, but in their directive uses."[18] Whatever our position on the question of whether the *over-all* emphasis in, say, a history course should be on history as an activity or skill rather than on history as a body of knowledge, we clearly expect our students to learn some facts of history. As we have seen, we cannot assume that a student who knows how to search for and substantiate facts ("Knowing how, Type A") also knows the facts ("Knowing how, Type B"). We must be careful, then, how we interpret Moore's argument or any argument that all subjects be viewed as activities or skills. Insofar as a subject involves facts to be learned (or tendencies to be acquired), it cannot be reduced without remainder to "Knowing how, Type A." We might, however, understand Moore and others who have advocated what has sometimes been called an "activity program" as simply recommending a particular emphasis in teaching and curriculum planning. On this interpretation they have not attempted an unjustified reduction of "Knowing how, Type B" to "Knowing how, Type A" but, rather, they have singled out for emphasis the elements of each subject which involve capacities falling under "Knowing how, Type A" and have given little attention to the capacities which fall under "Knowing how, Type B."

It follows from our analysis of various types of "know" sentences that to know a subject like history or mathematics is to have acquired many different kinds of capacities and tendencies. Which ones shall be made central to any given course is a matter for decision in the particular case; this question cannot be decided on the grounds of a reduction of "Knowing how, Type B" to "Knowing how, Type A" or by a reduction of "Knowing how, Type A" to "Knowing how, Type B."

These are some of the ways in which an analysis of "knowing how" and "knowing that" sentences bears on problems of teaching and learning. A great many other "knowing how" and "knowing that" sentences, as well as "knowing why," "knowing what," and "knowing about" sentences, remain to be examined. Hence, it must not be imagined that a classification of all "know" dispositions will contain only the two categories we have suggested. Indeed, upon further analysis it may turn out that the two categories proposed here must be altered. The purpose of this paper will have been achieved, however, if it is recognized that "know" dispositions are varied and that it is of practical as well as theoretical importance to sort out the different kinds of cases.

[17] Ernest Carroll Moore, *What is Education?* (Boston: Ginn and Company, 1915), pp. 344–45.
[18] Moore, p. 345.

Gilbert Ryle

GILBERT RYLE is Waynflete Professor of Metaphysical Philosophy at Oxford University. He is one of the most important figures in the development of analytic philosophy, and his classic book *The Concept of Mind* has served as a basis for much of the work that has been done both in philosophy of mind and analytic philosophy of education.

It is his distinction between "knowing how" and "knowing that" which was utilized in the previous essay by Professor Martin, and it is a related distinction between "teaching" and "training" which he employs in the following essay as a means of solving a central paradox in educational theory. As Ryle states it, "though the teacher in teaching is doing something to his pupil, yet the pupil has learned virtually nothing unless he becomes able and ready to do things of his own motion other than what the teacher exported to him."

Ryle's belief was put into practice by one mathematics professor who delighted in presenting his students with especially difficult problems. When he would place one of these problems on the blackboard, a student was sure to complain, "But I don't know how to solve this problem." To this the professor would reply, "I don't have to teach you what to do when you *know* how to solve a problem. I want to teach you what to do when you *don't* know how to solve a problem."

Ryle demonstrates how it is conceptually possible for one person to teach another to think things out for himself. He concludes that "I can introduce you to a way or the way of doing something, and still your actual essays in the exercise of this craft or competence are yours and not mine. I do not literally make you do them, but I do enable you to do them."

Ryle's article is a fitting conclusion to this book, for it is hoped that the reader is now able to consider criti-

cally the fundamental issues which are at the heart of
the crucial and complex inquiry referred to as philosophy of education.

TEACHING
AND TRAINING

I have no teaching tricks or pedagogic maxims to impart to you, and I should not impart them to you if I had any. What I want to do is to sort out and locate a notion which is cardinal to the notions of teaching, training, education, etc. about which too little is ordinarily said. This notion is that of *teaching oneself* which goes hand in glove with the notion of *thinking for oneself.* You will all agree, I think, that teaching fails, that is, either the teacher is a failure or the pupil is a failure, if the pupil does not sooner or later become able and apt to arrive at his own solutions to problems. But how, in logic, can anyone be taught to do untaught things? I repeat, how, in logic, can anyone be taught to do untaught things?

To clear the air, let me begin by quickly putting on one side an unimportant but familiar notion, that of the self-taught man. Normally when we describe someone as a self-taught man we think of a man who having been deprived of tuition from other teachers tries to make himself an historian, say, or a linguist or an astronomer, without criticism, advice or stimulation from anyone else, save from the authors of such textbooks, encyclopaedia articles and linguaphone records as he may happen to hit on. He hits on these, of course, randomly, without having anyone or anything to tell him whether they are good ones, silly ones, old-fashioned ones or cranky ones. We admire the devotion with which he studies, but, save for the rare exception, we pity him for having been the devoted pupil only of that solitary and untrained teacher, himself. However, I am not interested in him.

What I am interested in is this. Take the case of an ordinary unbrilliant, unstupid boy who is learning to read. He has learned to spell and read monosyllables like "bat," "bad," "at," "ring," sing," etc., and some two-syllable words like "running," "dagger" and a few others. We have never taught him, say, the word "batting." Yet we find him quite soon reading and spelling unhesitantly the word "batting." We ask him who taught him this word and, if he remembers, he says that he had found it out for himself. He has learned from himself how the word "batting" looks in print, how to write it down on paper and how to spell it out aloud, so in a sense he has taught himself this word—taught it to himself without yet knowing it. How can this be? How can a boy who does not know what "b-a-t-t-i-n-g" spells teach himself what it spells?

From *The Concept of Education* by R. S. Peters (ed.), London, Routledge & Kegan Paul, Ltd.; New York, Humanities Press, Inc., 1967, pp. 105–119. Reprinted by permission of both publishers.

In real life we are not a bit puzzled. It is just what we expect of a not totally stupid child. Yet there is the semblance of a conceptual paradox here, for we seem to be describing him as at a certain stage being able to teach himself something new, which *ipso facto* was not yet in his repertoire to teach. Here his teacher was as ignorant as the pupil, for they were the same boy. So how can the one learn something from the other?

What should we say? Well, clearly we want to say that the prior things that we *had* taught him, namely words like "bat," "bad," "rat" and longer words like "butter," "running," etc., enabled him and perhaps encouraged him to make a new bit of independent, uncoached progress on his own. We had taught him *how* to read some monosyllables, *how* to run some of them together in dissyllables, and so on. We had taught him a way or some ways of coping with combinations of printed letters, though not in their particular application to this new word "batting." He had made this particular application himself. So to speak, we had previously from the deck shown him the ropes and now he climbs one of them with his own hands and feet; that is to say, not being totally stupid, he was able and ready to employ this slightly general knowledge that we had given to him on a new concrete and particular problem that we had not solved for him. We had given him the wherewithal with which to think it out for himself—and this thinking out was his doing and not ours. I could just as well have taken an example from the much more sophisticated stratum where a brilliant undergraduate makes a good philosophical move that no one else has ever taught him, and maybe no one else has ever made.

Naturally, most often the boy or the undergraduate, if asked Who taught you that? would reply not that he had taught it to himself or that he had learned it from himself, but rather that he had found it out or thought it out or worked it out for himself. Just this brings out a big part of what interests me, namely, that though in one way it is obviously impossible for one person's own discovery, whether trivial or important, to be simply what someone else had previously taught him—since it would then not be his discovery—, yet in another way it is and ought to be one main business of a teacher precisely to get his pupils to advance beyond their instructions and to discover new things for themselves, that is, to get them to think things out for themselves. I teach Tommy to read a few words like "bat," "run" and "running" in order that he may then, of his own motion, find out how to read lots and lots of other words, like "batting," that we have not taught to him. Indeed we do not deem him really able to spell or read until he can spell and read things that he has not been introduced to. Nor, to leave the schoolroom for the moment, do I think that Tommy has learned to bicycle until he can do things on his bicycle far more elaborate, speedy, tricky and delicate than the things I drilled him in on the first morning. I taught him the few elements on the first morning just in order that he might then find out for himself how to cope with hosts of non-elementary tasks. I gave him a few stereotyped exercises, and, as I had hoped and expected, in a couple of days he had developed for himself on this basis a fair wealth of boyish skills and dexterities, though he acquired these while I was away in London.

However, there remains a slight feeling of a puzzle or paradox here, and it comes, I think, from this source. A familiar and indispensable part or sort of teaching consists in teaching by rote lists of truths or facts, for example the proposition that 7 × 7 is 49, etc., the proposition that Waterloo was fought in 1815, etc., and the proposition that Madrid is the capital of Spain, etc. That the pupil has learned a lesson of this propositional sort is shown, in the first instance, by his being able and reasonably ready to reproduce word-perfectly these pieces of information. He gets them by heart, and he can come out with them on demand. Now every teacher knows that only a vanishingly small fraction of his teaching-day really consists in simply reciting lists of such snippets of information to pupils, but very unfortunately, it happens to be the solitary part which unschooled parents, Sergeant Majors, some silly publicists and some educationalists always think of when they think of teaching and learning. They think or half-think that the request "Recite what you have learned in school today, Tommy" is a natural and proper one, as if all that Tommy could or should have learned is a number of memorizable propositions; or as if to have learned anything consisted simply in being able to echo it, like a gramophone. As you all know, most teaching has nothing whatsoever in common with this crude, semi-surgical picture of teaching as the forcible insertion into the pupil's memory of strings of officially approved propositions; and I hope to show before long that even that small and of course indispensable part of instruction which is the imparting of factual information is grossly mis-pictured when pictured as literal cramming. Yet, bad as the picture is, it has a powerful hold over people's general theorizings about teaching and learning. Even Tommy's father, after spending the morning in teaching Tommy to swim, to dribble the football or to diagnose and repair what is wrong with the kitchen clock, in the afternoon cheerfully writes to the newspapers letters which take it for granted that all lessons are strings of memorizable propositions. His practice is perfectly sensible, yet still his theory is as silly as it could be.

Perhaps the prevalence of this very thin and partial notion of teaching and learning inherits something from the teaching and learning that are done in the nursery, where things such as "Hickory Dickory Dock" and simple tunes are learned by heart from that mere vocal repetition which enables the parrot to pick them up too.

Well, in opposition to this shibboleth, I want to switch the centre of gravity of the whole topic on to the notions of Teaching-to so and so, and Learning-to so and so, that is, on to the notion of the development of abilities and competences. Let us forget for a while the memorization of truths, and, of course, of rhymes and tunes, and attend, instead, to the acquisition of skills, knacks and efficiencies. Consider, for example, lessons in drawing, arithmetic and cricket—and, if you like, in philosophy. These lessons cannot consist of and cannot even contain much of dictated propositions. However many true propositions the child has got by heart, he has not begun to learn to draw or play cricket until he has been given a pencil or a bat and a ball and has practised doing things with them; and even if he progresses magnificently in these arts, he will have little or nothing to reply to his parents if they ask him in the evening to recite to them the propositions that he has learned. He can *exhibit* what he has begun to master, but he cannot *quote* it. To avoid the ambiguity between "teach" in the sense of "teach that" and "teach" in the sense of "teach to" or "teach how to," I shall now sometimes use the word "train." The drawing-master, the language-teacher or the cricket-coach *trains* his pupils in drawing or in French pronunciation or in batting or bowling, and this training incorporates only a few items of quotable information. The same is true of philosophy.

Part, but only part of this notion of training is the notion of drilling, i.e., putting the pupil through stereotyped exercises which he masters by sheer repetition. Thus the recruit learns to slope arms just by going through the same sequence of motions time after time, until he can, so to speak, perform them in his sleep. Circus-dogs and circus-seals are trained in the same way. At the start piano-playing, counting and gear-changing are also taught by simple habituation. But disciplines do not reduce to such sheer drills. Sheer drill, though it is the indispensable beginning of training, is, for most abilities, only their very beginning. Having become able to do certain low-level things automatically and without thinking, the pupil is expected to advance beyond this point and to employ his inculcated automatisms in higher level tasks which are not automatic, and cannot be done without thinking. Skills, tastes and scruples are more than mere habits, and the disciplines and the self-disciplines which develop them are more than mere rote-exercises.

His translators and commentators have been very unjust to Aristotle on this matter. Though he was the first thinker and is still the best, systematically to study the notions of ability, skill, training, character, learning, discipline, self-discipline, etc., the translators of his works nearly always render his key-ideas by such terms as "habit" and "habituation"—as if, for example, a person who has been trained and self-trained to play the violin, or to behave scrupulously in his dealings with other people acts from sheer habit, in the way in which I do tie up my shoelaces quite automatically and without thinking what I am doing or how to do it. Of course Aristotle knew better than this, and the Greek words that he used are quite grossly mis-translated when rendered merely by such words as "habit" and "habituation." The well-disciplined soldier, who does indeed slope arms automatically, does not also shoot automatically or scout by blind habit or read maps like a marionette.

Nor is Tommy's control of his bicycle merely a rote-performance, though he cannot begin to control his bicycle until he has got some movements by rote. Having learned through sheer habit-formation to keep his balance on his bicycle with both hands on the handlebars, Tommy can now try to ride with one hand off, and later still with both hands in his pockets and his feet off the pedals. He now progresses by experimentation. Or, having got by heart the run of the alphabet from ABC through to XYZ, he can now, but not without thinking, tell you what three letters run *backwards* from RQP, though he has never learned by heart this reversed sequence.

I suggest that our initial seeming paradox, that a learner can sometimes of himself, after a bit of instruction, better his instructions, is beginning to seem less formidable. The possibility of it is of the same pattern as the familiar fact that the toddler who has this morning taken a few aided steps, tries this afternoon with or without success to take some unaided steps. The swimmer who can now keep himself up in salt water, comes by himself, at first with a bit of extra splashing, to keep himself up in fresh water. How do any formerly difficult things change into now easy things? Or any once untried things into now feasible ones? The answer is just in terms of the familiar notions of the development of abilities by practice, that is trying and failing and then trying again and not failing so often or so badly, and so on.

Notoriously a very few pupils are, over some tasks, so stupid, idle, scared, hostile, bored or defective, that they make no efforts of their own beyond those imposed on them as drill by their trainer. But to be non-stupid, vigorous and interested *is* to be inclined to make, if only as a game, moves beyond the drilled moves, and to practise of oneself, e.g., to multiply beyond 12 × 12, to run through the alphabet backwards, to bicycle with one hand off the handlebar, or to slope arms in the dark with a walking-stick when no drill-sergeant is there. As Aristotle says "the things that we have got to do when we have learned to do them, we learn to do by doing them." What I can do today I could not do easily or well or successfully yesterday; and the day before I could not even try to do them; and if I had not tried unsuccessfully yesterday, I should not be succeeding today.

Before returning to go further into some of these key notions of ability, practice, trying, learning to, teaching to, and so on, I want to look back for a moment to the two over-influential notions of teaching *that* so and so, i.e., telling or informing, and of learning *that* so and so, i.e., the old notion of propositional cramming. In a number of nursery, school and university subjects, there are necessarily some or many true propositions to be accumulated by the student. He must, for example, learn that Oslo is the capital of Norway, Stockholm is the capital of Sweden and Copenhagen is the capital of Denmark. Or he must learn that the Battle of Trafalgar was fought in 1805 and that of Waterloo in 1815. Or that $7 + 5 = 12$, $7 - 6 = 13$, $7 + 7 = 14$, etc.

At the very start, maybe, the child just memorizes these strings of propositions as he memorizes "Hickory Dickory Dock," the alphabet or "Thirty days hath September." But so long as parroting is all he can do, he does not yet know the geographical fact, say, that Stockholm is the capital of Sweden, since if you ask him what Stockholm is the capital of, or whether Madrid is the capital of Sweden, he has no idea how to move. He can repeat, but he cannot yet use, the memorized dictum. All he can do is to go through the memorized sequence of European capitals from start through to the required one. He does not qualify as knowing that Stockholm is the capital of Sweden until he can detach this proposition from the memorized rigmarole; and can, for example, answer new-type questions like "of which country out of the three, Italy, Spain and Sweden is Stockholm the capital?" or "Here is Stockholm on the globe—whereabouts is Sweden?" and so on. To know the geographical fact requires having taken it in, i.e., being able and ready to operate with it, from it, around it and upon it. To possess a piece of information is to be able to mobilize it apart from its rote-neighbours and out of its rote-formulation in unhackneyed and *ad hoc* tasks. Nor does the pupil know that $7+7 = 14$ while this is for him only a still undetachable bit of a memorized sing-song, but only when, for example, he can find fault with someone's assertion that $7 + 8 = 14$, or can answer the new-type question, How many 7s are there in 14?, or the new-type question "If there are seven boys and seven girls in a room, how many children are in the room?" etc. Only then has he taken it in.

In other words, even to have learned the piece of information *that something is so* is more than merely to be able to parrot the original telling of it—somewhat as to have digested a biscuit is more than merely to have had it popped into one's mouth. Can he or can he not infer from the information that Madrid is the capital of Spain that Madrid is not in Sweden? Can he or can he not tell us what sea-battle occurred ten years before Waterloo?

Notice that I am not in the least deprecating the inculcation of rotes like the alphabet, the figures of the syllogism, "Hickory Dickory Dock," the dates of the Kings of England, or sloping arms. A person who has not acquired such rotes cannot progress from and beyond them. All that I am arguing is that he does not qualify as knowing even that Waterloo was fought in 1815 if all that he can do is to sing out this sentence inside the sing-song of a memorized string of such sentences. If he can only echo the syllables that he has heard, he has not yet taken in the information meant to be conveyed by them. He has not grasped it if he cannot handle it. But if he could not even echo things told to him, *a fortiori* he could not operate with, from or upon their informative content. One cannot digest a biscuit unless it is first popped into one's mouth. So we see that even to have learned a true proposition is to have learned *to do* things other than repeating the words in which the truth had been dictated. To have learned even a simple geographical fact is to have become able to cope with some unhabitual geographical tasks, however elementary.

We must now come back to our central question: How is it possible that a person should learn from himself something which he previously did not know, and had not, e.g., been taught by someone else? This question is or embodies the apparently perplexing question: How can one person teach another person to think things out for himself, since if he gives him, say, the new arithmetical thoughts, then they are not the pupil's own thoughts; or if they are his own thoughts, then he did not get them from his teacher? Having led the horse to the water, how can we make him drink? But I have, I hope, shifted the centre of gravity of this seeming puzzle, by making the notions of *learning-to* and *teaching-to* the primary notions. In its new form the question is: How, on the basis of some tuition, can a person today get himself to do something which he had not been able to do yesterday or last year? How can competences, abilities and skills develop? How can trying ever succeed? We are so familiar, in practice, with the fact that abilities do develop, and that tryings can succeed that we find little to puzzle us in the idea that they do.

Looked at from the end of the teacher the question is: How can the teacher get his pupil to make independent moves of his own? If this question is tortured into the shape: How can the teacher make or force his pupil to do things which he is not made or forced to do? i.e., How can the teacher be the initiator of the pupil's initiatives? the answer is obvious. He cannot. I cannot compel the horse to drink thirstily. I cannot coerce Tommy into doing spontaneous things. Either he is not coerced, or they are not spontaneous.

As every teacher, like every drill-sergeant or animal trainer knows in his practice, teaching and training have virtually not yet begun, so long as the pupil is too young, too stupid, too scared or too sulky to respond—and to respond is not just to yield. Where there is a modicum of alacrity, interest or anyhow docility in the pupil, where he tries, however faintheartedly, to get things right rather than wrong, fast rather than slow, neat rather than awkward, where, even, he registers even a slight contempt for the poor performances of others or chagrin at his own, pleasure at his own successes and envy of those of others, then he is, in however slight a degree, cooperating and so self-moving. He is doing something, though very likely not much, and is not merely having things done to him. He is, however unambitiously and however desultorily, attempting the still difficult. He has at least a little impetus of his own. A corner, however small a corner of his heart is now in the task. The eager pupil is, of course, the one who, when taught, say, to read or spell a few words like "at," "bat" and "mat" travels home on the bus trying out, just for fun, all the other monosyllables that rhyme with "at," to see which of them are words. When taught to read and spell a dissyllable or two, he tries his hand, just for fun and often but not always unsuccessfully, on the polysyllables on the advertisement-hoardings; and just for fun he challenges his father to spell long words when he gets home. He does this for fun; but like much play it is spontaneous self-practising. When he returns to school after the holidays, although his spelling and reading are now far in advance of their peak of last term, he will stoutly deny that he has done any work during the holidays. It has not been work, it has been absorption in a new hobby, like exercising a new limb.

His over-modest teacher may say that he has taught this boy next to nothing —nor has he, save for the very beginnings of everything.

However, we should remember that although a total absence of eagerness or even willingness spells total unteachability, the presence of energy, adventurousness and self-motion is not by itself enough. The wild guesser and the haphazard plunger have freedom of movement of a sort, but not of the best sort. Learning how to do new and therefore more or less difficult things does indeed require trying things out for oneself, but if this trying-out is not controlled by any testing or making sure, then its adventurousness is recklessness and not enterprise. He is like the gambler, not like the investor. The moves made, though spontaneous, are irresponsible and they yield no dividends. Nothing can be learned by him from their unsuccesses or from their occasional fortuitous successes. He shoots away, but learns nothing from his misses—or from his fluke hits.

It is just here, with the notion of taking care when taking risks, that there enters on the scenes the cardinal notion of *method*, i.e., of techniques, *modi operandi*, rules, canons, procedures, knacks, and even tricks of the trade. In doing a thing that he has never done before, a person may, but need not, operate according to a method, sometimes, even according to a sheer drill that he has adhered to before. If he does, then his action is still an innovation, although the pattern of his action is a familiar and inculcated one. The poet composes a sonnet, taking care to adhere to the regulation 14 lines, to the regulation rhyming scheme, to the regulation metrical pattern, or else perhaps to one of the several permitted patterns—yet, nonetheless, his sonnet is a new one. No one has ever composed *it* before. His teacher who taught him how to compose sonnets had not and could not have made him compose this sonnet, else it would be the teacher's and not the pupil's sonnet. Teaching people how to do things just *is* teaching them methods or *modi operandi;* and it is just because it is one thing to have learned a method and another thing to essay a new application of it that we can say without paradox that the learner's new move is his own move and yet that he may have learned the *how* of making it from someone else. The cook's pudding is a new one and piping hot, but its recipe was known to Mrs. Beeton in the days of Queen Victoria.

Well, then, what sort of a thing is a method? First for what it is not. Despite what many folk would say, a method is not a stereotyped sequence-pattern or routine of actions, inculcatable by pure rote, like sloping arms or going through the alphabet. The parrot that can run through "Hickory Dickory Dock" has not learned how to do anything or therefore how not to do it. There is nothing that he takes care not to do.

A method is a learnable way of doing something, where the word "way" connotes more than mere rote or routine. A way of doing something, or a *modus operandi*, is something general, and general in at least two dimensions. First, the way in which you do a thing, say mount your bicycle, can be the way or a way in which some other people or perhaps most other people mount or try to mount their bicycles. Even if you happen to be the only person who yet does something in a certain way, it is possible that others should in future learn from you or find out for themselves the very same way of doing it. *Modi operandi* are, in principle, public property, though a particular action performed in this way is my action and not yours, or else it is your action and not mine. We mount our bicycles in the same way, but my bicycle-mounting is my action and not yours. You do not make my mincepies, even though we both follow the same Victorian recipe.

The second way in which a method is something general is the obvious one, that there is no limit to the number of actions that may be done in that way. The method is, roughly, applicable anywhere and anywhen, as well as by anyone. For however many people are known by me to have mounted their bicycles in a certain way, I know that there could have been and there could be going to be any number of other bicycle-mountings performed by myself and others in the same way.

Next, methods can be helpfully, if apparently cynically, thought of as systems of avoidances or as patterns of "don'ts." The rules, say, of English grammar do not tell us positively what to say or write; they tell us negatively not to say or write such things as "A dog *are . . .*" and "Those dogs *is . . .*", and learning the art of rock-climbing or tree-climbing is, among hundreds of other things, learning never, or hardly ever, to trust one's whole weight to an untried projection or to a branch that is leafless in summer time.

People sometimes grumble at the Ten Commandments on the score that most of them are prohibitions, and not positive injunctions. They have not realized that the notice "Keep off the grass" licenses us to walk anywhere else we choose; where the notice "Keep to the gravel" leaves us with almost no freedom of movement. Similarly to have learned a method is to have learned to take care against certain specified kinds of risk, muddle, blind alley, waste, etc. But carefully keeping away from this cliff and from that morass leaves the rest of the countryside open for us to walk lightheartedly in. If I teach you even twenty kinds of things that would make your sonnet a bad sonnet or your argument a bad argument, I have still left you an indefinite amount of elbow-room within which you can construct your own sonnet or argument, and this sonnet or argument of yours, whether brilliant or ordinary or weak, will at least be free of faults of those twenty kinds.

There exists in some quarters the sentimental idea that the teacher who teaches his pupils how to do things is hindering them, as if his apron-strings coerced their leg-movements. We should think of the inculcation of methods rather as training the pupils to avoid specified muddles, blockages, sidetracks and thin ice by training them to recognize these for what they are. Enabling them to avoid troubles, disasters, nuisances and wasted efforts is helping them to move where they want to move. Road signs are not, for the most part, impediments to the flow of traffic. They are preventives of impediments to the flow of traffic.

Of course we can easily think of silly ways of doing things which continue to be taught by grown-ups to children and adhered to by the grown-ups themselves. Not all methods are good methods, or all recipes good recipes. For example, the traditional ban on splitting the infinitive was a silly rule. But the gratuitous though trivial bother of conforming to this particular veto was negligible compared with the handicap that would be suffered by the child who had never been taught or picked up for himself any of the procedures for composing or construing sentences. He would have been kept back at the level of total infancy. He could not say or follow anything at all if, for example, he had not mastered conjunctions, or even verbs, and mastering them involves learning how *not* to make hashes of them.

How does one teach methods or ways of doing things? Well, there is no simple answer to this. Different arts and crafts require different kinds of disciplines; and in some one particular field, say drawing, one teacher works very differently from another. Sometimes a little, sometimes a lot can be told; there is much that cannot be told, but can be shown by example, by caricature and so on. But one thing is indispensable. The pupil himself must, whether under pressure or from interest or ambition or conscientiousness, practise doing what he is learning how to do. Whether in his exercises in the art he religiously models his strokes after Bradman, or whether he tries to win the praise or avoid the strictures or sarcasms of a feared, respected or loved coach, he learns by performing and improves by trying to better his own and his fellows' previous performances by eradicating their faults. The methods of operating taught to him become his personal methods of operating by his own criticized and self-criticized practice. Whether in spelling, in Latin grammar, fencing, arithmetic or philosophy, he learns the ropes, not much by gazing at them or hearing about them, but by trying to climb them—and by trying to climb them less awkwardly, slowly and riskily today than he did yesterday.

So far I have been, for simplicity, dividing the contributions of the teacher and the pupil by saying that the teacher in teaching how to so and so is teaching a method or way of operating, while the pupil keeps his initiative by making his own at the start somewhat arduous, because new applications of that method. The teacher introduces the pupil to the ropes, but it is for the pupil to try to climb them.

But now we should pay some attention to the fact that pretty soon the pupil has become familiar with the quite general fact that for lots and lots of widely different kinds of operations—spelling, say, skating and bowling at cricket—there exist different *modi operandi*. There are spelling-mistakes and there are bowling-faults, and neither spelling nor bowling can go right unless these faults are systematically avoided. So now, when he undertakes an altogether new kind of operation, canoeing, say, he from the start expects there to be *modi operandi* here too. This too will be a thing that he will have to learn how to do, partly by learning how not to do it. But this time, it may be, there is no one to teach him, and not even any other canoeist to imitate. He has got to find out for himself the way, or anyhow a way, of balancing, propelling and steering his canoe. Well, at first he tries a lot of random things, and nearly all of them end in immersion or collision; but he does after a time find out some ways of managing his craft. He may not achieve elegance or speed, but he does find out how not to topple over and how not to run into obstacles. He is trained, this time purely self-trained, regularly to avoid some kinds of faulty watermanship. But it is because he had previously learned by practice, coaching and imitation the "hows" of lots of other things such as tree-climbing, spelling and skating, that he now takes it for granted that canoeing has its "hows" as well, which similarly can be learned by practice, trial and error, and looking for ways of avoiding the repetition of errors. Here, as elsewhere, he has to study in order to improve; but this time he has nothing to study save his own unsuccesses and successes.

His more reckless and impatient brother, though full of go, just makes a dash at it, and then another quite different dash at it, and learns nothing or almost nothing from the failures which generally result, or even from the successes which sometimes just happen to result. He is not a self-trainer.

The third brother is uninterested, slow in the uptake, scared or idle. He never chances his arm. He tries nothing, and so initiates nothing either successfully or unsuccessfully. So he never learns to canoe; never, perhaps, even regrets not having learned it or envies those who have. There is no question of his training himself in this particular art, or even, if he is a very bad case, of his being trained by anyone else; just as there was fifty years ago no real question of me training myself or of my being trained by anyone else in the arts of cricket or music.

The supreme reward of the teacher is to turn out from time to time the student who comes to be not merely abreast of his teacher but ahead of him, the student, namely, who advances his subject or his craft not just by adding to it further applications of the established ways of operating, but by discovering new methods or procedures of types which no one could have taught to him. He has given to his subject or his craft a new idea or a battery of new ideas. He is original. He himself, if of a grateful nature, will say that his original idea just grew of itself out of what he had learned from his teachers, his competitors and his colleagues; while they, if of a grateful nature, will say that the new idea was his discovery. Both will be right. His new idea is the fruit of a tree that others had planted and pruned. It is really his own fruit and he is really their tree.

We started off with the apparent paradox that though the teacher in teaching is doing something to his pupil, yet the pupil has learned virtually nothing unless he becomes able and ready to do things of his own motion other than what the teacher exported to him. We asked, How in logic can the teacher dragoon his pupil into thinking for himself, impose initiative upon him, drive him into self-motion, conscript him into volunteering, enforce originality upon him, or make him operate spontaneously? The answer is that he cannot—and the reason why we half felt that he must do so was that we were unwittingly enslaved by the crude, semi-hydraulic idea that in essence to teach is to pump propositions, like "Waterloo, 1815" into the pupils' ears, until they regurgitate them automatically.

When we switched from the notion of "hydraulic injection" to the notion of "teaching to" or "teaching how to," the paradox began to disappear. I can introduce you to a way or the way of doing something, and still your actual essays in the exercise of this craft or competence are yours and not mine. I do not literally make you do them, but I do enable you to do them. I give you the *modus operandi*, but your operatings or tryings to operate according to this *modus* are your own doings and not my inflictings and the practising by which you master the method is your exertion and not mine. I have given you some equipment against failing, *if* you try. But that you try is not something that I can coerce. Teaching is not gate-shutting but gate-opening, yet still the dull or the scared or the lame calf does not walk out into the open field. All this does not imply the popular sentimental corollary that teachers should never be strict, demanding, peremptory or uncondoning. It is often the hard task-master who alone succeeds in instilling mistrust of primrose paths. The father may enlarge the child's freedom of movement by refusing to hold his hand, and the boxing-instructor or the philosophy-tutor may enlarge his pupil's powers of defence and attack by hitting him hard and often. It is not the chocolates and the sponge-cakes that strengthen the child's jaw-muscles. They have other virtues, but not this one.

BIBLIOGRAPHICAL NOTES

An exhaustive bibliography of work in virtually every aspect of philosophy of education is *Philosophy of Education: An Organization of Topics and Selected Sources*, Harry S. Broudy, Michael J. Parsons, *et al.* (eds.), Chicago, University of Illinois Press, 1967.

Provocative essays on the aims and content of philosophy of education are to be found in a symposium in the *Harvard Educational Review*, 1956, vol. XXVI, no. 2.

An excellent survey of historical work in philosophy of education is Kingsley Price, "Philosophy of Education, History of" in *The Encyclopedia of Philosophy*, New York, Macmillan and Free Press, 1967, vol. VI.

Informative essays on the educational philosophies of Plato, Aristotle, Rousseau, Kant, Dewey, and Whitehead are contained in Robert S. Brumbaugh and Nathaniel M. Lawrence, *Philosophers on Education: Six Essays on the Foundations of Western Thought*, Boston, Houghton Mifflin, 1963. Somewhat lengthier and more detailed studies of the educational philosophies of Aristotle, Kant, and Dewey can be found in William K. Frankena, *Three Historical Philosophies of Education*, Chicago, Scott, Foresman, 1965. A classic full-length study of Plato's educational philosophy is R. L. Nettleship, *The Theory of Education in Plato's Republic*, London, Oxford, 1935.

Good collections of essays in analytic philosophy of education are *Language and Concepts in Education*, B. Othanel Smith and Robert H. Ennis (eds.), Chicago, Rand McNally, 1961; *Philosophical Analysis and Education*, Reginald D. Archambault (ed.), London, Routledge, 1965; *Philosophy and Education*, 2d ed., Israel Scheffler (ed.), Boston, Allyn and Bacon, 1966; and *The Concept of Education*, R. S. Peters (ed.), London, Routledge, 1967.

INDEX